EXTREMISM IN AMERICA

EXTREMISM IN AMERICA

A Reader

Edited by
LYMAN TOWER SARGENT

NEW YORK UNIVERSITY PRESS
New York and London

Every effort was made to reach the copyright holders of the documents included herein. Any oversights will be corrected in subsequent reprints.

NEW YORK UNIVERSITY PRESS
New York and London

Library of Congress Cataloging-in-Publication Data
Extremism in America : a reader / edited by Lyman Tower Sargent.
p.   cm.
Includes bibliographical references.
ISBN 0-8147-7978-6 (acid-free paper). —ISBN 0-8147-8011-3 (acid-free paper)
1. Radicalism—United States.   2. Social movements—United States.
3. Ideology—United States.   4. Right and left (Political science)
I. Sargent, Lyman Tower, 1940-
HN90.R3E95   1995
320.5'3—dc20   95-7676
CIP

New York University Press books are printed on acid-free paper, and their binding materials are chosen for strength and durability.

Manufactured in the United States of America

10   9   8   7   6   5   4   3   2   1

To
Evan, Jennifer, and Ian

CONTENTS

10. TACTICS   359

BIBLIOGRAPHY   367

PREFACE

The Wilcox Collection of Contemporary Political Movements at the University of Kansas is one of the most important collections of extremist literature in the United States today. The collection is the work of Laird Wilcox, a retired carpenter, who began it while a student at the university. He sold the basis of the collection (three file drawers of material) to the university in 1965, and since then has donated nearly as much material most months. The Wilcox Collection now contains over one hundred thousand items, including books and periodicals as well as extremely rare ephemera, posters, leaflets, and numerous audio tapes, many of which hold interviews that Wilcox held with both leaders and members of extremist groups.

The Wilcox Collection is overwhelmingly American, but there is substantial material from other countries, most of it from Canada and Britain. The collection is stronger on the right than on the left but includes a wide range of material representing a vast number of groups from both extremes, with over eight thousand organizations represented.

While Wilcox has pointed out that many of the groups are tiny and some probably consist of only one person, the collection as a whole represents the resentments and dreams of thousands of people from the 1920s to the present and allows us a view into minds that are frequently ignored or belittled. We should take these people seriously, not only because no one's dreams should be belittled, but because we need to try to understand both those dreams and the resentments that are the more common focus of interest for those studying extremes in politics. Some of what will be found in this book is shocking, particularly the intensity of the racism, but it is best not to hide from the reality of the hatreds that exist.

ACKNOWLEDGMENTS

Working in the Wilcox Collection is a pleasure in itself, and I wish to thank the staff and students who were unfailingly helpful and frequently made suggestions that made my work easier and more productive. Sheryl K. Williams, Curator of the Kansas Collection, and Rebecca Schulte, Assistant Curator, oversee the collection and keep it safe while making it readily accessible to users, and they have created a friendly, pleasant place to work. Mary Linn, who was overseeing the Photographic Collection when I last worked there, was constantly helpful and a pleasure to get to know. Two students, Chris Hansen and Sarah Ruhlen, expeditiously brought me the hundreds of items I needed to see with constant good humor. In addition, friends on the faculty at the University of Kansas—Deborah Altus, Richard DeGeorge, James Gunn, Rex Martin, and Timothy Miller—made my visits very pleasant.

My office staff—Jan Frantzen, Lana Vierdag, and Kristine Brooks—made it possible for a department head to get some research done, and Christine Goedart, my undergraduate research assistant, transcribed the documents and efficiently brought me hundreds of books from the library that helped fill in the background.

The research was carried out under a grant from the University of Missouri Research Board, without which it could not have been completed.

INTRODUCTION

The varied social movements and political thought produced in any country may be imagined as existing along a line with midpoint and ends, although sometimes they are represented by a curve that illustrates the number of people holding the various positions, with most people in the vicinity of the middle, while the ends hold gradually fewer and fewer people. This book concentrates on the ends. This political spectrum can be defined in a variety of ways that puts different groups at the end; here the ends are defined as what was generally perceived as the ends at the time of writing by the people in the middle.

These ends are sometimes called radicalism or reaction, to imply a set of attitudes about the middle, but these labels, and the label "extremism," are as seen from the middle. To someone at one of the ends, those in the middle (let alone the other end) are frustratingly obtuse and unable to understand the dangers inherent in the positions they take. As Barry Goldwater said in 1964, "Extremism in the defense of liberty is no vice." Even though most of the people found in this book would see Goldwater as a representative of the middle, they might agree with his statement. Some, of course, would reject the label "extreme" for themselves. Others happily accept the label, usually in a spirit like that expressed by Goldwater. If there is something seriously wrong with the world—and everyone in this book believes there is—it is only sensible to go to whatever lengths are necessary to correct that wrong or those wrongs.

But from the middle, the meaning of extremism is quite simple: the extremes are the ends of the line representing political beliefs and attitudes, or those sections of the curve with relatively few people, and those in the middle believe that everyone at either end is seriously out of touch with reality. People do change positions, so that it is possible for an extreme to become popular; this is the goal of many, but not all, who hold extremist views.

Different readers of these texts will find some essays extreme that others will perceive as in the center of the political spectrum. For example, when they were written, the three essays from John Birch Society journal *American Opinion* were considered "extreme" even by most conservatives. Today, the arguments made are very similar to the arguments made by the leadership of the Republican Party. On the other hand, the documents from the National Welfare Rights Organization appeared conservative to the left and extreme to the right at the time of publication. Today these policies, without changing a word, have moved dramatically to the left and would be rejected by most liberals as too "extreme."

The authors of the documents found in this book disagree profoundly about what is wrong with the world and about what needs to be done to bring the world to its collective senses. Many don't care about "the world" at all; they care only about the United States. For these, "the world" and its institutions are the enemy. There is always an enemy. For others the problem is that the United States has lost its way and must be brought back to the correct path or led to a new and better path. For some the problems are deeply rooted in history; for others the causes of our problems are more recent.

Many extremists believe in the existence of a conspiracy, which, when identified, allows one to know who the enemy is.[1] For most the conspiracy is a well-thought-out plot that reaches far into the past and is under the control of identifiable groups; but there are many conspiracies operating at different levels of awareness, and there are many dupes or, in a phrase once popular, fellow travelers, who probably wouldn't behave as they do if they only knew better. For others there is no conspiracy as such, or it is a conspiracy that reflects the desire of certain people to keep the power they have, and at least some of the conspirators don't know that they are part of a conspiracy. That may sound odd, but if one accepts the argument that the formation of an individual's beliefs and attitudes is influenced more by social position than conscious choice, it is possible to be part of a conspiracy about which one knows little or nothing.

For some the issues are more fundamental: the problem is that there is a war between God and Satan, with the human race as the battleground. Others put the same point more generally, seeing the battle as one between good and evil, but for them good and evil are real, live presences, and the conflict between them is the most important issue in life.

One of the difficulties for someone trying to understand extremism in the United States is that all of the above views may be held by a single writer or movement. Thus, for some, Satan long ago chose his disciples, who have ever since been conspiring to control the human race using a variety of human tools, both knowing and unknowing. Some of these tools are people with power who want to keep it; others are people without power who want to change their position. It all gets very complicated.

The extremes are often called the far right and the far left. (The labels "left" and "right" appear to have originated in the French National Assembly of 1789, when the radicals sat to the left of the presiding officer and the conservatives to the right.) But these labels, while sometimes useful, are problematic. First, few conservatives want to be associated with the far right as presented here; they might prefer the label "reactionary" (the belief that the past was better than the present and that society should be turned completely around) for these groups. But many of the people here described on the right don't believe that; they believe there is need for radical change in the direction of some ideal, just what we usually think of as the definition of a radical on the left. Second, there are different issues on which people are conservative or radical. The question of equality, however, is one issue that can be used to distinguish the far right from the far left. On the whole, the left believes that greater equality is desirable, and the right believes that human beings simply aren't equal and that any attempt to achieve equality is doomed to failure. On other dimensions, however, some parts of the two extremes are similar; the line becomes a circle. For example, some on both extremes believe the only way to achieve their goals is to abolish or severely restrict governmental power.

DEBATES OVER THE LOCUS OF GOVERNMENTAL POWER

Many on both the left and the right believe they are supporting the ideals of the so-called Founding Fathers and the United States Constitution and Bill of Rights. This is possible for two main reasons. First, the Founding Fathers profoundly disagreed with each other and, therefore, created a Constitution that was the result of hundreds of compromises. They were also forced to add the Bill of Rights (opposed by many of the Founding Fathers). Second, the left and right focus on specific parts of the Constitution and Bill of Rights and frequently read the same parts very differently.

One of the central disputes, whose history predates the Constitution, concerns where power should reside—the local area, the state, or the national government.[2] Article 2 of the Articles of Confederation reads: "Each State retains its sovereignty, freedom and independence, and every power, jurisdiction and right, which is not by this confederation expressly delegated to the United States, in Congress assembled." This can be contrasted with the Tenth Amendment to the United States Constitution, which reads: "The powers not delegated to the United States by the Constitution, nor prohibited by it to the States, are reserved to the States respectively, or to the people." That phrase "to the people," which is often unnoticed or ignored, makes the intent of the amendment unclear, but it is clear that the central issues were, first, the various powers of the central government, the state governments, and the people; and second, the best way to limit power and corruption.

The argument that the Articles of Confederation were too democratic, i.e., allowed power to be decentralized and, some would argue, in the hands of the lower classes, provided a major justification for centralized, limited, and divided power, with only one house of the legislature directly elected. The Constitution, which took this form, was, it can be argued, a reflection of the classical republican tradition that a government balanced among the one, the few, and the many was the best way to limit power. In the Revolution, the one (the monarch) was eliminated, and the drafting of the Articles was a battle between advocates of the few and the many, with the latter generally winning at that time, while the Constitution later reasserted a balance.

The Articles were certainly not a balanced constitution, but they still reflected some of the concerns of classical republicanism. Their very lack of balance was based on the overriding concern to limit power and, hence, the possibility of corruption. Americans were intensely aware of the corruption of the British and became even more intensely aware of the possibility of corruption in their own midst as a result of the activities of many entrepreneurs during the Revolution. Thus, an overriding motivation of the drafters of the Articles was to avoid unchecked power.

The men writing both the Articles and many of the new state constitutions were most concerned with the problem of centralized power. Thus, the Articles had a weak to nonexistent executive, and even Congress had little power. In addition, delegates to Congress were "annually appointed" and "no person shall be capable of being a delegate for more than three years in any term of six years; nor shall any person, being a delegate, be capable of holding any office under the United States, for which he, or any other for his benefit, receives any salary, fees, or emolument of any kind" (Art. 5). All these rules were designed to check corruption by limiting the possibility of using one's office for personal gain.

The limitations on central power in the Articles were so great that it is necessary to look at the states to see where power resided. Since delegates to Congress were "appointed, in such manner as the legislature of each state shall direct" (Art. 5), those legislatures would appear to hold the most power. Since it was shortly to become a common argument that corruption at the state level was the real problem under the Articles, this would seem doubly appropriate. Consequently, the proponents of the Constitution argued that it was too much democracy in the states that led to the corruption.

Many Americans who had fought against centralized power found, not too much to their surprise, that power corrupts wherever it is placed. Probably the most famous result of this was Shays's Rebellion, an armed revolt in Western Massachusetts in 1786–87, sparked after debt-ridden farmers who had appealed to the state legislature for relief were rebuffed. Daniel Shays (1747?–1825) and others forcibly prevented county courts from meeting to make judgments for debt. Although suppressed, the rebellion gained considerable support and realized some of its goals. Since Shays and others argued that the state legislature, and particularly the state senate, was in the hands of the upper classes and was being used for their benefit, the Rebellion worried many in the upper classes in other states.

Looked at from the point of view of advocates of the Constitution, the problem was that too much power rested with the popularly elected house of the state legislatures or, as many put it at the time, too much democracy. But, from the point of view of Daniel Shays and some opponents of the Constitution, the problem was that the state legislatures had institutionalized the rule of state elites, abolished popularly controlled local institutions, and ignored the wishes of the people, i.e., too little democracy. Here, the differences within the republican ideology come sharply into focus, and it is clear that there were those who, while accepting that corruption and the creation of virtuous citizens were the central issues, rejected the idea that a balanced government was the solution. Between these extremes lay the Articles.

But the question of sovereignty was complicated by an additional factor in the South. While the North and particularly New England fought over state elite versus local popular government, and while the same battle raged in parts of the South, a very different central concern existed in the South. State sovereignty there meant greater protection for the Southern way of life, particularly the institution of slavery. As a result, two models of states' rights developed.

With some oversimplifications, these two models can be identified with New England and the South. In the South, states' rights were defended as part of the defense of slavery, or put more generally, as the defense of a set of social and economic institutions that included slavery. In New England, states' rights were part of a more general argument for the greater decentralization of political power. It was used to attack the existing social, political, and economic institutions. In other words, at the time of the Articles, the New England model was radical and the Southern model was conservative. In the Articles the two forces combined to protect the power of the states. But neither model proved adequate to its assigned task or capable of eliminating corruption and producing the virtuous citizen.

This oversimplification obscures three points. First, within its defense of state sovereignty, New England was divided over where the ultimate power should lie in the state. As a result, the more conservative New Englanders, whatever their position on slavery, were not that different from the dominant Southern position. Second, there were radicals in the South who wanted state power out of the hands of the state elites. Third, there were, of course, people in both sections who opposed state sovereignty altogether and wanted greater centralization of power. These people were shortly to defeat the proponents of state sovereignty, although they had to compromise to do so.

The Constitution that replaced the Articles was widely opposed in the United States as removing sovereignty from the thirteen state governments and creating a powerful, centralized, national government. The debate over the adoption of the Constitution produced a group of people that history has labeled the Anti-Federalists. As with any group of people united by opposition, they had little in common except the belief that the centralized government of the Constitution was not the balanced government described by its proponents, but a device for stripping power from the states and the people.

We know what happened to the Articles, but the central debate on the focus of sovereignty continued, as did the argument about how to limit power and avoid corruption. While the Federalists established a national government with considerable power, the Tenth Amendment was added to confuse the issue. The period of Jeffersonian democracy shifted power very slightly away from the center, and the period of Jacksonian democracy appears on the surface to have shifted power significantly back to the people. As the franchise was broadened and more states were added to the union—states perforce further from the centers of national power—the whole issue opened up again. Moreover, slavery made the issue of the locus of sovereignty particularly salient in the South.

In the period we call Jacksonian democracy the defenders of states' rights and decentralization would seem to have won a major victory. Andrew Jackson became a symbol of the power of the people, and a wave of democratic fervor swept the land. Popular democracy seemed about to be established. But as usual with symbols, this one was multifaceted. Jackson was a national hero and president, and, as a result, the focus of the popular democracy was not on local or state centers of power. On the other hand, if travelers' tales and the newspapers are to be believed, politics seemed to become a national pastime, and in this way decentralized institutions were reinvigorated.

Classical republicanism was given its most coherent nineteenth-century expression by John C. Calhoun. Calhoun traced his intellectual ancestry back to Aristotle and used him to defend both a balanced constitution and slavery. Calhoun argued that the Constitution did not provide a sufficient set of checks and balances in that it allowed a national majority to override the deeply held beliefs of a regional majority. Thus, he preferred his system of "concurrent majorities" (a system that provided for a veto over legislation by certain groups) as a mechanism for controlling power and obtaining a better balanced constitution.

As we know but tend to forget, a part of the United States lived for a time under what was called a confederation, and that confederation had a constitution. To a very great extent the Constitution of the Confederate States of America is identical to the U.S. Constitution, with the early amendments incorporated into the text. The Confederate States were no less centralized than the United States, but the differences between the two constitutions are sometimes interesting. Some differences are not directly related to this book, such as the item veto and the provision for question time for heads of executive departments, but there are differences that do relate to the combined issue of checked power and states' rights, clear issues for both left and right. For example, the Confederate Constitution prohibits the central government from any involvement in any promotion of industry by either import taxes or duties (Art. 1, sec. 8.1) or by construction projects except those directly related to navigation (Art. 1, sec. 8.3). Such prohibitions appear to be aimed at keeping government totally out of commerce, and there are a number of provisions strictly limiting the power of Congress to spend money. Since it is generally believed that the real impact of Adam Smith was felt in the US about this time, it is reasonable to conclude that these provisions are simply a reflection of *laissez-faire* thought. But it should also be recognized that the provisions are directed at the central government, not the state government, and they are the only limitations on the central government that the Confederacy added to the U.S. Constitution, except those directly related to slavery.

At the end of the Civil War, amendments to the Constitution were passed that limited the powers of the states. Legally the states' rights debate would appear to have ended on July 21, 1868, when the Fourteenth Amendment was adopted. But the debate certainly did not end politically. The period we call Reconstruction was short-lived, and after that few attempts were made to enforce the provisions of the Fourteenth Amendment. It was not until the 1960s that this amendment became a force in U.S. politics.

In the twentieth century the two models of states' rights have been expressed in many ways. The Southern model has been invoked in arguments over racial segregation, prayer in schools, sex education, abortion, and the so-called New Federalism. Obviously, the Southern model is now national. The New England model was expressed by the New Left in its concern with participatory democracy. The New England model is also now national. On the other hand, rhetoric aside, the arguments are not really about states' rights anymore, if they ever were. The arguments are about power and who should have it. The arguments are about what is necessary to create a virtuous citizen and how to avoid corruption.

Most radical thought, both left and right in the United States, which has generally been placed outside the debate over how to best check power and avoid corruption, belongs solidly inside it. Radicals tend to reject the balance of republicanism, but they do so precisely because they see it as incapable of providing the conditions in which a virtuous citizen can be nurtured. The different views of power and corruption found in the debates over the Articles and in the issues that come after them show that we still have much to learn about the relationship between political ideas and how they are worked out in practice.

Today parts of both the extreme left and the extreme right argue for radical decentralization, although they expect different results from it. Both have created small intentional communities to put their ideas into practice (this is well known about the left but generally unknown about the right), and both have argued for local control of political decision making.

POPULISM AND THE ROOTS OF EXTREMISM IN THE UNITED STATES

Most scholars trace the American right from early anti-immigrant or "nativist" movements that actually originated in the colonial period. Perhaps the best way to generalize the phenomenon is to call it "anti-alien," with the "alien" being not just foreigners but any group noticeably different, although in a nation of immigrants the most recent arrivals have frequently been the target of major concern and have been seen as carrying noxious beliefs and practices that would undermine the American way of life of the older immigrants.

While there are foreign roots for some of the social and political movements and ideologies of both left and right (Marxism for the left and fascism and National Socialism for the right), there was an indigenous movement—populism—which is the source of much on both the contemporary American left and right, as will be demonstrated by the documents reprinted in the next chapter.

Populism was a late-nineteenth-century social and political movement centered in the rural and small-town Midwest and South. The character of early American populism shows us how populism can be the basis for both contemporary extremes. On the one hand, late-nineteenth-century American populists demanded government action to help farmers and small businesses. Specifically, they asked for such things as the abolition of national banks (still a major issue for the right), free coinage of silver, paper money, a graduated income tax (now anathema to the right, while the left is concerned that it is being replaced by "repressive" taxes like the sales tax, generally favored by the right), government ownership of all means of transportation and communication (favorite themes of a good part of the left), election of senators by a direct vote of the people (achieved by the Seventeenth Amendment), civil service reform, restrictions on land ownership by foreigners, and an eight-hour workday. Many of the specific reforms reflect long-standing interests of the left, but they were designed to help the constituencies that at least now generally support the right in America.

In addition, populists asked for specific political reforms that would give the average citizen more power. Both the right and the left devoutly believe that "power to the people" means power to their supporters, and both have considerable evidence to back up their claims. The implementation of voter initiatives, referendums, and recalls, all means of taking power away from legislatures, had been advocated by populists. All three mechanisms have been used and are being used very effectively by both the left and the right.

A key to the bifurcated influence of populism is that nineteenth-century populism was divided over race, and people who call themselves populists today are still so divided. In the South and the southern part of the Midwest, populists were generally racist. In the northern Midwest, race was generally not an important issue, although there is some disagreement regarding the positions taken by various populist leaders.

This difference is today central to the character of both extremes. The extreme left generally strongly favors racial assimilation, and the extreme right generally strongly favors racial separation. A substantial part, but not all, of the extreme right identifies America as a quintessentially white nation with its roots in northern Europe.

An important aspect of the debate over race relations in the post–Civil War period related to states' rights, or, more generally, where power should reside in the American political system, a long-standing issue in this country, as we have seen from the previous section. William Lloyd Garrison (1805–1879), one of the leaders of the abolitionist movement, provides an excellent example of the dual theme of race relations and the locus of power. After an impassioned statement of the evils of slavery, he went on to say, "We fully and unanimously recognize the sovereignty of each State, to legislate exclusively within its limits; we concede that Congress, under the present national compact, has no right to interfere with any of the slave States in relation to this momentous subject."[3]

The most extreme response to the question of the locus of power was taken by the anarchists, who argued that power should reside either in the individual or in the small face-to-face community. The former is a fairly rare position in anarchism in general but is common in the United States in the form known as anarcho-capitalism. The earliest clear statement of anarcho-capitalism was made by Lysander Spooner (1808–1887), who argued that "two men have no more natural right to exercise any kind of authority over one, than one has to exercise authority over two. A man's natural rights are his own, against the whole world."[4] He went on to argue that continuing consent is the only basis for government; if an individual does not consent, then that individual is not bound.

Within American anarchism there was considerable debate over the locus of social decision making, because most anarchists recognized that after a wide range of questions were taken from community decision making and placed in the hands of individuals, there would still be some decisions that would have to be made collectively. In general anarchists wanted decision making at the lowest level possible, with cooperation among these levels to deal with questions that affected larger groups. But there were real disagreements about the identity of the groups. For example, the Industrial Workers of the World (IWW) wanted to bring all unions into "One Big Union," with decision making structured within the organization so that the local union would make all those decisions that affected only the local level, and cooperation at higher levels would occur as needed. This was a form of what is known as "workers' control." Except for the anarcho-capitalists, most anarchists argued that workers should control the workplace, but they did not accept the idea that work was the only basis for social decision making. Most anarchists, such as Emma Goldman (1869–1940), argued for a broader definition of the community so that all people living in an area would be involved.

This book acts as a guide to American extremism, mostly in the latter half of the twentieth century. It samples some of the most telling and revealing documents—mostly unknown—to provide an overview of the political, economic, racial, and sexual ideologies of both the extreme right and left. These texts, generally left to speak for themselves, reflect little-known but important parts of the ideological spectrum in the United States. While some of the groups are small, collectively they represent significant groupings of people with a long history in this country.

Most people in the middle are upset or even horrified by the extremes. Some of what will be discussed here is not very pleasant, and many would rather think that it doesn't exist, or that it is merely the result of a few misguided or sick people. Some in the middle are at times tempted to think that the extremes are really a conspiracy.

It is not clear how many people agree with the theories discussed here, but it is naive to think that there are only a few misguided or sick or evil people involved. Some of the groups are tiny, but there are many groups. And, more importantly, tiny groups have been known to increase their membership very quickly when the circumstances are right. The most obvious case is Hitler's Nazi Party, which grew from fewer than a dozen individuals into a movement that controlled a country and, for a time, much of Europe.

Thus, for a variety of reasons it is important that we understand our extremes. That is the purpose of this book. The focus is on the last twenty-five years (an almost entirely arbitrary number based on the collecting done by Laird Wilcox), but background information will be discussed and documented.

While the extreme left is represented in this book, the extreme right is given more space, both because the Wilcox Collection is stronger on the extreme right than on the extreme left, and because the extreme left has often been taken seriously by writers while the extreme right has usually been presented as the ravings of a few deluded people. It is imperative that we rid ourselves of that simplistic approach.

In understanding any thinker or movement we need to understand both what they are against and what they are for. In the past, the extreme right has been presented almost entirely for what it is against; the extreme left, interestingly, has been presented both in a more balanced fashion and, on the whole, more for what it is for. Here we will look at both sides, but particularly at what the extreme right is for.

In what follows I have tried to do a number of things. First, I provide a brief historical background, in which I note that the extremes have long histories in the United States. Second, while the two extremes coalesce around certain issues and ideas, there are differences both of emphasis and issues among the various groups, and I try to illustrate at least some of the range of positions taken on each extreme. Thus, third, I try to show the major issues that concern the extremes. As a result, I hope it will be possible to see the complexity of these movements.

In the chapters that follow, my commentary is given in italics to distinguish it from the documents reprinted here. Where a document contains footnotes or endnotes, these are indicated by superscript letters, presented as endnotes after the document, and labeled "Author's Notes." My own endnotes occur at the end of the chapter. I have retained the inconsistencies and irregularities of style, word capitalization, grammar, and punctuation found in the original documents. Obvious spelling mistakes or typographical errors are followed by my note *[sic]*.

NOTES

1. On conspiracy theories, see David Brion Davis, ed., *The Fear of Conspiracy: Images of Un-American Subversion from the Revolution to the Present Day* (Ithaca, N.Y.: Cornell University Press, 1971); Richard Orr Curry, comp., *Conspiracy: The Fear of Subversion in American History* (New York: Holt, Rinehart and Winston, 1972); and George Johnson, *Architects of Fear: Conspiracy Theories and Paranoia in American Politics* (Los Angeles: J. P. Tarcher, 1983).
2. The section on the Articles of Confederation is based on my "Articles of Confederation in American Political Thought," in *The American Constitution: The First Two Hundred Years 1787–1987,* ed. Joseph Smith, Exeter Studies in History Number 16 (Exeter, England: University of Exeter, 1987), 35–48.
3. William Lloyd Garrison, "Declaration of Sentiments (1833)," in *Selections from the Writings and Speeches of William Lloyd Garrison* (New York: Negro Universities Press, 1968), 412.
4. Lysander Spooner, *No Treason* (Boston: n.p., 1867).

1

POPULISM: AN AMERICAN ROOT OF BOTH LEFT AND RIGHT

Jacob Coxey

One excellent example of the continuity of American reform movements and their populist roots is Coxey's Army.[1] Jacob Sechler Coxey (1854–1951) was a wealthy businessman who became the symbol of the movement of the unemployed at the turn of the century, although there were a number of such armies. Coxey came out of the Greenback tradition (a movement to put more money into the economy by printing more money), and his reform proposals reflect that tradition, but his major influence was to develop the idea that legislatures could pass legislation to help create jobs. His two major bills are excellent examples:

I. The Good Roads Bill—53rd Congress, 2d Session, H.R. 7438, June 12, 1894.

A BILL to provide for the improvement of public roads, and for other purposes.

Be it enacted by the Senate and the House of Representatives of the United

From *Cause and Cure* 2, no. 2 (1894).

States of America in Congress assembled, That the Secretary of the Treasury of the United States is hereby authorized and instructed to have engraved and have printed, immediately after the passage of this bill, five hundred millions of dollars of Treasury notes, a legal tender for all debts, public and private, said notes to be in denominations of one, two, five and ten dollars, and to be placed in a fund to be known as the "general county-road fund system of the United States," and to be expended solely for said purpose.

Sec. 2. That it shall be the duty of the Secretary of War to take charge of the construction of the said general county-road system of the United States, and said construction to commence as soon as the Secretary of the Treasury shall inform the Secretary of War that the said fund is available, which shall not be later than sixty days from and after the passage of this bill, when it shall be the duty of the Secretary of War to inaugurate the work and expend the sum of twenty millions of dollars per month pro rata with the number of miles of road in each State and Territory in the United States.

Sec. 3. That all labor other than that of the office of the Secretary of War, "whose compensations are already fixed by law," shall be paid by the day, and that the rate be not less than one dollar and fifty cents per day for common labor and three dollars and fifty cents for team and labor, and that eight hours per day shall constitute a day's labor under the provisions of this bill, and that all citizens of the United States making application to labor shall be employed.

II. The Non-Interest-Bearing Bond Bill.—53rd Congress, 2d Session, H. R. 7463, June 15, 1894.

A BILL to provide for public improvements and employment of the citizens of the United States.

Be it enacted by the Senate and House of Representatives of the United States of America in Congress assembled, That whenever any State, Territory, county, township, municipality, or incorporated town or village deem it necessary to make any public improvements they shall deposit with the Secretary of the Treasury of the United States of America a non-interest-bearing twenty-five-year bond, not to exceed one-half of the assessed valuation of the property in said State, Territory, county, township, municipality, or incorporated town or village, and said bond to be retired at the rate of four per centum per annum.

Sec. 2. That whenever the foregoing section of this act has been complied with it shall be mandatory upon the Secretary of the Treasury of the United States to have engraved and printed Treasury notes in the denominations of one, two, five and ten dollars each, which shall be a full legal tender for all debts, public and private, to the face value of said bond and deliver to said State, Territory, county, township, municipality, or incorporated town or village ninety-nine per centum of said notes, and retain one per centum for expense of engraving and printing same.

Sec. 3. That after the passage of this act it shall be compulsory upon every incorporated town or village, municipality, township, county, State or Territory to give employment to any idle man applying for work, and that the rate be not less than one dollar and fifty cents per day for common labor and three dollars and fifty cents per day for team and labor, and that eight hours per day shall constitute a day's labor under the provisions of this act.

Socialist Party

Most of the left in the United States identifies itself as socialist and does not consider socialism "extreme," thus making the point that extremism depends on, among other things, where one is standing. Socialism is considered extreme by many Americans, but it has a rich history in the United States. That history includes one of the best selling novels, Looking Backward, 2000–1887 *(1888) by Edward Bellamy, in which he used the label "nationalism" rather than socialism because even in 1888 the word socialism was not acceptable. While there are a wide variety of socialisms that include a range of positions on the locus of power, most Americans think of a system with considerable power at the national level when they use the word. An example of this type of socialism can be seen in the following items from the 1912 platform of the Socialist Party, which contains proposals very similar to those of the left side of American populism.*

COLLECTIVE OWNERSHIP

1. The collective ownership and democratic management of railroads, wire and wireless telegraphs and telephones, express services, steamboat lines and all other social means of transportation and communication and of all large-scale industries.

2. The immediate acquirement by the municipalities, the states or the federal government of all grain elevators, stock yards, storage warehouses, and other distributing agencies, in order to reduce the present extortionate cost of living.

3. The extension of the public domain to include mines, quarries, oil wells, forests and water power. . . .

5. The collective ownership of land wherever practicable, and in cases where such ownership is impracticable, the appropriation by taxation of the annual rental value of all land held for speculation or exploitation.

6. The collective ownership and democratic management of the banking and currency system.

Populist Party

Recent political parties on both the right and the left have called themselves populist. People on both the left and the right, including the Liberty Lobby, a major right organization that had its roots in the right wing of populism, supported Ross Perot in his presidential campaign because of the populist elements in his platform. Prior to Perot the best-known populist presidential political campaign was that of George Wallace in 1972 who, at least at the time, was generally thought of as on the right and was then supported by the Liberty Lobby as a populist.

An example of a modern populist group is the Populist Party. Its platform for 1984 as reported by the Liberty Lobby stipulates abolition of the privately owned Federal Reserve System; repudiation of the national debt; repeal of the federal income tax on individuals; enactment of tariff laws; restriction of immigration; non-involvement in foreign wars; and revitalization of the family farm. In 1986 the Liberty Lobby split from the Populist Party because it had been, so they said, taken over by a clique that ejected the early leaders, including Willis Carto, the founder and leader of the Liberty Lobby. In 1988 David Duke was the presidential nominee of the Populist Party.

The following items from the Populist Party of 1984 and 1988 illustrate the connections between early and late Populism and sketch in a number of the themes that will follow.

THE POPULIST PARTY OF THE UNITED STATES PLATFORM 1984

POWER TO THE PEOPLE

The following is the platform of the Populist party of the United States, adopted on February 29, 1984 by the National Committee of the Populist Party.

ECONOMIC

REPEAL THE INCOME TAX. Paid almost entirely by the productive middle class, the super rich pay very little of it and the indolent poor none of it. Endorsed by the Communist Manifesto and by corrupt capitalists bent on buying the votes of the welfarites it has become the main prop for socialism.

REASSERT SOVEREIGNTY by abolishing the privately owned and controlled Federal Reserve System. The international bankers operate the greatest scam in history. They create their funny money literally out of thin air—**and then charge us interest on it!** Thus, we have ever-higher interest rates, unending inflation, perpetual war and an interest bearing "national debt" of more than $6,000 for every man, woman, and child in America. The *per capita* interest on this fraudulent debt is $600 per year—**and you pay it with your income tax!** The Populist Party will end this swindle, give America real money and solid prosperity.

REPUDIATE THE NATIONAL DEBT. The taxpayers have the moral and legal right to repudiate all federal debt except that held by investors who have actually paid for government securities with money they have earned. The official national debt now stands at approximately $1,400,000,000,000 (one trillion, four hundred billion dollars). The interest alone on this debt now stands at approximately $130 billion per year and is steadily rising along with the principal. Interest paid each year to the unconstitutional, privately owned Federal Reserve Bank accounts for the third highest item in the

From "The Populist Party of the United States: Platform, 1984" (Washington, D.C.: Populist Party of the United States, [1984], flyer).

national budget. National survival requires that this debt be extinguished and we will do it. Failure to do so will bring either runaway inflation and the total destruction of our economy or a depression far worse than the one of the 1930's. Approximately ½ of the official federal debt consists of securities owned by organizations which did not (repeat, DID NOT) invest earned money in them but which literally manufactured "funny money" out of thin air to "buy" said investments! One of the purposes of the Populist Party is to EXPUNGE this fraudulent debt the same way it was created—by a stroke of the pen. The Supreme Court or Congress could abolish the Federal Reserve at any time and the federal government could begin issuing debt-free, interest-free money as the Constitution intended instead of borrowing it from mattoid [insane] international bank.

REACTIVATE ANTI-USURY LAWS. When a person buys a house these days he often pays lending agencies for three houses. Interest paid on funny money created out of thin air is the main cause of inflation and recession. Private lending agencies, if they are allowed to exist at all, should be strictly controlled by restored anti-usury laws.

REJUVENATE AMERICAN INDUSTRY BY THE ENACTMENT OF FAIR TARIFF LAWS. The Populist Party will protect American manufacturers and workers by enacting tariff legislation to equalize cost at the water's edge, thus bringing back millions of jobs for Americans.

REVITALIZE THE FAMILY FARM. To save America's most precious resource—the vanishing landed American family farm—the Populist Party promises price parity to family farmers but not agri-business corporations or absentee owners. Foreign ownership of land will be prohibited. The foolish system of paying farmers not to farm in the midst of a starving world will be brought to an end.

REBUILD AMERICA INTERNALLY. Many of our highways and bridges are in bad need of repair even as the Democrats and Republicans send billions of dollars overseas. Hundreds of thousands of unemployed will be put to work rebuilding America's vital transportation and communication systems.

RECLAIM FREE ENTERPRISE. International parasitic capitalism is incompatible with nationalism and with free enterprise. Business should be free of government interference except when it tends toward monopoly, when law is used to reestablish competition. Government regulations such as are found in OSHA [Occupational Safety and Health Administration] and the mountains of red-tape now hampering businessmen will be eliminated. Except for regulated public utilities, no business will be permitted to dominate the market.

THE FAMILY

RESURRECT ANTI-DEGENERACY LAWS AND CRACK DOWN ON CRIME. America was founded on the values of traditional Christian morality. Until recently states and local government and in some cases the national government were able to enact and enforce laws against pornography and lewdness. These powers should be reinstated. An immediate crackdown on illegal drugs, street crime and organized crime followed by sure and swift punishment will once again make our beloved country a safe and moral place for all law-abiding citizens.

REJECT ERA AND GAY RIGHTS. Legally woman already have more rights than men, and that is the way the Populist Party intends to keep it. Homosexuality is not only immoral, it is perversion and should not be recognized as a legitimate life style deserving special legislation and forcing normal people to accept them. The Populist Party recognizes a responsibility to fight this growing social disease.

CULTURE

RESTORE FREEDOM OF CHOICE. Forced racial busing must end. Government interference with religious schools must cease. State's rights with regard to public schools and universal freedom of choice with regard to property rights must be restored. Restore medical freedom (see below).

RESPECT RACIAL AND CULTURAL DIVERSITY. Every race has both the right and duty to pursue its destiny free from interference by another race. The Populist Party opposes slavery, imperialist exploitation, social programs which would radically modify another race's behavior, demands by one race for another to subsidize it financially or politically as long as it remains on American soil, forced segregation or integration. The Populist Party will not permit any racial minority, through control of the media, culture distortion or revolutionary political activity, to divide or factionalize the majority of the society-nation in which the minority lives.

REPULSE IMMIGRATION. Repeal the Third-World-oriented immigration law of 1965 and replace it with one which works to preserve America's cultural heritage in the face of a population explosion among backward peoples and a no-population growth among the founding stock of the nation. At present there are an estimated 15 million illegal aliens in our midst. They should be found and deported. Our borders must be sealed off from this traffic at all cost or the country will be destroyed from within after it has first been bankrupted.

RECONSIDER THE WELFARE PROGRAM. Welfare for the truly needy only. Deny the franchise to persons on welfare for more than one year. Welfare will cost the taxpayers $70 billion this year, and is rising fast, with some 30 million on welfare today. Indians on reservations—wards of the government—don't vote. Why should other government wards vote? Rebuild democracy, help bring prosperity back to the producers of society and bless the taxpayers by getting this vast class of socialist-voting, taxpayer-financed drones off the voting rolls. No representation without taxation.

LEGAL

RENEW CONSTITUTIONAL GOVERNMENT BY RESTRICTING JUDICIAL REVIEW. Thomas Jefferson, the first great populist, saw the seeds of the destruction of the Republic in usurpation of power by federal judges. These alleged protectors of our liberties have now become their chief destroyers. Congress should curb the power of these dictatorial judges to interfere in the reserved rights of the states. Court decisions regarding such issues as school prayer, abortion, criminal rights which have strayed far from public wishes would be negated. All federal judges—including Supreme Court justices—should be elected.

REAFFIRM THE RIGHT TO KEEP AND BEAR ARMS. The second Amendment must be vigorously protected from the criminal element both private and public.

RESERVE THE RIGHTS OF INDIVIDUALS TO SEEK MEDICAL HELP FREE OF GOVERNMENT INTERFERENCE. Limit the power of government to say who can and who can't engage in a particular profession. Stop the unconscionable denial of health foods and vitamins to people who want and need them. Permit cancer victims the treatment of choice.

REASSERT AMERICAN CREATIVITY. Inventiveness should be encouraged. Make this country energy independent, economically secure and healthy by providing for more freedom of choice and less bureaucratic hampering of creativity.

REJUVENATE DEMOCRACY BY ALLOWING MORE PARTICI- PATION IN GOVERNMENT BY THE PEOPLE. Amend the Constitution to provide for the direct election of the president after regional primaries and the direct election of federal judges. Initiative, referendum and recall should be encouraged at all levels of government and in all states. The people themselves should be able to vote directly on vital issues. Bring proportional representation to America.

FOREIGN POLICY

REESTABLISH THE AMERICA FIRST TRADITION OF ARMED NEUTRALITY. First laid down by President George Washington, our national policy of nonintervention in foreign wars in which the United States is not directly endangered served us well. Our reckless intervention in two European wars served only to strengthen the power of our communist and internationalist enemies. Two wars in Asia have been bogged down in a no-win, no gain, foreign policy that has made us the laughing stock of the world. Our allies in Europe and Asia should be forced to provide for their own defense as we gradually withdraw our armed forces. Our aggressive meddling in the Middle East must cease. The Western Hemisphere is within our sphere of influence and should be defended from communist subversion.

RESTRICT FOREIGN PRESSURE GROUPS. There can be but two foreign policies: nationalist or internationalist. The America First Populist Party will curb foreign influence in our government. "One World" is treason so it follows that internationalists at the executive level must be removed from office. Banker's front groups, like the one world-oriented Council on Foreign Relations, the Trilateral Commission and the Bilderbergers, set our foreign policy at the present time. The United States should withdraw from the United Nations and remove the United Nations from American soil.

REDUCE FOREIGN AID and use it only where our vital national interests are at stake. Now it is little more than another way for the international bankers to rip off the taxpayers. We should help backward economies by showing them the advantages of the free-enterprise system and helping them to become self-sufficient. Military aid should be given only to dependable allies and surplus foodstuffs bought directly from our farmers and shipped overseas must be kept from falling into hands of corrupt officials. Shipping advanced technology and military equipment to our enemies is treason. American capitalists virtually built the Soviet war machine, fulfilling Lenin's prophecy that the capitalist would sell the rope to hang himself if he can make a profit on it.

REVITALIZE AMERICA'S NATIONAL DEFENSE. Any arms control agreement would require on-the-site inspections. We distrust our enemies. We cannot afford to be at a disadvantage in any way on military matters. The Populist Party seeks no conflict with other nations and will work to stay out of their affairs but we are not pacifist. We demand no less than a second to none defense force. Waste, inefficiency, and non-military extravagance should be weeded from the Pentagon. Because we are not a police state that fears its own people the Populist Party opposes a peacetime draft.

REWARD FRIENDS, not enemies. The Soviet empire could easily be destroyed simply by aiding dozens of ethnic dissident groups inside the Iron Curtain. But the mattoids need communism to scare the people into tolerating massive taxes and a huge war budget, *a la* George Orwell's "1984." Proof: They send billions of your tax dollars to communist leaning countries like Zimbabwe but criminally ignore the needs of the heroic nationalists in Afghanistan waging a bloody struggle for independence.

HERE'S WHERE DAVID DUKE AND THE POPULIST PARTY STAND ON THE ISSUES

. . . a Ten Point Program For Keeping America Strong.

* RESTRICT IMMIGRATION to protect employment for American workers, and to preserve the spirit, the heritage and traditional values of our nation.

* ABOLISH "AFFIRMATIVE ACTION" AND RACIAL QUOTAS in hiring and education. Return to Thomas Jefferson's principle of "Equal Rights for All; Special Privilege for None." Eliminate forced racial busing and forced racial integration.

From "Here's Where David Duke and the Populist Party Stand on the Issues" (Ford City, Pa.: Populist Party, 1988, flyer).

* REFORM THE WELFARE SYSTEM. Require able-bodied welfare recipients to perform community work in order to receive welfare payments. Enforce family planning among welfare recipients and to stop rewarding those who continue to give birth to illegitimate children.

* CRACK DOWN ON CRIME by instituting the death penalty for drug dealers, murderers, rapists, and those involved in violent crime. Protect the right of law-abiding citizens to keep and bear arms as guaranteed by our U.S. Constitution.

* REDUCE FEDERAL INCOME TAXES on America's middle income wage earners. A recent congressional study demonstrates that even with exempting the poor from taxes, a flat rate of approximately 10% would bring in the same revenues as our current graduated system.

* PROTECT AMERICAN FARMERS AND WORKERS from slave-labor foreign imports by instituting protective tariffs. Revenues from tariffs would help make up budget deficits and bring in additional federal revenues.

* PLACE AMERICA'S INTERESTS FIRST in foreign policy making. Stand behind anti-communist allies such as South Africa and the Nicaraguan "contra" freedom fighters. Stop siding with Israel in its endless Middle East war mongering.

* REFORM WALL STREET. Enforce sweeping revisions of current trading regulations. Support free enterprise, not monopoly capitalism. Protect small business from government regulations that smother competition and prop up the multinational conglomerates. Defend consumers from price-fixing and artificial manipulation of the economy.

* ESTABLISH THE STRONGEST DEFENSE IN THE WORLD. Cease shipments of advanced technology and military equipment to enemy nations. Build an invincible national defense by maintaining a posture of armed neutrality.

* BRING DOWN INTEREST RATES by abolishing the privately-owned banking monopoly known as the Federal Reserve System. Replace the Fed with a national bank committed strictly to the interests of the nation as a whole.

NOTE

1. On Coxey, see Donald L. McMurry, *Coxey's Army: A Study of the Industrial Army Movement of 1894* (1929; reprint, Seattle: University of Washington Press,

1968). In " 'Coxey's Army' as a Millennial Movement," *Religion* 18 (1988): 363–389, Michael Barkun demonstrates that Coxey's Army had millenarian content, another connection with some of the contemporary movements presented here.

2

THE BEGINNINGS OF THE DEBATE IN THE TWENTIETH CENTURY

Father Charles E. Coughlin

As a starting point for the materials that are the focus of this chapter my choice is Father Charles E. Coughlin (1891–1979), a Roman Catholic priest who was one of the first of the radio preachers. He has been called a fascist—he was anti-Semitic, he spoke favorably of Germany during World War II, and his newspaper was suppressed for sedition—but he is more accurately thought of as a populist. This can be seen in the platform of the party he formed in 1936 to oppose Franklin Roosevelt. The party did very poorly at the polls.

1936 Platform of the Union Party

1. America shall be self-contained and self-sustained—no foreign entanglements, be they political, financial or military.

Kirk H. Porter and Donald Bruce Johnson, comps., *National Party Platforms 1840–1968* (Urbana: University of Illinois Press, 1970).

2. Congress and Congress alone shall coin, issue and regulate all the money and credit in the United States through a central bank of issue.

3. Immediately following the establishment of the central bank of issue, Congress shall provide for the retirement of all tax-exempt, interest-bearing bonds and certificates of indebtedness of the Federal Government, and shall refinance all the present agricultural mortgage indebtedness for the farmer and all the home mortgage indebtedness for the city owner by the use of its money and credit which it now gives to the control of private bankers.

4. Congress shall legislate that there will be an assurance of a living wage for all laborers capable of working and willing to work.

5. Congress shall legislate that there will be an assurance of production at a profit for the farmer.

6. Congress shall legislate that there will be assurance of reasonable and decent security for the aged, who, through no fault of their own, have been victimized and exploited by an unjust economic system which has so concentrated wealth in the hands of a few that it has impoverished great masses of our people.

7. Congress shall legislate that American agricultural, industrial and commercial markets will be protected from manipulation of foreign monies and from all raw material and processed goods produced abroad at less than a living wage.

8. Congress shall establish an adequate and perfect defense for our country from foreign aggression either by air, by land, or by sea, but with the understanding that our naval, air and military forces must not be used under any consideration in foreign fields or in foreign waters whether alone or in conjunction with any foreign power. If there must be conscription, there shall be conscription of wealth as well as of men.

9. Congress shall so legislate that all federal offices and positions of every nature shall be distributed through civil service qualifications and not through a system of party spoils and corrupt patronage.

10. Congress shall restore representative government to the people of the United States to preserve the sovereignty of the individual States of the United States by the ruthless eradication of bureaucracies.

11. Congress shall organize and institute federal works for the conservation of public lands, waters and forests, thereby creating billions of dollars of wealth, millions of jobs at the prevailing wage, and thousands of homes.

12. Congress shall protect small industry and private enterprise by control-

ling and decentralizing the economic domination of monopolies to the end that these small industries and enterprises may not only survive and prosper but that they may be multiplied.

13. Congress shall protect private property from confiscation through unnecessary taxation with the understanding that the human rights of the masses take precedence over the financial rights of the classes.

14. Congress shall set a limitation upon the net income of any individual in any one year and a limitation of the amount that such an individual may receive as a gift or as an inheritance, which limitation shall be executed through taxation.

15. Congress shall re-establish conditions so that the youths of the nation as they emerge from schools and colleges, will have the opportunity to earn a decent living while in the process of perfecting themselves in a trade or profession.

Other early contributors to the development of the right wing in America included William Dudley Pelley (1890–1965), a spiritualist who believed in reincarnation. His The New Liberator *(early 1930s) contained materials "received 'clairaudiently' via the Psychic Radio from Great Souls who have graduated out of this Three-Dimensional world into other areas of Time and Space." He later became the editor of Pelley's* "The Silvershirt Weekly" *and led the Silver Shirts, an anti-Semitic, anti-communist, Christian movement that he "revealed" on the day Hitler gained power in Germany. Another early leader was Gerald B. Winrod (1900–1957), who was an active supporter of Father Coughlin. Winrod argued that the communist conspiracy went back to the Illuminati, an organization he described as based on the occult and black magic, founded by Adam Weishaupt in 1776. Winrod, who called Weishaupt* "a human devil," *connected the Illuminati to the Jesuits, Masons, and Jews and said that Karl Marx had taken his teachings from Weishaupt.[1] In Winrod's newspaper,* The Revealer, *one author argued that communism is against both private property and monogamous marriage: "Economic collectivism comes <u>first</u>; marital collectivism <u>later</u>. The regimentation of business comes <u>first</u>; the regimentation of women and children, of family life comes <u>later</u>. The collectivization of wealth comes <u>first</u>; the collectivization of human life comes <u>later</u>."[2]*

Gerald L. K. Smith

The most important of Coughlin's compatriots was Gerald L. K. Smith (1898–1976), who called his position Christian Nationalism. In many ways Smith was the foremost precursor of the modern far right, and he was immensely influential. In addition to his extreme anti-Semitism, he came out strongly against integration because he saw African Americans as clearly inferior. He believed that fluoridation of water was a Soviet plot and part of a guerrilla war that was enveloping America.[3] He also believed that "there are about a million people in this country that will have to be put away into work camps and guarded concentration camps if we are to save America."[4] The following selections show the range of his concerns, and the issues he addresses will be found throughout the rest of the book.

1946
For These
We Work—Fight—Pray

1. Preservation of America as a Christian Nation.
2. Expose and fight Communism.
3. Safeguard American liberty against menace of bureaucratic Fascism.
4. Maintain a government set up by the majority which abuses no minority and is abused by no minority.
5. Protect and earmark national resources for our own citizenry first.
6. Maintain the George Washington Foreign Policy of friendship with all nations, trade with all nations, entangling alliances with none.
7. Oppose a world government and a super state.
8. Prove that the Worker, the Farmer, the Businessman, the Veteran, the Unemployed, the Aged, and the Infirm can enjoy more abundance under the true American system than any alien system now being proposed by foreign propagandists.
9. Stop immigration until all veterans have jobs.
10. Abolish the corrupt money system.

Gerald L. K. Smith, "1946: For These We Work—Fight—Pray," *The Cross and The Flag* 4, no. 10 (January 1946): 685.

IF I WERE PRESIDENT

1. I would recognize the true racial traditions of our people. In campaigning for the Presidency, I would encourage every human being, regardless of his race, creed or color to believe that he was entitled to the maximum of wealth, happiness and opportunity guaranteed under our Constitution; but I would remind every citizen that the reason America is so great, so rich, and so creative is because her tradition is the tradition of the white man. This is not something for which to boast. It is something for which to be grateful. It isn't a conviction to be used for the purposes of enslavement or oppression; but it is a conviction which should inspire us to preserve the strength and the genius which has come only from the white race. To the black man, we should say: "If you doubt our judgment in this matter, contrast our background with yours. Do you want the future environment of America to be determined by the traditions of dark Africa, or by the refinements and attributes of the civilization which characterize our forebears?

2. I would approach my responsibilities to high office in the knowledge that the dynamic of this civilization and the tradition of this Nation is fundamentally Christian. This conviction would not imply hatred or scorn for the unbeliever, the Jew, the pagan, or the indifferent. Everyone of these are entitled to the liberties guaranteed under the Constitution, but as President of the United States, I would lift up the name of Jesus Christ and I would plant the Cross beside the flag, both figuratively and literally. Intelligent observers know that in recent years the name of Christ has been "outlawed" by an unwritten law among politicians and public officials. A President being inaugurated, or a Governor accepting his high office, is permitted to use the word God, but never the name of Christ—or Christian. If by a slip of the tongue he gives mild and passing honor to our Lord Jesus Christ, he is immediately viewed with suspicion by the professional Jews who are determined that no tax-supported official shall be permitted to give public honor in relationship to his official duties to the name of Jesus Christ. Occasionally there is a violation of this rule by a limited number of clergymen who are called on to pray in political meetings and at Government functions. The Bible is opened to a text in the Old Testament when our President is

Gerald L. K. Smith, "If I Were President" (Los Angeles: Christian Nationalist Crusade, 1956, pamphlet).

inaugurated, because no risk must be run that might offend the professional Jew who shudders with contempt when the name of Jesus Christ is mentioned. If I were to become President of the United States, I would insist that at the inauguration ceremony the Bible be opened to Peter's confession as recorded in Mark 8:29: "Thou art the Christ".

I would avoid in this address anything that sounded sanctimonious and self-righteous, but it is my firm conviction that America will rise or fall based upon its attitude toward Christ.

I favor continued complete separation of church and state. If any public official or citizen as a result of his personal conviction prefers to omit any reference to his Lord, that is his Constitutional privilege, but the situation we face in America today is not of that sort. Thousands of men coming to high office are Christian believers in their personal life. They attend church. They are raising their families in the Church, but when they come to positions of high authority they deny their Lord by refusing to give Him honor and by refusing to mention His name "for fear of the Jews." . . .

3. I would insist that the unexplained and mysterious events of the past 25 years in relationship to our Government be faced without fear or favor. Some time back I prepared a handbook which deals with the great unanswered questions. Among these unanswered questions were listed the following: (1) Why was General Douglas MacArthur removed from his command? (2) Who is the mysterious Anna M. Rosenberg? (3) Who persuaded Franklin Roosevelt to recognize Communist Russia against the advice of all Intelligence agencies? (4) What is the mystery in the Morgenthau Diaries? (5) Who is protecting Alger Hiss from further questioning? (6) Is there a super-secret apparatus within the United States Government? (7) Who engineered the transfer of atomic-hydrogen bomb secrets from the United States to Russia? (8) What is the real unpublicized purpose of the United Nations? (9) Why have the greatest Generals and Admirals, who were engaged in the Korean conflict, been ignored? (10) What is the mystery behind the appearance in America of phenomenal quantities of currency? (11) What happened to General Lawton? (12) Why is official Jewry unanimously on one side? (13) If General Mark Clark was correct when he said that he received mysterious orders while in the Far East, signed by high officials in Washington, only to be told by those same high officials that they did not sign these orders which helped to effect defeat—if General Clark's report is correct, why have we not been told the truth concerning these forgeries? (14) Who are the masterminds of appeasement and co-existence? (15) Why have we permitted the

Communists to break their Armistice agreement in Korea? (16) Who initiated the conspiracy against McCarthy? (17) Why does the death of General Patton and his relatives remain a mystery? (18) What is behind the new national policy of cowardice? (19) Is Harry Dexter White (Weis) dead or alive? (20) Who was responsible for permitting spies, posing as British agents, to see our most deadly military and diplomatic secrets in Washington? (21) What organization is in a deliberate campaign to eliminate the name of Jesus Christ in relationship to all public institutions, including the removal of crosses in military cemeteries? Is there an organized campaign by pro-Communists and appeasers to capture the influence of organized church denominations? (22) Who is responsible for our squandering one billion dollars on Tito in Yugoslavia? (23) What powerful organizations are raising millions of dollars to be used in what they call the quarantine treatment of patriots—patriots who are intelligent enough and brave enough to try to get the answers to these questions out to the people? (24) Is it true that the same undercover elements that kidnapped the Democratic Party have now kidnapped the Republican Party, to the end that traditional Democrats and traditional Republicans are both outside the area of effective leadership? (25) What force has power to determine what the American people shall and shall not know concerning their affairs? (26) Why the mania to break down racial self-respect and degenerate the purity of the white race by a program of mongrelization—integration? (27) Who is engineering the campaign to destroy the original and full purpose of the Declaration of Independence? (28) Why are millions of dollars being spent by lobbyists and propagandists to break down our immigration barriers and flood the Nation with aliens? (29) Why did President Eisenhower send a message of congratulations to the Kremlin on the most recent anniversary of the bloody Red Revolution? (30) Why have the American people never been told the true story about the millions of Russian refugees that were rounded up in Europe after World War II and returned forcibly to slave labor, torture and death? (31) What is the explanation for the fact that every chairman of every Congressional Committee that has really investigated and exposed Communism has been smeared, persecuted, threatened with death, and held up to ridicule by the most prominent newspaper and ether-wave commentators? (32) What about the treasonable secrecy at Yalta? (33) What is the truth behind the General George Marshall mystery?

I would go on radio and television and I would give satisfactory explanation of all matters that had heretofore been scientifically and purposely hidden from the people. Wherever there was no satisfactory information available I would release the proper law enforcement officials, to the end that the manipulators of deceitful chicaneries be exposed and brought to justice.

4. I would call on the Congress of the United States to resume its rightful position of authority as provided for in the Constitution. In recent years the Executive Department of our Government has built up terrific bureaucracies. These bureaucracies are manned and directed by full-time bureaucrats who draw on the Treasury of the United States almost without limit. They are surrounded by hundreds and thousands of expensive helpers, and the combination has resulted in a government of the bureaucrats by the bureaucrats and for the bureaucrats.

Strange as it may seem, the members of Congress are the most impoverished section of our Government. Recently they have been given some increases in personal salaries, but that constitutes the smallest part of the problem. They lack research help. They lack access to facts necessary to fulfill their representative responsibility. Thus, when they come in conflict with a bureaucrat who is likely to be only concerned with his own job and his own budget, they are overwhelmed. The result is that the decisions are usually made in favor of the bureaucrat instead of the elected representative of the people.

5. I would call on Congress and the various States to establish by Constitutional amendment whatever regulation was necessary to maintain our racial traditions and outlaw mongrelization. I would ask that it be made a criminal offense for blacks and whites to intermarry. In expressing my convictions concerning this matter, I would do so as a Christian man with no hate in his heart whatsoever. I would call on America to respect the tradition of nature as originally set in motion by God Almighty. I would call attention to the fact that the separation of the races of color from the white race was not a modern invention of the 20th Century fanatic, but was established by God Almighty in the unique arrangements by which the races were made separate in the beginning. I would not deny the Negro his opportunity to work and improve his situation, and I would suggest that he be encouraged as long as he made no attempt to cross the color line as it involved marriage and reproduction. I would advocate segregation in the school system, and I would advocate that public sentiment, as well as laws of the land, forbid all forms of social intermixture. I would advocate that these gestures be made in the spirit of compassion and Christian love, and I would not brand an exponent of these constructive policies as a hatemonger any more than I would brand a farmer a hatemonger because he chose to raise pure-bred stock rather than

cross-bred mongrels. I would point out that the people who have exercised demagoguery in exciting the Negro vote were the real hatemongers. I would point out that they are the ones who are creating ill-will and bad blood between the races. . . .

6. I would give all the moral support at my command to the great McCarran-Walter Immigration Act. This act has grown out of the hearts of the American people in their determination to preserve the racial traditions of our Nation. It restricts immigration in such a way as to protect America against criminals and conspirators. It recognizes the fact that Nordic nations and the Anglo-Saxon nations have furnished the foundation structure of our population. This Act is a magnificent protection against the threat of a flood of immigration which could destroy America without the firing of a shot. The Act was passed and it has survived in spite of the opposition of Roosevelt, Truman and Eisenhower. The most aggressive opponents of the Act are the organized professional Jews. They have vowed to destroy it, and under the leadership of their spokesmen they have declared time and again that the McCarran Immigration Act must go. Those of us who believe vigorously in the rich traditions of America are equally as determined that it must remain.

7. I would urge the Congress of the United States in harmony with an awakened public to return to the governments of the 48 states all the functions that have been usurped by the over-ambitious bureaucracies during the terms of office of Roosevelt, Truman and Eisenhower. I would go to the American people via the press, radio and television and enlighten them concerning the responsibilities of the states in relationship to the responsibility of the United States Government.

8. I would drive the money-changers out of the 'Temple'. We have been enslaved by usury. We have involved ourselves in debt for an amount twice the value of all our property. We pay to the money-changers each year $15,000,000,000.00 (fifteen billion dollars) in interest. This is the equivalent to the assessed valuation of all our real estate and real property every ten years. Some hold the conviction that Abraham Lincoln was slain not at the instigation of the South, but at the instigation of the money-changers who feared the monetary philosophy of Abraham Lincoln. Lincoln, it will be remembered, issued currency in harmony with the Constitution of the United States and free from the tribute such as we now pay to the money-changers via the Federal Reserve Bank. Why should we out of our blood, sweat and tears pay tribute to the usurers when the very money that they loan us by their trick manipulations is underwritten by the credit and the substance of

the United States Government? Recently President Eisenhower recommended a $25,000,000,000.00 road-building program to be financed by usurious bonds. Fortunately this bill was defeated, but if it had passed the interest rates would have been such that by the time the bonds had been retired we would have paid in interest another $25,000,000,000.00. This usurious technique for financing public projects has become virtually the law of the land whether it has to do with a municipality or the Federal Government. We are being eaten up with the collectors of interest, and the whole matter being manipulated by the same sort of people whom Jesus whipped out of the Temple when He said: "Ye shall not make of my Father's house a den of thieves."

9. I would revive the term "America First", and I would encourage every intelligent patriotic soldier in a position of authority to give first consideration to America's defense. I would recognize the fact that President Monroe was right when he expressed his doctrine in relationship to our Western Hemisphere neighbors. I would discourage any letting of blood to satisfy the century-old factions of the old world. I am no pacifist. I do not believe that there is any substitute for a strong, vigorous national defense. As President of the United States I would have access to the great intelligence secrets concerning world affairs, and if I became convinced that the atom-hydrogen bomb was available to all our friends and foes, then I would assume that as a matter of intelligent self-interest any nation would avoid using this deadly instrument of annihilation. This mutual fear of the atom and hydrogen bombs re-emphasizes the importance of conventional equipment for the protection of our nation, and I would insist that we maintain a defense in harmony with the best intelligence of the most patriotic students of world affairs.

10. I would remove from every government job and office under my appointment every traitor and every individual who had even the smell of treason upon him. I would not deny him any of his Constitutional liberties except as they were denied by due process of law, but I would insist that every department has the authority to remove any individual unwise enough to fraternize with traitors.

11. I would ask for the abolition of Civil Service. The principle of Civil Service was originally intended to protect America from the spoils system of political preference. It has degenerated into a "feather bed" racket in government which makes it virtually impossible for a President to assume his responsibilities and to take responsibility. People cannot be fired from Government office without long and laborious hearings. I believe when a new

Administration goes into the Government that the Party in power should assume responsibility for everything that goes on in every office and in every department, and I believe that if the Party wants to remove the most insignificant jobholder in the most insignificant spot, he should have the authority and the responsibility of doing so, if necessary. When the Truman regime was defeated, the same jobholders moved over into the Eisenhower organization, and instead of the Republicans coming to power the bureaucrats which had been frozen in office by Roosevelt and Truman continued to manipulate with very little interference and with practically no turn-over.

12. I would encourage the exposure of treason and the symptoms of treason. I would give full cooperation to such committees as the so-called McCarthy Committee and the Un-American Activities Committee of the House of Representatives. Strange enough, these committees which have been headed in recent years by men of patriotism and courage have almost without exception been smeared, discouraged and sabotaged by the President of the United States whether that President happened to be Franklin Roosevelt, Harry Truman or Dwight David Eisenhower. In fact, it is my opinion that McCarthy made as much headway, if not more, during the Presidential term of Truman than he did when Eisenhower came to office. Nothing in American history has been more vicious than what the White House, under Eisenhower, attempted to do and did do to Senator McCarthy. What happened to his key witness General Lawton is still one of the real unsolved mysteries of this generation.

13. I would deliver a special address concerning the treasonable potentialities and the diabolical qualities of the United Nations and its affiliated auxiliaries, including UNESCO. . . .

14. I would call on the Congress of the United States to investigate and expose all privately financed "OGPU" organizations, seeking to coerce and intimidate private citizens. I would dwell on the activities of the Anti-Defamation League of the B'nai B'rith. This is a powerful Jewish investigative agency which specializes in smearing and sabotaging the activities of patriots. Recently a group of citizens in New Orleans, Louisiana revealed that this Anti-Defamation League was planting literature in the school system which was enigmatic to the best welfare of their patriotic citizenry and the environment of the school children. The Board of Education accepted the recommendation of these patriotic citizens and the ADL propaganda was thrown out. At the very moment that this address was being reproduced in print, the Jewish Anti-Defamation League with unlimited sums of money

was releasing upon the patriots of New Orleans a campaign of persecution and abuse which they alone know how to put into motion. . . .

15. I would call on the people of the United States to support their Congress in the repeal of the income tax by a new Constitutional amendment that would re-establish the free enterprise that we had in the United States before the days of Baruch and Wilson. I would advocate the substitution of a manufacturers sales tax. This would put an end to income tax reports and all of those coercive methods now being employed by a bureaucracy which has terrorized the American public with a constant threat of harassment, assessment, indictment, incarceration and embarrassment. The income tax as a philosophy originated in the minds of Karl Marx and his associates. I rejoice over the fact that there exists in the United States an organization especially dedicated to the repeal of this abortive and tyrannical tax. If we were taxed as we spent, then every night as we went to bed, our taxes would be fully paid and there would be no reports to make out.

16. I would call on the Congress and all authorities concerned with the matter to establish the traditional liberty of free speech over radio and television. I would remind the people of America that the air and the ether waves belong to all of us and that these facilities are not monopolies to be used recklessly or arrogantly by the molders of propaganda and arbitrary opinion. I would assume that the American people were wise enough, when given all sides of important questions, to make their own decisions and never again would I let it be said that men were denied the right to purchase television and use television and radio merely because their opinions were not in harmony with those in authority or with the "hidden hand" manipulators operating behind the scenes. The American Jewish Committee some years ago created a formula for quarantine, and they pronounced this "sentence" upon me. The result of this arrogant Jewish manipulation has been that I cannot buy radio time and television time even though a full copy of my manuscripts are submitted in advance. Some years ago I contracted in behalf of the Christian Nationalist Crusade for $25,000.00 worth of time on a Mexican radio station. I was allowed to speak only twice. My messages were very satisfactory to the ownership of the station, but the Jews, functioning by way of the Mexican Government, brought pressure on the station, making it necessary for them to cancel my contract.

17. I would ask for an investigation of the most powerful and ruthless political organization on earth; namely, Jew Zionism. I would point out that millions and millions of dollars are raised by this organization and that their

members carry on lobbying and political activity in every capital on the face of the earth. I would point out that the reason this organization is not well known is because their members have been able to coerce press, radio and television to the point of great silence except to flatter and boost. Perhaps in the history of man there has never been an organization as tyrannical, as coercive and as intolerant as world Zionism. This is the organization which has given us the abortive state of Jew Palestine which calls itself Israel. I refuse to refer to it as Israel because I believe that Israel was a body of humanity out of which God gave us our Lord Jesus Christ. I furthermore believe that every Christian is an heir to God's promise to Abraham. These so-called Jews who deny Jesus Christ forfeit completely their inheritance by endorsing the condemnation of our Lord who said: "He that believeth not shall be damned" . . . .

IF THE CRUSADER QUITS, WHAT HAPPENS?

Below I summarize what is planned for us and the blueprints of conspiracy in the great centers of satanic power the world over.

1. A revolutionary savage on the order of the Black Panthers or a campus killer or a street mugger comes to your door demanding that you prepare to turn your home over to him as a gift. You will be given one hour or less to vacate.
2. Money, as an instrument, will be abolished and all your available resources will be handled by computers through central clearing houses.
3. The great monopolies which now control our economy, about 200 in number, will be merged with the revolutionary government after their executives have been assassinated. This will complete the pattern of *state* capitalism.
4. Religion will be completely outlawed and as a sop the people will be permitted to exercise their faith in a limited way only inside church buildings.
5. All communication will be cleared from the headquarters of tyranny. Nothing can be spoken on the air or written or printed or published except under the direction of the dictatorial machine.

Gerald L. K. Smith, "If the Crusader Quits, What Happens?" (Los Angeles: Christian Nationalist Crusade, [1980s], pamphlet).

6. All protestors will be immediately incarcerated as prisoners or assassinated as traitors to the new revolution.

7. Racial distinctions will be abolished and a formula for forced intermarriage, or at least forced breeding, will be so designed as to abolish black, white, brown, yellow and red and merge it all into a mongrel color designed to wipe out all racial tradition. Opposition will meet with prison or death.

8. All private schools and colleges will disappear and be merged into the state controlled educational system where all textbooks and reference books will be abolished that contradict the program of revolutionary tyranny. Christian faith especially will be downgraded and ridiculed. Children and young people will be taught to hate the name of Jesus Christ.

9. All babies will be numbered at birth. This number will serve as a permanent identification during the entire life of the individual. It is very likely that the number will be tattooed on the child.

10. The birth of babies will be outlawed beyond the second child. It will be made a crime to have more than two babies.

11. Compulsory abortion will be effective after two children have been born. Parents ignoring this rule will face criminal procedures.

12. Without any excuse except to get them out of the way, the old people will be put to sleep and buried. Mercy killing, like abortion, is already being proposed by those who would substitute humanism for Christianity.

13. There will be no independent choice of occupation. The state-controlled psychiatrists will make mental tests and assign people to occupations that fit into their charts. We are on the edge of that thing right now in America.

14. All people will be subject to permanent conscription. Even during the term of Franklin Roosevelt that was attempted, so that individuals, both men and women, can be assigned by the state in the name of the national need, to whatever occupation fits into the blueprint of tyranny.

15. The independent family physician will be abolished. All medical treatment will be computerized and all individuals will be assigned to the doctor whose number comes up.

16. There will be no income or property. Every individual will be subject to the will of the state and allowances in food and computerized credit cards will provide shelter, clothing and food.

17. Commercial entertainment will be prohibited and everything that comes out in the name of entertainment will be cleared first by the state.
18. Children will be kidnapped away from the family in the name of Child Care. The state will take care of the child while the mother and father work. In this way, parental care will disappear and the children will become mindwashed robots. This system was recently approved by Congress and under pressure the President vetoed it.
19. Sex 'equality' will be established to the point where women will be collecting garbage, plowing fields, digging ditches, cleaning the streets. Respect for gentle, tender, motherly femininity will be downgraded and will eventually disappear.
20. The purity of womanhood will be made obsolete and women will be encouraged to breed under the direction of the state.
21. If the men associated with the women are not as strong and vital as the state thinks they should be, they will be bred by capsules as cattle are now bred. Husbands and wives may be allowed to co-habit, but when reproduction is planned, they will be ordered to use the breeding capsule as directed by the authorities.
22. Population adjustment will be completely controlled and no one will be allowed to move from one community to the other without certification, based on computerized statistics. The individual family will have no right of decision and when they are officially located, they will not be able to travel from one community to the other without consent.
23. The masses will be kept subdued by tranquilizers, strange drugs, including marijuana and other nullifying potions.
24. Advertising and merchandising will be abolished. There will be no stores, no sales programs. There will be only storehouses where the rudiments of life will be dealt out according to computerized certification.
25. That which was once called the United States of America will be merged into a World Government dominated by the savage complex of Communism. Red China and the Soviet Union now dominate the United Nations which they hope to graduate into a tyrannical World Government that will abolish anything that looks like national sovereignty or governmental independence.
26. All so-called county and city governments will be rendered innocuous and federal bureaucrats acting under the dictatorship will operate in assigned areas of authority.

27. Elections will become meaningless. There will be no secret vote. The tyrants can check the voting record and the people who are voting will be merely voting "Yes" or "No" for the dictatorship, knowing that if they vote "No" they will be the victims of some formula of liquidation.
28. All telephone calls will be monitored and there will be no such a thing as a private conversation.
29. Even with the limited amount of money for negotiable credit that is made available to the individual, central clearing houses will make a complete record. Even now this bureaucracy is requesting that all checks of any size be photographed so that there will be no such thing as private business between two men.

IS CHRISTIAN CIVILIZATION MENACED?
A FEARLESS ANSWER

Evil is not new. Sin is not original with this generation. Treason and apostasy are as old as the human race. Disobedience began in the Garden of Eden, and sin forgiven characterized Bible characters all the way from David to the Apostle Peter.

Even so, as a veteran observer and as one who has studied the American scene and the world scene constantly and consistently across the years, I find myself shocked and overwhelmed by the evil manifestations that have projected themselves in the past few months and in the past two or three years.

I see and hear things every day that would have shocked the worst sinner in my hometown when I was a boy. I see and hear about things being done that would have caused individuals to be driven out of town or virtually banished from the state, or ridden out on a rail fifty years ago.

I am not a student of prophecy, and I am not bold enough to make any definite proclamations as to the termination of this world or as to when the last day shall be manifested, or when our Lord shall return, but I am bold to say that unless there is a miraculous intervention through the instrumentality of believing men and women, this civilization will go down the drain within five years, and we will become a chaotic, decaying nation, gobbled up by similar satanic forces to those which destroyed the empires of the past.

From Gerald L. K. Smith, "Is Christian Civilization Menaced? A Fearless Answer" (Los Angeles: Christian Nationalist Crusade, [1950s], pamphlet).

Here are five deadly enemies which threaten the preservation of our nation, our Constitutional traditions, our racial self-respect, and our Christian faith.

LETHAL FACTOR NO 1: THE RISE OF THE ANTICHRIST. In recent days and weeks and months sophisticated writers and clergyman and journalists in general as well as educators and international figures have concentrated on the destruction of man's faith in Jesus Christ. Through the years it has manifested itself by doctrinal attacks and academic assaults. Now we are being faced every day with brazen repudiations of Christ and the threat of a political and military tyranny controlled by the enemies of Christ. Only the naive and the uninitiated and the stupid and the intellectually dishonest would dare contend that the organized Jew is not in a world-wide campaign to shrink and belittle and evaporate the influence of the personality of Jesus Christ in the life of our nation, our culture and our social structure. We have been flooded by highly subsidized propaganda campaigns which have resulted in political action and academic pressures designed to outlaw Christian prayers in public institutions, outlaw the glorification of Christ in many of our governmental affairs, even to the forbidding of Christian carols and nativity scenes on public property. But beyond that we see now the hand of a giant military machine controlled absolutely by Jews. . . .

LETHAL FACTOR NO. 2. BLACK BARBARIANS. The day was when the Christian dynamic controlled the behavior of the majority of the American people. The un-civilized Negro brought here from Africa, sold into slavery by his own tribal chiefs, had an open heart to the simple teachings of the Christian faith, and for years the overwhelming majority of American Negroes had some sort of association with the church. The Negro churches were presided over by preachers who pronounced the simple doctrines of Christian faith, and the behavior of the average Negro was consistent with his understanding of Christian faith. Then it was that the Jews and the Communists moved in. The Jews took control of the organizations that were advertised as Negro organizations, but in the background there was always a Jewish director or a Jewish treasurer or a Jewish manipulator. They began to agitate and upset. The Communists came in and tried to reach the American working man and could not reach the American working man, because he was too intelligent concerning the traditions of our faith and of our Constitution. The agitators with the help of the left-wing Jews and their rich subsidizers began then to concentrate on the Negro preachers, and their formula for this concentration was successful, and they came out with agitators and revolutionists on the order of Martin Luther King who, at one time, received special training in a Communist school in Tennessee.

LETHAL FACTOR NO. 3. THE PERVERT. When the cities of Sodom and Gomorrah were destroyed tradition tells us that they went down because of their sex perversions. The sex relations of men with men have since that time been defined as sodomy, named after the behavior of those who lived in Sodom and Gomorrah. Remember, these cities were completely consumed with evil; so much so that God said: "If there had been ten just men, these cities would have been spared."

LETHAL FACTOR NO. 4. WEAKNESS AT THE TOP. Always before there have been strong men in positions of influence and power, such as great clergymen, great senators, great governors, great statesmen—men of influence and character who would speak out on these subjects and influence the American people. We have degeneration at the top. We have a president who is so weak and vacillating that he was referred to not long ago by cynical journalists as having a face that looked like an "underwater real estate agent." We have a few men who are strong by comparison. We hear an occasional announcement which gives us some slight encouragement, but we have no man in position in public life such as a movie hero or a dominant clergyman or a fighting congressman. We have no such men making pronouncements designed to set the American public on the track toward recovery and redemption and preservation.

LETHAL FACTOR NO. 5: THE APOSTATES. Every day I am shocked by men who are dressed like clergymen and who behave like atheists and unbelievers. These apostates have infiltrated the Evangelical churches, the Anglican churches, and the Roman Church.

THIS IS NATIONALISM

1 PRESERVATION OF AMERICA AS A CHRISTIAN NATION

Christ should be the head of our Nation. It was the intention of the founders of America that this Nation under God should be a Christian nation. Christian principle inspired the pioneers. Christian tradition gave us our Constitution. Christian character undergirded our way of life with self-re-

Gerald L. K. Smith, "This Is Nationalism," *The Cross and the Flag* 4, no. 11 (February 1946).

spect. Jews, unbelievers, Mohammedans, Shintoists, Confucianists, atheists and others have been permitted to come to America and enjoy their Constitutional right to believe what they pleased or to not believe at all. However, the teachings of Christ lie at the foundation of America.

2 EXPOSE AND FIGHT COMMUNISM

Red revolution is the real issue of the hour. J. Edgar Hoover, head of the F.B.I., in recent statements has manifested deep concern over the growth of Communism in the U.S.A. The tragedy lies in the fact that Communism controls nearly 1,000 front organizations which have taken on impressive names in order to deceive the public and snare the unsuspecting. Every Communist should be registered as a foreign agent and identified as a servant of Moscow. The knowledge concerning front organizations should not be limited to Congressional Committees and expert students of the subject. Newspapers, schools and radio commentators must begin to enlighten our people so that the conspiracy of the traitors who promote Red revolution shall become a matter of common knowledge among the young and the old. Communism reigns supreme in Europe and Asia. It is altogether too powerful in America. We must fight it. Expose it. Exterminate it. Its promoters must be branded as traitors.

Strikes against government, public utilities, transportation, communication and food production are merely rehearsals being used by the Red manipulators who long for the day of the general strike when midst chaos and bloodshed, street fighting and terrorism, they can seize the instruments of production and communication and consummate their much hoped for revolution.

3 SAFEGUARD AMERICAN LIBERTY AGAINST THE MENACE OF BUREAUCRATIC FASCISM.

Traditional liberty must be preserved. Bureaucratic encroachment upon family life, community life, social and business intercourse, is Fascism. The dictators of Europe rose to power merely because a sleepy citizenry and rubber-stamp legislative bodies delegated to small groups of men and individuals authority which should have remained in the hands of the people.

4 MAINTAIN A GOVERNMENT SET UP BY THE MAJORITY WHICH ABUSES NO MINORITY AND IS ABUSED BY NO MINORITY.

This Nation was designed to be a Republic whose officers were to be chosen democratically. Our Constitution and our election laws provide that those who rule over us shall be chosen by a majority of qualified voters. The popular term for this system is majority rule. Just as our Constitution provides that the minority shall not be abused by the majority, so it also provides that no minority, no clique, no little groups, shall be allowed to develop a power with which they can abuse, mis-use and exploit the majority. Today, opportunists, racketeers, and political manipulators have specialized in developing coercive and gestapo-like organizations financed by certain minorities for the purpose of purging, boycotting, and bankrupting individuals not pleasing to these minority manipulators. We want no gestapo in America no matter who operates it.

5 PROTECT AND EARMARK NATIONAL RESOURCES FOR OUR OWN CITIZENRY FIRST.

Citizens of our own country should have the first chance at our natural and accumulated resources. Why should any American go hungry and be in want while we loan and donate billions of interest-free dollars to foreign countries? Why should we send thousands of prefabricated houses to Europe while our own veterans are walking the streets? Why should we loan six billion interest-free dollars to Russia, which they very likely will never pay back, while charging our own wounded and other veterans 4% to 6%? Simple patriotism, which is pure Nationalism, requires that Americans come first in America.

6 MAINTAIN THE GEORGE WASHINGTON FOREIGN POLICY OF FRIENDSHIP WITH ALL NATIONS, TRADE WITH ALL NATIONS, ENTANGLING ALLIANCES WITH NONE.

Nationalism does not mean separation from the rest of the world. It means just what Washington stood for. Our sovereignty must stand unimpaired. It must never be shared with any foreign nation or any super government. The Washington system has been very fine so far, and the only time we have gotten into real trouble is when we have violated the admonition of the father of our country.

America must always maintain strong military equipment on the land, on the sea and in the air. Scientific discoveries contributing to this equipment and to our national defense must be shared with no other nation.

7 OPPOSE A WORLD GOVERNMENT AND A SUPER STATE

International Bankers, international politicians and globe-trotting manipulators want a world government. They want a super state. They want an international police force. They would like to remove the function of this super state as far from the will of the people as possible. If they have their way the Congress of the United States and especially the United States Senate, which is charged with the responsibility of confirming treaties, will delegate their functions as pertains to world affairs to a super parliament, a super congress. The authority to send our boys into battle and to tax money out of our pockets must remain in Washington and must not be delegated in part or in full.

8 PROVE THAT THE WORKER, THE FARMER, THE BUSINESSMAN, THE VETERAN, THE UNEMPLOYED, THE AGED, AND THE INFIRM CAN ENJOY MORE ABUNDANCE UNDER THE TRUE AMERICAN SYSTEM THAN ANY ALIEN SYSTEM NOW BEING PROPOSED BY FOREIGN PROPAGANDISTS.

True Nationalists are not reactionary. They hate feudalism just as they hate Communism. We seek abundance for the common man, but believe this abundance can best be obtained under the American system of free enterprise, which means an America (1) free from monopoly, (2) free from Communism, (3) free from the manipulations of the money-changer.

9 STOP IMMIGRATION UNTIL ALL VETERANS HAVE JOBS

In recent years America has been flooded by foreigners who begin tearing down our way of life before they even learn how to speak our language. We recognize the fact that our best citizenry includes foreign-born. We are not against foreigners just because they are foreigners, but during the war thousands of refugees have come into this country legally and illegally, and thousands more are being slipped in. These refugees should be sent back to Europe and no more immigrants should be admitted until we have solved the unemployment problem of not only our veterans but all our citizens. American jobs belong to Americans first.

10 ABOLISH THE CORRUPT MONEY SYSTEM.

The Federal Reserve Bank is not a national institution. It is a private corporation which creates booms, busts and depressions at will. It plays the game of the Rothschilds, the Kuhns, the Loebs, and the Morgans. It is Wall Street's baby. It is America's taskmaster. It is un-Constitutional. Money should be released for circulation under the direction and supervision of the Congress of the United States as provided for in the Constitution. This is the Abraham Lincoln plan which he instituted shortly before he was assassinated.

AMERICA, AWAKE! BEFORE IT IS EVERLASTINGLY TOO LATE. The acid test of every political theory and every piece of proposed legislation should be: Is it best for America? Nationalism is the natural development among a people of that impulse which causes a self-respecting citizen to be the husband of one wife, to provide for his own family first, in harmony with the word of God which reads: *"He that careth not for his own is worse than an infidel."*

NOTES

1. Gerald B. Winrod, *Adam Weishaupt: A Human Devil* (Metairie, La.: Sons of Liberty, n.d.).
2. Dan Gilbert, "The New Deal and Morals," *The Revealer* 3, no. 6 (September 15, 1936): 10. Emphasis in original.

3. Gerald L. K. Smith, "Fluoridation: The Crime of the Century. Exposing the Doctoring of Water," *The Letter*, no. 197 (1950): 4.

4. Gerald L. K. Smith, "The Big X—The Unknown Quantity: The Reader Has the Answer" ([Los Angeles]: Christian Nationalist Crusade, n.d., pamphlet), 15.

3

REWRITING THE FOUNDING FATHERS

A NEW BILL OF RIGHTS

Constitutional Revival

One of the most interesting pieces found in the Wilcox Collection is the following rewriting of the Bill of Rights to fit contemporary conditions. The history suggested by the title is a bit confused, since Jefferson was out of the country, Madison was opposed to having a Bill of Rights, and Hancock was not a member of the Constitutional Convention. George Mason (1725– 1792), the least known of the men cited, is the one who belongs here. He refused to sign the Constitution produced by the Convention, fought to have a Bill of Rights added, and drafted the document that served as a basis for the Bill of Rights that was adopted. It should also be noted that the actual Bill of Rights is shorter than Article 1 of this document, and that the entire United States Constitution is considerably shorter than this document.

This recasting of the Bill of Rights—in fact of the Constitution—is a particularly good place to begin because it includes a wide range of the positions of the modern American far right without any of the racial or religious concerns that divide so much of the far right both from each other and from mainstream conservatism. But it is precisely those racial and religious concerns, already seen in Smith, that will dominate in what follows later. Here the concern is with individual freedom against the government and with what might be called economic rights, the rejection of virtually all limits on the use of private property. This is a major concern of the right and the central difference from the left, which generally wants government to be actively involved in the economy either through ownership or regulation.

One of the most interesting points found here and in a number of later documents is the stress on the jury system as the basis of justice.

IF WASHINGTON, JEFFERSON, MADISON, HANCOCK AND MASON WERE ALIVE TODAY HERE IS HOW OUR BILL OF RIGHTS WOULD LOOK

Dear Fellow American:

There are very few of us now, who are not aware that our country is in serious trouble. Most people have difficulty in determining what that trouble is, so are unable to start or support meaningful corrective action. These basic principles, the heart of our U.S. Constitution, are being ignored by our "leaders."

1. Every person must be free to do whatever he pleases with his life and property as long as he does not interfere with the right of his fellow man to do the same.

2. If there is no threat to life, liberty or property, government has no business in our affairs.

3. Government MAY have business in our affairs where there is a clear threat to life, or property.

4. Government has no right to spend tax money other than for the protection of life, and property.

These laws frame the true meaning of freedom. . . .

From "If Washington, Jefferson, Madison, Hancock and Mason Were Alive Today, Here Is How Our New Bill of Rights Would Look." Compiled and edited by Andrew J. Melechinsky with the advice and support of Rabbi Marvin S. Antelman, Ralph J. Lombardi, Norman Rochon and numerous others (Enfield, Conn.: Constitutional Revival, 1979, pamphlet).

.

THE UNIVERSAL BILL OF RIGHTS
PREAMBLE

This Universal Bill of Rights is promulgated under the authority of the Universal Supreme Law: the Law of God; the Law of Nature; the Law of the Constitution; and the Law of Common Sense.

The Highest Law is:

"Every person has an absolute right to do anything that is not a provable threat to others."

INTRODUCTORY PROVISIONS

Under the provisions of Article IV, Sec. 2, Article VI, Par. 2 and Amendments IX, X, and XIV of the United States Constitution, *this* Universal *Bill of Rights has the standing and force of Constitutional Law in the United States of America.* It shall serve as a standard for all of the world.

The Bill of Rights is supported by various provisions of the Constitutions of the several United States of America which, in turn, support and are supported by the Constitution of the United States of America. It is applicable in all courts.

We the people are the only possessors of police power, which we have delegated to the government for limited purposes of defense. *So-called "police of the state" is abhorrent to a free society and will not be allowed to exist.*

Legislative acts which violate this Bill of Rights are void; the Judiciary shall so declare them, and the Executive branch shall refrain from enforcement.

Where the meaning of this Bill of Rights is clear and unambiguous, there can be no resort to construction to attribute to the founders a purpose or intent not manifest in its letter.

Should the meaning of, or between, provisions of this Bill of Rights be not clear, the conflict can be resolved by the application of the following question: Is there a clear threat to life, physical safety, liberty or property? If not, the question must be decided in favor of no government action. If there is a clear threat, such threat must be confirmed by a jury; the jury may retroactively sanction whatever protective action was taken by the government; provided, any such protective action not so sanctioned must be penalized if harm to an individual results therefrom.

Where conflict remains, the resolution must favor the defendant individual.

Stated simply, *as long as an individual does not threaten or harm others by his actions, no human agency has a right to bother him in any way.*

This Bill of Rights has been developed by and on behalf of We the People in order to assert our rights; to prevent misconstruction or abuse of power by government; and to insure the beneficent ends of its institution.

No provision of the Constitution or laws of any Country or other geographic or civic entity shall ever be construed or applied in any way which would deny to any person or agency the protections enumerated herein.

The essential and unquestionable rights and principles herein mentioned shall be established, maintained and preserved, and shall be of paramount obligation in all legislative, judicial and executive proceedings.

No law-making body of any Nation shall ever pass a law contrary to the intent and words of this Bill of Rights. Any such contrary laws which may exist are null and void, and morally unenforceable.

This Bill of Rights is a BARRIER, to protect the individual against arbitrary exactions of majorities, executives, legislatures, courts, sheriffs, and prosecutors.

The individual is Sovereign.

NOTE: Many provisions herein are reprinted verbatim from individual (U.S.) State Constitutions, in the interest of historical accuracy. A certain amount of redundancy and irregular grammar can be expected. Where the word "man" or "men" appears it shall be understood to include women and children, as applicable. The placement of rights in specific categories herein for convenience, shall not detract from their application elsewhere.

ARTICLE I—GENERAL PRINCIPLES

1. The enumeration in this Bill of Rights of certain rights, shall not be construed to deny, impair, or disparage others, all of which are retained by the people individually. Permits or permission are not needed to exercise rights.

2. All rights and powers not herein enumerated, remain with the people.

3. All powers not unanimously granted to the government are retained by those individuals who elect to reserve such powers.

4. The provisions of this Bill of Rights are mandatory, prohibitory and sacredly obligatory upon all; and all laws contrary thereto shall be void.

5. This enumeration of rights shall not be construed to deny or disparage others retained by the people; and to guard against any encroachment on the rights herein retained, or any transgression of any of the higher powers herein delegated, we declare that everything in this Bill of Rights is excepted out of the general powers of the government; and shall forever remain inviolate; and that all laws contrary thereto or to the other provisions herein contained shall be void.

6. The body politic is formed by a *voluntary* association of individuals.

7. There exists no hereditary entitlement to emoluments, honors or privileges. All men and corporations are equal in rights; and no man or set of men are entitled to exclusive public emoluments or privileges under the law.

8. All men and corporations are equal in rights; and no man or set of men are entitled to exclusive public emoluments or privileges under law.

9. The right of complaint, and of the people peaceably to assemble to consult for the common good, and to make known their opinions, shall never be denied or abridged.

10. The right of the people to revolt individually or collectively against any agency, including government, which seeks to suppress the rights guaranteed by this Bill of Rights, shall exist forever.

11. Zoning and planning laws, motor vehicle laws, building codes and other similar statutes are guides and shall not be used as a basis for prosecution unless harm or a clear threat of harm to life, liberty or property results from their being ignored.

12. It is a crime to claim a defense of "obedience to orders" for violations of this Bill of Rights, except to produce evidence of public protest against such violations.

13. Treason against a government shall consist only in participating in active, unprovoked aggression against it. No person shall be convicted of treason without the testimony of at least two witnesses before a jury, or on confession in open court.

14. This Bill of Rights may be expanded and/or updated at any time by any person, in a manner not inconsistent with the principles enumerated

herein. In the event of conflict the individual or the accused shall prevail unless and until a jury deems otherwise.

15. Simply stated, in any argument between an individual and the government, the individual wins.

ARTICLE II—GOVERNMENTAL RESPONSIBILITY

1. The sole object and only legitimate end of government is to protect each individual in the enjoyment of life, liberty, and property, and when the government assumes other functions it is usurpation and oppression. This protection shall be impartial and complete.

2. The rights enumerated in this Bill of Rights are inalienable and shall be preserved inviolate by the government.

3. All power is inherent in the people, and all free governments are founded on their authority, and instituted to protect their lives, liberty, and property, equally and to maintain individual rights; for the advancement of these ends, the people have at all times an inalienable and indefeasible right to alter, reform or abolish the government in such manner as they may think proper.

4. Public officials shall not be immune from prosecution for violation of this Bill of Rights whether or not perpetrated in the performance of their duties.

5. No judicial, executive or legislative immunity shall exist, and any government official who claims immunity shall be deemed to have committed a crime.

6. All persons in government positions, elected or appointed and regardless of official capacity, are public servants and subservient to each non-governmental individual.

7. Defenses through trial by jury shall be available to governmental officials, in the same manner as to all other persons.

8. To justify its existence, a government must be prepared and anxious to preserve, protect and defend the life, liberty, property and other rights of all persons, equally.

9. To justify its existence, a government must guarantee that all persons shall have access to a justice system in which all immunities enumerated in this Bill of Rights shall be protected.

10. All government agencies shall abide by and be subject to this Bill of Rights and/or shall be subject to penalties for failure to do so.

ARTICLE III—OBLIGATIONS OF PUBLIC OFFICIALS

1. Decency, security, and liberty alike demand that government officials shall be subjected to the same rules of conduct that are commands to the individual.
2. All government officials, elected or appointed, must take an Oath of Affirmation to, and be bound by the laws incorporated in this Bill of Rights.
3. All officials at all levels of government are bound by the United States Constitution and all federal, state, county and municipal statutes which conform thereto, as well as the State Constitution of the jurisdiction wherein they work and reside.
4. It is more important for the government to obey the law than it is for the people to do so.
5. Government may not prohibit or control the conduct of a person for reasons that infringe upon freedoms guaranteed by this Bill of Rights.
6. Magistrates and other officials are trustees and servants of the people and at all times accountable to them.
7. The benefits of a free government can only be maintained by a firm adherence of all public officials to justice, moderation, temperance, frugality and frequent recurrence to fundamental principles.
8. Disobedience or evasion of this Bill of Rights may not be tolerated, even though such disobedience may promote in some respects the best interests of the public.
9. It is a crime for any agent or agency of government to interrupt a sovereign citizen in the exercise of free speech.

ARTICLE IV—OBLIGATIONS OF INDIVIDUALS

1. All men have a natural, inherent and inalienable right to enjoy and defend their lives and liberties; to acquire, possess and protect property; to worship or not worship according to the dictates of their consciences; to assemble peaceably, protest against wrongs and claim redress of grievances; to communicate freely their thoughts and opinions, being responsible for the abuse of that right.
2. All persons have the inherent right to the enjoyment of the gains of their own (lawful) industry.

3. All men when they form a social compact, are equal in rights; and no man, or set of men are entitled to exclusive emoluments or privileges from the community.

4. All men are, by nature, equally free and independent, and have certain inherent rights of which, when they enter into a state of society, they cannot by any compact, deprive or divest their posterity, namely; The enjoyment of life and liberty, with the means of acquiring and possessing property and of pursuing and obtaining happiness and safety.

5. By nature, complete equality cannot exist; nevertheless all persons are entitled to equal rights, opportunities, and protection under the law.

6. In their inherent right to liberty and to acquire property (the pursuit of happiness), all members of the human race are equal.

7. Parents and guardians have the right to act for children to the extent that the children do not yet possess the maturity to act for themselves.

8. The individual owes nothing to the public as long as he does not trespass upon rights of others.

9. One need not be a criminal to claim rights.

10. There shall be no distinction between persons because of race, color, religion, ideology, sex, physical handicap, circumstance or condition whatsoever (other than individual incompetency as determined by a jury) in the application of this Bill of Rights.

11. The right of private discrimination cannot be condoned or condemned by the law.

12. Mentally incompetent persons may not be imprisoned, nor deprived of life, liberty or property unless shown to be a clear threat to others, to the satisfaction of a jury.

13. Generally, adults found by a jury to be mentally incompetent shall be treated by the law in the same manner as minor children.

ARTICLE V—RIGHTS AND PROHIBITIONS

SECTION ONE—FREEDOM AND FREE ENTERPRISE

1. Firms, corporations and other voluntary associations have the same rights and liabilities as persons under this Bill of Rights.

2. Members of a corporation shall not be deprived of their liberties or property, unless by a trial by jury as in other cases.
3. Absolute and arbitrary power over the lives, liberty and property of free men exists nowhere in a free society, not even in the largest majority.
4. A person may not be bound by any law to which he has not assented as long as he is not a clear threat to others.
5. Every member of the community has a right to be protected by it, in the enjoyment of the rights enumerated herein.
6. Where rights secured by this Bill of Rights are involved, there can be no rule making or legislation which would abrogate them.
7. There can be no sanction or penalty imposed upon one because of his exercise of basic rights.
8. No person shall ever be required to surrender one basic right in order to assert another.
9. Slavery shall not be allowed to exist, anywhere.
10. Involuntary servitude shall not be allowed to exist, except for the purpose of requiring an aggressor to compensate a victim of his crime, whereof the aggressor shall have been duly convicted. Taxes for "welfare" are a form of involuntary servitude.
11. The right of persons to work, shall not be denied; or abridged on account of membership or non-membership in any labor union, bar association or other such organization.

SECTION TWO—LIMITATIONS OF GOVERNMENT

1. Public employees shall not have the right to strike. Because all public employees are presumed to be engaged in the protection of life, as well as liberty and property; any person accepting such employment must be willing and shall be expected to waive the right to strike as a condition of employment.
2. No person or agency, including government shall make or enforce any law which shall abridge the immunities (rights) and protections of this Bill of Rights.
3. No person or agency, including government, shall deprive any person of life, physical safety, liberty, property or any other rights guaranteed by this Bill of Rights, without the sanction of a jury.
4. No person or agency, including government, shall ever deny to any

person within its jurisdiction the equal protection of all rights guaranteed by this Bill of Rights.

5. There shall be no nobility or titles of nobility created by law.
6. Except where funds are donated, no government employee shall be paid at a rate higher than his counterpart on the non-government job market.
7. No person shall be entitled to a government pension unless he shall have been engaged in a function directly concerned with the protection of life, physical safety, liberty and property in which his life shall have been under threat; such as a soldier or a policeman.
8. Government pensions must not be paid with involuntary tax dollars.
9. Government subsidies are not allowed except when funds are donated for specific subsidy purposes; such funds to be used for the administration as well as implementation of the specific program.
10. All government agencies are prohibited from sponsoring gambling activities except for the purpose of raising funds for the protection of life, physical safety, liberty and property under this Bill of Rights.
11. There can be no restrictions on voluntary private gambling.
12. The rights of emigration and immigration of all persons shall not be infringed or restricted in any way.
13. The use of passports and other identification must be voluntary on the part of the individual.
14. Importation or exportation of any product or service related to the sustenance of life shall not be infringed or restricted in any way.
15. Competition with government activities is an inalienable right and may not be prohibited or restricted.
16. Opening and closing hours of private activities may not be decreed.
17. The right to bring suit against a government is inviolate; and no judge or any other official shall be immune from suit.
18. Governmental entities shall have no immunity from suit for injury to person or property.
19. Government immunity violates the common law maxim that everyone shall have remedy for an injury done to his person or property.
20. Immunity fosters neglect and breeds irresponsibility, while liability promotes care and caution, which caution and care is owed by government to its people.

SECTION THREE
PROHIBITIONS AGAINST GOVERNMENT COERCION

1. There can be no infringements of activities related to individual procurement of the necessities of life, unless such infringement is clearly authorized by this Bill of Rights.
2. It is a crime for any person or agency to confiscate property or other possessions of any other person or agency, without the other's consent or the unanimous consent of a jury.
3. No person can be held responsible for any debts incurred by any legislative or other government body, unless he has affirmatively and consciously agreed, in advance, to shoulder such debts.
4. No person or agency, including government, shall issue currency which is not redeemable in coin of value or other universally recognized medium of exchange with intrinsic value of its own, such as gold and silver.
5. No government agency will initiate or impose any policy which would result in inflation; a devaluation of a unit of currency. Currency must be kept stable.

SECTION FOUR—INDIVIDUAL LIBERTIES

1. Every person has a right to keep and bear arms and this right shall never be questioned.
2. All persons have and shall retain the right to keep and bear arms without restriction; but shall be responsible for any abuse of that right.
3. No person shall be disturbed in his private affairs, or his home invaded, without his own consent or the authority of a jury decision.
4. No part of the property of any individual can be taken from him or applied to public uses, without his own consent.
5. The right of property is before and higher than constitutional sanction. Private property shall not be taken for private use without just compensation being first made therefore; and not in any case until after a jury shall have agreed unanimously that such taking is vital to the protection of the lives, liberty and property of everyone, including the owner.
6. There is no right of eminent domain.
7. No soldier shall ever be quartered in any house, without the consent of the owner or lawful occupant.
8. No person shall be harmed in his life, physical safety, liberty, property,

or other rights by any other person or agency as long as his actions are not a clear, provable threat to others.

9. The claim and exercise of any right cannot be converted to a crime.
10. The right of individual privacy is essential to the well-being of a free society and shall not be infringed without the showing of a compelling state interest to the satisfaction of a jury.
11. No Bill of Pains and Penalties shall be passed or enforced.
12. No Bill of Attainder shall be passed or enforced.
13. A person may not be penalized for ignoring a Bill of Attainder or a Bill of Pains and Penalties.
14. A person may not be penalized for ignoring any law, statute, ordinance, regulation or custom which would tend to deprive him of his rights (immunities) as enumerated in this Bill of Rights.
15. Retroactive laws, punishing acts committed before the existence of such laws and by them only declared criminal, are oppressive, unjust, and incompatible with liberty, and therefore no ex post facto law shall be enacted, or enforced; nor any retroactive oath or restriction be imposed, or required.
16. All persons are entitled to at least the immunities secured to all other persons, everywhere.
17. No person can be subjected to any liabilities prohibited by this Bill of Rights.
18. No person shall be bound by a judicial or quasi-judicial decision of an administrative agency; nor shall he be subject to the same person for both prosecution and adjudication; nor shall he be deprived of the right to judicial review.
19. A person may not be deprived of (or restricted in) his right to do as he pleases with his own life, liberty or property, so long as he does not become a clear and provable threat to the equal rights of others.
20. Except in self defense, including defense of rights, the use of armed force against other persons is prohibited.
21. No person shall be bound to obey any law, statute, ordinance, regulation or custom which is contrary to this Bill of Rights.
22. Every person shall be free to speak, write or publish or otherwise communicate his sentiments on any subject and shall be responsible for the abuse of that right; but, the truth by itself shall be sufficient defense in any charge of libel or slander.
23. No person can be held permanently to a contract which requires waiver

of basic rights and to which he would not have agreed had he known such waiver was involved; provided only a jury can cancel such a contract and the burden of proof must be on the person claiming relief.

24. Service in the military shall be voluntary. No person shall be compelled to bear arms.
25. No man shall be compelled to send his child to any school to which he may be conscientiously opposed.
26. No person shall be imprisoned for debt or tort except in cases of fraud, absconding debtor, libel judgment, slander judgment or where no other means of redress is available; but in no case shall any person be imprisoned for debt unless opportunity is provided for retiring the debt through a voluntary work program.

SECTION FIVE—RELIGIOUS LIBERTIES

1. The civil and political rights, privileges and capacities of no person shall be diminished or enlarged on account of his religious belief.
2. The rights of conscience shall never be infringed; nor shall any man be compelled to attend, erect or support any place of worship, or to maintain any ministry against his consent, nor shall any control of, or interference with, the rights of conscience be permitted, or any preference be given by law to any religious establishment or modes of worship; nor shall any money be drawn from the treasury or appropriated for or applied to any religious worship, exercise or instruction, or for the support of any ecclesiastical establishment.

SECTION SIX—TAXATION

1. The only lawful mandatory tax is a poll tax, for those who choose to vote. A person may not be compelled to vote.
2. There is no other right of mandatory taxation.
3. No subsidy, charge, tax, impost, or duty, shall be established, fixed, laid or levied, under any pretext whatsoever, without the consent of the people, individually and any taxation shall be equal and uniform.
4. There can be no tax on the necessities of life.
5. Taxation is based on voluntary assessment and payment, not upon distraint.
6. Tax monies may not be used to compete with private enterprise.

7. To lay with one hand the power of government on the property of the individual and with the other to bestow it on favored individuals, is none the less robbery because it was done under the forms of law and is called taxation.

SECTION SEVEN—PROPERTY AND COMMERCE

1. No government shall control water or any other natural resource.
2. No government shall own land, buildings or other property not in active use.
3. Private property shall not be taken for private [*sic*] use unless by consent of the owner, except for public ways of necessity, after a jury shall determine that such taking will alleviate a clear threat to the lives, liberty and property of all; private property shall not be taken or damaged without just compensation.
4. All navigable waters shall remain forever public highways, free to all persons, without tax, impost or toll; and no tax, toll, impost or wharfage shall be demanded or received from the owner of any merchandise or commodity for the use of the shores or any wharf erected on the shores with tax monies, or in or over the waters of any navigable streams.
5. There can be no toll or other charge for the use of any public highway, bridge, building or other public enterprise.
6. Though perpetuities and monopolies can be contrary to the genius of a free state, corporations shall enjoy the same rights and incur the same obligations as individual persons.
7. Licenses are evidence of monopoly and may not be required by law.
8. No distinction shall ever be made by law between aliens and citizens as to the possession, enjoyment and descent of property, and all other natural rights.

SECTION EIGHT—MISCELLANEOUS

1. Any civic body which claims to represent the general populace, is prohibited from holding secret sessions.
2. Any secret vote, including an election, which could result in violations of this Bill of Rights, is automatically invalid.
3. The doctrine of non-resistance against arbitrary power and oppression is absurd, slavish and destructive of the good and happiness of mankind.

ARTICLE VI—EXECUTIVE RESPONSIBILITY

1. Any government which claims the loyalty of the people must abide by this Bill of Rights and must be divided into three distinct departments: The legislative, executive and judicial, and no person or collection of persons charged with the exercise of powers properly belonging to one of these departments shall exercise any powers properly belonging to either of the others.
2. This Bill of Rights is mandatory, prohibitory and obligatory on all three departments of government.
3. Any governmental official who implements or supports in any way a law or statute which is contrary to this Bill of Rights shall be subject to prosecution.
4. It shall be the responsibility of the Executive department to see that violators of this Bill of Rights are prosecuted.
5. It is a crime for any Executive Officer to implement or enforce any law or statute in such a manner as to violate this Bill of Rights.
6. The Executive Officer is expected and required to resist and oppose any usurpation of power on the part of the Legislative or Judicial branches of government.
7. The Executive Officer is expected and required to invoke all laws and prosecute all cases in which the Legislature or Judiciary become a threat to individuals in violation of this Bill of Rights.
8. There can be no time limit for prosecution of public officials, including judges, for violations of this Bill of Rights. Public officials who continue to violate the provisions herein after they have been presented with a copy, shall be subject to additional penalties upon conviction.

ARTICLE VII—LEGISLATIVE RESPONSIBILITY

1. This Bill of Rights is superior to any ordinary act of the Legislature; the Bill of Rights and not such ordinary act, must govern the case to which they both apply.
2. All laws which are repugnant to this Bill of Rights are null and void.
3. It is a crime for any legislator to propose a law or statute which is contrary to this Bill of Rights.

4. All acts of a Legislature contrary to natural right and justice are void.
5. The Legislature shall make no law abridging, curtailing or restraining the freedom of speech, or of the press.
6. The Legislature is expected and required to resist and oppose any usurpation of power on the part of the Executive or Judicial branches of government.
7. No legislature shall make any law respecting an establishment of religion, or prohibiting the free exercise thereof. No preference shall be given by law to any sect or mode of worship, nor shall any person be rendered incompetent to hold office or serve as witness or juror because of his religious belief.
8. No religious test shall be required as a qualification for any office or public trust.
9. The social status of persons shall never be the subject of legislation.
10. No special privileges or immunities shall ever be granted by the Legislature.
11. Individual legislators who vote in favor, are liable for all debts incurred in violation of this Bill of Rights.
12. It shall be unlawful for any legislator to propose the circulation of currency which is less than 100% redeemable in gold, silver or other universally recognized medium of exchange which has intrinsic value of its own.
13. The Legislature may not authorize the trial of the issue of mental incompetency without a jury.
14. No law shall delegate to any commission, bureau, board or other administrative agency authority to make any rule fixing a fine, imprisonment or any other penalty as punishment for its violation.
15. Any law, statute, ordinance or regulation "passed" by any Legislature which is contrary to this Bill of Rights is null and void from the time of its enactment. Such a law or statute is as inoperative as if it had never been passed.
16. Any law, statute, ordinance or regulation "passed" by any Legislature in violation of this Bill of Rights imposes no duties, confers no rights, creates no office, bestows no power or authority on anyone, affords no protection and justifies no acts performed under it.
17. The Legislature shall make no law setting government standards for professional behavior and no law, statute, ordinance or regulation establishing mandatory public licensing shall be passed or enforced.

18. The Legislature shall make no law restricting the right of any person to work at a rate of compensation agreeable to himself and his employer.
19. The Legislature shall make no law fixing prices or otherwise regulating the market.
20. The Legislature shall make no law abridging the right of the people peaceably to assemble or to claim a redress for grievances. This right includes the right of remonstrance.
21. The Legislature shall make no law restricting the right of fishery and access to shorelines.
22. There can be no law or enforcement of law which would impair the right of the people to gamble; there can be no law which would impair other activities in which there is no involuntary participant.
23. There can be no law or enforcement of law, which would impair the obligation of contracts, including marriage contracts.
24. The rights of the citizens to opportunities for education should have practical recognition. The Legislature shall suitably encourage education by means not at variance with this Bill of Rights and without the expenditure of tax monies.
25. The Legislature shall make no law which would shift the burden of proof from the accuser to the accused. It is the responsibility of the accuser to overcome the presumption of innocence enjoyed by all.
26. Votes on legislation which might have an impact on We the People shall be by roll call and shall be recorded.

ARTICLE VIII—JUDICIAL RESPONSIBILITY

SECTION ONE—JUDICIAL PROCEDURE

1. The Judiciary is expected and required to resist and oppose any usurpation of power on the part of the Executive and Legislative branches of government.
2. After a charge has been ignored by a grand or petit jury no person shall be held to answer, or for trial therefor.
3. All courts shall be open and every person, for an injury or wrong done to him in his person, property, immunities, privacy, or reputation, shall have remedy and right and justice administered without sale, denial, delay or prejudice. This includes his movable and immovable possessions.

4. In no instance shall any accused person before final judgment be compelled to advance money or fees to secure the rights herein guaranteed.
5. No court shall be secret. Justice in all cases shall be administered openly, promptly, and without delay.
6. Ex parte (one-sided) actions are prohibited, except in cases of default or where habeas corpus proceedings might be delayed in cases of unlawful prosecution.
7. No statutes, rules, or court decisions shall ever be a bar to justice.
8. No person shall be liable to be transported out of a district for trial for any offense committed within the same, without his consent.
9. It is the right of every person to be tried by judges (and jurors) who are as free, impartial and independent as the lot of humanity will admit.
10. The jury acts not only as a safeguard against judicial excesses, but also as a barrier to legislative and executive oppression. The jury is designed to protect Defendants against oppressive governmental practices.
11. The jury has an unreviewable and unreversible power to acquit in disregard of the instructions on the law given by the trial judge.
12. The common law right of the jury to determine the law as well as the facts remains unimpaired. The jury will be reminded of this right (and obligation) in each case.
13. Justice in all cases shall be administered openly and without necessary delay.
14. The right of the Writ of Habeas Corpus shall never be suspended. Judges, Magistrates, Justices of the Peace, etc., must consider and respond to all such writs, freely, without delay and without cost; at any time of day or night.
15. The right to record public proceedings is inalienable.
16. The judicial branch has only one duty—to lay this Bill of Rights beside the statute which is challenged and to decide whether the latter squares with the former. The only power the court has is the power of judgment.
17. When any court violates the clear and unambiguous language of this Bill of Rights, a fraud is perpetrated and no one is bound to obey the court.
18. It is the duty of the courts to be watchful for the rights of all persons against any stealthy encroachments thereon.
19. All oaths or affirmations shall be administered in the mode most binding upon the conscience and shall be taken subject to the pains and penalties of perjury.
20. In all courts persons of all persuasions may freely appear in their own

way, and according to their own causes themselves, or if unable, by their friends.

SECTION TWO—RIGHTS OF ACCUSED

1. All Defendants are entitled to free access, without cost, to the transcript or tapes of all proceedings.
2. The accused shall have the right to full voir dire examination (interrogation) of prospective jurors and to challenge jurors peremptorily. There shall be no limit to the number of challenges for cause, if cause is shown.
3. Every person is presumed innocent of any wrongdoing until he is pronounced guilty by the unanimous decision of a jury of his peers.
4. In matters in which principles are involved, there shall never be any restrictions on the right of trial by jury.
5. There can be no abridgement of the right of the accused to present to the jury any and all evidence and testimony which might induce a vote in his favor. So-called rules of evidence can apply only to the prosecution and (possibly) to the accuser.
6. Any person accused of violating or disobeying any order of injunction, or restraint, made or entered by any court or judge shall, before penalty or punishment is imposed, be entitled to a trial by jury as to the guilt or innocence of the accused. In no case shall a penalty or punishment be imposed for contempt, until an opportunity to be heard by a jury is given.
7. No person shall ever be arrested, detained, or punished, except for violation of this Bill of Rights.
8. Waiver of basic rights must not be presumed.
9. Courts must indulge every reasonable presumption against waiver of fundamental rights, and not presume acquiescence in the loss of fundamental rights.
10. When any person has been arrested in connection with the investigation or commission of any offense, he shall be advised fully of the reason for his arrest or detention, his right to remain silent, his right against self incrimination, his right to assistance of counsel and his right to court appointed counsel. In all prosecutions, an accused shall be informed of the nature and cause of the accusation against him. At each stage of the proceedings, every person is entitled to assistance of counsel of his

choice (including himself) or appointed by the court if he elects not to choose his own. The legislature shall provide for a uniform system for securing and compensating qualified counsel for this purpose.

11. The right of the people to be secure in their persons, against searches, seizures, or invasions of property, shall not be violated, except by the authority of a proper warrant, signed by a judge after jury authorization.

12. The right of the people to be secure in their houses and businesses against searches and seizures shall not be violated except by the authority of a proper warrant, signed by a judge, after jury authorization.

13. The right of the people to be secure in their papers and possessions against searches and seizures shall not be violated except by the authority of a proper warrant, signed by a judge, after jury authorization.

14. Any person adversely affected by a search or seizure conducted in violation of this Bill of Rights shall have standing to raise its illegality and to claim redress and damages in the court in which the case is prosecuted or in any other appropriate court.

15. The people shall have a right to be secure against invasions of privacy or interceptions of communications by eavesdropping devices or other means.

16. No warrants shall issue, but upon probable cause, supported by Oath of Affirmation, charging violations of this Bill of Rights and particularly describing the place to be searched and the persons or things to be seized.

17. No person shall be held to answer for a capital or otherwise infamous crime, unless on indictment of a Grand Jury.

18. No person shall be required to answer for a misdemeanor, infraction or other lesser crime or offense, unless on indictment of a Petit-Jury.

19. The accused shall be entitled to a copy of the indictment, before arrest.

20. No finding of probable cause shall ever be issued before the accused shall have been given an opportunity to respond to the charges and to the evidence.

21. No person shall, for the same alleged crime or offense be twice put in jeopardy of life, physical safety, liberty or property; except for his or her own motion for a new trial after conviction.

22. No person shall after acquittal, be tried for the same offense. Any finding of innocence or non-finding of guilt by any jury, shall constitute a final action.

23. Any dismissal or finding of innocence (not guilty) by a judge shall constitute a final action.

24. No person shall in any case be compelled to give evidence or testimony against himself in any manner. The same right shall apply to private agencies.

25. No person shall be deprived of life or physical safety without due process, including the unanimous consent (judgment) of a jury of his peers.

26. No person shall be deprived of liberty without due process including the unanimous consent (judgment) of a jury of his peers.

27. No person shall be deprived of property or other rights without due process, including the unanimous consent (judgment) of a jury of his peers.

28. In all civil cases the right of Trial by Jury shall remain inviolate, as in criminal cases, without regard to the amount in controversy. This right includes all controversies concerning property.

29. Whenever an attempt is made to take private property for a use alleged to be public, the question whether the contemplated use be really public shall be a judicial question and determined as such by a jury, without regard to any legislative assertion that the use is public.

30. In all prosecutions, criminal or civil, the accused shall enjoy the right to a speedy and public trial by an impartial jury of the district wherein the alleged crime or offense shall have been committed, which district shall have been previously ascertained by law and to be informed of the nature and cause of the accusation.

31. The accused shall have reasonable time to prepare a defense and must be brought to trial within three working days after announcing his readiness for trial; otherwise the prosecution shall be in default and the accused shall not again be placed in jeopardy under the charge.

32. The accused shall enjoy a right to change a venue, whenever fair treatment is not assured.

33. In all prosecutions, criminal or civil, the accused shall enjoy the right to be confronted by his accuser and by the witnesses against him and the accuser and witnesses must be required to be present in court whenever the accused is required to be present in court.

34. The accused shall enjoy the right to meet the witnesses in their examination face to face and to have compulsory process on application by himself, his friends, or counsel, for obtaining witnesses in his favor.

35. In all prosecutions, criminal or civil the accused shall have compulsory process for obtaining evidence in his favor.

36. In all criminal and civil prosecutions the accused shall have a right to prosecute or be heard by himself or counsel or both. The court shall be obligated to see to it that the accused shall have counsel available for his defense. Should the accused not be satisfied with counsel provided by the court, he shall have the option to hire counsel of his choice with no restrictions on the right of such counsel to defend the accused in a manner agreeable to the accused.

37. In all prosecutions, criminal or civil, no person shall be barred from prosecuting or defending before any tribunal, by himself or counsel of his choice.

38. Such counsel need not be licensed or otherwise approved by the government.

39. Bail or imprisonment may be allowed where a person is accused of the commission of a felony while on probation or parole, or while free on bail awaiting trial on a previous felony charge except where the proof is evident or the presumption strong that a clear threat to life or property would thereby occur.

40. No accused, who has not previously failed to appear for trial, shall be required to post bail, unless in the case of a capital crime, it can be proven to the satisfaction of all of the Grand Jury members that the accused is not likely to appear to answer to the charges.

41. No person shall be interfered with in his normal pursuits and no vehicle shall be required to pull to the side of any road or highway, except to alleviate a clear threat to life, physical safety, liberty or property.

SECTION THREE—JURIES

1. The right of trial by jury shall be and remain inviolate and shall extend to all cases at law.

2. There can be no equity jurisdiction to which all parties have not consciously and voluntarily agreed.

3. In all trials, the jury after being informed of the law by the judge, shall have a right to determine, at their discretion, the law and the facts. The jurors shall be informed of their right to interrogate witnesses.

4. The jury and/or judge must disregard all "laws" which do not conform to this Bill of Rights.

5. Jury service shall be voluntary.

6. All guilty verdicts must be unanimous to be valid.

7. No person shall be convicted of any crime but by the unanimous verdict of a jury in open court. This right may be voluntarily waived; if conscious and recorded.

8. In all trials the members of the jury may not retire or consult with one another before reaching a decision, but must publicly cast a ballot into a suitable container; such ballot to be secret. The ballots must be withdrawn and read one at a time, in public, and the trial shall end in an acquittal at any time that one ballot is withdrawn on which the single word, guilty, does not appear.

9. Any person who serves on a jury which convicts (or finds against) the Defendant, shall be ineligible for further jury duty unless acceptable to both prosecution and defense.

10. The highest court shall be a jury of not less than twelve persons, randomly selected, who shall have demonstrated a knowledge of the principles of law contained in this Bill of Rights.

11. The right to be heard in all criminal and civil cases in this court of last resort, by appeal, error, or otherwise, shall not be denied.

12. No jury shall consist of less than twelve persons.

SECTION FOUR—PUNISHMENT AND APPEAL

1. Capital punishment shall not be allowed if the state can achieve its legitimate goals of deterrence and punishment through life imprisonment or other humane methods.

2. Neither banishment nor whipping, as a punishment for crime, shall be allowed; nor shall any person be abused in being arrested, while under arrest, or in prison.

3. The penal code shall be framed on the humane principles of reformation and prevention.

4. No person confined in jail shall be treated with unnecessary rigor. The erection of safe and comfortable prisons and inspections of prisons and the humane treatment of prisoners shall be provided for.

5. Indefinite imprisonment is prohibited, except upon conviction for a capital crime.

6. Excessive bail shall not be required, nor shall bail be required before conviction; except by the authority of a Grand or Petit Jury, unless the bailee is clearly a threat to life, liberty or property.

7. In any imprisonment for protective custody or probable cause the inmate

has an inalienable and unrestricted right to be visited by friends and counsel.

8. Excessive fines shall not be imposed.

9. No law shall subject any person to euthanasia, to torture or to cruel, excessive or unusual punishment.

10. The law must treat euthanasia and abortion in the same manner as all other forms of murder.

11. The Defendant's right of appeal shall not be restricted until he has exhausted all avenues of appeal and then been convicted a second time by a jury.

12. Any person appearing before the Supreme Court on appeal shall be presumed innocent and shall be released if the court fails to act or if any verdict against him is not unanimous.

13. The right of appeal to the Supreme Court shall not be abridged in any way.

14. The announcement by a defendant of an intent to appeal, acts as an automatic stay of execution of sentence.

15. Certiorari (required forwarding of appeal) shall be mandatory for all defendant appellants.

16. In any court action in which a person shall have been convicted on the basis of evidence which was obtained through the violation of any of the rights enumerated in this Bill of Rights, sentence may not be imposed until the persons who violated the said rights shall have been tried, convicted and sentenced. Such evidence must not be suppressed.

17. No conviction shall work corruption of blood or forfeiture of estate.

18. All costs of all court actions shall be borne by the court, unless a jury shall determine other liability based on this Bill of Rights.

19. In any case, no person shall be compelled to pay costs except after conviction on final trial.

20. In no instance shall any accused person before final judgment be compelled to advance money or fees to secure the rights herein guaranteed.

21. Persons inconvenienced by government agents or agencies, if not convicted or held liable by a jury, will be entitled to compensation for all losses.

22. It is a crime for any judge to fail to dismiss any charge based on a law or statute which violates this Bill of Rights.

23. It is a crime for any judge to impose a punishment for contempt of court without the authority of a jury decision.

24. Judges have no immunity from prosecution for their judicial acts which violate this Bill of Rights and may be punished criminally for deprivation of rights.

SECTION FIVE—MISCELLANEOUS

1. No person shall be imprisoned for the purpose of securing his testimony.
2. No person shall be detained without his consent, as a witness in any prosecution; nor any longer than may be necessary to take his testimony or deposition; nor be confined in any room where criminals are imprisoned.
3. No person shall be compelled to testify in matters of conscience. No human authority can in any case whatever control or interfere with the rights of conscience.
4. No person shall be rendered incompetent as a witness, in consequence of his opinions on matters of religion.
5. The power of Grand Juries to inquire into the wilful misconduct in office of public officers, and to find indictments in connection with such inquiries, shall never be suspended or impaired by law.
6. No Grand or Petit Jury shall return an indictment without offering the accused an opportunity to respond to the evidence against him.
7. Grand and Petit Jury hearings shall be private unless the accused shall deem otherwise.
8. All persons shall have direct and easy access to grand and petit juries for the purpose of securing indictments for violations of rights.
9. Should the right to trial by jury be denied to an accused for any reason, the right to be vindicated by a compurgator jury is, and shall remain, inviolate.

A NEW DECLARATION OF INDEPENDENCE

Robert McCurry

Another very interesting general statement from the right is a new Declaration of Independence, modeled on and quoting from the original.

From Robert McCurry, "A Declaration and Demand for Redress of Grievances" (East Point, Ga.: n.p., 1983, pamphlet).

A DECLARATION
AND
DEMAND FOR REDRESS OF GRIEVANCES
To The
PRESIDENT OF THE UNITED STATES
And All
CONGRESSMEN AND SENATORS OF THE UNITED STATES
And All
GOVERNORS AND LEGISLATORS OF THE FIFTY STATES

IN THE SAME SPIRIT AS OUR FOREFATHERS who were the authors of the Declaration of Independence. . .

WE HOLD THESE TRUTHS TO BE SELF-EVIDENT:—that all men are created by the Lord God; that they are endowed by their Creator with certain inalienable rights; that among these are life, liberty, property, and the pursuit of happiness; that, to secure these rights, governments are instituted among men, deriving their just powers from the consent of the governed; that whenever any form of government becomes destructive to these ends, it is the right of the people to alter or abolish it, and to institute a new government, laying its foundation on such principles, and organizing its powers in such form, as to them shall seem most likely to effect their safety and happiness. Prudence, indeed, will dictate that governments long established should not be changed for light and transient causes; and accordingly all experience hath shown that mankind are more disposed to suffer, while evils are sufferable, than to right themselves by abolishing the forms to which they are accustomed. But when a long train of abuses and usurpations, pursuing invariably the same object, evinces a design to reduce them under absolute despotism, it is their right, it is their duty, to throw off such government, and to provide new guards for their future security.

ON BEHALF OF OURSELVES AND OUR POSTERITY, we now declare that for the past seventy years the American people have patiently suffered similar grievances as those suffered by our forefathers; and such is now the necessity which constrains us to call upon the President of the United States and all members of the House of Representatives of the United States and all members of the Senate of the United States and all Governors and Legislators of the Fifty States to immediately return America to the original purpose of this great nation as envisioned and structured by the founding fathers in the Constitution of the United States and the Bill of Rights.

The history of the present government—including the Executive, Legislative, Judicial, and the unelected and unconstitutional fourth branch of government, the bureaucracy—for the past seventy years is a history of repeated injuries and usurpations, all having in direct object the establishment of an absolute tyranny over the citizens. To prove this, let facts be submitted to all citizens of these United States.

1. The Constitution of the United States and the Bill of Rights as envisioned and structured by the founding fathers have been declared null and void by Acts of Congress, the bureaucracy, and the courts. Many courts have banned the reading of or any reference to the Constitution and the Bill of Rights in courtroom litigation.

2. The courts are endorsing and supporting the unelected bureaucracies at virtually every level in investigating, approving or disapproving, licensing and controlling religion, churches, and their God-ordained ministries. This, among many other abuses, has resulted in the jailing of pastors (some for refusing to surrender church records to unelected bureaucracies and the courts, and other for conducting church ministries of preaching and teaching the Gospel), the padlocking of a church, and worshipers being dragged from a church building by law enforcement officers.

3. The courts have returned to the Star Chamber and have assumed a role of self-appointed sovereign supremacy and thus have become tyrannical and despotic in their actions by ignoring the Constitution of the United States and the Bill of Rights while protecting themselves with a self-imposed cloak of so-called sovereign immunity.

4. The courts have assumed a legislative role and are imposing upon the citizens "judicial legislation" based upon so-called "public policy" and "overriding government interest" that violates the very Constitution they have sworn to uphold.

5. The Supreme Court of the United States has decreed that justice will be meted out in light of current public sentiment and without regard to Divine absolutes.

6. The Supreme Court of the United States has assumed a self-imposed role of deity and authorized the murder of over twelve million babies by way of abortion since 1973.

7. Citizens are forced to pay for the murder of babies by way of tax-funded abortion in violation of their religious convictions.

8. Citizens are forced to pay for the funding of sodomite organizations through taxation in violation of their religious convictions.

9. Citizens are forced to pay for the funding of slothfulness, fornication, adultery, illegitimacy, and a multitude of other wicked sins through taxation in violation of their religious convictions.

10. Citizens are forced to pay for a humanistic public educational system that is anti-God, anti-Christ, anti-Bible, anti-Family, anti-American, and anti-Constitutional through taxation in violation of their religious convictions.

11. Congress, legislatures, and the courts have combined with the bureaucracies to subject the citizens to a jurisdiction foreign to our Constitution and the Bill of Rights and unacknowledged by the founding fathers.

12. Our government has formed a multitude of new bureaucratic offices that send swarms of officers across America to harass the citizens and eat out their substance.

13. The bureaucrats have become a standing army that wages war against the citizens and invades the privacy and security of the citizens in their persons, houses, papers, effects, businesses, families, and religion.

14. The coinage of gold and silver has been unlawfully suspended in violation of Article 1, Section 8, Clause 5, and Article 1, Section 10, Clause 1 of the Constitution of the United States by Executive Order, Acts of Congress, and Judicial Rulings; and the circulating medium of exchange has been replaced with irredeemable paper currency called Federal Reserve Notes.

15. The monetary policy of America is controlled by a privately-owned and secretly-operated corporation—the Federal Reserve System.

16. Government contrived and controlled inflation is destroying America and the hopes of our children and grandchildren of ever owning homes or lands of their own.

17. Taxes are imposed upon us without our consent.

18. The oppressive boot of the communist-designed graduated income tax grinds more and more heavily on our necks and is destroying the producers of America.

19. The Internal Revenue Service is enforcing social and public policy rules and regulations of its own design and formulation in violation of the Constitutional principle of separation of powers.

20. The Internal Revenue Service regularly resorts to Gestapo-like tactics

in the collection of "taxes"; this strategy has reduced the majority of our citizens to the fearful and whimpering state of common slaves.

21. Churches have been unlawfully brought under the jurisdiction and control of government by Congress, the President, the Supreme Court of the United States, State Legislatures, and the unelected bureaucracies.

22. Churches are required to have federal tax identification numbers and to collect and pay social security taxes in violation of their religious convictions.

23. Congress, with few exceptions, has abdicated its Constitutional function by failing to guard against the erosion and destruction of the rights, privileges, and liberties of the citizens and by passing legislation that violates the letter and the spirit of the Constitution of the United States and the Bill of Rights.

IN EVERY STAGE OF THESE OPPRESSIONS, we have warned time and time again of the unwarranted jurisdiction which these acts extend over us and have petitioned for redress in the most humble terms; our petitions have been answered only by a deaf ear and repeated injury. A government whose character is thus marked by every act which may define tyranny is unfit to be the government of a free people.

WE, THEREFORE, the undersigned, now humbly petition the President of the United States, the House of Representatives of the United States, the Senate of the United States, and the Governors and Legislatures of the Fifty States for a redress of grievances and for immediate relief and freedom from these tyrannical and despotic acts and oppressions of a government which is foreign to the republic envisioned and structured by the founding fathers and which has usurped the rights, privileges, and liberties of the American people as guaranteed and protected by the Constitution of the United States and the Bill of Rights.

AS DID THE FOUNDING FATHERS, we place as a priority the restoration of our God-given rights and liberties as protected by the First Amendment to the Constitution of the United States, to wit, that by virtue of Divine Authority from God, existing before the United States became a nation, the church has rights and responsibilities over and above the limitations handed down by men's constantly changing opinions, philosophies, and laws which too often seek to prevail against the church and her mission on earth through time.

THEREFORE, BY VIRTUE OF THE FIRST AMENDMENT to the Constitution of the United States, it shall be recognized by all branches and at all levels of government, including the courts, that all religions, churches, and their ministries cannot and must not come under the jurisdiction of federal, state, or local governments or any of their agencies, except, when a religion or church or their ministries choose to voluntarily:

1. Accept said jurisdiction
2. Accept direct public tax funds
3. Commit acts to a person against the will of the person or his legal guardian, which result in a crime against said person's life, liberty, or property.

NOTICE IS HEREBY GIVEN to the President and all Congressmen, Senators, Judges, and Magistrates of the United States; Governors, Legislators, Judges, and Magistrates of the Fifty States, and all others in governmental positions; if our demand for Redress of Grievances is met with deaf ears and repeated injuries, we will use whatever Biblical and Constitutional means are necessary to protect and defend our God-ordained families, homes, religious liberties, churches, and the Constitution and the Bill of Rights of the United States.

WE THE UNDERSIGNED, humbly affix our signatures to this petition with the purest of motives and the belief that this nation, under God, must once again be brought under the restrictions of Constitutional mandates. Our purpose is to rebuild, not to destroy. We appeal to our elected officials not to again answer us with deaf ears and repeated injuries.

FINALLY, FOR THE SUPPORT OF THIS DECLARATION, with a firm reliance on the Divine Protection of our Sovereign Lord and Saviour Jesus Christ, we mutually pledge to our God, to each other, and to our posterity: our lives, our fortunes, and our sacred honor.

4

COMMUNISM AND ANTI-COMMUNISM

COMMUNISM

One of the central concerns of the right in midcentury was communism, which was identified with the Soviet Union and the conflict for dominance in world affairs between it and the United States, but which more basically was seen as the greatest threat to the central American value—individualism.

Communist Party of America

Before we look at the main anti-communists of the fifties and sixties, it is a good idea to see how the communists presented themselves.

From *The American Way to Jobs, Peace, Equal Rights and Democracy: Program of the Communist Party* (New York: New Century Publishers, 1954).

THE AMERICAN WAY TO JOBS, PEACE, EQUAL RIGHTS AND DEMOCRACY

To the Reader

THIS PROGRAM of the Communist Party was ratified unanimously by the delegates to the Party's National Election Conference, held in New York, August 7–8, 1954.

THE COMMUNIST PROGRAM FOR JOBS, PEACE, EQUAL RIGHTS AND DEMOCRACY

The American Communists propose for our nation a five point program of Human Welfare, Democratic Freedoms and Peaceful Co-existence.

1. Raise the Purchasing Power of the People and Curb the Power and Profits of the Trusts!

* To combat depression we urge the defeat of all wage-cut attempts and a militant struggle by labor to raise wages on all levels, to shorten the work week without a reduction in weekly earnings, and to curb speed-up. We oppose the Eisenhower policy of tax relief for the rich. We demand a drastic revision of this policy and a shift of the tax burden to the monopolists. We oppose the Administration's "give-away" of our nation's natural resources and publicly financed utilities and industrial plants to the monopolists. We advocate the lowering of consumer prices, and an end to rent gouging.

* An anti-depression program requires government protection of home owners, small farmers and small business from mortgage foreclosures and bankruptcy. It requires a government guarantee of 100 per cent price parity and crop insurance for small and middle sized farmers and government loans and credit at low interest rates to small business and needy farmers.

* To end the economic backwardness of the South and to raise the purchasing power of the people of that region, the government should institute agricultural reform measures aimed at helping the sharecroppers and tenant farmers, Negro and white, to become independent producers who own the soil they till. The wage differentials between North and South and

between men and women workers should be ended and equal pay for equal work guaranteed to all, regardless of race, nationality, religion, sex, age, or political belief.

2. Spend for Human Welfare, not Warfare; for Homes and Schools, not Bombs and Battleships!

The government has the responsibility to guarantee jobs and living standards. The giant plants which have been erected for the production of planes, tanks, atom and hydrogen bombs for war, need not be shut down. They can be converted to peacetime uses. For example, the giant war-time aircraft plants can be converted into huge factories for producing pre-fabricated homes on an assembly line basis. A government-supported program of this kind can produce a minimum of 1,500,000 additional modern private dwellings a year. This would help wipe out the rat-infested fire-traps in which so many of our people live and die. The government which built these giant war producing plants with the people's money must guarantee their continued operation, but for peaceful purposes. If private industry cannot or will not do so, the government can and must!

* We propose a substantial increase in unemployment and old-age benefits, including the payment of unemployment insurance to new job seekers. We advocate special measures to keep our youth from becoming a jobless generation and to guarantee all our youth free and equal educational opportunities. We urge the labor movement to carry on a struggle against the mass ousting of women from industry and a program to protect women's economic rights. We call for a federal health program and a large scale federal program of public school construction, flood and drought control, conservation, power dam development and rural road building.

3. End the "Cold War" and Promote Friendship and Trade!

There can be no hope for a lasting peace and world disarmament without the principle of peaceful co-existence between the capitalist U.S.A. and the socialist Soviet Union and People's China. This is necessary whether one agrees or disagrees with Socialism, whether one likes or dislikes these countries.

Peaceful co-existence does not preclude, but includes, a peaceful competition between the different social systems. It does exclude, however, a settlement by force of arms of the question as to which social system is superior.

To ease world tension and to restore the United Nations as an instrument for lasting peace we propose:

* A return to President Roosevelt's policy of big power negotiation and agreement. This must include the admission of People's China, the established and effective government of the great Chinese nation, to the U.N. and its recognition by the U.S.

* An end to the arms race and to the policy of encircling the globe with U.S. military bases. What is needed is a world ban on the use of all atomic weapons and an agreement for a drastic reduction in all types of armaments. We oppose the militarization of our youth and Universal Military Training.

* The widest promotion of peaceful world trade. Our country, in its own interests, must take advantage of the immense markets for American goods available in the Soviet Union, China and Eastern Europe. These markets can provide millions of jobs for American workmen for years to come. We favor the extension of credit to bolster world trade and to help overcome the hunger and under-development of the colonial lands. The colonial and semi-colonial countries need machine tools, agriculture implements and farm products. But they rightfully reject fraudulent "Point 4" programs which aim at robbing them of their national independence, natural resources, and keeping them as backward hinterlands.

* An end to the policy of remilitarized West Germany and Japan. The lessons of World War II prove that a remilitarized Germany is a threat to world peace and the security of the U.S. We stand for a united, democratic and peaceful Germany.

* No intervention in the internal affairs of other nations and the recognition of the right of all nations to govern themselves. . . . The right of all nations to restrict and control all foreign investments on their territories should be recognized and respected. We favor a policy of the good neighbor to the Latin American lands and to all nations.

4. Defend and Strengthen Democracy!

We call for the defense of the Constitution and its Bill of Rights, for an end to the "dictatorship of fear," and for a turning back of the evil tide of McCarthyism. This requires the defense of the constitutional rights of all, including the Communists. To deny the Communists their constitutional rights is the first step to denying these rights for all Americans. This is the lesson of Nazi Germany. It is the lesson of the witch-hunt in this country. Labor leaders and former New Dealers are learning that they cannot obtain immunity from the witch hunters by crawling on their knees and Redbaiting. In the words of Benjamin Franklin, "They that can give up essential liberty to obtain a little temporary safety deserve neither liberty nor safety."

* We urge an end to the witch-hunting, the abolition of all Congressional witch-hunting committees, and the prosecution of their perjured informers, and a halt to the Gestapo-like political activities of the F.B.I. Political arrests and deportations must cease. . . .

* Labor's right to organize and strike must be protected and all anti-labor legislation such as the infamous Taft-Hartley act must be repealed and defeated. Strike-breaking by court injunctions or government decrees should be stopped.

* End discrimination against all minority groups. Outlaw anti-Semitism and wipe out all discrimination against Mexican-Americans, Puerto Ricans and American Indians.

* Academic freedom and freedom of inquiry should be restored for America's youth. Young people should be given the right to vote at 18. The time has come to put a stop to the cult of violence in our movies, TV and literature, and to promote culture for peace and democracy.

5. Win Equal Rights for the Negro People! For Full Economic Political and Social Equality!

All progressive forces should give full support to the valiant fight of the Negro people for their rights. This is necessary because the fight for Negro freedom, for the rights of all the Negro people is an integral part of the fight for democracy, for peace, for the rights and living standards of labor and all the people.

* We urge prompt federal action to wipe out every form of discrimination in employment and job opportunities for Negro workers in government service and industry. This can help end the practice of hiring Negro workers last and firing them first, of denying them opportunities for advancement as skilled workers or of employment as white-collar workers or professionals. A federal FEPC, strictly enforced, can help prevent the corporations from pitting one group of workers against another and from reducing wage standards for all workers.

* We further urge federal legislation to outlaw poll-taxes and all restrictions on registration, voting and election activity which operate to disfranchise the Negro citizens in the south.

* We urge federal civil rights legislation and executive and administrative orders to outlaw lynching, segregation and Jim Crow. We urge an immediate end to segregation in the educational system, health and hospitalization services, in transportation and housing, in meeting houses and public parks in the south and throughout the land.

Socialist Labor Party

A bit later one of the many socialist parties in America outlined its goal of industrial democracy.

Industrial Democracy—Complete Democracy
Arnold Petersen

Like its forerunner, political democracy, *Industrial Democracy* will be organized on a representative basis. Having dispensed with the old, worn out Political State, which derived its representation from geographic units (town, county, state), geographic or territorial demarcations and boundary lines are now discarded. Industrial Democracy, then, derives its representation from industrial units, and from industry generally. It will be organized from the bottom up, that is, an ascending scale of organization—single plant or group of plants, Local Industrial Union of a given industry, National Industrial Union of the given industry, and finally the All-Industrial Congress, representing all industries. This All-Industrial Union Congress will be the governing board, or the Industrial Government of the Socialist Republic. Its task would, in the words of [Daniel] De Leon, be "the easy one which can be summed up in the statistics of the wealth needed, the wealth producible, and the work required." In short, how much of this or that article do we need, how much can be produced of that article with present equipment, and how many hours of labor will the workers have to render on the basis of need and capacity? The answers lie close at hand.

From Arnold Petersen, *Democracy Past, Present and Future* (New York: New York Labor News Co., 1962).

The workers, in the ascending scale of industrial organization, will elect their own foremen and managers, their representatives to the local and national unions, and finally to the All-Industrial Union Congress, with the power of recall never surrendered, and complete democracy—Industrial Democracy—prevailing. This democracy—though necessarily representative—will be a complete democracy such as the world has never before enjoyed—one is tempted to say a "pure" or "perfect" democracy, though it may be best not to yield to the temptation by reason of the manner in which defenders of the acquisitive society have misrepresented these terms. Certainly it will be an infinitely purer and vastly more "perfect" democracy than any the human race has ever known. And with its institution the golden age of mankind will begin. . . . True democracy, not qualified democracy, nor a democracy cancelled by the limitations inevitably imposed by a class society resting on an economy of scarcity, will be at last enthroned and made secure by that strongest of bonds, the bond of the enlightened material interests of man, united in a common brotherhood made possible by the rendering unnecessary of individual acquisitiveness, and the rendering superfluous of petty motives of personal selfishness.

Marxist-Leninist Party

One of the parties that split off from the Communist Party is the Marxist-Leninist Party, which was supported by the Communist Party of Albania and saw Albania as the only pure communist country. The jargon used in this document is typical of the period.

COMMUNIQUE ON THE SECOND CONGRESS OF THE MLP, USA

—FALL 1983—

To meet the challenge of the capitalist offensive, the times demand one thing: steadfast revolutionary work

The Second Congress of the Marxist-Leninist Party was convened in

From "Communique on the Second Congress of the MLP, Fall 1983," *The Workers' Advocate* 14, no. 1 (January 1, 1984).

the fall of 1983. It met at a time when the U.S. stands at the brink of big class battles. It is a time when the capitalist bourgeoisie is on a Reaganite rampage, when the revolutionary path is neither easy nor fashionable, when the fainthearted cower around the fringes of the bloodstained Democratic Party. But it is also a time when the class lines are sharpening to a fine point, when the working masses are profoundly skeptical of the old reformist leaders, and when all the prerequisites for a new mass upsurge are maturing.

In this difficult period, when the battle lines are being drawn but the masses are often stunned by the ferocity of the capitalist offensive and handcuffed by the treachery of the reformist leaders, the Second Congress spoke up for the proletariat and all toilers. It put forward the revolutionary alternative to slavish submission to this capitalist hell. It looked back with pride at the firm stand and solid work of the Party in the four years since its founding at the First Congress, and it took, with supreme confidence in Marxism-Leninism and the historic mission of the proletariat, a series of daring decisions to direct the work in the future.

The Second Congress raised four main slogans:

FIGHT THE CAPITALIST OFFENSIVE—BUILD THE INDEPEN-DENT MOVEMENT OF THE WORKING CLASS!

AGAINST SOCIAL-DEMOCRACY AND LIQUIDATIONISM—FOR STEADFAST REVOLUTIONARY WORK!

ORGANIZE THE PROLETARIAT, BUILD THE MARXIST-LE-NINIST PARTY!

UPHOLD THE RED BANNER OF COMMUNISM—BACK TO THE CLASSIC TEACHINGS OF MARXISM-LENINISM!

The Second Congress resolutely declared: "To meet the challenge of the capitalist offensive, to make the necessary preparations in organization and consciousness for the coming class battles, the times demand one thing: steadfast revolutionary work."

Fight the Capitalist Offensive—Build the Independent Movement of the Working Class!

The 1980's have opened with the capitalists running amok against the working masses. There is a capitalist offensive of starvation, militarism, racism and lies against the working people at home. And there is stepped-up warmongering, intervention, CIA subversion and lies against the working people of other countries.

The Marxist-Leninist Party is the party of revolutionary action, the party of the class struggle, and it has thrown itself heart and soul into battle against the capitalist offensive. It leads the masses to rise up against oppression and exploitation. The Second Congress summed up the lessons of the struggle and charted out the path ahead. . . .

The Second Congress brought the class basis of politics to the fore. Reaganism and the capitalist offensive are the bipartisan program of the capitalist class. Democrat and Republican, liberal capitalist and conservative capitalist, are united in waging war on the working masses, slashing wages, arming the Pentagon to the hilt and stepping up racist attacks. The Democrats and Republicans, however, also have their own specific roles in the overall capitalist program. The Democrats have been given the job of being the main deceiver of the working masses. They present themselves as the "party of labor and the minorities" in order to paint up each capitalist atrocity, each Reaganite proposal, with a liberal facade and thus mislead and pacify the masses.

Today the American working class still finds itself mainly ensnared in the chains of bourgeois politics. For decades the liberal politicians, the labor bureaucrats, the social-democrats, the revisionists, and the other reformists have worked day and night to tie the workers' movement and all popular struggles to the coattails of the capitalist politicians. This system of class collaboration has been the main factor tying the masses down in the face of the Reaganite attacks. Breaking the grip of the capitalist parties and building the independent movement of the working class is the immediate task of the fight against the capitalist offensive.

Building the independent movement of the working class is decisive because the working class is the truly revolutionary class which can defeat the capitalist reaction. Because of its revolutionary dynamism and stamina, its capacity for organization, and its economic position and numbers, the working class is the oppressed class with the greatest potential strength in history. The working class must stand up to play its historic role as the champion of all the exploited and oppressed. It must place a mighty proletarian stamp on all the struggles of the masses against exploitation, reaction and war. The degree to which the working class organizes itself and rises in struggle, the degree to which it establishes its political independence in the struggle against the capitalists, will determine whether or not the capitalist offensive is defeated. It is this that will determine whether the fruits of the mass struggles are frittered away, or whether they serve to build up the forces for the socialist revolution which will emancipate the working masses from capitalist exploitation and oppression once and for all.

Against Social-Democracy and Liquidationism—
For Steadfast Revolutionary Work!

The capitalists themselves are aware of the great potential for struggle that resides in the working class. They see the storm of indignation that is building up in the hearts of the oppressed. They are building more and more prisons, passing harsher laws and organizing racist gangs and fascist storm troopers, but they know that this alone cannot keep the working masses down. So they are making more and more use of the reformist forces to misdirect, divert, disorganize and demoralize the working masses. Reformism does not mean improving the conditions of the masses; on the contrary, the vital role that reformism has played in the capitalist offensive shows that reformism means collaborating with the bourgeoisie in suppressing the mass struggle and implementing the capitalist program. The social-democrats, reformists, labor bureaucrats and the bourgeois misleaders of the oppressed nationalities are a screen to divert the anger of the masses.

The Second Congress denounced the treacherous role of the social-democratic and revisionist forces.

The capitalists have had a special fondness for social-democracy for decades. In the situation where the masses are more and more disgusted with the bourgeois politicians, the social-democrats make it their job to give the Democratic Party a "socialist" tinge and to assure the workers that the Democratic Party hacks are really on their side. The social-democrats perform the same service for the labor bureaucrats, who are rabid capitalist agents and strikebreakers in the workers' movement. All in all, the social-democrats are nothing but firefighters for the bourgeoisie, dressing up the capitalist program in "socialist" colors and fighting tooth and nail against the political independence of the working masses.

The Second Congress showed that liquidationism—working to obliterate (liquidate) the independent organization of the working class—is today the main feature of all the revisionist and opportunist currents in the revolutionary movement. The pro-Soviet revisionists, the pro-Chinese revisionists and the trotskyites have, despite their quarrels, a common platform of liquidationism and merger with social-democracy. The revisionist and trotskyite liquidators accommodate themselves to social-democracy, merge with social-democracy in the "left" wing of the Democratic Party, and adopt the traditional social-democratic style and methods.

The maintenance of a revolutionary stand is impossible without a relentless struggle against social-democracy and liquidationism.

The Second Congress also noted that, in those situations where the masses have gone to the left and sections of activists have become disgusted with various of the more blatant capitulationist stands of the social-democrats and of the revisionist liquidators, a trend has generally come up that sees itself as to the left of the reformists, but which refuses to break with them. This trend, which is composed of diverse elements, can be generally characterized with regard to its ideology and political practice as "left" social-democracy, although it does not usually call itself that. Activists under the influence of such "left" social-democratic ideas are willing, to a greater or lesser extent to take up the more popular militant slogans, but they still cherish illusions in the "left" wing of the Democratic Party and they keep their activities within the general bounds of what is acceptable to the reformist forces. The Second Congress showed that breaking the influence of the "left" social-democratic ideology is part and parcel of the fight for the political independence of the working class, part and parcel of the fight against social-democracy and liquidationism.

The work of the Marxist-Leninist Party has been a beacon against the opportunism of the liquidationist and social-democratic trends. The Marxist-Leninist Party has persevered in steadfast revolutionary struggle, while the opportunists, as fair-weather "revolutionaries," are reveling in despondency and renegacy, are denouncing the revolutionary traditions from the mass upsurge that reached its height in the 1960's and early 1970's, and are cowering behind the liberals, the labor bureaucrats and any bourgeois who is willing to throw them a crumb. It is not difficult to be a "revolutionary" when the revolutionary movement is at its height, when everybody talks about revolution just because they are carried away, because it is the fashion, and sometimes even out of direct careerist motives. It is far more difficult—and of far greater value—to be able to champion the interests of the revolution when the mass upsurge is not yet present. It is far more difficult—and of far greater value—to be able to work for the revolution by agitation among the masses, by theoretical work and through building organization, during the preparatory period when the majority of the masses do not yet appreciate the need for direct revolutionary action. This is the task which the revolutionary vanguard, rallied around the Marxist-Leninist Party, has taken upon itself and handled with skill and heroism in the first years of the 1980's. It is this work which is essential to clear the way for a new mass upsurge and to ensure that the mass struggle is not wasted, but is used to establish the class independence of the working masses.

The Second Congress held that the Marxist-Leninist Party has been able to uphold the banners of class struggle and revolution because it has known how to maintain close contact with the masses. The Second Congress opposed both those who renounce the revolution and the phrasemongers who, in the name of revolution, denounce work among the masses. These phrasemongers are nothing but "liquidators from the left," whose "revolutionary" words are nothing but anarchist posturing to hide their agreement with the other liquidators on all major questions of political practice. The Marxist-Leninist Party, on the other hand, has known how to judge the mood of the masses and find methods of approach to them so that, even in the midst of difficult periods, it is possible to carry out revolutionary agitation and to fight the capitalists and their opportunist servants.

Organize the Proletariat— Build the Marxist-Leninist Party

Steadfast revolutionary work requires the building of solid organization. The highest form of class organization is the proletarian political party, the Marxist-Leninist Party itself. The Second Congress stressed that the specific tasks of building up the proletarian party and rallying the masses around it must not be neglected in the general work of building up the independent political movement of the working class. On the contrary, without a political party of its own, the working class can not constitute itself as a class for itself, a class with its own independent class aims. The extent to which the working class consolidates its political party and acts as a unified force under its leadership is, in the final analysis, the extent to which it has achieved an independent class stand. The Second Congress was a resounding call to persevere on the road of party-building. . . .

Uphold the Red Banner of Communism—
Back to the Classic Teachings of Marxism-Leninism!

Without a revolutionary theory, there can be no revolutionary movement. The workers' movement faces many complex questions today in its struggle against the bourgeoisie. Marxist-Leninist theory is an essential weapon to answer these questions. Marxism-Leninism is not some hidebound catechism. It is above all a guide to revolutionary work. It is the revolutionary science of the working class, providing workers and activists with consciousness of the socialist goal of the revolution and a comprehensive summation of the experience of the world revolutionary movement. . . .

Another essential feature of communism is proletarian internationalism. A permanent feature of the work of the Marxist-Leninist Party has been its enthusiasm for the world revolutionary movement. The Second Congress declared that:

"The struggle between exploiter and exploited, oppressor and oppressed, lies behind the tangle of world events. . . . On one side stands the old world of capitalist exploitation, reaction, imperialism and aggressive war. On the other side stands the world of revolutionary struggle, of the working masses who are striving for a new world without exploitation, oppression and enslaving wars."

The Resolutions of the Second Congress denounced world imperialism, including the two superpowers, U.S. imperialism and Soviet social-imperialism, and the lesser imperialist powers. They laid special stress on thoroughly denouncing the crimes of "our own" U.S. imperialists throughout the world. They hailed the world proletarian movement, the revolutionary movements in the oppressed and dependent countries and the international upsurge of the anti-war movement in the imperialist metropolises. And they declared the Party's resolute support for socialist Albania, the only genuinely socialist country in the world today, and for the Party of Labor of Albania. . . .

Hail the Second Congress of the Marxist-Leninist Party!

Let the rich tremble at the doom and gloom that confronts them, at the sight of their capitalist system bogged down in economic crisis, unending inter-imperialist rivalry, racism and decay. Let the fainthearted cower under the supposed protection of the liberal imperialists and the Democratic Party of the millionaires. The class conscious proletariat, for its part, is organizing and preparing itself for the great storms that lie ahead.

Let all working people unite in the class struggle against the exploiters and oppressors. Let the perspective of the socialist revolution inspire and encourage the downtrodden. For the day is coming when the proletariat, at the head of all the working people, will rise up to smash to dust the iron chains of bourgeois slavery, the chains of starvation, militarism, imperialism, racism and exploitation. The working class is organizing itself as an independent force, and it will rush forward on the road of proletarian revolution to build a new world, a world free of misery and oppression, free of the exploitation of man by man. Despite the capitalist clouds that now cover the sky, the revolutionary ferment among the masses is growing and the new socialist sun is preparing to emerge.

ANTI-COMMUNISM

These parties and ideas are the main concerns of the anti-communists. Their focus is as much on the idea that communism was connected with the Soviet Union and the People's Republic of China, opponents of the United States on the world stage, as it was on the content of the beliefs. One of the most famous anti-communist books was None Dare Call It Treason *(1964)[1] by John Stormer, who saw America permeated by collectivist values. Stormer traced America's problems to John Dewey and the Social Gospel Movement. Dewey, a favorite target of the right, is blamed for stressing the need for children to get along in groups. Followers of Dewey are believed to have developed a vision of the school system as a means of achieving socialism, creating class hatred, and teaching internationalism. The Social Gospel Movement, a movement that had argued that Christians should actively try to improve social conditions, is depicted as the root of all modern religious problems.*

Minutemen

The platform of the Patriotic Party was written by Robert DePugh, the founder of the Minutemen. It presents a detailed plan for the transition from the present situation to one in which the extreme right holds political power; as such, it demonstrates that even the most virulent of anti-communists looked to positive change beyond simply ridding the country of communists.

The Minutemen were a small paramilitary group located in Missouri. They were forerunners to many of the survivalist paramilitary groups today, but they saw themselves as the real bulwark against a communist invasion. The selections that follow the platform show something of their organization.

POLITICAL PLATFORM OF THE PATRIOTIC PARTY
Robert B. DePugh

Whereas the sovereignty of our nation and the liberty of its citizens are in grave and immediate danger; the officers, candidates, and members of the Patriotic Party advocate the following emergency measures:

1. Genuinely loyal, patriotic and pro-American candidates must be elected to federal, state and local offices as fast as is humanly possible.

2. As soon as a Patriotic President can be elected, he should create and appoint committees made up of private citizens well known for their loyalty, integrity and administrative ability to supervise and put into effect the further measures listed in this platform under the following five categories.

Regarding National Defense—

3. Our Armed Forces should be put on an immediate alert to guard against surprise attack by any foreign aggressor.

4. The Armed Forces of the United States now stationed in Europe and Asia should be returned to the Western Hemisphere except for small balanced units equipped with atomic weapons which should remain as long as advisable to support the Armed Forces of loyal and cooperative allies.

5. The military installations existing within territories of the United States which have been closed during the past ten years should be re-opened, modernized and additional installations be prepared where needed.

6. Our Armed Forces now stationed in the United States should be quickly dispersed into small self sufficient combat groups so that a maximum percentage of our military strength would survive any surprise atomic attack.

From Robert B[olivar] DePugh, *Blueprint for Victory* (Norborne, Mo.: n.p., 1966).

7. All our present military aircraft, naval vessels and army equipment should be quickly repaired and put into active service as a stop-gap measure until more modern weapons systems can be manufactured and delivered to the Armed Forces.

8. Patriotism, experience and ability should be the criteria by which our top military officers and advisors are selected. The citizens freedom of speech is not forfeited just because he happens to be a military officer.

9. An effective civil defense program should be put into effect, managed by competent reserve officers and civilian administrators. The civilian population should be prepared psychologically as well as militarily to 'roll with the punch' of any surprise attack and come back fighting. New defense industries should be scattered through those parts of the United States most easily defendable. This would automatically cause the civilian population to disperse and thus become less vulnerable to atomic attack. Suitable treaties might be made with Canada to scatter our industry even further to the mutual benefit of both nations.

10. Our government, industry and people must combine their efforts to build an impregnable defense against foreign aggression and to develop our Armed Forces into the most powerful military force in the world.

11. Once our defences and military forces have reached a stage of development comparable to our nations industrial might in other fields, we should then make no further effort to maintain a static defense of Europe, Asia or Africa. Instead we should notify the communist powers that any further invasion, direct or indirect, into those areas will result in their prompt destruction.

Regarding Internal Security—

12. All known or suspected communists now holding jobs in government or in any essential industry should be immediately discharged from such positions and subpoenaed to appear before appropriate Grand Juries for investigation. Where reasonable grounds are found to believe that such persons have been guilty of treasonous activity such cases should be referred to the courts for prompt legal action.

13. All persons suspected of treason against the constitution of the United States should be placed under arrest, tried by jury and if found guilty should be confined for such a time and in such a manner as to protect our national security.

14. An extensive investigation should be made as to the loyalty of all the officials in government, defense industry, tax free foundations, labor unions, the communications industry, news media and similar fields vital to the nations internal security, such investigations being made for the most part by Grand Juries composed of private citizens of substance and good repute.

15. Past and present activities of all government agencies and departments should be closely scrutinized by appropriate committees of the senate and the congress [*sic*] to make certain that all such activities have been and will be in the nations best interest. These investigations should include not only the Departments of State, Defense, Health, Education and Welfare, Agriculture and Labor but also the Treasury, the Justice Department, the F.B.I. and the C.I.A.

16. Where evidence of treason is found, those suspected of such acts should be tried before civilian courts but if it is found that the courts themselves have been infiltrated to such an extent as to make the conviction of traitors impossible, then the Constitution should be amended to allow such persons to be tried before military courts or before new federal judges especially appointed for this purpose.

17. All the present members of the Supreme Court should be removed from office; new justices should be elected by the people to take their place and all future replacements should be made by election rather than by political appointment.

18. A new Department of Internal Security should be formed under the joint direction of appropriate committees of the Senate and Congress with legal authority to investigate all other government agencies and departments and to report any evidence of disloyalty or subversion to the elected representatives of the people.

Regarding Foreign Affairs—

19. All relationships between this nation and other nations should be designed: first, to protect the freedom, prosperity and security of our own citizens; secondly, to strengthen and encourage worthy allies, and third to work toward the eventual freedom of the captive nations.

20. This nation should immediately withdraw from the United Nations, reclaim the land on which the United Nations building is constructed, and deport all foreign personnel now working for the United Nations in this country.

21. The sale or shipment of any material, strategic or non-strategic to any of the communist block nations or to their satellites should be considered an act of treason and punished as such.

22. All foreign aid, military and economic, should be immediately stopped to any nation that continues to trade with the communist block nations or allows their facilities of transportation to be used in such trade.

23. Mutual defense agreements should be continued only with those nations who fully reciprocate those efforts and who maintain a strong anti-communist position in both their foreign and domestic affairs.

24. Trade relationships with other friendly nations must be of mutual benefit but must also be arranged as to protect the welfare of American business and labor, to maintain favorable financial balance, to expand foreign markets for American made products and assure reliable sources of strategic materials. Those factors that effect the balance of payments between this and other nations must be quickly altered to prevent further drain on our national gold reserves. In no case should gold be transferred to any nation that has failed to repay in full all past loans made to them by the United States.

25. The Monroe Doctrine must be enforced. Where communist controlled governments exist in the Western hemisphere, 'free governments in exile' should be given prompt diplomatic recognition and the people of those nations should be given whatever help may be necessary to regain their political freedom.

26. Having prepared for our national defense and provided internal security against espionage and subversion, we should then begin an all out psychological, political and economic warfare against the communist conspiracy. Our goal is not only the freedom and safety of our own people but also the freedom and dignity of mankind everywhere.

Regarding Government Economy —

27. The government should buy back the Federal Reserve System as has been provided for by law. The right 'to coin money and set the value thereof' should be returned to Congress as the Constitution provides. All money now in circulation as federal reserve notes should be recalled in an orderly manner and United States notes should be issued in their place. This new currency should be backed not only with the governments present reserves of gold and silver but by government stock piles of other strategic metals such as platinum,

manganese, tin, nickel, tungsten, mercury, copper, aluminum, etc. so that their actual value will correspond as nearly as possible to their face value. The price of gold paid to private miners in this country should be considerably increased so as to encourage production, increase our national gold reserves and further strengthen United States currency in the World Market.

28. The entire mechanism whereby the National debt has been acquired should be declared null and void as an illegal contract. Payment of interest on the national debt should be stopped at once. A computation of past interest paid on this debt should be made and that amount deducted from the balance owed to the Federal Reserve Systems, other agencies of government, international bankers, etc. In most cases it will be found that the interest already paid exceeds the amount originally owed.

29. In the fastest and most efficient manner, the Government should take itself out of competition with private industry. All non-military transportation facilities, all power producing facilities and similar government owned industry should be sold to private citizens or companies.

30. The federal government has no constitutional right to make or guarantee loans to private companies, individuals or cooperatives or to states, counties or cities. All such debts should be collected in a firm but orderly manner and the funds received used to pay off that part of the national debt legally owed to private citizens and companies that hold government bonds.

31. The federal government should make no further loans, gifts or grants to either state or local governments or to any institution, public or private. In this manner unwanted federal control can be avoided in such fields as education, and in the administration of local political affairs.

32. The federal government has no constitutional right to own land. Title to all the so-called 'public lands' now controlled by the federal government should be transferred to the states. If these lands are 'purchased' by the states at a modest rate the money would provide an emergency reserve fund that the federal government could draw on temporarily when its expenses unavoidably exceeded its income. Thus, the government would have no excuse for going in debt. When this happened it should be mandatory that either the tax structure or the federal budget be adjusted so that the amount drawn from the fund would be repaid in not more than two years. Where limited tracts are needed for defense purposes, they can be leased by the federal government from the states.

33. All government subsidies, regardless of their form should be reduced

by one-third for each of three succeeding years and thereafter outlawed entirely. This will allow the proven principles of the free enterprise system to operate most efficiently, free from government control and regimentation.

34. Those departments of the federal government which deal with internal affairs, such as the department of Agriculture, Department of Commerce, the Department of Health, Education and Welfare, etc. should be required to reduce the number of persons employed by them by 20 percent per year for the first three years and by 10 percent per year for the next three succeeding years. After that time these agencies would be limited to a small staff of administrative and technical personnel that would be available on an advisory basis only when requested by comparable state agencies.

35. Tax on income encourages waste and extravagance while tax on purchases encourages thrift and savings. All hidden taxes such as corporation taxes, business taxes, real estate taxes, personal income taxes, etc. should be made unconstitutional. All governments, at every level should be required to raise their necessary revenues by sales taxes, which, regardless of how high they must be, will be plainly labeled as such and added to each product purchased by the citizen. In this way the people will be constantly reminded of the cost of government and more likely to insist on government honesty, efficiency and moderation.

36. The privilege of tax exemption for certain foundations and organizations should be carefully limited because such organizations are automatically subsidized in part by other citizens. As a condition to tax free status those foundations and organizations having capital funds of over one million dollars, should have half of their directors selected by a committee of congress from among private citizens who volunteer to serve in such positions without pay and who will make certain that such funds are in no way used to the detriment of the Constitutional Republic or the freedom of its citizens. If an educational, charitable or religious organization wishes to receive tax free gifts, then all its funds must be used within the territorial limits of the United States They may, of course, spend such funds elsewhere but in so doing forfeit their tax exempt status. No one person should be allowed to serve as officer or director of more than one tax free organization.

37. The laws relating to the formation and regulation of corporation need modification. Under our free enterprise system, there is no theoretical limit to the amount of wealth that may be acquired by any citizen. This is as it should be. In recent decades however, the economic rights of the workers, and of other citizens also, has [*sic*] been endangered by the development of

vast self perpetuating corporations. It is not the size of these corporations that constitutes a danger so much as the fact that they are often managed by persons who are hardly controlled at all by the owner-stockholders and who have only an academic interest in the welfare of the employees. Corporations enjoy definite tax and business advantages. To qualify for these advantages all corporations should meet one of these requirements: one, the management team (president, vice-president, secretary and treasurer) should between them, own at least ten percent of the companies stock, or two, the corporation should be limited to owning property in one state and to conducting business in only one basic type of business or industry. In no case should more than 20% of any corporation stock be owned by interests outside the United States.

38. If the power and extent of corporations is to be restricted then labor unions should be restricted in a like manner. Unions should be restricted to one of two situations: either all members of one union should work in the same state, or all members of one union should work for the same company. Unions should be allowed to bargain collectively only with the management of corporations and not with the individual owners of small business. In no case should union membership be compulsory for the obtaining of employment.

39. In no way should government be allowed to restrict freedom of the press or similar news media. At the same time, every precaution should be taken that these news media are not controlled by any foreign ideology or special interest group. The best way of doing this is to provide maximum competition between different parts of the industry and by legally limiting the number of newspapers, radio or television stations that can be owned by any one person or company.

Regarding Limited Government—

40. The power of government must be limited in every possible way without seriously weakening the national defense. A belief in this fact must be paramount in the selection of public officials and in the interpretation of the laws.

41. The size of government bureaucracies at every level must be greatly reduced. Each unnecessary regulation must be cancelled. Every obsolete office must be abolished. Every non-essential job must be eliminated. In some cases this may be done by acts of congress or the state legislature. Sometimes it can be done by conscientious public officials. Most often it can

be done only by cutting off the previously unlimited sources of money that have fed these bureaucracies and thereby forcing them to bring their own size under control.

42. When a truly pro-American government has been formed, some means of federal-state joint control must insure that Armed Forces of the United States will never again be used against our own citizens. The Air Force, intercontinental ballistic missiles, the Navy and the Marines could remain under federal control. The pay scale, living conditions and educational opportunities of these units should be such as to encourage the enlistment of well qualified personnel who would make these Armed Forces their lifetime career. Troops of the United States Army would be recruited by the states themselves and maintained in numbers according to the state population, equipped according to uniform standards. They would be commanded at the national level by a 'General Staff' of professional officers who would coordinate with the other services in the national defense. Replacement of members of the General Staff would be selected from among the career officers by the remaining staff members and confirmed by the senate. They would have under their control all the weapons of ground warfare, including short and medium range missiles, anti-aircraft missiles, tanks, artillery, etc. as well as such aircraft as required for defense against other aircraft and as normal air support for ground troops.

43. At present the federal government is composed of three major branches: the executive, the legislative and the judicial. The military should become a fourth major branch of government. Although still under control of civilian authority, including the states themselves, the general staff should have greater latitude in forming their own plans and deciding on the best weapons systems without the interference of inexperienced civilian advisors.

44. Government must be the servant of the people and not the master. Although the United States Constitution and the Bill of Rights are among the greatest documents ever written, there are places in which the wording is vague. The enemies of freedom have taken advantage of these generalities to greatly expand the power of the government and to restrict the freedom of the individual. There are several areas where the general wording of the constitution needs to be amended to make it more specific.

45. The clause in the Constitution which states 'and provide for the general welfare' has been used as an excuse by ambitious government officials to create a multitude of illegal agencies and laws that extend the government's power over the citizens. This clause serves no useful purpose

and should be stricken from the Constitution entirely. All agencies that have been formed under this clause should be abolished. All laws and federal regulations that have resulted from it should be declared null and void.

46. The right of the federal government to 'regulate commerce between the states' is another clause that has stretched far beyond its intended meaning and traditional interpretation. It has been used as an excuse to regulate and harass many small companies completely out of business. This part of the Constitution should be amended to read somewhat as follows: 'No state shall raise tariffs for export or import of merchandise to or from any other state or otherwise interfere with the free flow of commerce across its borders.'

47. The right of the citizens to own and bear arms is considered in the second amendment in the Bill of Rights. The wording of this amendment, however, is such that in many areas this right has been regulated almost out of existence. This important freedom should be fully guaranteed in a clear and straight forward manner such as: 'Any individual having the right to vote as a citizen of the United States shall in no way be restrained or prohibited from the ownership of firearms, or ammunition, nor shall any citizen be restrained from the bearing or transport of such arms or ammunition on property legally controlled by him, or on the public roads or on the public domain or on the property of others with their permission, provided of course, that he shall take reasonable and prudent care for the safety of other citizens and their property.

48. The present situation whereby the President can have his wish become law by simply having a statement printed in the Federal Register must be stopped at once. Either by Constitutional amendment or by an act of congress all such 'laws' should be declared illegal, and as having no effect. The Federal Register must be used only—as it was first intended—as a guide to federal employees in the accurate interpretation of the laws duly passed by the congress and the senate.

49. The right to buy and sell property or merchandise is a purely personal transaction. Neither the seller nor the buyer should be forced by government to either enter into or refrain from any such transaction against their personal wishes or desire.

50. Our nation's Christian heritage must be strengthened, its traditions of religious freedom, and the separation of church and state must be preserved. Unconstitutional government interference into local and individual religious beliefs must not be permitted.

51. Freedom from oppressive taxation, freedom from invasion of personal privacy, freedom of choice, freedom from bureaucratic restraint, freedom in the selection of employees, employers, friends or associates. These and many others should be the right of every citizen and they should be guaranteed by clear and concise amendments to the United States Constitution.

PRACTICAL SECURITY MEASURES

1. Anyone who wishes to prevent identification as a member of this organization should avoid the use of checks or postal money orders. In modern banking practice all checks are microfilmed and such records are kept for years. Ordinary cash is the best thing to send because the risk of a small financial loss in the mail is much less than the possible loss of your life when the communists take complete control.

2. Use deceptive measures. Subscribe to one or more left-wing periodicals or get on the mailing list of some 'peace movement.' This will keep the postal inspectors guessing as to which side you are really on. See the December issue of On Target for names and addresses of many left-wing organizations or write to National Headquarters for this information. While doing this our members can be of great assistance in searching this left-wing literature for names and addresses of fellow travelers and forwarding this information for our Central Intelligence files. We desperately need people to assist in this work. Please inquire as to detailed instructions for such activity.

3. Always use two envelopes in sending mail to any patriotic organization or to any other member of our organization. Do not put a return address on the outer envelope. Put your return address on the inside envelope with the words, 'Return postage guaranteed.'

4. Place some opaque material such as tin foil, carbon paper, etc. between the inner and outer envelopes to prevent your mail from being read by infra-red cameras.

5. Send all letters from corner mail boxes or from post offices where you are not known.

6. Be careful in the use of the telephone. Avoid telephone calls to Na-

"Practical Security Measures" ([Norborne, Mo.:] Minutemen, [1960s], pamphlet).

tional Headquarters or to known members of the organization as much as possible.

7. Prepare telephone codes ahead of time for future protection.

8. In recruiting new members always learn as much as you can about the prospective recruit and make sure he is not an infiltrator before you identify yourself as a member of the organization.

9. Members of the organization in each area should be divided into four groups.

A. Those who have been identified publicly or by law enforcement agencies as members of the Minutemen.
B. Those persons not known as members of this organization but who are generally known as being patriots.
C. Those persons who have kept their political beliefs hidden.
D. Members who profess to be liberal for the purpose of infiltrating enemy organizations.

All members should be very careful in making contact with persons in a different category than themselves. For example, people in Class D should be very secret in their contacts and communications with persons of Class A or Class B. Each member must respect the security of every other member. Do not, under any circumstances, identify one member of the organization even to other members without his expressed permission on each and every occasion.

10. Avoid loose talk. Do not discuss organizational plans in public places where you could be overheard. Do not even hint at such a discussion in the presence of non-members.

11. Do not write patriotic letters to newspapers or magazines under your own name. To do so achieves very little except to identify you to the enemy.

12. If you are already known as a patriot, or as a member of this organization you may find it advisable to spread the rumor that you have become disillusioned with the right wing or for you to pretend a gradual loss of interest.

13. Classify your various members addresses, your communications and your other activities as 'top secret', 'secret' or 'restricted'. Use your most secret lines of communication only for the most important messages rather than flooding them with unimportant material.

14. Demand obedience to all security measures from all members. Persistent disregard for security measures should be cause for disciplinary action.

15. Check your lines of communication from time to time by sending phoney messages to make certain they are not intercepted.

16. Change mail drops, meeting places, etc. frequently.

17. Prepare secret rendezvous points, mail drops, now that may be used in time of some future emergency.

18. Each band should assign some member the rank of Security officer and should set up a system of fines or other penalties for failure to comply with security precautions.

19. Observe the 'need to know' rule. Each member should be given only that information which is needed by him in the performance of his duty or which he will need in cooperating with other members of the band. No member should feel 'left out' because he is denied such information. Instead every member should willingly avoid information which he does not need.

20. Be careful that you are not followed in going to and from meeting places or in making contact with other members of the organization.

21. Keep all records and correspondence carefully hidden and in a manner that they can be easily destroyed. Records should be kept in code whenever possible.

22. Important as secrecy may be, it is not the only essential factor in successful underground movement. Morale and efficiency are equally important. Elaborate security measures always reduce efficiency to a greater or lesser degree. Unnecessary security can create an atmosphere of suspicion that is devastating to the esprit de corps of any organization. Find a proper balance between security and efficiency.

JOIN THE
"MINUTEMEN"

An organization of loyal Americans
dedicated to the preservation of both
national and individual freedom.

1. To prepare the means of personal defense and survival in case of enemy attack.

2. To resist and expose the spread of communist influence and propaganda within our own national boundaries.

"Join the 'Minutemen'" ([Norborne, Mo.:] Minutemen, [1960s], flyer).

3. To investigate, by means of our own secret memberships, the possible infiltration of communist sympathizers into American organizations of government, business, labor, religion and education.

4. To detect and expose waste, corruption or disloyalty in any American enterprise or activity that might subvert the defense effort.

5. To resist by all legal means the passage of laws which regulate the private ownership of firearms or which detract from the individual's ability to defend his own family and personal property.

6. To promote knowledge and skill in the use of arms by our own members and by the general public.

7. To form in advance of actual need a secret underground organization equipped to spy upon, harass and destroy troops of any foreign power that might occupy United States territory.

8. To extend this organization, wherever possible into other nations besieged by the threat of communist expansion or subversion.

9. To lend assistance and support of such kinds as our own government cannot officially extend to underground organizations now operating in Cuba and other communist occupied nations.

10. To pursue these programs as private citizens motivated only by patriotism and to remain entirely free of government subsidies or control.

John Birch Society

The John Birch Society, which still exists, was the best known and best financed of the anti-communist groups of the immediate postwar period. They are probably best remembered for their campaigns against General George Marshall, Chief Justice Earl Warren, and President Dwight D. Eisenhower, whom they labeled "dupes" of the Communist Party, "fellow travelers," or, it was implied, active members of the Party.

Beliefs and Principles of the John Birch Society

I

With very few exceptions the members of the John Birch Society are deeply religious people. A member's particular faith is entirely his own affair. Our

"Beliefs and Principles of the John Birch Society." *Congressional Record*, 87th Cong., 2d sess., June 12, 1962.

hope is to make better Catholics, better Protestants, better Jews—or better Moslems—out of those who belong to the society. Our never-ending concern is with morality, integrity, and purpose. Regardless of the differences between us in creed and dogma, we all believe that man is endowed by a Divine Creator with an innate desire and conscious purpose to improve both his world and himself. We believe that the direction which constitutes improvement is clearly visible and identifiable throughout man's known history, and that this God-given upward reach in the heart of man is a composite conscience to which we all must listen.

II

We believe that the Communists seek to drive their slaves and themselves along exactly the opposite and downward direction, to the Satanic debasement of both man and his universe. We believe that communism is as utterly incompatible with all religion as it is contemptuous of all morality and destructive of all freedom. It is intrinsically evil. It must be opposed, therefore, with equal firmness, on religious grounds, moral grounds, and political grounds. We believe that the continued coexistence of communism and a Christian-style civilization on one planet is impossible. The struggle between them must end with one completely triumphant and the other completely destroyed. We intend to do our part, therefore, to halt, weaken, rout, and eventually to bury, the whole international Communist conspiracy.

III

We believe that means are as important as ends in any civilized society. Of all the falsehoods that have been so widely and deliberately circulated about us, none is so viciously untrue as the charge that we are willing to condone foul means for the sake of achieving praiseworthy ends. We think that communism as a way of life, for instance, is completely wrong; but our ultimate quarrel with the Communists is that they insist on imposing that way of life on the rest of us by murder, treason, and cruelty rather than by persuasion. Even if our own use of force ever becomes necessary and morally acceptable because it is in self-defense, we must never lose sight of the legal, traditional, and humanitarian considerations of a compassionate civilization.

The Communists recognize no such compulsions, but this very ingredient of amoral brutishness will help to destroy them in the end.

IV

We believe in patriotism. Most of us will gladly concede that a parliament of nations, designed for the purpose of increasing the freedom and ease with which individuals, ideals, and goods might cross national boundaries, would be desirable. And we hope that in some future decade we may help to bring about such a step of progress in man's pursuit of peace, prosperity, and happiness. But we feel that the present United Nations was designed by its founders for the exactly opposite purpose of increasing the rigidity of Government controls over the lives and affairs of individual men. We believe it has become, as it was intended to become, a major instrumentality for the establishment of a one-world Communist tyranny over the population of the whole earth. One of our most immediate objectives, therefore, is to get the United States out of the United Nations, and the United Nations out of the United States. We seek thus to save our own country from the gradual and piecemeal surrender of its sovereignty to this Communist-controlled supergovernment, and to stop giving our support to the steady enslavement of other people through the machinations of this Communist agency.

V

We believe that a constitutional Republic, such as our founding Fathers gave us, is probably the best of all forms of government. We believe that a democracy, which they tried hard to obviate, and into which the liberals have been trying for 50 years to convert our Republic, is one of the worst of all forms of government. We call attention to the fact that up to 1928 the U.S. Army Training Manual still gave our men in uniform the following quite accurate definition, which would have been thoroughly approved by the Constitutional Convention that established our Republic. 'Democracy: A Government of the masses. Authority derived through mass meeting or any form of direct expression results in mobocracy. Attitude toward property is communistic—negating property rights. Attitude towards law is that the will of the majority shall regulate, whether it be based upon deliberation or governed by passion, prejudice, and impulse, without restraint or regard to consequences. Results in demagogism, license, agitation, discontent, anarchy.' It is because all history proves this to be true that we repeat so emphatically: 'This is a Republic, not a democracy; let's keep it that way.'

VI

We are opposed to collectivism as a political and economic system, even when it does not have the police-state features of communism. We are opposed to it no matter whether the collectivism be called socialism or the welfare state or the New Deal or the Fair Deal or the New Frontier, or advanced under some other semantic disguise. And we are opposed to it no matter what may be the framework or form of government under which collectivism is imposed. We believe that increasing the size of government, increasing the centralization of government, and increasing the functions of government all act as brakes on material progress and as destroyers of personal freedom.

VII

We believe that even where the size and functions of government are properly limited, as much of the power and duties of governmental units as possible should be retained in the hands of as small governmental units as possible, as close to the people served by such units as possible. For the tendencies of any government body to waste, expansion, and despotism all increase with the distance of that body from the people governed; the more closely any governing body can be kept under observation by those who pay its bills and provide its delegated authority, the more honestly responsible it will be. And the diffusion of governmental power and functions is one of the greatest safeguards against tyranny man has yet devised. For this reason it is extremely important in our case to keep our township, city, County and State governments from being bribed and coerced into coming under one direct chain of control from Washington.

VIII

We believe that for any people eternal vigilance is the price of liberty far more as against the insidious encroachment of internal tyranny than against the danger of subjugation from the outside or from the prospect of any sharp and decisive revolution. In a republic we must constantly seek to elect and to keep in power a government we can trust, manned by the people we can trust, maintaining a currency we can trust, and working for purposes we can trust (none of which we have today). We think it is even more important for the government to obey the laws than for the people to do so. But for 30 years we have had a steady stream of governments which increasingly have regarded our laws and even our Constitution as mere pieces of paper, which should not be allowed to stand in the way of what they, in their omniscient benevolence, considered to be 'for the greatest good of the greatest number.' (Or in their power-seeking plans pretended so to believe.) We want a restoration of a "government of laws, and not of men" in this country; and if a few impeachments are necessary to bring that about, then we are all for the impeachments.

IX

We believe that in a general way history repeats itself. For any combination of causes, similar to an earlier combination of causes, will lead as a rule to a combination of results somewhat similar to the one produced before. And history is simply a series of causes which produced results, and so on around cycles as clearly discernible as any of the dozens that take place elsewhere in the physical and biological sciences. But we believe that the most important history consists not of the repetitions but of the changes in these recurring links in the series. For the changes mark the extent to which man has either been able to improve himself and his environment, or has allowed both to deteriorate, since the last time around. We think that this true history is largely determined by ambitious individuals (both good and evil) and by small minorities who really know what they want. And in the John Birch Society our sense of gratitude and responsibility (to God and to the noble men of the past), for what we have inherited makes us determined to exert our influence, labor, and sacrifice for changes which we think will constitute improvement.

X

In summary, we are striving, by all honorable means at our disposal and to the limits of our energies and abilities, to bring about less government, more responsibility, and a better world. Because the Communists seek, always and everywhere, to bring about more government, less individual responsibility, and a completely amoral world, we would have to oppose them at every turn, even on the philosophical level. Because they are seeking through a gigantically organized conspiracy to destroy all opposition, we must fight them even more aggressively on the plane of action. But our struggle with the Communists, while the most urgent and important task before us today, is basically only incidental to our more important long-range and constructive purposes. For that very reason we are likely to be more effective against the Communists than if we were merely an ad hoc group seeking to expose and destroy so huge and powerful a gang of criminals. In organization, dedication, and purpose we offer a new form of opposition to the Communists which they have not faced in any other country. We have tried to raise a standard to which the wise and the honest can repair. We welcome all honorable allies in this present unceasing war. And we hope that once they and we and millions like us have won a decisive victory at last, many of these same allies will join us in our long look toward the future.

Congress of Conservatives

The following is a classic statement of the anti-communist position by a lesser-known group.

Declaration Of Principles
With a firm reliance on the protection of Divine Providence, the
Congress of Conservatives
Chicago, May 1, 1965,

AFFIRMS its faith in the principles of the Declaration of Independence and the Constitution of the United States of America, as conceived and intended

From "Declaration of Principles" (Kirkwood, Mo.: American Conservative Party, 1965, pamphlet).

by the Founding Fathers. God created people; people created the States, the States created the Federal Government; and God, not government, is the rightful master of the people. We rededicate ourselves to the divinely inspired Ten Commandments and the Sermon on the Mount.

RECOGNIZES that an attempted world revolution—external and internal, violent and nonviolent—threatens to destroy the Union, subvert justice, incite domestic disorder, liquidate the common defense, abuse the general welfare, and steal the blessings of liberty from ourselves and our posterity.

DISCERNS the danger of our becoming a one-party nation, like all one-party Socialist nations under Communism, where no man's life, liberty, or property is safe from agents of the dictatorship.

RECALLS with rising hope that in November 1964, twenty-seven million Americans would not be seduced or intimidated by power, but voted the conscience of a Conservative—thus, in effect, constituting themselves a reserve army of freedom and, in review of subsequent capitulation, a virtual Committee of twenty-seven million for the formation of a new national party—the largest unled articulate minority in America.

RECORDS its conviction that most of the forty-three million who voted another way were equally dedicated to the principles of Americanism, but simply did not have the facts—or else did not have their votes counted right.

DECLARES its intention to participate in the formation of a national anti-Communist party. In this critical year we are confident that in every part of these United States, Americans by the millions are ready. We urge every patriot to prepare to make his own contribution to this party of faith, freedom, independence, and prosperity—the party of the future which will depose a corrupt Establishment and resurrect the hopes of anti-Communists throughout the world.

CONSTITUTES an Advance Committee to assist in every possible way all who support the principles of this declaration and the following Action Program. The Advance Committee will encourage the formation of appropriate new State parties, support existing independent parties, seek the achievement of a national committee, and encourage the appearance of potential candidates for the new national party's nomination. The final terms of the organization will, of course, be set by a new national convention. The Advance Committee will serve as a catalytic agent, and will not be an exclusive, divisive, or dictatorial body. It will have no chairman, but will have a secretary and treasurer. The treasurer shall be bonded, and decisions as to disbursements, placing of funds in escrow for the new national committee, or other disposition, shall be made by the full Advance Committee.

ATTACHES herewith a program of action recommended to the American people, to the new national convention, and to constituent State Parties.

ACTION PROGRAM FOR PRESERVATION OF THE CONSTITUTIONAL REPUBLIC OF THE UNITED STATES OF AMERICA

To return to sane national policy, the following action should be taken "with all deliberate speed":

1. Reappraise the political and military doctrines which have, during the past 20 years, reduced the United States from a position of incomparable power to a condition of national peril. This means stopping unilateral disarmament and reconsidering the whole arms-control-and-disarmament policies, program, and agency.
2. Withdraw from any and all projects looking to the establishment of World Government, as being at best futile, and at worst catastrophic. The United Nations has failed to keep the peace and is now being used as a smokescreen for Communist aggression. The UN should be developed away from the concept of the universal police agency under the Secretariat to a legitimate forum of free nations with equitably distributed financial support.
3. Break diplomatic, cultural, and trade relations with all governments which are openly creatures of the Communist Party. This means, in the first instance, Soviet Russia and her East European satellites. It should go without saying that it also means continued non-recognition of Red China.
4. Liberate Cuba from its Communist conquerors. In the achievement of this objective, which traditional American hemispheric policy, as contained in the Monroe Doctrine, requires, we should capture Chinese and Russian Communists now based on Cuba, and hold them as hostages pending release of Americans now being held by Russia and Red China. The importance of liberating Cuba is emphasized by its use as a base for military and paramilitary operations against the United States and the Western Hemisphere.

5. Re-establish free government on the main land of China as a permanent solution to Communist aggression in Southeast Asia.

6. Extend the frontiers of real freedom by judicious use of the financial, military, and moral power of the United States. Openly declare as an objective the liberation of the enslaved nations, both the so-called satellites, like Poland and Hungary, and those swallowed up and lost, like the Baltic Nations.

7. Manage foreign aid so as to assist only those nations which support the struggle against Communism, and so as to check the gold outflow which now threatens this nation with financial disaster.

8. Stop Federal support of Communist subversion of America through the agitation of racial turmoil in the streets.

9. End the news-management syndicate of Big Government, Big Business, Big Labor, and the monopolistic media of communications.

10. Revitalize the national economy through the recognition of the power of personal and private enterprise. This is the most effective approach to the problem of poverty. Socialism, in contrast, leads to Communism, with the far deeper poverty of abject slavery. Reduce the elephantine Federal Bureaucracy. Eliminate un-Constitutional and uneconomic business and industrial operations of the Federal Government, which elimination will make practical the repeal of the Marxist-oriented, graduated Federal Income Tax. Uphold the right to work. End Federal land grants. End programs of intervention in agriculture which make the American farmer at once a ward and a slave. Respect the integrity of the medical, legal, and other professions.

11. So long as we have significant unemployment, severely restrict permanent immigration. Establish immigration policies which protect the American freedom which sincere immigrants come here to find.

12. Renovate the program of internal security. To this end, support not only the anti-subversive work of the Federal Bureau of Investigation but also that of the House Committee on Un-American Activities and the Senate Internal Security Sub-Committee.

13. Restore the dignity of the Supreme Court. Restore the Constitutional balance of the coordinate branches of the Federal Government.

14. Uphold local law-enforcement officers in the performance of their duties.

15. Return control of education to the states and to the people.

16. In the American tradition of separation of church and state, resist the political activities of churches, and the quasi-religious activities of the

Federal Government. The best Peace Corps America ever had was conducted by private missionaries.

NOTE

1. John A. Stormer, *None Dare Call It Treason* (Florissant, Mo.: Liberty Bell Press, 1964). See also Julian Foster, *None Dare Call It Reason: A Critique of John Stormer's "None Dare Call It Treason"* (Placentia, Calif.: n.p., 1964).

5

RACE

Racial questions have been part of American history from the time Columbus commented on the racial characteristics of the first Caribbean islanders he met.[1] The struggle over slavery deeply divided the country from the time the first African slaves were brought to the colonies in 1619. Thomas Jefferson wanted the Declaration of Independence to include a statement against slavery, but lost to the Southern states. The Constitution recognized the existence of slavery and counted slaves (as three-fifths of a person) as part of the population in determining the number of members of the House of Representatives a state would have, but set an end to the slave trade in 1808, twenty years after the adoption of the Constitution. These compromises set the stage for the long conflict between those supporting slavery and those who wanted it abolished.

But it is clear that many who were opposed to slavery believed there were inherent differences among human beings based on race, and at least some of those opposed to slavery believed that those differences precluded any future integration of African Americans into the dominant culture. Moreover, racial concerns were never limited to African Americans. Any group that was identifiably different could, and usually was, labeled inferior by some segment of the population.

RACE ON THE RIGHT

Racism tends to be identified with the right, and that identification is generally correct. As will be noted, there are exceptions, but the right is much more likely to express a clearly racist point of view. The selections grouped here reflect three major groups with a racist position as a central point in their political program—National Socialists, the Ku Klux Klan, and the Aryan Nations—and some minor groups with some similar positions. It is important to note, though, that racism is not the only plank in their political platforms. It generally plays the role of explaining why the world is in the mess it is—the _____ (fill in the blank with the appropriate group or groups) control the economic or political system, are the cause of all the crime, and so forth. If only we (the whites) could reestablish our natural superiority, the world could be made better again, but "they" are stopping us. How to accomplish that and what the better world would look like are the concerns of these selections.

NATIONAL SOCIALISM

George Lincoln Rockwell

Although there were German and Italian National Socialist groups in the United States prior to World War II, a truly American National Socialism awaited the postwar period and George Lincoln Rockwell (1918–1967), who led the American Nazi Party until his assassination. The selections here include two from Rockwell, but National Socialism, with its glorification of Hitler, continued after Rockwell's death and now exists in varied forms and organizations. There is even a homosexual Nazi organization, which would have horrified both Hitler and Rockwell.

NATIONAL SOCIALISM

Hitler inspired, organized, and pulled off a relatively peaceful revolution, a revolution which took far fewer lives than the American Revolution, and

From George Lincoln Rockwell, *White Power*, 2d ed. Dallas: Ragnarok Press, 1967). Reprinted in part as *The White Primer: A Dynamic Racial Analysis of Present Day America From the Viewpoint of the White Majority* (n.p.: C. W. Bristol, [1977 or 1978]).

an insignificant number of lives compared to any ever pulled off by the Jewish Bolsheviks.

Not only that, but Hitler's revolution, as he promised in *Mein Kampf,* was 100% "legal"—legitimate—the formally expressed will of the majority of the German people, sanctioned by both the top executive officer of Germany, von Hindenburg, and by the German "congress", the Reichstag. Hitler had many opportunities to seize power by force and could have done it easily in 1931. But Hitler believed that a revolution against the will of the people, a revolution which gains power only by force, cannot long endure. Hitler, as I do, believed that a leader is an enemy of civilization unless he has the will of his people behind him.

How, then, can I be calling for "revolution"? How can I write of "killing and being killed"?

Is not the very essence of a revolution violence?

Not necessarily.

There may be an element of violence, yes. When you are attacked by a killer and faced with the choice of death or dealing death yourself, then violence is the only possibility. And Western Civilization is indeed under attack by an enemy who regularly, as a matter of policy, kills and massacres more ruthlessly than any other group in history.

So we must be violent enough to put a stop to the Communist enemy's killing and ruthless enough to smash his power.

But the essence of a real revolution is never JUST the bloodshed and upheaval. In a genuine and lasting revolution, violence and killing are only one expedient means to the end of a radical change in over-all spiritual outlook—the outward manifestation of a supreme human will to establish a new arrangement of physical affairs to conform with an inner ideal.

The authority exercised by most of those in power today is unadulterated tyranny, though it is hypocritically disguised as "democracy". It is not the benevolent, intelligent authority to maintain order and justice established by the Founding Fathers for the benefit of White men.

Our revolution must be based firmly on the ideal of destroying the illegal power of tyrants, and restoring a just social order which is based on a firm authority which comes straight from our people, and is freely granted to a leader.

That, believe it or not, is precisely what Adolph Hitler did for Germany, and what we must do for America.

Our revolution in short, must have as its driving force and goal, not merely the hatred and destruction of the enemy, but it must be imbued with an absolute determination to establish a just social order in which each man can achieve his maximum potential as a successful, happy, and productive part of our great White Race.

What is such a just order of society?

There is no need for this understanding of the scientific principles of successful group living among those in healthy societies where natural instincts are unimpaired. Animals, for instance, have orderly, successful "societies" because *Nature gives every social creature all the instincts he needs for successful group living.*

Wolves, ants, bees—and apes—for instance, have highly organized and thoroughly healthy, *orderly* societies.

Early men had healthy societies. Then man's growing control over Nature allowed him to escape his natural environment, surround himself with artificialities and luxury until he became decadent and full of arrogant conceit—a conceit which is today called "liberalism".

Only by going back to the simpler and more primitive life-situation of the unthinking and uncivilized animal world, and observing the workings of the instincts given them by the Creator, can we catch a glimpse of the wonders of what has also been given us—*and which we have thrown away.*

Nature has created "breeds" with which she can experiment and seek always better breeds, just as does a good farmer. The Creator, being an infinitely wiser farmer than any human, absolutely insists on the purity, the sanctity—the BIOLOGICAL INTEGRITY of each group.

But Nature, like a farmer breeding cows, can improve the breed only by fostering the breeding of the better type, and *eliminating* the poorer type. Nature accomplishes this task with the most powerful instincts we are given: LOVE of our own, and HATRED of those who intrude—or "outsiders".

These two instincts are *equally* important: Love is not "good" while hate is "evil"—which is the canard so dearly loved by the Jews, liberals, hippies, queers, and half-wits.

Love is indeed incredibly powerful, and good, when it is NATURAL.

LOVE, the natural, healthy kind, is indeed what makes the world go round, and is the most beautiful, holy miracle we ever see here on this earth.

BUT WITHOUT A DEADLY HATE OF THAT WHICH THREATENS WHAT WE LOVE, LOVE IS AN EMPTY WORD, A CATCHWORD FOR HIPPIES, QUEERS, AND COWARDS. . . .

BIOLOGICAL INTEGRITY is the essence, the be-all and end-all of

National Socialism when applied to Aryan society—and, indeed, of every healthy human society which has ever existed.

But there is not space in this work for the book that could be written on this subject alone. I can only sum up by saying that the *first* law of all group living by social creatures is BIOLOGICAL INTEGRITY; absolute, total and uncompromising loyalty to one's own racial group based on a consuming love, *and* absolute, uncompromising hatred of any outsiders who intrude and threaten to mix their genes with those of the females of one's own group.

The everyday way this law is manifested is love of one's own kind, and hatred of aggressive intruders (which is why most healthy Whites have such instinctive abhorrence of "niggers", Jews, and other "aliens").

* * * * *

The second most important law is the law of TERRITORY.

For example, ten or twenty males of the tiny tropical fish called "swordtails" will each stake out a section of a tank as soon as they are placed in it, and they will attack any intrusion by another male. If females are introduced into the tank, the males will fight over them, as expected. But the surprise to science was that sex is not the strongest motive in the life of these little fish.

If you start cooling the water in their tank, you can reach a point where the water is so cold the males no longer give much of a damn when you introduce the females. When the water gets so cold as almost to kill the little fish, they pay no attention at all to the females. *But even when they are on the point of almost freezing to death, they will still come out ferociously to defend their TERRITORY—their private property!*

National Socialism is based, among other things, on this concept of private property. The law of TERRITORY comes out as "Nationalism" and private property in human society.

* * * * *

Throughout the animal kingdom, the leader is never chosen by vote, but always by the natural selection established by Nature as the only sure method of insuring that the group is led by the best—*combat*. This I have called the law of LEADERSHIP.

* * * * *

Once each member of an animal society learns his or her place in the natural biological order of toughness, wisdom, and cleverness, each member settles down into his own niche and the group is relatively peaceful and orderly. Only when young males begin to mature and have to fight their way up or down the ladder is there serious battles. And then, as soon as each male learns who he can whip, and who can whip him, he settles down and lives peacefully and contentedly in that place he has found for himself.

Thus is established two more of the fundamental principles of laws of all group living—LEADERSHIP by the best, and a natural hierarchy or scale of leadership of all the other members of the group—STATUS.

Finally, a study of the animal world establishes that females stay out of the affairs of males, and specialize in producing and rearing the young by organizing healthy *families.*

To summarize: There are five basic laws of all group living, which I have called "THE LAWS OF THE TRIBE";

(1) the law of BIOLOGICAL INTEGRITY (love inside, hate outside);
(2) the law of TERRITORY (private property);
(3) the law of LEADERSHIP (by the best);
(4) the law of STATUS (or the natural place of every individual in a group); and
(5) MOTHERHOOD for females.

With these natural principles in operation, as they are throughout the whole world of social animals, there is a relative peace and order in the group.

It is only when the group somehow is forced into unnatural conditions that the God-given instincts to obey these iron laws of Nature fail.

NATIONAL SOCIALIST WORLD VIEW

I *WE BELIEVE that an honest man can never be happy in a naked scramble for material gain and comfort,* without any goal which he believes is greater than himself, and for which he is willing to sacrifice his own egotism. This goal was formerly provided by fundamentalist religions, but science and subversion have so weakened all traditional religions, and given

From George Lincoln Rockwell, "Program of the American Nazi Party" (Chicago: American Nazi Party, n.d., flyer).

man such an unwarranted, short-sighted conceit of his "power over Nature," that he has, in effect, become his own God. He is spiritually lost even if he will not yet admit it. We believe that the only realistic goal which can still lift man out of his present unhappy selfishness and into the radiance of self-sacrificing idealism, is the upward struggle of his race, the fight for the common good of his people.

II *WE BELIEVE that society can function successfully and therefore happily, only as an ORGANISM:* that all parts benefit when each part performs the function for which it is best suited to produce a unified, single-purposed WHOLE, which is then capable of out-performing any single part, the whole thus vastly increasing the powers of all cooperating parts, and the parts, therefore subordinating a part of their freedom to the whole; that the whole perishes and all parts therefore suffer whenever one part fails to perform its own function, usurps the function or interferes with the function of another part, or, like a cancer, devours all the nourishment and grows wildly and selfishly all out of proportion to its task—which latter is exactly the effect on society of the parasitic Jews and their Marxism.

III *WE BELIEVE that man makes a genuine progress only when he approaches Nature humbly, and accepts and applies her eternal laws,* instead of arrogantly assuming to ignore and conquer Nature, as do the Marxists, with their environmentalism, special laws of biological equality for humans only, and insane denial of the primitive and fundamental institution of private property.

IV *WE BELIEVE that struggle is the vital element of all evolutionary progress and the very essence of life itself;* that it is the only method we have won and can maintain dominion over the other animals of the earth; that we must therefore welcome struggle as a means of testing and improving us, and that we must despise weaklings who run away from struggle. We believe that life itself is awarded by Nature only to those who fight for and win it, not to those who wish or beg for it as a "right".

V *WE BELIEVE that no man is entitled to the services and products of the labor of his fellow men, unless he contributes at least an EQUAL amount of goods or services of his own production or invention.* We believe that the contribution by a member of society of NOTHING ELSE but the tokens called "money" is a fraud upon his fellows, and does not extuse [*sic*] a man capable of honest work of his responsibility to PRODUCE his share.

VI *WE BELIEVE that it is to the advantage of society to see that every honest man has freedom and opportunity to achieve his maximum potentials* by preserving his health, protecting him from unforeseeable and ruinous catastrophes, educating him to capacity in the areas of his abilities, and guarding him against economic and political exploitation.

VII *WE BELIEVE that Adolf Hitler was the gift of an inscrutable Providence to a world on the brink of Jewish-Bolshevik catastrophe,* and that only the blazing spirit of this heroic man can give us the strength and inspiration to rise, like the early Christians, from the depths of persecution and hatred, to bring the world a new birth of radiant idealism, realistic peace, international order, and social justice for all men.

American Nazi Party

American
NAZI
Party
official
stormtrooper's
MANUAL

PREFACE

The AMERICAN NAZI PARTY is not any different, fundamentally, from the original concepts of the Republican and Democratic Parties. All parties seek political power in order to carry out their ideas of how best to secure the most wholesome social, economic and political organization of their people. Actually, this is all the AMERICAN NAZI PARTY seeks to do, by lawful means.

But because the AMERICAN NAZI PARTY recognizes the vicious subversive and parasitic nature of many Jews and does not fear to tell the truth about this dangerous subject, the Party is brutally and unfairly attacked by every organ of public opinion and information, and ruthlessly persecuted by almost every social and governmental organization in America. Many of these attacks are not the result of sincere hostility to the AMERICAN NAZI PARTY. Most non-Jewish Americans hate Communism, race-mixing and

From "American Nazi Party Official Stormtrooper's Manual" (Arlington, Va.: American Nazi Party, 1972, pamphlet).

moral subversion as much as we do. But, because of what the Bible calls "fear of the Jews", non-Jewish officials in all sorts of organizations seek to save themselves from the wrath of the Jews by persecuting us. The more they unfairly send us to jail, lie about us and even attack us physically, the more they are praised in our Jew-ized newspapers, magazines and TV.

For this reason, the AMERICAN NAZI PARTY is forced to organize along military lines to DEFEND itself from this constant illegal and immoral harassment. When we are trying to express our honest opinions in public, as is our most fundamental right as Americans, we are almost always attacked by screaming mobs of hysterical Jews. They seek to prevent our public exposures of Jewish treason to the United States. Their pose as lovers of "tolerance" and "free-speech" disappears in an instant whenever anybody asks why so MANY of our convicted spies, traitors and Soviet sympathizers have been racial Jews (More than 85%).

When we are thus attacked with fists, clubs and tire irons, etc, it is impossible to hold a committee meeting to decide how to fight back. Our response to Jewish violence must be immediate and effective. For this reason, and others, we maintain an iron chain-of-command, with stern discipline and absolute responsibility up and down the line.

It is important for the new Trooper to notice that we are NOT Germans; we do not use German uniforms or insignia, and there is no "Goose-stepping" or use of German titles, etc. Such things are strictly prohibited in the AMERICAN NAZI PARTY. This is not because we do not greatly admire the Germans and the German Nazis,—but because we are AMERICANS. Most of us have fought in the Armed Forces for America. Our admiration for Adolf Hitler and the principles of his magnificent National Socialism do not make us Germans any more than a belief in Jesus Christ and Christianity make one "Hebrew".

The AMERICAN NAZI PARTY is actually the SHOCK TROOP of Americanism. Although the ignorant and blind "patriots" don't realize it yet, we are the vanguard of the "right wing revival" all over the world. In fact, we are the CAUSE of that revival. The opposite of Communism is NOT "Conservatism". Conservatism is almost pure Jewry with the defeatist slogan of worn-out old women, "Back to the old days!" The opposite of Communism is NAZI-ism,—as the Communists themselves recognize by their constant hysterical screaming about "Fascism"!

In spite of unbelievable persecutions from both the Jews and our own people, (the terrified and small-minded "conservatives" who imagine we are working for the Jews or Communists)—the AMERICAN NAZI PARTY is relentlessly driving to POWER. Nothing can now stop us, and the Jews are already talking about "smelling the gas".

Our motto is "the Jews Are Thru in '72!"—And with the help of our growing Storm Troop of dedicated American White Men, we will sweep into National Power in the elections of 1972!

Then the traitors and human scum will be swept into the garbage can of history with an iron broom, and our America will once again be a clean, wholesome, and HOLY place for AMERICANS. Our cities will be WHITE, our youth will be strong, healthy and full of FIGHT, and no red rat anywhere on the globe will dare lay a hand on our sacred American Stars and Stripes, or the holy Swastika banner of the WHITE RACE!

What's WHITE POWER All About?

The popular slogan, "White Power!" was not originated by any single man or organization. It came directly from the masses of Americans who assembled by the tens of thousands in the streets of Chicago during the hot summer of 1966, when Martin Luther King, Jr. and his filthy black hordes tramped into several White neighborhoods. It was the slogan hurled (together with bricks and bottles!) at the invaders by the White youth and workers. When Commander Lincoln Rockwell, leader of the American Nazi Party, saw the massive, popular outpouring of resistance to forced integration, he produced and distributed the first White Power posters to the teeming crowds in the streets. The people enthusiastically took up these radical posters and have since employed this powerful slogan wherever the sanctity and existence of their race is at stake, not only in Chicago, but all across America. Their battle cry which instinctively arose from the enraged masses has therefore returned to them as the most meaningful and effective slogan to unify and inspire them to defeat the enemies of their race and nation.

We use the term "White Power" because it best sums up just what we believe in and what we want. We believe that American and all civilized societies are the exclusive products of the White man's mind and muscle. We believe that the White race is the Master Race of the earth. This means that we are the Master Builders, the Master Minds and the Master Warriors

From "What's White Power All About?" (Chicago: American Nazi Party, ca. 1981, flyer).

of civilization. Without the White race, the world would still be a Stone Age swamp. The world is in trouble now only because the White man is divided, confused and misled. Once he is united, inspired by a great ideal and led by real men, his world will again become livable, safe and happy.

When we talk about White Power, we do not mean any particular class of White people. Nor any single religion. We are not appealing to one age group over another, nor favoring one special nationality. When we say WHITE Power, we mean ALL White people. Economic status means nothing to us. It is our whole RACE we must preserve, not just one class. Let a man believe in God any way he chooses. In our ranks, the Protestant and the Catholic, the believer and the skeptic march side by side in the common good of all for White America. in our Movement children as young as seven years old put up White Power stickers, while in high school youths battle niggers in the streets and college students write articles exposing the truth in our publications. Workers in their 20s, 30s, and 40s are members and Stormtroopers. Americans in their declining years support us with their few dollars. While we encourage pride in one's national heritage, the far more important issue is the unity and salvation of our whole White Race, of which each European nationality is only a part. Even national considerations must be subordinated to RACIAL imperatives. It makes no difference to us whether a White man's forefathers came from London, Paris, Berlin, Rome, Warsaw, Moscow or Dublin. The same blood flows through his veins, and that's all that matters.

Why then do we call ourselves "National Socialists?" We are national because we want a strong national government, not afraid to stand up to all the enemies of America. But a government based on the principles of liberty spelled out in the Constitution and the Bill of Rights. In working for national unity, we realized that such unity is impossible without first uniting the people themselves, and the only American people worthy of national unification are our WHITE people. There can be no national unity without social unity. And that is where our racial socialism comes in. We are social racists who, as we said earlier, want to unite our WHOLE White race, regardless of class, age, sex, nationality or religion. Nationalism stands for government, and socialism means people. Divided, these concepts are powerless. Together, they alone can restore our civilization to unity, happiness and greatness.

We believe in Adolf Hitler because he laid down the ideas of National Socialism, as is apparent in any of Hitler's writings or speeches. He united first Germany and then Europe in a common front against Asiatic Communism, a threat he knew was a danger to the whole civilized world.

Hitler used the Swastika and so do we. He resurrected it from the ancient past, not as a German symbol, but as an emblem standing for our race everywhere. We employ the Swastika for that reason too, but also to terrify our vicious enemies and arouse the attention of the White masses we are reaching with our program. Once we have their attention, the eloquence of our conviction will prove to them that we can lead them to victory for their race and nation.

White Power means just what it says. We want total power for our fellow White people. We reject the Communists, who say "Power comes out of the barrel of the gun." And we equally reject the Capitalists, who say "Money is power." True, long-lasting and legitimate power comes only from the will of the people themselves. We mean to get the whole-hearted, voluntary support of people by honestly winning them to our cause. Once we have power delegated by the masses of America, we will use it to scrub and wash clean our country of every trace of the anti-White forces unleashed throughout civilization.

These are the things White Power means to us. To the American worker, it means a permanent end to unemployment because, with the non-Whites gone, the labor market will no longer be over-crowded with unproductive niggers, spics and other racial low-life. It means an end to inflation eating up a man's paycheck faster than he can raise it because OUR economy will not be run by a criminal pack of international Jewish bankers, bent on using the White worker's tax money in selfish and even destructive schemes. It means that his tax money will no longer be used to integrate the schools of his children, and consequently a restoration of the formerly high standards of education our schools enjoyed before the inclusion of uneducatable non-Whites. It means a complete and total end of the "bad neighborhoods," because the sub-humans responsible for those dangerous slums will be gone forever. It means the end of urban guerilla warfare falsely portrayed by the news media as "a high crime rate." Our mothers, wives, lovers and sisters will no longer walk the streets of any city in America in fear of being raped, mugged or murdered. And finally, White Power means that as one, united, racial-national family, Americans will feel that their country has direction and purpose, not that it is drifting in the corruption and incompetence of the present System.

Someday our people must realize that they have but two choices: either an all-White and happy America, or a race-mixed and totally dead America.

As can be seen from the above selections, although Rockwell died, National Socialism in America continued. The two selections below are from more recent exponents of National Socialism and show both continuity with the Rockwell tradition (in the first selection) and some interesting changes (in the second).

Social Nationalist Aryan People's Party

Adolf Hitler Was Elijah
Keith D. Gilbert

TO: THE ARYAN NATION
Beloved kinsman:

In the Holy Bible in modern English as translated by Ferrar Fenton, in the Book of Malaki we read, "Then you will turn and distinguish between the righteous and the wicked, between who serves GOD, and who serves Him not. For be assured the day comes that will burn like an oven, when all the cruel, and all who practice vice, will be stubble, and will be burnt in that coming day," says the LORD OF HOSTS, "nor root not branch shall be left. But the Sun of Righteousness will shine forth to you with restoration on his wings, and you shall be brought out, and sport like a bullock from the stall, and tread down the wicked, for they will be dust under your feet, on the day when I perform it," says the LORD OF HOSTS.

"Remember the Laws of My servant Moses, which I communicated to him in Horeb, and the Institutions and Decrees for all Israel. I will assuredly send to you Elijah the Prophet before that Great and Terrible Day of the Lord arrives, and he will turn the hearts of the fathers toward their children, and

From Keith D. Gilbert, "Adolph Hitler Was Elijah" (Post Falls, Idaho: Social Nationalist Aryan People's Party, [early 1980s], pamphlet).

the children towards their fathers; lest I should come and strike the earth with a ban."

The coming of Elijah must be confronted before we can move on to the judgement of the Aryan Nation of Israel. We are told that Yhwh will send Elijah BEFORE the great and terrible day of destruction. That terrible day is now upon us, therefore, Elijah has already been made manifest. Two thousand years ago, the prophet, John the Baptist, was a manifestation of the spirit and power of Elijah. He spoke the powerful message of repentance and the condemnation of the King and his life. Then John identified the jews as vipers in Matthew 3:7. There was a great boldness and power manifested and many thought that John the Baptist was really the Prophet Elijah. He was manifesting the power and MESSAGE in the spirit of Elijah as a forerunner of the coming Yoshua and the events that were to take place.

For years I have known that the message of Identity brought the power of the Holy Spirit and the coming of Elijah as stated in the scriptures. A good thing to remember is that we must have two witnesses before judgement and punishment can be executed. Over fifty years ago this message went out to the world in the words of Adolf Hitler and the message lives in his second witness Rudolf Hess who at this writing is alive and true to the faith in spite of the lies and persecution of the murderous jews who pressed for his imprisonment and the ritual murder of eleven of the Saints who stood with this great peacemaker.

These men told our Racial Nation that the jews were turning the people away from God and His ways. They warned about the jews and the International Bankers and spoke against mongrelization and racial suicide. However, those who ruled over us in governments and "churches" didn't heed the warning; in fact, they supported integration and intermarriage of the races and accepted the massive use of usury banking and truly did Mystery Babylon take control.

The Beast of Desolation invested with the power of the Red Dragon of old, of Satan and his children, the mongrelizing jews of dark destruction, was wounded almost unto death by this great prophet of our Aryan people, Adolf Hitler, for he delivered the sword thrust and led the way for our deliverance and he said; "It is necessary that I should die for my people; but my spirit will rise from the grave and the world will know that I was right." Adolf

Hitler—1889-1945, born on April 20th, his great truths and prophesies live on in spite of the persecution of the jews who murdered our God and sought to kill all the Prophets and Saints.

But do not allow this to escape you Kinsmen, that with the Lord a single day is as a thousand years, and a thousand years as a single day. The Lord does not delay His promise, as some regard delaying; but extends His patience towards you, desiring that none should be lost, but that all should come to a change of mind. But the day of the Lord will approach like a thief, when the skies will pass away with a crash, and their constituents will be dissolved by heat; while the earth and what is upon it will be reorganized. All having to be thus dissolved, what ought you to be like in regard to pure conduct and piety, expecting and hastening on the appearance of the Day of God!— during which the burning skies will be dissolved, and their constituents melted by heat: yet according to his promise, we look for new skies and a new earth, in which righteousness will dwell. II Peter 3:8-13.

It is not without good cause that Adolf Hitler quoted the Holy Bible over five hundred times in his great work, *MEIN KAMPF*.

REMEMBER, our sacred writings describe the Last Covenant and its requirements. You are Saints, In your own eyes, and to the exclusion of all others, representatives of the only Covenant agreeable to our God, the eternal and final Covenant. We shall be, and with the communities which we establish, the "little remnant" foretold by the Prophets; the true Israel. We are all volunteers joined with our Assembly bringing all our wisdom, understanding, and powers, the wholeness of our possessions and wealth into a community of God in the valley of our decision.

We hold to TRUTH and it is our VICTORY! You will find no "fire escape theology" here among us nor will the libelous doctrine of a "rapture" be heard among our Assembly for we are "born from above" and as the children of ALMIGHTY GOD, YHWH, our father of old we will do only his bidding.

THE RESTORED CHURCH OF JESUS CHRIST is a SOCIETY OF SAINTS. We hold to and practice the ancient FAITH of our Aryan ancestors. We hold to no "religion" with its incense candles, rituals and vain repetitious chants. We have cast off the tricks of "priestcraft" and "churchanity" of the catholic and protestant "religions" that we might "be as little children" and true to the FAITH of our racial NATION!

ARYAN KINSMEN, this is my testimony unto you: that ADOLF HITLER was ELIJAH and that he did all that he came here to do. When he died on April 30, 1945, he set the date for THE GREAT DAY OF THE LORD!

This truth I leave with you. On May 1, 1985 will come THE GREAT DAY OF DESTRUCTION! This will be forty years after the great man's death and a high holiday in the Jew "Soviet" empire. Be true to the FAITH of our ARYAN racial NATION and may God keep you safe unto himself in his great storehouse as the tares now bundled together in the cities of Mystery Babylon burn.

American Program

An odd offshoot of National Socialism is found in the following selection, which is racist (citizenship will be racially based) and supports free enterprise but says that education, medical care, recreation, and legal costs will all be governmentally provided. Family management will become a profession and Universities of Family Management will be established.

AMERICAN PROGRAM

The Jewish Problem

We shall investigate, try and execute all Jews proved to have taken part in Marxist or Zionist plots of treason against their Nations or humanity.

We shall immediately remove all disloyal Jews from positions where they can control non-Jewish thoughts or actions, particularly from the press, government, education, entertainment, and courts.

We shall expose the criminal nature of the hate-book of the Jews, the Babylonian Talmud, by wide publication of its actual vicious words of hate and extermination of all non-Jews.

We shall cancel all debts owed to Jews by non-Jews, where there is evidence of unfair or immoral business methods or conspiracy.

From "American Program" (n.p.: n.p., n.d., flyer).

We shall establish an International Jewish Control Authority to carry out the above measures on a world-wide basis, to protect the rare honest Jews from the wrath of the people newly awakened to the truth about the Jews, and to make a long-term, scientific study to determine if the Jewish virus is a matter of environment and can be eliminated by education and training or if some other method must be developed to render Jews harmless to society.

We shall establish an International Treason Tribunal to investigate, try, and publicly hang, in front of the capitol, all non-Jews who are convicted of having acted consciously as fronts for Jewish treason or subversion, or who have violated their oaths of office, or participated in any form of treason against their Nation or humanity.

The Negro

We shall appropriate ten billion dollars a year for five years, from the money now being wasted fighting over integration, poured into foreign aid, and lost on Negro crime, and use the money to build a modern, industrial nation in Africa, complete with shopping centers, airlines, super-highways, cities, and handsome suburbs, and everything else to make it the finest in the world; and then grant $10,000 to every Negro family of five or more migrating to the new land to help them build a home and establish a business. We believe if this is done with ABSOLUTE SINCERITY, we can make up to our sorely oppressed "second-class citizens" some of the injury and degradation we have heaped upon them, and help them to regain their self-respect and dignity as first-class citizens who will lead their own Continent out of its Darkness with their American know-how and our sincere and generous help. It is inconceivable that any significant number of Negroes will resist such an inspiring and historical opportunity. But no Negroes will be FORCED to return to Africa.

However, Negroes remaining in America will be rigidly segregated noncitizens.

White Survival

We shall establish a National Eugenics Commission, to discourage the unlimited breeding of the least desirable elements, to sterilize those who are hopelessly insane or otherwise biologically dangerous to innocent unborn children, and to encourage, with early marriage subsidies and bonuses for childbirth, the reproduction of our best human stock.

Citizenship

We shall make citizenship a proud privilege to be earned, not a right carelessly awarded simply by birth in a certain geographical area. To be a citizen, an individual must have passed his eighteenth birthday, passed certain minimum tests of knowledge and ability to understand his government, be in the process of education, or be engaged in a productive enterprise, and be prepared to give his life in the defense of his Country and race. The conferring of citizenship shall be a major ceremony, to impress on all the precious privilege of membership in the greatest race and the greatest Nation ever to appear on the planet.

World Order

We shall assist all peoples to throw off the yokes of colonial oppression, and establish their own free National Socialist governments.

We shall abolish the Marxist United Nations, and establish, in its stead, an organic Union of Free Enterprise National Socialist States, with a world police force to maintain order, and to bring the blessings of REAL peace, international responsibility and political sanity to the peoples of the earth.

Social Sanity

We shall enact laws to protect every honest, working citizen from unforeseeable and ruinous catastrophes of all kinds; to assure him of education and training to the top level of his capacity (but ONLY to that level); to assure him of vital medical and hospital facilities by providing medical coupons usable with any physician and redeemed by the Government; to protect him from "easy-payments" debt by insuring that every working man can earn enough to live decently without mortgaging his future to do it; to make easily available to all citizens major recreation facilities such as vacation cruises, which give life zest and color, but which are presently dependent on wealth; to make all defense lawyers in criminal cases paid officers of the court, like the prosecutor, and not paid by the accused, to remove the weight of money from the processes of justice involving the life or liberty of a citizen; and to protect the people from political and economic exploitation by any individual or group.

Economics

We shall abolish the Federal Reserve Central Bank set up in violation of the Constitution, cancel all illegal debt resulting from the semi-private issuance of INTEREST-BEARING money instead of genuine National money, and issue all currency solely by the National Government, with no interest.

We shall establish a National Economic Integrity Commission to eliminate speculation, the immoral gambling by idle men in the labor of others, as a sole means of earning money. The commission will insure that no able man is permitted to enjoy a lion's share of the luxury products and services created by the labor of others without contributing his own share of goods and services by his own management, invention or labor. The mere delivery of some of the tokens called "money", with absolutely no productive effort by a man enjoying the goods and services of society, is a fraud on society, disintegrates the character of such an idle individual, and destroys the honesty and strength of the society which permits it.

No one man or group will be permitted to profit from the ownership of any public necessity which constitutes a monopoly. A monopoly shall be considered to exist whenever it would be impossible or impractical to have competition, and shall be owned only by the whole people.

We shall abolish the Marxist progressive income tax, and establish, in so far as possible, direct taxes on the users of schools, roads, etc., with a manufacturer's tax to finance the facilities needed by all the people.

Family, Homes, School

We shall take vigorous measures to restore to women the dignity and status they deserve as the creators of our citizens, and to eliminate the terribly disruptive idea that being the mother of a family is a job for an ignorant female, that she is just a drudging "housewife", that a woman must do something MORE, something masculine to prove she is "equal".

We shall elevate Family Management to the status of a genuine profession, which it should be, and establish Universities of Family Management to train women in a scientific and satisfying manner in pediatrics, gestation and birth, family economics, nutrition, family culture, philosophy and the arts, etc. Graduates will be granted degrees having the same status as Law or Medical degrees, and honored by every agency of the community for their accomplishments in the fields of their natural abilities and needs. We assert that a cultured, professional, thoroughly capable MOTHER is the equal of any man on earth, and we will see to it that society recognizes that fact.

On the other hand, we shall eliminate from our civilization the disruptive doctrines of false "equality"—meaning sameness with men—which is masculinizing and frustrating millions of our good women, breaking up our marriages, and wrecking our sacred family life. We shall encourage the restoration of the father as master of the home, grant subsidies where necessary to give the home and children a full-time mother, and promote in every way the re-building of the home and family as the very fountainhead of goodness in our people.

We shall put an end to the foolishness of "progressive education", and give our youth a disciplined ability to think and understand, rather than "social values" which they should get in the home. We shall establish a physical culture program with something more than desultory games and half-hearted calisthenics, to harden and steel our youth to maximum physical fitness and exuberant health.

Business, Farms, Labor

We shall remove all possible controls from labor, the businessman and the farmer, and allow free enterprise and free bargaining to produce the efficiency unobtainable with any bureaucratic controls. We shall assist each group to form its own control councils, on a local basis, to maintain order and communication, and national industrial councils to establish policies of mutual benefit. The government will keep hands off all honest enterprises, labor, and farmers, so long as they do not coerce one another, take unfair advantage, or threaten the whole people, when compulsory arbitration will take place.

As a temporary measure to protect all honest producers during the necessarily chaotic conditions following removal of the present crazy patch-work of controls and subsidies, we shall guarantee all honest producers a decent level of family income, until genuine free enterprise can bring genuine and natural order to the economy.

Honest Free Press

We shall make it a penitentiary offense for any medium of public information or entertainment to CONSCIOUSLY MISLEAD THE PUBLIC by lies, misrepresentations, omissions, deletions, or by any other method whatsoever.

To insure the real freedom of the press, which is presently only a myth in view of the need for millions of dollars to reach any significant segment of the population today, we shall establish a National Free Opinion Network of Newspapers, TV, Radio, Books and Magazines. These facilities will be available, upon petition to any group of 1,000 or more citizens of decent presentation of their views to the nation without cost; subject, of course, to the penalties of conscious lying.

Crime, Vice

We shall deal ruthlessly and efficiently with habitual and natural criminals, and drive them permanently out of existence, instead of the present tearful dabbling with them as "lost sheep". At the same time, we recognize that millions of our best people are driven, under the impossible chaos of our times, into situations where there is almost no escape from the pressures except some illegal action. We shall remove the pressures from these oppressed people with the rest of this program, and take every measure to help these basically good people, and restore them to a productive role in the community.

We shall rescue most of the growing hordes of criminal teenagers by dealing with their need for aggression, action, danger, and excitement realistically, by ending the nonsense of clubs and tea-parties and forming them into para-military volunteer Police Youth Auxiliaries, to patrol America's crime-ridden streets, and turn would-be muggers, etc. over to regular authorities.

Since we recognize that it is utterly impossible to suppress entirely drinking and gambling in society, we shall remove these two sources of much crime from the criminals, and establish a generous national lottery, and place the sale of alcoholic beverages under a control board. At the same time, we shall ruthlessly suppress all forms of vice such as prostitution, dope addiction, homosexuality, etc., which are NOT universal and necessary, and which cannot be tolerated in any form without breeding disintegration and disease.

Government

We shall use only legal, constitutional means to win power in the United States, because we know the people will demand our services in government when they finally awake to the Jewish subversion of our people. Until then, we must train, and be prepared to establish an orderly government when the present false prosperity, false peace, false welfare, and false government blow sky-high under the blows of the Jews, as they surely will.

In power, we shall reestablish the actual function of the electoral college as intended by the wise founding Fathers of our Country to protect us from demagoguery, and we shall return the election of Senators to the State Legislatures.

We shall make the pay of all government employees directly dependent on their efficiency, apply modern business methods to government operation, and ruthlessly eliminate the hordes of bureaucratic parasites who make our present government the world's most wasteful, inefficient and extravagant.

We shall call a constitutional convention to draw up amendments and strike out others to enable all the above program, and to insure that never again can any subversive conspiracy bring this great Nation to the very brink of extinction.

KU KLUX KLAN

The Ku Klux Klan was first organized in 1866 in Pulaski, Tennessee, and first flourished during Reconstruction after the Civil War or, as it is known

in the South, the War Between the States or the War for Southern Indepen-
dence. The Klan revived after World War I and was very powerful in the
South and Midwest for about fifteen years. It was then revived again in the
1960s in a number of small groups, each claiming to be the legitimate heir
to the early Klan movements. The selections here are from such groups. They
are small but numerous.

United Klans of America, Inc.

What We Believe

The men and women of the KU KLUX KLAN believe that the future is
what we make it. We believe that we, as free and conscious agents, have an
absolute responsibility for all those elements of the world around us over
which we are capable of exercising control: for the structure of our society
and its institutions; for the beauty and cleanliness of both our natural and
man-made environments; for the cultural and moral climate in which we live
and work; for the military and geo-political status of our nation relative to the
other nations of the earth; and, most of all, for the racial quality of the
coming generations of our people.

We believe that no multi-racial society can be a truly healthy society, and
no government which is not wholly responsible to a single racial entity can
be a good government. America's present deterioration stems from her loss
of racial homogeneity and racial consciousness, and from the consequent
alienation of most of our fellow citizens.

We believe that a good government is a government firmly based on
fundamental principles, the first of which must be that the long-range welfare, security, and racial quality of our people is the ultimate good. A
good government is a government which implements continuing, farsighted
programs consistent with this principle; it is not a government like the one
we have now, which embodies no coherent national purpose, which is
swayed by every minority pressure group, and which bases its policies on

From "What We Believe" (n.p.: United Klans of America, [1984], flyer).

shortsighted, partisan considerations, drifting from one crisis to another and seldom planning beyond the next election.

We believe that, in addition to a principled, responsible government, we must have a society which facilitates progress in all realms of life: that is, a society whose institutions and values are conducive to advancements not only in material efficiency, but also in artistic achievement, in moral and physical health, and in racial quality. And we believe that all of these things are closely bound together. We can have a healthy, vital artistic life once again only when we reject the false notion of artistic universalism and encourage our young artists and musicians to express the inherent values and feelings of our own people in their creative work. Likewise, our educational system should concern itself not only with training our young people in the basic skills of civilized life and giving them pride in their racial, cultural, and national heritage, but also with building character in them. Self-reliance, moral toughness, and a sense of personal honor, and physical fitness are qualities at least as important in our citizens as a knowledge of facts and techniques. All young people of our race must have instilled in them a sense of quality instead of equality; they must be taught to embrace discipline and order instead of being encouraged to succumb to permissiveness and chaos.

We believe that our people must be united by the common goal of building a better world and a better race. Today, without a common national-racial purpose, we are unable to focus our energies and achieve the great things which otherwise would be within our grasp. But once we are united on the basis of common blood, organized and disciplined within a progressive social order, and inspired by a common set of ideals, there will be no problem which we cannot overcome, no enemy whom we cannot vanquish, and no goal which we cannot attain.

We believe that the first step toward this goal must be the gathering together of all those men and women of our race who share our beliefs and who are willing to participate in our effort to raise the consciousness of others.

The Klan was one of the largest anti-Catholic movements in American history, and this part of Klan beliefs continues in some contemporary groups, as is shown in the following selection.

IDEALS OF A KLANSMAN

In the crisis of today, we have at our command the strength, the courage and inspiration which lay in the four great faiths of our founding fathers—faith in God—faith in ourselves—faith in our fellowman—faith in our freedom.

Our great Nation was founded upon these faiths. The patriots who signed the Constitution, men and women who braved the prairie, the forests and the mountains to pioneer our great Nation, they lived and died by those great faiths.

It is our children's birthright—ours to hand on to them and to their children.

It is not enough merely to declare our faiths. We must give them life and meaning—by words—by our works—in our daily lives.

WE THE KLAN BELIEVE:

We believe in God and the tenets of the Christian religion, and that a Godless nation cannot long prosper.

The Christian religion is founded on the teaching of Jesus Christ. An infidel or a person who rejects Jesus Christ and his teachings, cannot be a true Klansman. And the nation that rejects God and His word is sure to reap calamity of some kind.

We believe that a church that is not founded on the principles of morality and justice is a mockery to God and man.

There are churches, so-called, that do not require a high standard of morality and justice from their membership. Men who accept the teachings of such churches cannot be klansmen, in the true sense of the word. The genuine Christian is both moral and just.

We believe that any church that does not have the welfare of the common people at heart is unworthy.

Any church that is founded on the principles set forth in the teaching of Jesus Christ has the welfare of all the people at heart. There is no class

From "The Principle of the United Klans of America" (Tuscaloosa, Ala.: Office of the Imperial Wizard, [1974], pamphlet).

distinction, no subjection of the masses by a favored few, as has been the case for centuries in Mexico and other Romanized countries.

We believe in the eternal separation of the church and state:

Roman Catholicism teaches the union of church and state with the church controlling the state.

The Constitution of the United States declares that the church and state shall forever be separate. The church has its function, which is spiritual and the state its function, which is temporal. Each has its place, and while they should work in harmony, they should be separate.

We hold no allegiance to any foreign government, emperor, king, people or any other foreign political or religious power.

Every Roman Catholic holds allegiance to the Pope of Rome, and Catholicism teaches that this allegiance is superior to his allegiance to his country.

We believe in just laws and liberty.

By just laws is meant laws that apply equally to all, rich and poor, educated, men and women. Liberty does not mean license, as many seem to think, it does not mean to do as one pleases, regardless of others: it means that in the exercise of our privilege, the welfare of others and of society at large must be considered.

We hold allegiance to the Stars and Stripes next to our allegiance to the Almighty God: God should be honored and obeyed above all: but next to God we should hold allegiance to the Stars and Stripes, which is the emblem of our liberties.

We believe in the upholding of the Constitution of these United States.

By upholding the Constitution, is meant the whole Constitution, anyone who violates one clause of the Constitution, would as quickly break every other one if it served his purpose to do so.

We believe that our free public school system is the corner-stone of good government, and that whose who are seeking to destroy it are enemies of our Republic and are unworthy of citizenship to [sic] our republic.

Ignorance, superstition, immorality, and crime go hand in hand. Destroy our schools and the rule of our country will be placed in the hands of the few, as is the case where there are no public schools.

There are enemies within our gates who are trying to break down our system, which would put more stress on church dogma than general education, the result would be the ignorant masses controlled by the educated few.

We believe in freedom of speech: By this is meant the right of any citizen to express an opinion on any subject, either publicly or privately, so long as no other person's private character is assailed. Until the arising of the Knights of the KKK, this right was denied American citizens in many of our cities and towns.

We believe in a free press, uncontrolled by political or religious sects.

The press should be free to spread news without coloring it to suit any person or sect: But such is not the case, scarcely a newspaper anywhere dares to publish the truth: the whole truth and nothing but the truth. The press is largely controlled by the Roman Catholic priesthood and Judaism, and as a result the great masses of people are fed on propaganda instead of true facts. When an article is read in either a newspaper of [sic] magazine, one does not know but what there is a sinister motive back of it. And a paper that publishes nothing but the truth can hardly exist.

We believe in law and order; in other words, the Klan believes in keeping the laws and in enforcing the laws. Many accusations have been brought against the Klan as law-breakers. These accusations against the order are purely newspaper propaganda. So far we have not heard of a single instance where the Klan, by an official act, has violated any law.

We believe in white supremacy:

The Klan believes that America is a white man's country, and should be governed by whitemen. Yet the Klan is not anti-Negro, it is the Negro's friend. The Klan is eternally opposed to the mixing of the white and the colored races. Our creed: Let the white man remain white, the black man black, the yellow man yellow, the brown man brown, and the red man red. God drew the color line, and man should so let it remain, read Acts 17:26 if you please.

We believe in the protection of our pure womanhood, the home, the church, our public school system, our constitution, and our American way of life.

This is a stand for the purity of the home, for morality, for the protection of our mothers, our sisters, our wives, our daughters, against the white slaver, the home wrecker, the libertine. And to live up to this principle a Klansman must keep himself pure and above reproach. He must treat other women as he would have those of his own household treated.

We do not believe in mob violence, but we do believe that laws should be enacted to prevent the cause of mob violence.

Deaths by mob violence have fallen off very materially since the advent of the Klan. The Klan believes in law-enforcement, and if a person has committed a crime the law should take its course.

We believe in a closer relationship of capital and labor:

And that the leadership of the American labor movement be white American born with a knowledge of American customs and principles.

Instead of being antagonistic one towards the other, capital and labor should work in harmony, this would be the case if men observed the teaching of Christ in His word, and if they would observe the teachings embodied in the Klan motto: Non Silba Sed Anthar—(not for the self but for others.)

We believe in limitation of foreign immigration:

No nation can absorb an unlimited number of foreigners and retain its national integrity and traditions. Immigration should be controlled by the nation which the immigrants are entering. The nation should be judge as to whom it will receive.

The traditions of America have well-nigh been buried under the avalanche of foreign ideas and ideals.

But for the arising of the Knights of the KKK, they would now have been but a memory in some parts of our country.

We are native born American citizens, and we believe our rights in this country are superior to those of foreigners.

The Klan believes in England for Englishmen, France for Frenchman, Italy for Italians, and America for Americans: Is there anything objectionable in this? The Klan is not anti-Catholic, anti-Jew, anti-Negro, anti-foreign, the Klan is pro-Protestant, and pro-American.

The Klan does not oppose the foreigner who comes to our shores and becomes an American citizen, and an American at heart, but the Klan does oppose those who come here to drag America down to the level of the priest-ridden countries of Southern Europe, while hoarding up good American dollars and living under the protection of American laws.

We believe that the Supreme Court was in error when it attempted to legislate an act which would in effect, if adhered to, nullify the sovereignty of all states, and it is our purpose to seek by legal means the reversal of the United States Supreme Court.

We believe that the N.A.A.C.P. is a subversive organization, and is infiltrated with Communistic idealogies *[sic]* and should be abolished by legal means.

All true Klansmen and Klanswomen stand together on these American principles and will stake their lives on the perpetuation and protection of same.

We the Klan will never allow out *[sic]* blood bought liberties to be crucified on a Roman cross: and we will not yield to the integration of white and Negro races in our schools or any where else.

We will follow the teachings of the Bible, and not the unwise and one-sided rulings of the United States Supreme Court which is not in keeping with the Constitution of the United States of America.

Knights of the Ku Klux Klan

1. To prepare the means of defense and survival in case of civil emergency.
2. To resist and expose communist influence and propaganda in America.
3. To resist passage of gun control laws, which hinder an American from the ability to defend his home and family.
4. To establish a plan for mutual self-help between members, and to help them live economically.
5. To co-operate as much as we can, with law enforcement officials, towards exposing the plans of black militants, communists, and other types of "liberals", who are intent on destroying American society.
6. To stop racial busing, and all other plans to intergrate [sic] white children into the black movement, which includes all white children.
7. To support home rule in the fields of zoning, housing, jobs, also in the various branches of unions, schools, fraternal or service organizations, churches, or any other activities that our members may participate in.
8. To support state rights as political principle.
9. To emphasize and defend civil rights of white, American people.
10. To extend our help and encouragement, whenever possible, to white people in other non-communist countries, many of whom are facing the same problems as our-selves.
11. To obey all laws, but primarily the basic law of self-defense. This means we try to avoid violence, but, if violence is used against us, we may defend our-selves.
12. To recognize the Declaration of Independence and the U.S. Constitution as our guidelines, and supporting the original interpretation of the Constitution as the basic law of the land.
13. In general to initiate programs of public policy and private education,

From "Knights of the Ku Klux Klan" (Tuscaloosa, Ala.: United Klans of America, [1979], flyer).

which restore our damaged social and political institutions, and save our moral standards.

Other Klan Groups

A BRIEF HISTORY OF THE FIERY CROSS

Down through the history of the white race the lighted cross has always been used as a symbol of resistance to alien tyranny. In times past, our race was organized according to the family or tribal system of Clans, Kith, Kin, and Septs. The Celtic, Nordic, and Teutonic Clans maintained large stacks of wood and/or a large wooden cross upon the highest promotory [sic] in each tribal domain. At the first sign of alien invasion or strife, the cross was lighted as an alarm signal to the entire Clan. Thus alerted, the people armed for war and hurriedly gathered at the cross, often accompanied by the skirl of the great Warpipes (Bagpipes). The lighted cross also acted as a signal to distant allied chieftans [sic] to light their own crosses and to bring their clansmen quickly. They knew then, far better than we, that a peril to one was a peril to all. In this manner the alarm was sent speeding over the land. Likewise, down through the centuries, the lighted cross became a symbol of the determination of free men to guard their own birthrights.

Now, as so often in the past, we face an alien invasion of our lands. Under the sponsorship and with the aid of the Feds in Washington, our country is being inundated with a tidal wave of colored immigrants who are devouring our sustenance and displacing our own people off the land. Our race is being destroyed through miscegenation, no-win foreign wars (soon to be with us again), black crime, and anti-white tax policies which force the white man to support and subsidize these colored hordes. Because of the economic burden imposed upon him, the white man's birth rate is the lowest in the world. We are compelled against our will by the Zionist Occupation Government (ZOG) in Washington to feed, house, and arm these who are sworn to destroy us. We are forced to support an army of tax collectors and bureaucrats who wax fat off our sustenance and daily trod upon the laws which were intended to guarantee our common law rights (the Constitution).

From "A Brief History of the Fiery Cross" (n.p.: n.p., [early 1980s], flyer).

We are shackled with a judicial system and judges who's *[sic]* only purpose is to avoid justice at all costs. No white man in this land need be reminded of the sneering contempt and judicial tyranny which they daily heap upon us. The murderer, the thief, the rapist are extended unlimited consideration while the farmer, the worker, widows and the aged are turned out of their homes and off their land at the behest of the money boys.

Thus, we raise the standard of the fiery cross and proclaim a message unto our own people. We summon the Clans of our race to gather at the Standard to hear the Word and Law of God. Yes, we are militantly Christian and white . . . for the two are inseparable. God's law is the organic life-law of the White Race and that law demands total separation of the races!

SPECIAL RIGHTS FOR BLACK SAVAGES?

Do you believe that Blacks are entitled to special consideration because of the color of their skin?

Do you believe that law enforcement should be relaxed so Blacks can murder, rape, loot and burn without fear of punishment?

Do you believe that Black rioters and looters should be allowed to threaten and intimidate Congress and the American public?

Do you believe that Negro loafers and their illegitimate offspring are entitled to 90% of the welfare money poured out by politicians, while poor White people are regularly neglected?

Do you believe that arrogant Negroes should get the jobs of better qualified Whites?

Do you believe that White people who live in the cities of America should be required to submit to violence at the hands of Black criminals?

Do you believe that White children should be forced to go to integrated schools where they are shaken down, molested and assaulted by young Black thugs?

From "Special Rights for Black Savages?" (n.p.: n.p., n.d., pamphlet).

Do you believe that Black agitators should be free to incite to hate and violence against the White people of this country?

Do you believe that Black criminals should be permitted to stockpile arms and organize guerrilla warfare, while White citizens of this nation are systematically disarmed by new gun laws?

Do you believe that Negroes are indispensable to the harmonious and orderly functioning of our society?

If your answer to each of these questions is an emphatic NO, then contact:
KU KLUX KLAN

PRINCIPALS

* OUR LORD JESUS CHRIST
* DEFENSE OF STATE RIGHTS
* EXPULSION OF ALL COMMUNISTS
* RACIAL SEPARATION
* BUILD A POWERFUL WHITE AMERICA
* PRESERVATION OF THE WHITE CHRISTIAN RACE
* FULL POWER BACK TO OUR POLICE
* HONEST LEADERS

ARYAN NATIONS

Aryan Nations, centered in Hayden Lake, Idaho (where there is a community or compound), and led by Richard Girnt Butler, is probably the best known of the contemporary racist groups. Its focus is overwhelmingly on race with relatively few other concerns, but it has a religious basis in the Christian Identity Movement, which was founded in 1946 by Wesley Smith, a former Klan member. The Christian Identity Movement is based on British or Anglo-Israelism but adds elements of its own.[2]

Church of Jesus Christ Christian

This is *Aryan Nations*
R. G. Butler

This pamphlet is published to answer a few basic questions regarding the Kingdom Identity Message. We pray fervently that those who read these words will do so in an objective manner and will allow God's Holy Spirit to penetrate and enlighten.

Aryan Nations is not a new right-wing organization which has suddenly appeared on the scene. Aryan Nations is the on-going work of Jesus the Christ regathering His people, calling His people to a state for their nation to bring in His Kingdom! Hail His Victory!

WE BELIEVE the Bible is the true Word of God written for and about a specific people. The Bible is the family history of the White Race, the children of Yahweh placed here through the seedline of Adam.

WE BELIEVE that Adam-man of Genesis was the placing of the White Race upon this earth. All races did not descend from Adam. Adam is the father of the White Race only. (Adam in the original Hebrew is translated, "to show blood; flesh; turn rosy.")

WE BELIEVE that the true, literal children of the Bible are the 12 tribes of Israel which are now scattered throughout the world and are now known as the Anglo-Saxon, Celtic, Scandinavian, Teutonic people of this earth. We know that the Bible is written to the family of Abraham, descending from Shem, back to the man, Adam. God blessed Abraham and promised that he would be the "Father of Nations." This same promise continued through the seedline of Abraham's son, Isaac, and again to Isaac's son, Jacob, the Patriarch of the 12 tribes, whose name God changed to Israel (meaning "he will rule as God.")

WE BELIEVE that there are literal children of Satan in the world today. These children are the descendants of Cain, who was a result of Eve's original sin, her physical seduction by Satan. We know that because of this sin, there is a battle and a natural enmity between the children of Satan and the Children of the Most High God.

From R. G. Butler, "This is *Aryan Nations*" (Hayden Lake, Idaho: Church of Jesus Christ Christian, Aryan Nations, [1980s], pamphlet).

WE BELIEVE the Jew is the adversary of our race and God, as is attested to by all secular history as well as the word of God in scripture; that he will always do what he was born to do, that is, be the "cancer" invading the Aryan body politic to break down and destroy the dross from Aryan culture and racial purity; that those who are able to resist this satanic "disease" are the "called chosen and faithful."

WE BELIEVE there is a battle being fought this day between the children of darkness (today known as Jews) and the children of light (God), the Aryan race, the true Israel of the Bible.

WE BELIEVE that God created pure seed lines, races, and that each have a specific place in His order on this earth under the administration of His Life Law. We know that man (Adam) was given the command to have dominion over the earth and subdue it, but that, in great part our race has been deceived into rejecting this divine order. They have forgotten the words of Yahweh to Abraham, "In thee shall all the families of the earth be blessed." (Genesis 13:3) There is no race hatred in this statement. It was and is the plan of Yahweh to bless all, through the seed of Abraham. We believe in the preservation of our race individually and collectively as a people as demanded and directed by God. We believe a racial nation has a right and is under obligation to preserve itself and its members.

WE BELIEVE that the present world problems are a result of our disobedience to God's laws. God's intended purpose was that His racial kinsmen were to be in charge of this earth. Our race, within itself, holds divine power; and when we abrogate and violate divine law, we give power to our enemies. Evil is the result to all.

WE BELIEVE that the redemptive work of Jesus was finished on the cross. As His divine race, we have been commissioned to fulfill His divine purpose and plans—the restitution of all things.

WE BELIEVE that there is a day of reckoning. The usurper will be thrown out by the terrible might of Yahweh's people as they return to their roots and their special destiny. We know there is soon to be a day of judgment and a day when Christ's Kingdom (Government) will be established on earth as it is in heaven. "And in the days of these kings shall the God of heaven set up a kingdom which shall never be destroyed; and the kingdom shall not be left to other people, but it shall break in pieces and consume all these kingdoms and it shall stand forever. But the saints of the Most High shall take the kingdom and possess the kingdom forever, even for ever and ever. And the kingdom and dominion and greatness of the kingdom under the whole heaven shall be given to the people of the saints of the Most High, whose kingdom is an everlasting kingdom, and all dominions shall serve and obey Him." (Daniel 2:44; 7:18; 7:27)

Aryan Nations

TWELVE FOUNDATION STONES TO ESTABLISH A STATE FOR OUR ARYAN RACIAL NATION
R. G. Butler

1) The recognition that there exists no place on earth in any branch of the Adamic Aryan race, a State of our Racial Nation.
2) The recognition that an Aryan National State is an institution that has a single duty to itself and the people of the racial Nation; the preservation of the race, culture and people of the Nation.
3) The recognition that there exists a Law Order that governs the life of men and nations of men, in that obedience to this life law is life, disobedience is death.
4) The recognition of the fact that the creative "Life spirit" of the Adamic Aryan can only exist through the purity of the blood of the race in their generations.
5) That recognition is made of the fact that no compromise or adulteration of this basic organic life law principle can be made without violating all law.
6) That recognition is made of the fact that the only hope for redemption of the Aryan racial household is the total return to the fundamental life law.
7) That recognition is made that life is inseparable from the political government under which the Aryan racial family lives.
8) That recognition be made that only by the single united will of the people of the racial Nation can there exist a State or Government for the Nation.
9) That recognition be made of the fact that the people of the nation create the State, and that the State does not create the people.

From R. G. Butler, "Twelve Foundation Stones to Establish a State for Our Aryan Racial Nation" (Hayden Lake, Idaho: Aryan Nations, [1980s], pamphlet).

10) That recognition is made of the fact that a nation begins and ends as a race, and everything else is predicated upon this fact.
11) That recognition be made that there is and can be no separation of the "spiritual" worship, state, and the political state.
12) That recognition be made that we have but one hope as a Racial Nation and that is the Life Law of our Father and God.

The Aryan Warriors Stand

POPULATION AND RACE

The Aryan world-idea is accepted by Aryans universally both as revealed Christianity and legislative law. It is an idea comprising both the spiritual and the material, a Guide to nation-builders, and to the individual in his search for the truth.

The very foundation of faith and worship is Racial Truth, for with the Aryan, Christianity and Race are one. On this foundation arises the Will to power and World Leadership inherent in the soul of the seed of Adam. Through racial purity and an unfettered instinct in procreation the Aryan goes forward to the repeopling of his world.

The Aryan does not have a sexual union outside his own race, but seeks always the improvement of his own species.

Perfection in type is the union between men and women who are fair, with comely eyes and an open countenance. These traits constitute the Adamic ideal, in whom the Aryans acknowledge their heritage as the Israel of God.

The Aryan honors the science of eugenics founded by the English biologist, Sir Francis Galton, in the 19th century, which science continues today through those such as Dr. Shockley and Dr. E. O. Wilson.

PROPERTY

Property, in the form of land or industrial wealth, is subject to public control, and will be operated in the national and racial interest.

From "The Aryan Warriors Stand," *Aryan Nations,* no. 1 (1979).

Private ownership remains in name; but since all ownership is regarded as trusteeship for the nation, under God, exploitation must be effectively ended. There shall be no taxation on homes or farms of citizens.

Since economic security in all stages of life is guaranteed to every member of the nation the covetous pursuit of material wealth becomes unnecessary and, indeed, a despised social aim. A man will be honored for his children, rather than for his material riches.

A man shall own his home or farm and other personal possessions; but the exploitation of the national property to alien control for private profit is forbidden.

The Aryan community recognizes its most precious possession in its children. Where property is concerned, the aid will be towards the nation's citizens in ownership and benefit rather than alien private ownership and benefit.

INDUSTRY AND FINANCE

Aryan nationalism predicates a system in which all men are producers. Excepted only are the children and the aged who, together with those temporarily incapacitated receive and live upon the fruit of their labors with State help and allowances.

The financial system of International Jewish capitalism will be ended. There is no unearned income, or reward without service. Loans are made interest-free to industry, and worthy individuals, thus ending the system of usury or of debt-interest.

Within the framework of a usury-free system, Industry will be self-governing, with representatives of management, workers, and consumers co-operating to distribute equitably the proceeds of industry.

Industry and Finance will be subject to general control by central authority for the purpose of co-ordinating the national industrial system.

Production is wealth. There is no other economic criterion.

YOUTH

Aryan youth aims to be educated spiritually, mentally and physically for the service of the race so that our race may fulfill its manifest destiny and purpose.

Youth Movements, both for boys and girls, are a vital part of all Aryan States.

In young men the Aryan ideal is of physical and athletic fitness, reliability and determination of character, proficiency in chosen livelihood-occupation, and of general usefulness to the community.

In young women the accent is primarily on fitness for mother-hood and home-making, but also on athletics and arts.

Aryan youth regards its racial unity as indispensable to its continued strength. The concept of race and nation must dominate all other social divisions. In unity and comradeship is the strength of the whole Aryan order.

Aryan youth is sturdy and proof against all trials, is fearless and determined.

Aryan youth believes in action rather than in words; and in the principle that youth must be led by youth. The Aryan does not devote himself or herself exclusively to personal interest. The ideal of service to the community predominates. To steel the body, to prepare and fortify the mind in order to serve race and God, is the creed of Aryan youth.

Aryan youth knows first how to obey. Only he who knows how to obey can learn to command. Alongside the training and hardening of the body is the task of obedience and discipline in youth.

Aryan national discipline breeds love of order in the world, in contrast to the parliamentary democratic chaos.

Aryan youth is consciously idealistic and believes in sacrifices for the greater good of the community.

Aryan youth believes in the ideals and hard virtues necessary to the foundation of great peoples, which never surrender or weaken before the blows of life.

Aryan youth is God-believing, and abides in the laws of God.

WOMEN

Every child that an Aryan mother brings into the world is a battle waged for the existence of her people.

The program of the National Aryan Women's Movement has truly a single point—the child. The sphere and tasks of man and woman in life are separate but complementary. Mutual respect lies in the fact that both man and woman know that each is doing everything which is necessary to maintain the whole National community.

The Aryan way of life is determined not by material considerations but by the soul of a nation. Aryan women [sic] gives herself in conscious idealism to the concept of the national interest before private interest.

The thoughts of Aryan woman are dominated by the desire to enter family life.

A creed of the Aryan women is this: "We serve the life of our people. We regard our household tasks as a means for achieving and maintaining the physical and spiritual health of the nation."

Aryan woman brings true love and affection, and a happy, well-run home to refresh and inspire her man.

Aryan woman is treated with chivalry and respect by Aryan man.

The morality of the Aryan girl is very important. As girls you must learn to play your part in the national community and you have to school yourselves for the day when you shall become the wives of our men and the mothers of the new generation. For the men who are to shape the future of our race need women of your kind, women who in profound faith and brave in spirit, are prepared to share with their menfolk every hardship and sacrifice. That is a high aim for every girl, for the attainment of which it is very worth while to devote years to making oneself pure with a view to being able in all honesty to fulfill this mission.

There is a world of man and the world of woman. Nature has ordained that man should be the guardian of the family and the protector of the community. The world of contented womanhood is made up of family, husband, children, and home. Both man and woman form a totality in which a people is able to live and prosper.

Honored above all is the mother. It is far greater love and service, to be the mother of healthy Aryan children than to be a clever woman lawyer.

It is a duty to the Aryan state to safeguard the mother and child.

Aryan woman finds her joy and self-fulfillment in creative living, and in a conscious development of the higher culture of Aryan life under the Law of God.

Aryan woman guards the purity of her blood in which reposes her racial instinct and strength, the guarantor of Aryan culture.

ARYAN LAW

Aryan law honors the spirit more than the strict letter of its legal code. Judges are therefore given wide powers in the racial and national interest; and efficient, speedy working of the legal machine is always sought in the maintenance of community interest and in the punishment of wrongdoers. Aryan justice knows no compromise with evil, and least of all with the power of the purse. The law is clearly stated in the Holy Bible available to every citizen. The administration of this law will be an efficient process unhampered by the legal parasites of the capitalistic code.

THE ARMY

The Aryan believes in the armed forces of his people as responsible for their destiny and as the guarantor of the future.

The army is for the defense of a country and of a Divine ordained racial concept, not for the protection of a political and economic system.

This is the pledge of the Aryan soldier; "At the beginning of our struggle there stood a people; at the end of our struggle there will once more stand a people."

The fight for our race has always come and will always come from the world of Aryan soldiery.

The school of the Army teaches the Aryan in self confidence, to rely upon his own strength.

The Aryan Army exists not to deprive non-Aryans of their freedom, but to protect Aryan freedom.

There is nothing else in the whole of the Aryan state which is so rich in traditions as the Army.

In the indissoluble and sworn unity of People, State and Army lies the enduring strength of the Aryan and of the whole Aryan world destiny.

CONSTITUTION AND WORLD-OUTLOOK

The constitution of the Aryan world and National Aryan State is based upon the Leadership principle.

The Covenant combines the people's will with the authority of administering the law.

The best form of State and Constitution is that which, with natural sureness of hand, raises the best brains of the community to a position of leadership and predominant influence.

The end in view of all Aryan efforts and institutions is the preservation and increase of the race and people, for the purpose of their Father and God.

The Aryan Constitution is divinely ordained and based upon eternal life Law principles.

The Divine ordained Aryan Constitution creates a single, centralized authority. The heads of all departments carry full responsibility in their work, exercising control over subordinates and being subject to the general control of their superiors. Such is the executive foundation of the Aryan Nationalist State.

The Aryan United States represents the Leadership, or the control of its own destinies, by the entire community, as a nation and race. Neither the merchants nor the workers, private class nor group, can control a State for its own private interests.

Capitalism, or the lending and borrowing of money at interest, cannot be in the Aryan State. The economic system is under divine law, controlled towards the equation of production and consumption, and in which there is only income earned by work.

The starting point of Aryan National State is not the State, but the people. The supreme test of every institution is: Does it preserve the People?

Intolerance of opposing ideas is necessary to strength. Strength lies in the disciplined observance of rigid principles, based upon preservation of nation and race.

The Aryan political concept of government is by statesmen trained in natural Divine Law and administrators, advised by technical experts in the various fields of economic and cultural activity.

The Aryan views not only his state and nation, but his race throughout the earth; and he works for "understanding and union between the different language groups of the one ordained ruling race." Against the international organization of Jewry, he sets his World Aryan Christian Union.

Aryan Nationalism embraces the heroic Aryan principles. Sacrifice for the Cause, rather than personal pleasure, must be the guiding light. For on the foundation of Aryan strength and unity are built the only possibilities of individual fullness of life. To the anti-Christ doctrine of the prime importance of the individual, the Aryan Nationalist replies with the doctrine of the common racial interest before private interest. This concept, together with the leadership principle, forms the basis of this Christian Aryan Constitution, A Divine Compact.

The Aryan Nations Movement is not mere theory: it is the acknowledgement of the millions of our race that they are brothers and sisters.

The future of an Aryan America, as of the whole Aryan world, does not depend on the number of associations which work for this future, but it rather depends on the question whether the will of the many can be successfully brought to acknowledge our Father's single will and thus be limited in a Movement which will execute our purpose and ordained mission on earth.

AGRICULTURE

The foundation of a State is its farmers and agriculture.

The farming community has the right to State protection both as regards permanency of tenure and the sale of its produce.

Maximum production from the land, but without exhausting its fertility, is a primary aim of an Aryan State.

Land Settlement, with the creation of farm holdings for family inheritance, is the aim of an Aryan State, rather than the movement of population to the towns and cities.

Self-sufficiency in food production and consumption is the agrarian ideal to place before all Aryan Nations.

EDUCATION

The establishment of a national education based upon racial identity and culture, with control based upon scripture foundation for a unified political and philosophical outlook.

Education in an Aryan State should be consistently based upon the foundation of Aryan culture.

Aryan Nationalism insists upon the priority of life and action over all other systems of education and learning.

The Aryan concept is of practical rather than theoretical experience in education; and sees in political struggle in youth movements for both sexes, character builders of the first order.

Physical training and athletic accomplishment are an essential part of youthful training in Aryan peoples.

All forms of education in Aryan States have one aim: the shaping of the Aryan Nationalist man and woman.

Man is a Unity of Spirit, mind and body; and education should develop him as an integrated trinity.

The foundation of Aryan States is in an understanding of racial philosophy and biology.

Higher education should be determined by merit. Thus, strength of character and mind, physical fitness and marked racial traits are points insisted upon in this selection.

Intellectual capabilities alone are insufficient. To them should be added strong will-power, a sense of right behavior and of team work, and a consciousness of belonging to the Aryan racial stock.

The examples given in the Aryan States, in respect of Youth Movements, Labor and Military service in respect of vocational training both for young men and women, as additional to the general educational system are a guide to all Aryan peoples.

The function of education is not exclusively to fill the mind with knowledge, but to develop capabilities needed to occupy a position of responsibility.

Education for political posts should receive prime attention. For, whereas the power of money has determined political positions within the plutocracies, merit alone should count in an Aryan State. The science of politics requires first-class Aryan material and its technical schooling as does any other science.

The Aryan Nationalist principle of education places the main emphasis not on intellectual attainments, but on character.

ECONOMICS

Our education also trains men to respect intellectual achievement: we bring one to respect the spade, another to respect the compass or pen. "All now are but Aryan fellow countrymen, and it is their achievement which determines their value."

The pursuit of agriculture is the foundation of the Aryan State. The countryside produces men for the nation, and has been through the generations the eternal source of national strength.

In the sphere of economic life all action must be governed by one law: capital serves Industry; and Industry serves the people of the nation.

What is necessary is to teach each class and profession the importance of others. All together form one mighty body: laborers, farmers, and professional men.

All work which is necessary ennobles him who performs it. Only one thing is shameful, to contribute nothing to the community.

Nothing falls into a man's lap from heaven. It is from labor that life grows.

The wage of the people has meaning only when it arises from production. Every increase in production should benefit the whole people and raise the people's standard of living.

We renew the only true economic system and its basis is that capital is workpower, and the value of our money lies in our production.

ARYAN NATIONS THEOPOLITICAL PLATFORM

1. *ARYAN NATIONS* is a White Racial "THEOPOLITICAL" movement. It is a "GEOPOLITICAL" movement for the re-establishment of White Aryan sovereignty over the lands of Aryan settlement and occupation.
2. *ARYAN NATIONS* is a Racial National in that our Race is our Nation on earth and every White Aryan is a member of this Racial National body regardless of geographical location of birth.
3. *ARYAN NATIONS* is "RACIAL" NATIONALISM in that each country of our Race's inhabitation is an essential national member of our racial body on earth.
4. *ARYAN NATIONS* is "LAWFUL" in that it upholds and proclaims creation's supreme "LAW OF NATIONS" the Law of Nature's God.
5. *ARYAN NATIONS* is "PROGRESSIVE" in that it stands for the restoration of co-ordination of the nation's members of our racial body for the fulfillment of our race's purpose and reason for being on earth.

"Aryan Nations Theopolitical Platform" (Hayden Lake, Idaho: Aryan Nations, [1980s], broadsheet).

6. *ARYAN NATIONS* is "LIBERTY" in that only by the sovereign Aryan will to return to the Creator's Life Law, may all creation be liberated from its present pain of travail.
7. *ARYAN NATIONS* is "HOPE" in that the Plague of Death now upon our Nations may only be removed by restitution of God's Life Order.
8. *ARYAN NATIONS* is "CHRISTIANITY" in that by and through our Race, The Creator's Supreme, Sovereign Word became flesh, for the healing of the Nations.

Christian Defense League

The Christian Defense League is closely associated with Aryan Nations and can be virtually considered an affiliated organization. Richard Girnt Butler was its first National Director.

WHY WHAT WHO WHERE WHEN
Rev. James K. Warner

WHY

THE CHRISTIAN DEFENSE LEAGUE was formed in 1964 to assure for all time that we, the Christian majority of Americans, retain control of our own destiny—and of the destiny of the nation we founded.

We are closer each day to outright dictatorship by organized Jewry. Most of our major cities and our federal government are already under their yoke: A White Christian is not allowed to defend himself or speak for his Race. Our institutions—family, schools, churches, our government itself—have been first silently subverted and now are openly assaulted by organized Jewry which insists on its own special "rights" at the expense of time tested and blood hallowed traditions—even at the expense of common sense itself. Both major political parties, groveling at the altar of expediency and the prospect of Jewish votes and campaign financing, outbid each other in catering to the never ending demands of these hypernated *[sic]* "Americans."

The White Christian majority lies shattered divided into dozens of oppos-

From Rev. James K. Warner, "Why What Who Where When" (Baton Rouge, La.: Christian Defense League, [mid-1970s], pamphlet).

ing and neutralizing factions: Democrats vs. Republicans, North vs. South, Catholic vs. Protestant, rich vs. poor, farmer vs. city dweller, labor vs. capital. We are taught to despise our Race and true Christian IDENTITY— the only forces strong enough to forge us together.

Meanwhile, the power mad Jew, using minority groups organized around race, and riding the crest of cowardly concessions by compromising and weak-willed politicians, show clearly that they will not hesitate to trample and spit on every principle of our Constitution and of our White Christian society to perpetuate and extend their own selfish and destructive gains. Private property, the rights of states, freedom of association—the most precious jewels in the treasure-house of our national and racial heritage are tossed overboard like so much garbage before the raging flood of civil rights.

If we allow this mania to continue, we are only one fateful step from total tyranny and from the death of America as we know it.

THE JEWISH CONTROL OF AMERICA MUST BE STOPPED AND NOW!

America must re-identify herself with the Race which conceived her. The cause of our Race and our nation must overcome petty differences. The farmer from Iowa must unite with the businessman from New York, the miner from West Virginia with the folks from New Hampshire, the worker from Ohio with the World War II vet from California. Our forefathers left us a brave heritage: We have greater freedom better health, more material comforts, and greater opportunity for spiritual and intellectual expression than at any time in history. But the shadow of turmoil and race war darkens the future. Threatened from outside our borders by the terroristic colossus of Marxism—already astride half the globe, the marshaling the world's colored masses behind it—and from within by militant Jewish Zionism. America (civilization itself) is on the edge of extinction. Only with Zionist Jews dominating the American political scene, and the injection of racial minorities into the nation's bloodstream, was there even a possibility of being a "second-rate power" or "behind Russia." Our pluralistic society is bursting at the seams.

We can survive only if we unite beneath a common banner—but there can be no common cause where there is no common heritage, where there are no common values, no common blood—RACE is our key to unity, our touchstone—the dreaded enemy of our foe. We must rally to the banner of White Christianity!

IF YOU ARE A WHITE CHRISTIAN, THEN YOU BELONG IN THE CHRISTIAN DEFENSE LEAGUE!!

WHAT

THE CHRISTIAN DEFENSE LEAGUE is the voice of true Christianity in America. We shall speak most strongly against the Jewish attack on our churches and their attack against the Christian principles upon which this country was founded.

THE CHRISTIAN DEFENSE LEAGUE is non-denominational and both Catholics and Protestants hold leadership positions. The **CDL** is nonpartisan, but we feel it is our Christian DUTY to advocate the election of Christians to all political offices in America, and we consider it our Christian DUTY to fight against the election of any individual who practices a religion which is anti-Christian or uses the Babylonian Talmud as its "moral" and "spiritual" guide. The ultimate aim must be to organize the White Christian majority and to forge them into a force or movement that can sweep the anti-Christ from our churches and those that support the anti-Christ Jews from any political positions they may hold.

We believe that only a new, fresh wholesome CHRISTIAN MOVEMENT crystallized around the pure idealism of TRUE CHRISTIANITY and RACE as well as PATRIOTISM—one that springs from the grass roots of fundamental Christianity—can hope to win the fight ahead.

To achieve our aims will not be an easy task. We have arrayed ourselves against the power of Satan himself as embodied in the anti-Christ Jews living in our midst!

We will take our message to the White Christian majority in America. We will be more tireless than any missionary, more fanatic than any labor organizer, more impassioned than any socialist "do-gooder", more deadly determined than any communist agitator. We will go not only into the streets, but into factories and mines as well—into the dirt wherever White Christians toil, and into the shops wherever White Christians sweat. Where the enemy opens fire, there we will be: In the white neighborhoods living in the dread of the black deluge, in schools where White girls must study in the shadow of rape, on construction jobs where a White carpenter is fired so the boss can meet his "racial quota".

Our purpose is to right these wrongs. We will be the voice of the White Christian majority.

OTHER RECENT GROUPS

American Mobilizers

One of the more unusual groups is the American Mobilizers, which combines classic far-right positions with a rejection of materialism (usually but not always associated with the left), a strong environmental position, and an argument for an Indian state. Like a number of other far right groups (and the Articles of Confederation) this groups believes that, given a chance, Canada would leap at the chance of amalgamating with the United States, which suggests a lack of contact with Canadians.

PRINCIPLES FOR A NEW AMERICA

INTRODUCTION

The American Mobilizers believe in the application of forceful tactics in battling the enemies of White America. We believe we must organize the White people into one unified movement. To do this, we must recruit the young and the old, speak to the workers and prepare ourselves for the coming struggle. We believe that White America <u>must</u> survive, and that we must be prepared to <u>use any means whatsoever</u>—to combat the traitors and anarchists.

We do not believe that any of the politicians or major political parties can save America. We believe we must eventually find a political party which is new and clean and embodies the White Man's spirit of <u>Death before Dishonor</u>! Until such a party arises, we feel it is the duty of the American

From "Principles for a New America" (Mount Vernon, N.Y.: American Mobilizers, [1970s], pamphlet).

Mobilizers to win over and organize the people and prepare for the future awakening.

We do not believe that any of the "conservative" leaders or groups can succeed. For years conservatives have wasted time and money on safe, "responsible", and utterly useless projects, none of which have ever benefited the White people. These professional "patriots" speak loudly about the situation, but are the first to denounce men that FIGHT FOR AMERICA WITH THEIR FISTS instead of their mouths. We say it is time to face the brutal fact that America is too far gone to be rescued by safe, easy methods! Only an aggressive new political creed can lead America to victory, not the weak and thread-bare echoes of the past. We therefore turn our backs on the worn-out, cowardly and useless "conservatives", and aim for a vigorous FIGHTING movement.

1 A WHITE AMERICA

in which our people are the sole masters of their destiny.
WE MUST HAVE AN ALL-WHITE AMERICA; an America in which White children will play and go to school with other White children. An America in which they can grow up in an environment free from the destructive influence of Blacks. We must have an America in which our cultural, social, political and business life is free from African jungle life-style influences.

2 A NEW SOCIAL ORDER

where a man's worth is not judged by materialistic values.
WE MUST BUILD A NEW SOCIETY based on Racial-community values, rather than the corrupt materialism of the American "consumer society". We believe that a man's worth depends first of all upon the extent to which he applies his natural abilities to the service of his people—be it as a worker, administrator, artisan soldier, etc.—and NOT merely in the amount he has accumulated in the bank. We believe it is to the advantage of society to see that every productive individual has the freedom and opportunity to achieve his maximum potentials, by preserving his health, protecting him from ruin-

ous catastrophes, educating him in the areas of his abilities, and guarding him from political and economic exploitation.

3 AN HONEST ECONOMY

We must put an end to economic freeloading and exploitation.
THERE MUST BE NO PLACE FOR PARASITES who draw their sustenance from society without giving anything in return. Those who thrive on usury, speculation, manipulation and monopoly form a special class today whose primary interest is to maintain the system that allows their form of parasite to flourish in the first place. We must have an economy based on the long-term needs of our Race and geared to the interests of the working people—not the chronic loafer or the vermin that live by renting their capital. It is necessary for us to establish an economy that will function properly—without the armies of professional witch-doctors known as "economists"—so that working men will be protected from inflation and depressions. To do this, we must abolish the "Gold Standard" which is the basis of the Federal Reserve System, and instead base our currency on a National Production Standard, which will reflect the actual productive worth of our Nation.

4 GOVERNMENT BY LEADERS

not political hacks and incompetents.
WE MUST HAVE A GOVERNMENT OF RESPONSIBLE LEADERS— not demagogues and opportunists. If we are to survive as a Nation, we must put an end to the catastrophic system of irresponsible government, incompetent leadership, and self-serving party politics which rules today—a system in which none but the rich, the hypocritical, and unscrupulous may rise to the top. Instead we must have a strong National government that selects for every level of authority the best and wisest men America has to offer. We must establish a system that guarantees swift and ruthless punishment for any member of government, high or low, who does not carry out their oath of office, does not function efficiently, is incompetent, or in any way does not serve the best interests of the Nation.

5 SOLUTION OF THE BLACK QUESTION

that has caused so much strife and will yet tear America asunder.

AMERICA'S BLACKS MUST SEEK THEIR FUTURE IN AFRICA from whence they were brought by greedy and unscrupulous men. We must establish a program of repatriation to the existing Black Nations of Africa of America's teeming millions of Black people. The gulf between White people and Blacks is so vast that there can never be peace on the North American continent so long as our two Races are forced to live together. All the democratic schemes to "integrate" the Races failed. The end results of years of equality propaganda by the Establishment has been the realization by Blacks that they cannot compete successfully with Whites—in spite of massive governmental aid, lowered standards and special privileges. We must realize that the Black and White Races have nothing in common, and that the continued existence of the Black in America can only lead to Race-mixture or Race-war. We believe that our Race has the right to it's own identity and life-style and that the Black in America is a serious threat to our future. THEREFORE, WE DEMAND that all Black people be removed from the North American continent, and established in the various Black Nations of Africa. WE DEMAND the formation of a Back to Africa movement to be organized by sincere and responsible Blacks which will work in conjunction with the New American government to organize a swift and efficient repatriation. We pledge to aid in this undertaking by granting generous financial incentives to every Black family and individual, and to defray all re-establishment costs.

6 A STRONG FOREIGN POLICY

based exclusively on the best interests of the White Race.

AMERICA MUST NEVER AGAIN FIGHT ANOTHER WHITE NATION as we did twice before in this century at the behest of alien and parasitical minorities. Our foreign policy must reflect the good-will of the American people to her White Racial brothers in Europe, Africa, Australia and elsewhere. We must make alliances only with Nations that have proven their genuine friendship to America. ABOVE ALL we must never again become involved in no-win wars such as Korea and Vietnam. We must extend the hand of friendship to Nations of other Races ONLY if they are willing to defend their own lands, and not expect Americans to do the fighting. We must aid any and all people in revolutions to over throw communist, liberal, democratic and Zionist regimes in their countries such as the Cuban commandoes, Nationalist China, etc.

7 A HEALTHY ENVIRONMENT

We must protect at all costs our natural resources and eliminate the pollution of our environment.
WE MUST MAKE IT AN IMPERATIVE DUTY of the government to protect the gifts which nature has bestowed on America, and to insure the maintenance of a clean, wholesome and healthy environment for our people. Our government must be given absolute power to deal with the pollution problem. We must have programs instituted in which the massive amounts of refuse can be collected and reclaimed, such as waste metal, paper, cloth, even wood and plastics. This reclamation must be organized by the government and made compulsory throughout North America. These programs could be put into effect today, were it not for the weakness and collusion of the present regime with big business who claim that reclamation is "not profitable". We must gradually bring about a whole new mode of living in America—a mode with less emphasis on new cars, easy open packages, and throw-away bottles, etc. We must eventually reorganize the aimless, profit oriented, "American way-of-life"—a way of life which has attempted to force man into a mold determined by the necessities of a congested, neon and asphalt big-city rat-race. Instead we must remake that "mold" to accommodate the health and well-being of the White Race.

8 A REBIRTH OF WHITE CULTURE

We must encourage the rebirth of genuine cultural activities and advancement among our people.
WE MUST DESTROY THE DEGENERACY being peddled as "art" "music" and "literature". We must never again let the ethical syphilis of Hollywood or the moral leprosy of New York grow and master the lives of our people. We must instill in our youth the appreciation for beauty and order

that characterize a genuine White Man's culture. We must awaken a new understanding of our Racial and Cultural heritage so that the creative instincts can once again find expression in a direction that will continually renew and enrich that heritage instead of degrading and debasing it. We must make ourselves worthy of the heritage we have been blessed with—the legacy of Golden Age Greece, Rome, Europe—by guaranteeing to future generations a Nation in which they can accomplish even greater things. It is our task to provide a world of order, health, and beauty—a world in which life once again has meaning—that will encourage those future generations to search for the Destiny of our Race among the mighty and boundless frontiers of the stars!

9 A NORTH AMERICAN REPUBLIC

We believe that the similarities of the American and Canadian people dictate the necessity of an integrated Nation.
AMERICA AND CANADA MUST BECOME ONE CULTURAL AND POLITICAL UNIT. We must encourage the people of Canada to join America as one Political, Cultural and Racial State, with one common heritage and future. It is ridiculous to perpetuate the existence of an imaginary boundary between two "nations" that share as many things in common as do America and Canada. For Western Man to survive, all petty nationalism and regionalism must be abolished. We believe that the Union of America and Canada will encourage similar steps to be taken by our Racial brothers in Europe and elsewhere, and that the future will witness the foundations of a world-wide Western Imperium.

10 FORMATION OF A FREE "INDIAN" STATE

in which the Native American Indian can pursue his Racial and cultural life without interference.
THE AMERICAN INDIAN MUST BE ALLOWED TO FULFILL HIS DESTINY in a home fitting for the well being of his people. Of all the "minorities" in America, only the Indian has suffered genuine injustices. A proud people, the Indian has become the forgotten group in the land of his forefathers. The lying politicians and exploiting businessmen who have so

foully mistreated the White working people are responsible too, for the deceitful and disgusting treatment of the Red Man. Treaty after treaty were broken, until the White Man's word became worthless, all because of the greed of treacherous, raceless "businessmen". We recognize the fact that the Indian wishes to be able to live in the way he chooses and to have his children raised in an environment compatible to their best interests. THERE-FORE WE PROPOSE the establishment of a totally independent American Indian Nation on the North American continent, including a wide diversity of lands — mountains, forests, flatlands, seacoasts, etc. — in which the Red Man can organize his society according to National and Tribal wishes and Racial instinct. We propose the foundation of such a State to be organized as a joint project between the New American government and a representative council of American Indians. We further propose a program of generous financial and technical aid to establish industry and commerce in the new Nation at the expense of the American government, and pledge future aid if ever our continental neighbor needs such.

National Association for the Advancement of White People

Given the success of the National Association for the Advancement of Col-ored People, it is no surprise that a parallel organization was established. It has not met with similar success.

NAAWP

WHY WE NEED IT

The **NAAWP** is the National Association for the Advancement of White People. It maintains that there should be equal rights and opportunities for all **including whites**! It believes that white people need to defend and preserve their civil rights, heritage, and basic interests, just as blacks and other non-whites do.

White people now face the most extensive racial discrimination in Ameri-can history. It is true that some blacks faced discrimination in the past, but

From "NAAWP" (New Orleans: National Association for the Advancement of White People, 1980, flyer).

the discrimination was limited as it was primarily practiced in the private sector. Today, the federal government is **forcing** an across-the-board racial discrimination in employment, promotions, scholarships and in college and union admittance. This racial bias is pervading all sectors of our national life, including civil service, military, eduction, and business.

The U.S. Department of Labor boasts that over 175,000 major corporations have programs favoring blacks over whites in employment and promotions. "Affirmative action" is a euphemism for nothing more than **blatant racial discrimination.** And no one should harbor the illusion that it simply favors equally qualified blacks, for it consistently favors less qualified blacks over better qualified whites. Good examples of this practice are the Bakke and Weber Supreme Court decisions that sanctioned racial quotas. Bakke, who scored in the 90's on his tests for medical school, was denied entrance in deference to blacks who scored in the 30's. This kind of discrimination is driving down productivity and diminishing the quality of life.

Black pressure groups have not limited their attention to so-called affirmative action. They have brought about busing and forced integration, a program which is heightening racial tensions and drastically harming educational quality. They have forced higher taxes on productive Americans in order to finance exorbitant and wasteful welfare programs. They have practically handcuffed police and the courts, preventing them from dealing firmly with violent criminals (most of whom are black). They have opened the floodgates of unrestricted immigration which is increasing unemployment, and adding to already high welfare costs and crime.

Groups like the NAACP have litigated and lobbied untiringly on issues they perceive as important to blacks. On the other hand, there has been no organization that forthrightly worked to defend the civil rights of whites. Our people must come to the realization that unless we also organize to defend our heritage, and even our very right to exist as a people, we will lose everything we care about.

Much more is at stake than even our rights; indeed, the continuation of our way of life is in question. Last year, by the lowest estimates, 2 million aliens entered America. Over 90% were non-white! Blacks and browns, a majority of whom are on welfare, have birthrates 2 to 3 times higher than white people.

If immigration and welfare financed birthrates continue, America will soon become outnumbered and totally vulnerable to the political control of blacks and other non-whites. The same kind of population change is also going on in Canada and Europe. There are 24 all-black countries, but there are no all white nations except Iceland, and Iceland is not enough! There is no threat to the continued existence of the black race, but there is a real threat to the white.

If breeds of life like the blue whale, the rocky mountain cougar, or even the tiny breed of fish called the snail darter are worth preserving, shouldn't a beautiful and creative people such as the white race also be worthy of our concern?

There is no doubt that our people have lost and continue to lose many of their civil rights every day, that our people are often victims of violent racist assaults, that our culture and history are being twisted and denigrated by the mass media, that hard working, productive Americans are being financially stripped by high taxes for wasteful welfare programs and that our nation is being swamped by immigration. Each of these conditions should make it abundantly clear why we need the **NAAWP . . . to change them!**

The **NAAWP** is absolutely necessary if the rights of our people are to be defended, if our heritage is to be preserved, and if our magnificent potentialities are to be realized.

NAAWP PRINCIPLES

EQUAL RIGHTS FOR WHITES

We demand an immediate end to racial discrimination and quotas against white people in employment, promotions, scholarships, and in union and college admittance. We want American government, military, education and business to make **excellence** the sole criterion for advancement.

AN END TO FORCED BUSING

We want an end to busing and forced integration. We believe that forcing the races together has resulted in a marked decline in educational quality and increased racial tension and violence. Additionally, busing constitutes a tremendous waste of tax money and precious energy resources.

TOTAL WELFARE REFORM

We believe that the present welfare system is taking advantage of productive and hard-working Americans and that instead of alleviating poverty, it is only increasing it. We see two fundamental solutions to the growing welfare problem:

1) **Workfare instead of welfare.** Under this program, able bodied welfare recipients would have to perform work for the community in order to receive their welfare benefits.

2) **Welfare family planning.** A vigorous promotion of family planning must be instituted for welfare recipients in which they would be given financial incentives to have smaller families. Such a program would be humanitarian by bringing fewer children into intolerable conditions, and it would allow more money to be applied to training and guidance programs for the poor. Thus, such a program would be beneficial to the indigent, while progressively reducing the number of poor each generation, and thus lessening the tax burden shouldered by productive Americans.

CRACKDOWN ON VIOLENT CRIME

We want swift and sure punishment of violent criminals and an end to special consideration for rioters and other violent criminals who are black. We believe that local police should be given more community support in their defense of the potential victim.

NO MORE IMMIGRATION

We believe that America, Canada, and Europe already have the maximum population for the maintenance of good economic health. Legal and illegal aliens are increasing unemployment among citizens, adding to already overburdened welfare rolls, and contributing to violent crime. The time has come to demand enforcement of our laws concerning illegal immigration and to severely limit legal immigration.

AN END TO RACE HATRED IN THE MEDIA

We want an end to the chronic portrayal of white people as exploiters and oppressors of blacks and other minorities. Such portrayals instill guilt in white children and hatred in young blacks that often manifests itself in violent crime against white people.

PRESERVATION OF THE WHITE RACE AND ITS HERITAGE

We believe that all peoples on this planet must have the right to life, that is, the right to exist and preserve their cultural integrity. We do not object to black groups having black beauty contests, black radio stations, black colleges, or black scholarships. Nor do we object to blacks teaching their young about black heritage and instilling black pride in them, but we do demand the same rights for our own people, for we deeply love the beauty, culture, and heritage of the white race, and want to preserve them.

EXCELLENCE IN ALL THINGS

We believe in a society where the young are educated to the best of their ability, a society in which the best qualified, hardest working, and most talented are rewarded commensurate with their contribution to the nation. We believe in equal justice under the law, equal opportunity, and equal rights as the fairest means of determining the best in any field. True equality in opportunity will enable the men and women of quality to step forward and serve the ideal of a high humanity.

National States' Rights Party

As seen earlier, the promotion of states' rights has been used for a variety of purposes, but in the last half of the twentieth century, it has primarily been a slogan of the right. In the platform reproduced below, the first concern of the party is race.

PLATFORM
OF THE
NATIONAL STATES' RIGHTS PARTY

RACIAL POLICY

1. We believe in the creation of a wholesome White Folk Community, with a deep spiritual consciousness of a common past and a determination to share a common future.

From "Platform of the National States' Rights Party" (n.p.: National States' Rights Party, [1980], flyer).

2. We favor complete separation of all non-Whites and dissatisfied racial minorities from our White Folk Community.
3. We demand that intermarriage between Whites and non-Whites be outlawed, in all states not already having such restrictions.
4. We demand that total segregation be maintained in the nation's schools, and that only members of the White Folk Community be allowed to engage in the educational and cultural activities of our White society.
5. We believe that segregation should be restored in the nation's armed forces, to rebuild morale and fighting efficiency.
6. We believe it better that only members of our White Folk Community be allowed to take part in the affairs of government or serve in the courts.
7. We demand a policy of non-interference in the cultural affairs of other races.
8. We favor creation of a National Repatriation Commission, to encourage the voluntary resettlement of Negroes in their African homeland, with fullest financial and economic assistance toward that end.
9. We approve the removal of all alien minorities, dissatisfied with our American way of life and the republic for which we stand.
10. We favor the preservation of Indian national life in America, and the unlimited development of reservation facilities.
11. We believe that immigration should be restricted to select White individuals.
12. We demand the impeachment or removal from office otherwise of any public official who advocates race-mixing or mongrelization.

ECONOMIC POLICY

1. We believe that the workers, farmers, businessmen and professional people of our nation should work together as a team, placing the greater good of our White Folk Community above any individual or group interest.
2. We approve of labor unions, run by honest White men and free of subversive influence.
3. We believe that the farmer should get a fair price for his product in a free market.
4. We believe that the government should refrain from competing with private enterprise, and from interfering in the hiring policies of private business.

5. We demand that Congress alone exercise its constitutional right to issue debt and interest-free currency, based on the production of goods and rendition of services in America.
6. We favor protection of the White American producer by limiting foreign trade to the direct exchange of surplus products.
7. We believe that the purchasing power of the consumer should be raised proportionately as science increases the power to produce.
8. We demand that the confiscatory taxation policies of the federal government be ended immediately.

SOCIAL POLICY

1. We favor combined civic effort in every individual state to eliminate slum, flood and dust-bowl conditions.
2. We favor creation of proper outlets for the White youth of our nation to encourage the development of mind and muscle, and provide for instruction in the highest racial ideals.
3. We demand the complete reorganization of our educational system, so that every individual White citizen is afforded full opportunity to realize his vocational ambitions.
4. We demand the elimination of all ideology and influences from the movies, television, radio, newspaper and all other phases of our national life, which tend to cause the degeneration and disintegration of our White Folk Community.
5. We demand the creation of a clean and honest White government, which will provide the basis for a sound economy, with full employment and improved living conditions for White citizens of every age.

STATES' RIGHTS POLICY

1. We demand that the federal government cease interfering with the sovereign rights of the states, as guaranteed by the Constitution.
2. We demand that the federal government stop issuing judicial decrees which violate state sovereignty.

3. We demand that the federal government stop fostering thought-control, and refrain from violating the traditional social customs of the individual states.
4. We demand the removal of all federal control over the national guard units and law enforcement agencies of the states.
5. We demand that all states exercise their authority to stop the secret-police tactics employed against them by the federal government.
6. We demand that the states uphold their right to investigate, prosecute and obtain conviction of subversives within their borders.

FOREIGN POLICY

1. We approve the strengthening of cultural and moral ties among all White nations, in view of the world-wide survival crisis which the White Man faces.
2. We demand that White Christian boys never again be sent to fight and die on foreign soil to appease the interests of an alien minority.
3. We demand that all financial and moral support to the State of Israel cease, as a basis for the rebuilding of Arab-American friendship.
4. We demand an end to the policy of foreign give-aways.
5. We oppose any international entanglement whereby this Republic would tend to lose its sovereignty and freedom.

WHITE MEN UNITE!

William L. Pierce

One of the most important figues on the racist right today is William L. Pierce, the author of The Turner Diaries *(1978, under the pseudonym Andrew Macdonald), considered by many to be the American equivalent of Adolf Hitler's* Mein Kampf, *in that it outlines a future strategy for America's racist right. Pierce publishes the influential* National Vanguard *and is one of racist America's most outspoken advocates.*

A PROGRAM FOR SURVIVAL

There are two things fundamental to every society: the quality of its human stock—that is, the vitality, intelligence, creativity, courage, and will of its people—and the values which guide it.

One may be tempted to reduce these two fundamentals to a single determinant—namely, to the racial character of the society's people—since the most basic values are innate. That reduction, however, ignores the all-too-evident fact that the values which guide a society may not be the innate values of the race which founded it.

Innate values express themselves subtly—and, in most cases, unconsciously. A homogeneous population permitted to develop in isolation over a long period of time will usually have a society which reflects faithfully the people's innate values, whether they consciously recognize them as such or not. But when a society, without being conscious of its own value, is subjected almost constantly to extraneous influences, it will often be the case that some of its guiding values become extraneous. And, of course, when the population base of a society loses its homogeneity, then the very concept of innate values becomes ill-defined for that society.

Only when a homogeneous people, living in accord with its innate values, has become conscious of those values and translated them from feeling to knowledge does it gain a degree of immunity from extraneous influences, because only then can it surely distinguish what is extraneous from what is its own and reject the former while continuing to shape its society and guide its development in accord with the latter.

I had come to understand this by 1974, the year in which the National Alliance was founded. This understanding gave me the basis for the program of the new organization with a strategy quite different from any of the right-wing strategies I had evaluated and rejected in the preceding decade.

It was—and is—an organization for racial survival and progress. Its strategy rests on several assumptions about the course of national and world events over the next couple of decades:

* There will be no sudden collapse of U.S. governmental authority, due

The foregoing selection was excerpted from the August 1984 issue of *National Vanguard*, a magazine published by the National Alliance, Post Office Box 90, Hillsboro, West Virginia, 24946.

either to an economic catastrophe or to military action by a foreign government.

* There will be a continuation of the present trend toward more governmental cynicism, corruption, and inefficiency. As the present generation of senior, White civil servants retires and "affirmative action" brings more non-Whites into the bureaucracy, along with a more permissively raised and less-responsible generation of Whites, there will be more waste, bungling, and minor breakdowns, until the level of governmental efficiency and integrity approaches that in El Salvador.

* At the same time the government will grow more repressive, with eventual bans on private firearms and any exercise of free speech deemed threatening to the established order.

* Despite their growing unpopularity in some segments of society, the Jews will retain their control of the mass media, the affections of most of organized Christianity, and their influence over the political process. As by far the best organized, most purposeful, and most intelligent pressure group, they will become even more powerful and dangerous as the standards and institutions of the host society continue to decay, and as the growing power of other non-White minorities provides more leverage to use against the dwindling White majority.

* Although technocratic and bureaucratic elites—scientists and engineers; lawyers, public office-holders, and top corporate administrators—along with the wealthier members of the entrepreneurial class, will have enough money and mobility to insulate themselves, more or less, from worsening social conditions, and although increases in the productivity of some sectors of the economy as a result of further advances and applications of the microelectronics revolution will continue to provide a high material standard of living for many others, life for most White Americans will become increasingly ignoble, unnatural, and restricted. In addition, White workers in many occupational sectors will find their material living standard declining along with other standards.

* There will be reactions among the White population to the continued decay of their society and the worsening of their living conditions—minor (or even major) taxpayer revolts, organized protests and demonstrations by farmers or other occupational groups, occasional assassinations of leading politicians, and the popping up of all sorts of fads, cults, and new ideological movements either implicitly or explicitly hostile to the policies of the authorities—but the media, the churches, and the government, working in tandem,

will be able to keep most of the population obedient most of the time, so long as there is not a catastrophic collapse of the economy.

   * Most White Americans will continue to drift morally in the same direction they have been moving since the Second World War, toward a greater acceptance of miscegenation, the presence of more non-Whites in their midst, and such evils as drug abuse and homosexuality. Their standards for both public and private behavior will continue to decline. Even racially conscious White parents will have little success, on the average, in preventing their children from being swept along with this tide.

   If the above assumptions are sound, and if no unforeseen developments arise to cause a radical change in the course of events, then sometime in the next century America will pass the point of no return; at least, it will be too late for any further holding back of the flood by way of the democratic electoral process, even if a strong White leader capable of arousing racial consciousness in the breasts of White voters should appear. The White majority will become a White minority, thoroughly Judaized morally, and this remnant will miscegenate ever more rapidly with the non-White majority, until there is nothing left capable of saving itself—or worth being saved.

   Unforeseen developments always arise, of course. History is full of surprises, and there can be no doubt that the future will be too. It is only prudent to expect the unexpected and to maintain readiness to take advantage of it, whatever it may be. But a people in imminent danger of extinction had better rely on something besides an act of Providence to pull itself back from the brink. It had better have a program.

   After this lengthy and highly personal introduction, the program of the National Alliance can be stated succinctly. It consists of the following steps, or phases: first, cadre-building; second, community-building; and third, community action. Although these phases must be initiated in the indicated sequence, they will overlap; that is, the activities associated with earlier phases will continue even as new phases begin.

   Cadre-building is the task of attracting the strongest, ablest, and spiritually soundest individuals who can be found and functionally integrating them into a structured organization. The principal function of the organization, prior to the initiation of the third phase, is the generation of propaganda for the purpose of attracting more members to the cadre.

   Such propaganda is different from that intended to change public opinion or public behavior. Both types of propaganda consist of facts and ideas which can move and inspire people as well as enlighten them. But cadre-building propaganda is addressed to an elite, while third-phase propaganda is addressed to the general (White) public. The former is designed to attract, the latter to persuade or agitate.

Most important, whereas third-phase propaganda typically concerns itself with people's everyday personal concerns—with their fears for their physical safety or their economic security, with their resentment against those who offend their sense of propriety or fairness, with their hopes for relief from an oppressive or threatening situation—first-phase propaganda must appeal much more strongly at a spiritual level.

Propaganda addressed to the average man may say: "Vote (or go on strike, or whatever) for us, and in return we'll give you something that you want." But to the potential cadre member it must say instead: "Your conscience will not rest unless you accept your responsibility as a White man or woman and do what you know must be done, even if it means giving up everything, including your life."

Finally, whereas first-phase propaganda can be conducted effectively even on a small scale, third-phase propaganda is practically useless unless it can be conducted on a massive scale and can be sustained for a relatively long period of time.

Actually, the preceding paragraphs somewhat oversimplify the distinction between first-phase and third-phase propaganda. Even during the first phase, it is essential that propaganda involve many persons who are not suitable cadre material. If books, magazines, and other printed materials are to be published and distributed on a large enough scale to be economically feasible, for example, they must be purchased by others than potential cadre members. In addition, it is useful to place cadre-recruiting material into as many hands as possible; even those who will not themselves be recruited by it often pass on its message to those who will.

The first phase of the National Alliance program is not markedly different from the programs of other organizations. Every movement which aims at changing the world must first recruit a cadre of true believers before it can hope to move the masses effectively. But in its second phase the program of the National Alliance departs from the others. That phase, community-building, is dictated by the unique nature of the National Alliance task and by the conditions under which it must be performed. The task is to ensure that, even as the society around us remains on its course toward a degraded, mulatto future, the physical and spiritual basis for a rebirth of civilization will be preserved and nurtured. That is, a reservoir of the best human material, consciously guided by its innate values, must be available when conditions are such that it can serve as the seed for a new flowering of the race—and as the agent for preparing the soil for that flowering.

Human material, in the form of frozen sperm and eggs (or even frozen embryos) can be hidden away and preserved under refrigeration for centuries if necessary. But unless both the motivation and the means to thaw and utilize that material is also preserved, the exercise is pointless. Only a community of living men and women conscious of their identity and their purpose, can serve the latter need.

The second phase of the program, then, is the building of a community which is sufficiently well isolated from the larger society that it is able to live in accord with its own values and to maintain those values over the course of several generations, and which is structured in a way suitable to its role as both the bearer of the seed of a rebirth and as the agent to prepare the soil for it.

Other communities—Shakers, Jehovah's Witnesses, and Amish are examples—have been formed deliberately to preserve values over the course of generations, with different degrees of isolation and of success. The most successful example of such an endeavor is provided by the Jews, who have managed to preserve values, purpose, and, to a lesser extent, a particular human type over a remarkably long period of time.

Undoubtedly, there are lessons to be learned from the experience of all such communities. But the task of the National Alliance is unique, as are the conditions under which its community is taking form and under which that community must survive. At least to the degree of any past community ours must keep its values intact; and much more than any other it must maintain—and, to the extent possible, improve—its genetic basis.

To achieve these things it is not necessary to isolate the entire community on a remote island, although a degree of physical isolation for at least the core of the community is almost indispensable. What is necessary for the entire community is a very high degree of spiritual and social isolation. It must be a community which wholly rejects the values and the forms of the larger society, while holding faithfully to its own. It can do this only through the most rigorous possible education and discipline, based in a purpose-oriented social structure whose institutions are tailored specifically to the desired end.

Merely maintaining a good home—individual members teaching their children to be racially conscious and providing them with moral training—is insufficient; peer influence is nearly always stronger than parental influence. When there is a bad environment outside the home, it is often the preacher's son who is arrested for drunken driving first.

The community must provide a total moral environment for its members— an environment which builds character in the young, tests character in the mature, and keeps everyone conscious of and committed to its values and goals. Children must be raised, virtually from the cradle, with the sole aim of fitting them to their purpose. When an adult member goes forth into the larger society, whether on business matters or for the sake of continued recruiting for the community, the training he has received in his youth must serve him as an untarnishable coat of moral armor, so that the corruption and decay all around him leave him unchanged.

Most important of all is the moral quality of the community's leaders. It is inconceivable that they should be selected on the basis of their promises to the venal and the credulous or their ability to charm the gullible, as in the larger society. Instead, they must be trained, tested, and selected in a continuing, lifelong process, just as the other members of the community are for their various roles. This implies a structure which is hierarchical and meritocratic, both for the community as a whole and for its leadership cadre.

Building such a community is vastly more difficult than organizing an election campaign for the next George Wallace or Barry Goldwater who offers himself as God's gift to distraught conservatives—which may explain why the latter is tried so much more frequently than the former. But it is the former which is necessary—not only to preserve values and genes, but to act when the time comes to act.

The time for the third phase of the National Alliance program—outward-directed community action—will be determined as much by the ripeness of conditions in the larger society as by the size and strength of the community. And the action more likely will be a gradual encroachment in those domains where the enemy is weakest than a sudden, frontal assault on his citadel.

An example of such community action is the use of community resources to acquire mass media—local radio or television stations, daily newspapers—and, if necessary, operate them at a loss in order to be able to exercise the political and ideological influence inherent in them.

Another example is the expansion of territorial sovereignty: the acquisition of a new territory within which members of the community exercise the dominant political, economic, and moral power and are able to prevent others from taking it away from them. This may involve continued recruiting, and a combination of colonization and natural increase.

A third example is the infiltration of members into the power structure of the larger society—into the military command structure, key governmental investigative or law enforcement agencies, and communications networks— where they will be able to compensate, to some degree, for the numerical superiority of hostile elements.

All of these actions have been used by other communities to advance their ends. Whether or not they also can be used successfully by us will depend upon how well we build our own community. What is certain is that without a well-trained, well-disciplined, thoroughly conscious, and utterly determined community made up of the best men and women available we will not be able to sustain any program for more than a few years. And no program which depends upon bringing about a radical, long-lasting change in America's or the West's racial, political, and spiritual environment in only a few years can succeed.

The war in the Persian Gulf caused considerable difficulty for some on the right. The protection of Israel was unacceptable to anti-Semites, but the nationalist fervor aroused by the war was music to their ears. The following essay by Pierce reflects this confusion and is particularly interesting in that, except for the strident racism, many on the left would clearly agree with parts of the analysis.

THE LESSON OF DESERT STORM

Most of the yellow ribbons are down now, a year after the great victory. Perhaps passions have cooled enough for us to think objectively about America's latest "good war." Perhaps it is even possible to say a few things aloud without having some good ol' boy snarl "commie bastard!" at us and mutter darkly about what should be done with people who don't "support our troops."

First, I'll not waste any time with an explanation of why the blasting of

The following selection was excerpted from the January–February 1992 issue of *National Vanguard*, a magazine published by the National Alliance, Post Office Box 90, Hillsboro, West Virginia, 24946.

Iraq was a "good war" (that is, a war which serves the interests of the Jews). Everyone reading this should understand that already, and I've gone into the matter with my "Open Letter to George Bush" and a half dozen other flyers distributed to the public by National Alliance members during the past year.

The lesson I want to draw from the war now is about democracy. It is a lesson based on the way the American people reacted to the war.

My task is made easier by the fact that the public reaction was so overwhelmingly one-sided. Depending on which poll one goes by, something between 86 and 94 per cent of Americans approved of Mr. Bush's campaign to chase the Iraqis out of Kuwait and teach Saddam Hussein not to get uppity again. Even if one doesn't trust the pollsters, it was clear enough from the sheer tonnage of yellow ribbons adorning every power pole, lamppost, tree, fire hydrant, parking meter, gatepost, and porch pillar in the country that most of the citizenry approved wholeheartedly of our high-tech slaughter of the Iraqis. Bureaucrats from Washington weren't being sent around the country to tie those ribbons; the people themselves were doing it. I don't know how it was everywhere else, but out here in hillbilly country even slow-moving pedestrians were in danger of being beribboned by patriotic yahoos. Seldom have the rubes been so solidly in agreement on anything.

Interestingly enough, however, if one discusses the issue now with some of the folks whose premises were decorated with ribbons then, one notes an almost apologetic tone. Ask: "Say, Clem, I wonder when the Emir of Kuwait is going to start dishing out some of that freedom we went over there to give him?" The answer is likely to be, "Well-l-l, shucks. I dunno. Who cares?" Or: "Hey Billy Bob, do you reckon any of those American jobs we fought to save in the Gulf War will be coming our way soon?" Billy Bob will study his bootlaces for a minute, spit, and change the subject.

Now, to be fair to the Clems and Billy Bobs we should acknowledge that most of them weren't tying up yellow ribbons last year as an expression of bloodlust. With a few exceptions, they weren't saying, "Go George, go! Kill them towheads, Blast them Iraqis to smithereens!" Most of them were saying instead, "Hey, I'm an American. I'm patriotic. Our soldiers are risking their lives over in the Persian Gulf to protect the American way of life here, and I'm behind them 100 per cent." That's what TV told them to say, and they said it.

After a few false starts, the media masters hit on the right set of clichés and were able to evoke the conditioned reflexes they wanted from most Americans. The clichés that worked were the ones about being patriotic, about "supporting our troops," about not tolerating aggression, about restoring freedom and democracy, about protecting the "American way of life." The fact that all of these reasons for supporting the war were based on obvious lies didn't matter. Only a relatively small minority of the public was receptive to the arguments that there's nothing patriotic about fighting a war that's contrary to America's national interests, that the best way of supporting our troops would be to tell them the truth about the war and then bring them home without further shooting and bombing, that if we really wanted to punish aggression in the Middle East we should be aiming our bombs and missiles at Tel Aviv instead of Baghdad, that there never had been any freedom or democracy in Kuwait to restore, and that there was no conceivable way that Saddam Hussein, even if we simply left him alone to do his damnedest, could ever threaten the "American way of life."

Not only were most Americans not receptive to such arguments, but they'd become angry if one tried to reason with them. It was not uncommon to see otherwise intelligent people nodding soberly and agreeing with media assertions that "it's better to stop Saddam in Baghdad than to wait until we have to stop him in America."

What we saw a year ago was a herd being manipulated at a sub-rational level. Sub-rational manipulation of one sort or another is omnipresent in our society: for example, advertising people try very hard to find ways to push the correct sub-rational buttons which will lead consumers to buy their products. Politicians and preachers do the same sort of thing.

What made last year's manifestation of sub-rational herd behavior especially striking was the fact that the stakes were so much higher than in an advertising campaign designed to make us feel like unlovable slobs if we don't run out and buy the sponsor's brand of toothpaste. The stakes were not just the few hundred lives lost by American troops (after all, they're paid to accept risks, and more of them died in accidents than in combat anyway) or the few tens of billions of dollars of our taxes spent on the war by our government.

Supporting the war meant supporting a lie: a whole pack of lies, in fact. What's worse, they were transparent lies, which should have fooled no one. The idea of national honor has pretty well become a joke these days, but it certainly didn't do what might have been left of it any good to let ourselves be used once again to do Israel's butcher-work and then to pat ourselves on the back and swagger around as if we thought we were heroes for having done it. Our behavior showed more than a lack of honor; it also showed an appalling lack of national maturity and good sense.

And then there's the matter of the 150,000 or so Iraqi men, women, and children we slaughtered. Lest I seem hypocritical, I will confess now that, although my natural inclination is not to bother anyone who isn't bothering me, I have no really strong objection to killing Semites, whether they be Arabs or Jews; they're all a greasy lot, and the fewer of them in the world the better. I wouldn't mind seeing the whole Middle East nuked, were it not for the wildlife and the priceless antiquities which would be destroyed. That sentiment, however, is contrary to the one professed publicly by most of the supporters of the war, from Commander-in-Chief George Bush down to the Rotary Club types tying yellow ribbons on their front porches and the tatooed yahoos strutting about in Desert Storm T-shirts. They acted then and they act now as if America had sent its troops to the Persian Gulf for some sort of bloodless exercise in patriotism.

This total lack of concern for the tens of thousands of Iraqis we slaughtered is the most interesting aspect of the whole, shameful, bloody affair. Americans just aren't like that. They're basically a sentimental bunch. Remember what a degree of public revulsion the media were able to stir up two decades ago when they filled the front pages with those photographs of the 200 or so Vietnamese civilians our troops had massacred at My Lai? Remember all of the American tears that were shed over starving Ethiopian children just a couple of years ago when African famine was a regular TV news feature?

The Bush government, of course has been very careful not to talk about Iraqi casualties or to release photographs showing dead Iraqis. The news media have, for the most part, ignored the issue as well. And the public certainly isn't demanding the gory details; they're still feeling good about having restored democracy to Kuwait, or whatever, and they don't want to spoil the feeling. And yet we all know that if the controlled media did make an issue of it—if they started showing photographs of the corpses of Iraqi children incinerated by our bombs, of the arms and legs of dead Iraqi soldiers sticking out of the sand in those miles of collapsed Iraqi bunkers—and kept it up, night after night, with interviews with Iraqi survivors who had lost their families, Americans would begin having quite different thoughts about the war.

What it boils down to is that mass murder is real only when it can be seen on TV; it is real only when Dan Rather or Tom Brokaw or Peter Jennings says it is and asks us, with the proper tone of voice and facial expression, to be indignant about it. Every American knows that we slaughtered tens of thousands of Iraqis, but most don't let it bother them. This is as true of the bleeding hearts who weep buckets over starving children in Africa and would be horrified if our Coast Guard used those boats full of invading Haitians now headed toward our shores for gunnery practice as it is of most of the rest of the population.

The point is that it's not just a matter of the government or the media telling lies or suppressing information in order to fool the public. It's a matter of the public being manipulated just like a herd of sheep. Maybe Joe Sixpack really believed that baloney about restoring democracy to Kuwait, but no intelligent, knowledgeable American did. Yet most of them marched in a lockstep with Joe. If they felt sheepish about it, they kept it a secret. They let not only their opinions be manipulated, but their morality as well.

And what does all of this say about democracy as a system of government? Democracy, remember, is the system which is based on the assumption that most citizens are able to decide what they want and make responsible choices; it is the system which pretends that if people are given the opportunity to go into a voting booth and pull a few levers every year or so they are in control of their government. Democracy is "rule by the majority." Democracy is "freedom."

Actually, democracy is a hoax. The majority never has ruled and never will. A minority always rules, because only a minority of men have the capacity for independent thought and action; the rest are capable only of thinking and acting with the herd. Those who rule in a democracy are those with the ability to manipulate the herd, and in this last decade of the 20th century they are the ones who control the medium of television.

It is true, of course, that the masses are permitted to participate in popularity contests. They are permitted to express themselves in numerous polls as to whether or not they approve of various government policies, and on special occasions they can go into the voting booths and let it be known which of the candidates presented to them they like best. There is no doubt that the politicians involved take these polls seriously; their careers depend on them. The media masters take the polls seriously too; polling is their way of finding out what the herd is thinking, what the herd is unhappy about at the moment, what the herd wants.

That doesn't mean that the herd will get what it wants, of course. If a poll reveals that the public is beginning to develop a hankering for something that the media bosses don't want it to have, they will simply shift their persuasion in the necessary direction to squelch the hankering. If the polls a year ago had shown that a majority of the voters disapproved of the war against Iraq the rulers certainly wouldn't have halted the bombing and left Saddam Hussein as a threat to the further expansion of Greater Israel; instead they would have trotted out "Stormin'" Norman Schwarzkopf, "Magic" Johnson (before his AIDS infection became public knowledge), and a few other media idols to tell us soberly on prime time that Saddam Hussein had to be stopped, for the sake of God, Mom, and apple pie. Then they would have Secretary of State James Baker warn us grimly on all of the network news programs of how many American jobs would be lost if we did not continue killing Iraqis around the clock. If that didn't get an acceptable level of bellicose sentiment from the next poll, they would give us a few more reruns of WWII films designed to stir patriotism to a fever pitch. It works every time. It certainly worked last year.

It works so well, in general, that the media bosses can even tolerate an occasional unapproved candidate—a David Duke, say—participating in the democratic process. They only had to run their persuasion machine at about half throttle to keep pro-Duke sentiment in check during the recent gubernatorial election in Louisiana.

Democracy really isn't such a bad system, considering the nature of people. It's a bit wasteful staging all of those election campaigns, but it's probably worth it just to give the masses the illusion that they have a say in things. The great danger of democracy, of course, is the same danger that exists with any other form of government: namely, that the wrong minority will be in the driver's seat. That's the problem we must overcome now—or perish as a race.

Before the advent of television, it wouldn't have been feasible to run a truly progressive nation democratically; the process of control simply was too awkward. That's why the United States drifted the way it did, subject to various pressure groups, until the worst of all possible groups elbowed the others aside and took over. These days the process of control is reasonably efficient, and if we ever manage to break the grip of the present media bosses we can look forward to the use of the same process to speed America along the upward path again.

Desert Storm taught us that the task of straightening things out can be much easier than we might have thought. If the Bible beaters and liberals could be made to cheer and wave the flag right along with the good ol' boys while we butchered 150,000 folks who had never done us a lick of harm, then we certainly can make them cheer while we sort out America's godawful racial problem and settle the hash of the people who have done us grievous harm indeed. It's something to look forward to.

White American Resistance

If it weren't for the racist premises, some of the points in the following selection, from the newspaper WAR: White American Resistance, *might have come from the far left. The right's ambivalence about capitalism is obvious here. On the one hand, it is argued that the free market will act as a limit on corporations; on the other hand, it is argued that wars should not be fought to support capitalism. The platform also supports taxing businesses run by churches, penal reform, and publicly provided education and job training programs.*

Whiteman's Platform

* Self determination for enlightened White racial nationalists, ending the destructive practice of money-breeding, which leads to loss of home, business and country. Usury is the bastard child of such practices.
* The use of political action or force to wrest millions of livable acres from the federal system to be allotted to middle and low income Whites. No corporations or syndicates may purchase such lands.
* Small business and healthy competition will flourish due to our program of government neutrality in the market place. Government will not permit the rise of megacorporations that base their power on shoddy products, unfair labor practices and government bribery. A healthy business climate will be possible due to the elimination of inflation that robs the worker of his or her security in old age.

From "Whiteman's Platform," *WAR: White American Resistance* (Fallbrook, Ca. [?]: n.p., 1984).

* The elimination of inflation will be a direct result of the end of economic wars that in the past were camouflaged as national security brush fire wars.
* Schools will teach money mechanics and not the witch doctor pseudoscience of economics. Every child will understand the direct cause of inflation and other maladies, so as to always know if their government is honest and true.
* A respect for our natural heritage. Redevelop a system promoting small farming, which protects the land from corporate destruction. Outlaw foreign ownership of U.S. farms. Only those who live on the land can adequately show love of the land.
* Revitalization of U.S technology and manufacturing. Seizing the assets of all corporations who openly flaunt the people's interest, i.e. shipping manufacturing out of the country or politically influencing the importation of non-white foreign workers.
* The end to economic wars disguised as national defense. Those that have business interests in Third World nations that endanger the economic well-being of White American workers, must accept the consequences of Wars of Liberation.
* Outlaw fratricidal war (Whites against Whites), including all White nations in the Northern Hemisphere—the United States, Europe, European Russia. Australia, South Africa, and New Zealand in the Southern Hemisphere. (Whenever White men go to war they weaken their race).
* Non-intervention in Third World non-White nations, as long as White racial survival is respected. Any non-White alien invasion of White homelands by military or economic invasion, such as now exists, will be taken as an act of war. Swift and adequate measures will be taken.
* A 20 year plan for re-vitalization and expansion of an economical means of speedy travel, such as trains. Working people who retire should receive low cost or free travel allowances.
* National testing of all school age children to channel the genetically gifted to a superior university education, regardless of financial status. Applicants must also be eager, aggressive and industrious. Superior college age students should be subsidized to produce children, even during the time of their formal education.
* Corporations doing business with the government will set aside a percentage of their profits to establish a national system of universities and technical schools. A system of dormitories to be made available to student

technical schools should be a close distance to manufacturing facilities to allow on the job training.

* An aggressive program of space exploration along with a crash program to advance the arts and sciences.
* The taxing of all religious corporations in the same manner other businesses are taxed. Adequate land on which a worship site is located would not be taxed, since there should be no profit in simple worship.
* Major White collar crime may be limited by the death penalty, thus installing justice in the minds of poorer elements of our society.
* Complete change of penal philosophy. For crimes against the race, lethal injection. For all lesser crimes, work corps to work on national projects such as aquaducts [*sic*] from White Canadian neighbors to make our deserts bloom. Any man or woman so beastial [*sic*] as to be kept in a cage, should be shown mercy and executed by lethal injection.

Positive eugenics will lead to the virtual elimination of birth defects as opposed to the present plunge into disease, birth defects, and low intellect that plagues society.

RACE ON THE LEFT

On racial questions the left generally advocates integration and acceptance of difference. There are exceptions, however, most of which, not surprisingly, are found among African American groups who see separation as the only response to the history of race relations in the United States.

African People's Party

AFRICAN PEOPLE'S PARTY TEN POINT PROGRAM

1. We want self determination and independent nationhood. We believe African captives in America will not have freedom until they have land of their own and a government; a nation that we govern and run and

From "African People's Party Ten Point Program," *This Is The Black World* 1, no. 5 (May 1971).

control. We demand the states of Mississippi Georgia, South Carolina Alabama and Louisiana as partial repayment for injustices done to us for over 400 years.

2. We want an independent self governing economy to guarantee full employment for our people. We believe the U.S. federal government owes us for 400 years of slavery and 100 years of forced citizenship-servitude. We demand the U.S. government pay the colonialized captive African 400 billion dollars, including the five states stated in point one and the said sum of 400 billion dollars for ten years as partial repayment for its crimes of genocide against our people.

To organize pressure for this demand we advocate the forming of Black unions and the convening of a national Black strike to make our demands met. We advocate the establishment of an independent Black communalist economy because from suffering under the capitalist system for years we have learned that capitalism cannot meet the overall needs of our people.

3. We want community control of all businesses in the Black community and an end to the economic, political and cultural exploitation by the capitalist class waged against our people. We demand of the U.S. government, the long overdue debt of forty acres and two mules; we demand this repayment in land, the territory stated in point one and currency and period stated in point two. We also demand Black community control of all businesses located in the Black community. We advocate nationalization by our people of all businesses inside the Black community. We want all businesses in the Black community to be termed *[sic]* into community cooperatives.

4. We want community control of housing and community planning of Black communities. We believe all housing and land in the Black community should be turned over to the Black community to be developed into communal-communities we call communes. We advocate the formation of Black housing cooperatives wherever possible. We believe urban renewal for the Black community has meant Black removal. We, therefore, demand 100% control of all planning boards that are planning housing and other project relocations of the Black community. We believe we are the best qualified to plan our own community.

5. We want to control the education of our children. We want an educator that teaches us the true history of Black people and of our racist oppressors. We believe because the present racist educational system is inade-

quate to the needs of our people, Black people must form an educational system of their own. We advocate the establishment in every Black community of Black institutes that teach and train youth and adults alike in the knowledge of self and prepares them in job retraining and in the scientific and technical fields.

6. We want all Black men to be exempt from military service. We believe that Black people should not be forced to fight in the military service to defend a racist government that does not protect us. We believe until racial abuses and police brutality; racial genocide is stopped being waged against our people right here in America, "America's The Blackman's Battleground." We, therefore, call for the formation of a Black People's Liberation Army and seed *[sic]* to organize Black youth into Black Guards.

7. We want an immediate end to the racist war of genocide that is being waged against the African held in captive colonial bondage inside the United States. We believe Black people living inside the U.S. who are called citizens are actually colonial captives because after the emancia- tion *[sic]* proclamation was signed so-called freeing us from chattel slavery a vote was never taken among the so-called freedmen to deter- mine whether we wanted to be citizens of the U.S. government or not. Therefore, the last 100 years of forced citizenship has been one of citizenship slavery and we are, therefore, still captives of war. We have also in the last 100 years been victims of a systematic plan to destroy our captive nation. We believe the responsibility of racial injustice lies in the hand of the U.S. federal government and feel the U.S. government should be brought before the United Nations and indicted for crimes of genocide and violation of the U.N. human rights charter. To stop this war of extermination and genocide we advocate the formation of thou- sands of self defense Black Guards units.

8. We want freedom for all Black people held in federal, state, county, and city prisons and jails. We believe under the present system that no Black people have received a fair and impartial trial. We believe that this racist system is organized in all ways against Black people. We especially demand the release from prisons and jails of all Black political prisoners. We believe all Black people should be tried in court by a jury of their peer group, meaning people from Black communities.

9. We want an end to the social degradation of our community. We want to rid our community of drug addiction, prostitution and other social

evils that destroy the moral fiber of our community. We believe these evils which are controlled by organized crime is a vice that is controlled by police who accept bribes and graft. We feel these evils are allowed to exist to lower the moral fiber and to weaken our community.

10. We want independence, self-determination and Black state power. We believe Black people in the U.S. will not have true freedom until we control and govern a government and nation of our own. We advocate the formation of a national Congress of African People's run by Black people to determine the destiny of the Black nation. We feel the decision (vote) of this congress should be taken to the U.N. to present our case of self determination to the World Court. We, the African-People's Party of National Liberation, call on all Black leaders and organizations to unite to form a Black Liberation Front that would serve as a centralizing committee of a national Black congress.

Junta of Militant Organizations

WHAT J.O.M.O. BELIEVES

1. The united states of america is a colonial power where African people are being colonized by america.

2. African people have no responsibility—morally nor legally—to perpetuate, sustain or protect this country which is actively oppressing us.

3. Because of the fact of our colonization, African people have no responsibility to the law, which was made without our consent, and without consideration for our interest.

4. All African people in jails and prisons throughout this country are therefore political prisoners and not criminals.

5. America is a criminal society which has historically and traditionally made it her unspoken and unwritten foreign and domestic policy to enslave, destroy and wipe out from this earth all non-white peoples she comes into contact with.

6. America is an all-white nation in fact, and plans to eliminate the so-called negro problem by eliminating the so-called negro.

From "What J.O.M.O. Believes," *The Burning Spear* 2, no. 2 (February 23–March 8, 1971).

7. African people must begin to control the political, economic and social power of our colony.

8. African people must begin to acquire land, which is the basis for revolution and liberation and must establish independent businesses which will make it possible to employ our people and will help to prepare us for the day when it may be necessary to build our own nation and separate from this brutal racist nation.

9. African people must form alliances with all other oppressed peoples all over the world, so we will be able to depend on support much greater than the Africans here in this country.

10. African people must broaden our struggle beyond the arena of civil rights and move into the field of human rights, so we can bring this racist nation before the world body called the United Nations and air our grievances before the world and have america condemned before all the other non-white nations of the world.

11. African people must view this racist, oppressive nation just as we view any other enemy we have. We must view this nation just as this nation views its enemies, and we must be prepared to react to her oppression and brutality toward our people accordingly.

12. African people must not allow ourselves to be drafted into the racist wars of america which are generally directed toward other oppressed peoples anyway. We must refuse to fight for a nation which refuses to recognize the humanity of millions of African people right here on this continent.

13. The battle ground for Africans in america is in the streets of america.

14. It is the duty of all African people to arm ourselves so we will be able to protect our families when this racist white power structure decides to revert to the "good old days" and swoop down into the African colony to eliminate Black people.

J.O.M.O.'S 10-POINT PROGRAM

1. WE DEMAND GUARANTEED EMPLOYMENT THAT PAYS DECENT WAGES FOR ALL BLACK COLONIAL SUBJECTS.

* The country that supports this illegitimate government was built on the whip-scarred bodies of African people. During and since slavery, African people have been denied the just wages for our labor. We demand decent jobs and decent wages during the days of our life in this country.

2. WE DEMAND LOCAL, COUNTY, STATE, AND FEDERAL COUNTER-GERRYMANDERING TO GUARANTEE BLACK REPRESENTATION FOR BLACK PEOPLE.

* We demand the right to equal representation according to our numbers and living patterns. We are not represented now by white racist gangsters and their colored lackeys who depend on white gangsters for election. We demand that all areas where black people live be counter gerrymandered, making all areas where Black people live a political district, to guarantee Black representation for Black people on the local, county, state and national levels.

3. WE DEMAND THE CONTROL OF ALL TENEMENT BUILDINGS OWNED BY WHITE SLUMLORDS AND OCCUPIED BY AFRICAN PEOPLE.

* We demand the right for Black people to have decent housing and since most African people are not property owners and must rent unlivable housing from white racists, we demand that Black people have control of these dwellings, through ownership, so they can be made into dwellings fit for human habitation, and free African people from another source of gangster oppression.

4. WE DEMAND CONTROL OF ALL BLACK PUBLIC HOUSING.

* We demand the right to guarantee all African people who life in public housing and who want to live in public housing the right to do so in dignity, without the racist criminal and dehumanizing pressure; without the graft, payoffs, and sexual exploitation that now occurs while racist, government controlled gangsters administer black public housing.

5. WE DEMAND THE CONTROL OF ALL COURT PROCEEDINGS THAT AFFECT BLACK PEOPLE.

* Every day white racist gangsters are legally lynching African people in their so-called courts of law. Black people can get no justice from white judges and prosecutors whose jobs are designed to contain the African

Liberation Struggle and protect white citizens and their interests. If Black people are to have justice from courts, Black people must control the courts administering justice to Black people.

6. WE DEMAND CONTROL OF ALL POLICE FORCES USED TO MAINTAIN ORDER IN THE AFRICAN COLONY.

* We demand the right to move about in our colony free from the white terror of foreign occupying troops, who are in the colony to suppress our just demand for liberation, and to protect the property of white criminal merchants and absentee landlords.

7. WE DEMAND THE CONTROL OF OUR SCHOOLS—THE CURRICULUM, THE HIRING AND FIRING AND THE DETERMINATION OF HOW MUCH MONEY IS TO BE ALLOTTED TO THE SCHOOLS.

* We demand a proper and progressive education for our Black children that clearly reveals the richness of our history and is designed to offer alternatives which will take us from this despicable condition of servitude and make us masters of our own destiny.

8. WE DEMAND AN END TO EXPLOITATION BY WHITE MERCHANTS AND THE RIGHT TO TAX WHITE MERCHANTS WHO SET UP BUSINESSES IN OUR COLONY.

* We demand that the economy of our colony be stabilized and protected. We have the same right of all people to protection from the theiving *[sic]* merchants and petty capitalists. We understand that white merchants are racist and come to our colony out of greed and not out of any need to serve our people.

9. WE DEMAND THE CONTROL OF ALL WELFARE AND GOVERNMENT FUNDING USED FOR BLACK PEOPLE.

* We demand the right to speak to the needs and aspirations of Black people as they are determined by Black people, based on objective conditions. Government funding and welfare are controlled by white gangsters who have proved historically to be the enemies of Black people. All their decisions and grants are based on their own racist outlook and serves to dehumanize Black people and sink us deeper into a state of slave-like dependency.

10. WE DEMAND THE RIGHT OF SELF DETERMINATION FOR ALL BLACK COLONIZED SUBJECTS OF THE UNITED STATES GOVERNMENT.

* All Black people in this country are colonized Africans. We are not, nor were we ever, american citizens. We demand our just and democratic right to Self Determination; to speak to our own needs and aspirations as we define them; to walk among other peoples, and other nations, truly free, truly liberated from cold racist white colonialism; to stretch out our hands in friendship to other hands stretched out in friendship, and to pursue all policies designed to lift up and unite African people wherever we may be.

NOTES

1. For example, see *The Journals and Other Documents on the Life and Voyages of Christopher Columbus,* ed. and trans. Samuel Eliot Morison (New York: Limited Editions Club, 1963), 287.
2. For a careful study of Christian Identity and its roots, see Michael Barkun, *Religion and the Racist Right: The Origins of the Christian Identity Movement* (Chapel Hill: University of North Carolina Press, 1994).

6

SOCIAL CONCERNS

Among the primary concerns of the extreme right are relations between men and women, the family, child care, and education. These concerns are less central to the left, although gender relations (to use the current phrase) and the role of women in society are issues for the left and a particular focus for attacks from the right on the left.

For the right these issues are basic to their conception of the moral system that is necessary for American greatness. Sex should be only within marriage and, of course, only between men and women. Women should stay home and out of the workplace and remain subservient to their husbands and devoted to their children. Hence, child care should be in the home. Education should be controlled by parents rather than by educational professionals.

The left stresses individual moral choice, arguing that no single moral system is appropriate for everyone. For them sex should be among consenting adults of any sexual orientation. Women should be equal to their partners and able to choose to enter the workplace; therefore, child care needs to be widely available. The left, while having some doubts about educational fads, generally believes that educational professionals should set the educational agenda; they are more worried about the effects of education controlled by the untrained.

At one point the debate came to focus on the Equal Rights Amendment, which reads as follows:

Section 1. Equality of rights under the law shall not be denied by the United States or by any State on account of sex.

Section 2. The Congress shall have the power to enforce, by appropriate legislation, the provisions of this article.

Section 3. This amendment shall take effect two years after the ratification.

The right represented this as requiring everything from unisex bathrooms to the service of women in the military, and successfully opposed its adoption. The left, who saw the ERA as a relatively minor reform that did none of the things suggested by the right, seemed at a loss over how to deal with the accusations.[1]

FAMILY

The right is concerned that the left is trying to destabilize the family in order to get control of the children. In addition, a major target is sensitivity training, which many see as a Jewish plot "to aid in making White Christians uninhibited about other immoral 'programs'." "The aim is to make him or her more receptive ('sensitive') to the colored, the ne'er-do-wells, to the worst and weakest features of society."[2] Such training is believed to be central to the desire of the left to replace the family with government control.

Phyllis Schlafly, her Eagle Forum, and her STOP ERA organization have been consistently in the forefront of right activities concerning the family and gender relations.

Eagle Forum

We Support your RIGHTS . . .

We support the Declaration of Independence and its fundamental doctrine that we owe our existence to a creator who has endowed each of us with inalienable rights and we support the U.S. Constitution as the instrument of securing those God given rights.

From "We Support Your Rights" (n.p.: Eagle Forum, [1970s], flyer).

We support the Holy Scriptures as providing the best code of moral conduct yet devised.

In addition we support:

1. The right of citizens to have the federal government provide for the common defense against aggression by any other nation.
2. The right to live in a community where state and local government and judges maintain law and order by a system of justice under due process, and punishment that is swift and certain.
3. The right to equal opportunity in employment and education for all persons regardless of race, creed, sex, or national origin.
4. The right to life of all innocent persons from conception to natural death.
5. The right of a community to prevent the distribution of printed or pictorial materials that degrade women or children in a pornographic, perverted, or sadistic manner.
6. The right of a community to protect itself and its members from those who abuse their own bodies with poisonous drugs.

We Support the FAMILY . . .

WE SUPPORT THE FAMILY AS THE BASIC UNIT OF SOCIETY, WITH CERTAIN RIGHTS AND RESPONSIBILITIES INCLUDING:

1. The responsibility of society to have laws and taxes that encourage mothers to care for their own children and encourage fathers to provide for them, rather than laws and taxes that impose disincentives on the role of motherhood and the traditional family.
2. The responsibility of the parents (not the government) for the care of pre-school children. Parents have the right to expect schools to:

   a. teach basic educational skills such as reading and arithmetic before time and money are spent on frills.
   b. use textbooks and hire teachers that do not offend the religious and moral values of the parents.
   c. use textbooks that teach the truth about the family, monogamous marriage, motherhood, American History and Constitution, and the private enterprise system.

d. teach the fourth "R" (right and wrong) and permit voluntary prayer.
e. respect gender identity: and separate the sexes for sex education, gym, and other classes if so desired.

3. The right of parents to send their children to private or religious schools free from arbitrary government regulations and control.
4. The right of all religious bodies to designate different roles among their members for men and women.

John Birch Society

CHILD CARE
THE GREAT FEDERAL KIDNAP CONSPIRACY
Medford Evans

What is the most precious possession of human beings?
Their children.

God himself "so loved the world that He gave His only Son" for the redemption of all His created and fallen children.

Among His other creatures, too, no drive is so strong—not even hunger or sex—as the imperative to protect the young, whether of songbird or tiger.

King David, "a man after God's own heart," was emotionally intense in all things. Greatest of Hebrew poets, author of the Psalms, David was irresistible in war, faithful in friendship, ardent in the love of women—but above all devoted in his love for his children, from Solomon the wise to Absalom the rebel, and including as not least that nameless elder brother of Solomon who perished in infancy. (See II *Samuel* XII: 14–24.)

The supreme value of children has been recognized by all men, not only by beneficiaries of divine revelation. The ultimate plague upon Pharaoh's Egyptians derived its effective terror from the degree to which the firstborn was cherished.

Nor are all the examples Biblical. The epic sorrow of *Sohrab And Rustum* was in the unwitting slaying of the son by the father. The most terrible of Shakespeare's tragedies displayed the betrayal of King Lear by his daughters

From Medford Evans, "Child Care: The Great Federal Kidnap Conspiracy," *American Opinion* 15, no. 6 (June 1972).

Goneril and Regan. The poignant consolation was the devotion of one daughter, Cordelia. In every age of man the fabric of life has been sustained by ties of family, and of these ties the most essential is the responsibility of the parent for the child. "Honor thy father and thy mother" was written into the Ten Commandments, but the Almighty evidently did not consider it necessary to command parents specifically to love and protect their children. If this were not done, there would simply be no race of man.

Men and women who have no children of their own often, as Bacon observed, make mankind their heirs and labor for the benefit of posterity in general. It was no doubt for this among other reasons that the Catholic Church enjoined celibacy upon its priests, who are significantly called Father.

What then do parents—either literally or figuratively so called—desire for their children? They desire: **The well being of the child—of each child.**

No other love so nearly approximates the unselfish. You recall how Solomon judged which of two women was the true mother of a child in dispute between them. He feigned an order that the child be divided in two and given half to one woman, half to the other. Immediately the true mother withdrew her claim, and said, "Give her the living child, and in no wise slay it." The false mother, in contrast, was ready to accept the judgment. Solomon then said straightway that the one whose first thought was of the child's life, not her own victory in the contest, was the true mother, and should have the child. You may not recall that both these women were harlots, so that neither could be suspected of acting from indoctrination in conventional virtue. It was natural love at work.

That case of the lying harlot reminds us that there have been, and obviously still are, people in the world who desire to act *in loco parentis* for one or more of any number of reasons other than unselfish parental love. But seldom are such reasons so explicitly stated as they are in the well-known utterance of the United Nations Educational, Scientific and Cultural Organization (U.N.E.S.C.O.), in its publication, *Toward World Understanding,* from which we read in part as follows:

The kindergarten or infant school has a significant part to play in the child's education. . . . Not only can it correct the errors of home training [these are assumed], *but it can also prepare the child for membership . . . in the world society.*

Membership in the world society! That is the objective of the currently dominant educational, scientific, and cultural fraternity for "the child."

What the child may feel, what the parents may feel, is a matter of no consequence to the social engineers of the new order, or to their political puppets. The latter, comprising executive and legislative personnel, but most notably judges (since it is they who give the commands in specific cases), still work primarily within existing frameworks of state and nation—which are, however, altered at every opportunity in the direction of a consolidated world society as envisioned by the current intellectual establishment.

It is hard for a normal American citizen to realize ordinarily what the intelligentsia and their government hacks are up to. The verbalisms of the professors sound generally incomprehensible, or when understood are dismissed as visionary and impractical. That is why so many good people are shocked by so many contemporary court decisions. *I just don't understand why they do that!* Such is the typical response of "Middle America" to busing decrees in Richmond, Detroit, and other scenes of recent juristic outrage.

"They" do it because they are preparing to incorporate America (very much including, of course, "Middle America") into their projected world society. They have told you time and again that they are going to do it. Why are you surprised?

Not that they don't recognize difficulties. The thing will take some time. That is why they are now concentrating on children. Members of the new world society will have a totally different psychology from that of the majority of present-day adults. The latter have been conditioned to value the near and the familiar—their neighborhood, their region, their own country. Local loyalties, patriotic and ethnic sentiments, cannot be eradicated from the mature. But perhaps they can be prevented in the young.

The scenarists of the proposed world order have several more or less cryptic terms for the kinds of loyalty they intend to eradicate. Often they call it chauvinism, but perhaps their oldest and weightiest term of derogation is *nationalism.* That this is not just a term of abuse and revilement only emphasize the seriousness with which it is condemned in such a passage as the following from the previously cited U.N.E.S.C.O. tract:

> *It is sufficient to note that it is most frequently in the family that the children are infected with nationalism by hearing what is national extolled and what is foreign disparaged. . . . The school should therefore . . . combat family attitudes. . . . As long as the child breathes the poisoned air of nationalism, education in world mindedness can produce only rather precarious results.*

We scarcely need labor the point that the same family setting which exudes the "poisoned air of nationalism" is liable to be similarly fetid with ethnocentricity and racism, not to mention clannishness and subliminal "hate." But give U.N.E.S.C.O. credit. There is indeed an inherent and indestructible relationship between the very concept of family and that of nation. The word *nation* is derived from the past participle of the Latin verb *nascor, nati, natus,* meaning to be born. Which is reminiscent of the fact that *patriotism* is derived from the Latin *patria,* fatherland, from *pater,* father. There can be no denial that the very idea of political sovereignty, and thus of all lesser legal authority, is inextricably fused with the idea of blood kin, of family, of parental responsibility and authority.

The difference between the sanity of the ordinary man and the madness of the excessively learned is that the former recognizes that the family is more basic than the state, while the latter not only believes that existing states (i.e., nation states, not states of the Union) should be regarded as more basic than the family, but that they in turn should be superseded by a new world order, created by "Man" (meaning the intellectual elite), and appropriating all functions formerly associated with the nation-state—and/or the family.

Today's conflict in America between the family and the world Leviathan (the latter represented for the time being by the federal government) is in a sense more primal than that between the government and the individual, for the individual obviously cannot survive alone, whereas both the family and the government can do so. The difference between the two groupings is that the family is of natural—and divine—origin, whereas government is of the nature of a compact. We are accustomed to think of it as a compact between individuals, but government is more properly thought of (considering the reason of viability already alleged) as a compact between families. Yet neither individuals nor families have or ever had the right to make a compact to destroy themselves. Government can take over the fundamental family duty of child-rearing only by usurpation.

Just such a usurpation is now being vigorously attempted. That the great "Middle American" public senses this fact is attested by the surge of "anti-busing" sentiment across the country. To the average American it does not seem right, and it certainly is not right, for courts to require children to be taken, against the will of their parents, away from accustomed "neighbor-hood schools" into what is admitted alien territory, for of course the whole avowed purpose of court-ordered busing is to mingle children from one kind of cultural environment with those of another and very different kind. The expected cultural blend is the precise and explicit justification of the expense and effort involved.

The larger and implicit justification is that breaking down traditional racial barriers and mingling black and white in America today may be regarded as a major rehearsal for breaking down national barriers and mingling Americans with all other races and nations in the future. Once the "separate and equal" facilities of segregation have been liquidated, the "separate and equal station" of the Declaration of Independence can also be liquidated. Busing is prologue.

Until mid-April the busing atrocity was thought of largely in general terms. It discriminated between North and South, it was at best a needless extravagance, it was potentially injurious to children and their parents, it was a nightmare for school administrators, and in addition to everything else it had—serious as it was—an air of the ridiculous. Then on April 12, 1972, a probate judge in Oakland County, Michigan, brought the brunt of the forced-busing operation to bear, not on a community in general, not on a school board, but on an individual child.

Thirteen-year-old Cari Merchant lived with her parents, the Carl E. Merchants, in the predominantly white northwest section of Pontiac, Michigan. Mr. Merchant is an inspector at General Motors Corp. Fisher Body Plant. He and his wife, Constance, are both in their mid-thirties. Judging by an A.P. Wirephoto of April 14, they are as typical and attractive a couple as you are likely to find in any given cross section of Middle America. In spite of the juridical ordeal to which they had just been subjected they were both smiling with unforced heartiness in the photo, and we shall say a word or two about that in just a moment. First, the basic facts in the case.

Last September, as was widely publicized at the time, Federal Judge Damon Keith of Detroit ordered the Pontiac school district to bus children to achieve racial integration. You recall that there were protests in Pontiac. But when school started September ninth, the *New York Times* proclaimed the desegregation-by-busing a success. Protests continued, however, as demonstrative women, led by Mrs. Irene McCabe, for example, staged rallies and even an overland hike to Washington, D.C. The attractive Mrs. McCabe has been quoted as branding President Nixon's anti-busing talk as mere "political rhetoric," the sagacity of which observation suggests that the women of Pontiac will not be easily bought off.

Meanwhile, Carl and Constance Merchant had simply and quietly kept Cari at home, rather than send her to Jefferson Junior High School, some eight to ten miles across town, on the predominantly Negro side of southeast Pontiac, as Judge Keith had ordered. They requested that their daughter be admitted to the (largely white) Avondale School, east of Pontiac, but officials had ruled that this was an attempt to evade compliance with Judge Keith's order (which I, too, should think it was, and why not, for heaven's sake!—a perfectly legitimate attempt), and the request was refused. The Merchant's still would not allow Cari to go to Jefferson Junior. The school, they said, was in a high crime area. They contended that they had a right—as a matter of fact, they had a duty—to look out for the safety of their child. They had bought their home on the northwest side of Pontiac because of, among other reasons, its proximity to a (then) perfectly safe junior high school.

But who are parents to judge whether their child is safe? Pontiac School Superintendent Dana Whitmer brought suit against Carl and Constance Merchant, alleging child neglect for failure to comply with Michigan's compulsory education act.

Neglect! That was the charge. The Merchant's stuck their necks out, as the saying goes, to resist an unreasonable, vicious, and basically un-Constitutional court order. Not only did they face the certainty of painful and expensive litigation, but you know they could have expected nothing but (at best) Pharisaical silence or (at worst) organizational censure from General Motors *and* the United Auto Workers. For such gallant resistance to the encroachment of the federal industrial behemoth, Carl and Constance Merchant could have no possible motive except concern for their child. It was no doubt *therefore* inevitable that an Orwellian bureaucracy should charge them with *neglect* of the child.

The case came to trial Monday, April 10, 1972, before Oakland County Probate Judge Norman Barnard, who—to judge *him* on the basis of his reported ruling in this matter—is the quintessential opposite of Solomon. Judge Barnard and a jury of six (all whites, as it happened) heard Merchant's testimony and his attorney Richard Kuhn's argument that the parents had acted out of concern for their child's safety. Jefferson Junior High School, they contended, was in a high-crime area. Certainly all children there—who at junior-high age would be just old enough to get the picture, but not old enough to be really part of the picture—are scared to death of that high-crime environment around school.

But we shall never know what the jury, which is normally the judge of facts in a case, would have decided—for it was never allowed to weigh the testimony. Incredibly, Judge Barnard took the matter out of the jury's hands and directed a verdict of guilty. Guilty of "neglect"! All the testimony as to the facts of the character of the school was, according to the anti-Solomon on the bench, irrelevant. Assuming that all that Carl Merchant had said about the high-crime area was true, it would make no difference, for parents' "fear of a neighborhood" is no reason, ruled Judge Barnard, to keep a child out of the neighborhood if a federal judge has ordered the child to go to a school in that neighborhood.

A child in the age brackets for compulsory school attendance is like a combat soldier in the draft-age brackets. If the commanding officer tells a boy to go into the D.M.Z. (after all, it is demilitarized!), neither he nor his parents can say, *But, Sir, it is dangerous there!* And if a federal judge tells a thirteen-year old girl to go into a ghetto area of an industrial city, no one can remonstrate—however truly—that the area is dangerous. In the new order of things, your foremost duty as a parent is to turn your child over to the proper authorities of the state, and don't interfere. Nobody wants to hear your opinion as to the propriety or safety or wisdom of what the authorities are going to do with or to your child. Pay your taxes and shut up.

You will want to know that, ironically, the Cari Merchant story has a sort of happy ending for Cari and her parents—and grandparents. Luckily she has grandparents. What happened was that when Carl and Constance Merchant were judged guilty of child neglect, their daughter Cari became a ward of the court. So Judge Barnard, *in loco parentis* (loco, all right), went into a 45-minute huddle "in chambers" with the Merchants, their counsel Richard Kuhn, and Superintendent Whitmer and his counsel, and came out with the solution of placing Cari in the custody of her grandparents, who live in the Avondale School District where Carl and Constance tried to put Cari last fall! Now she can go there. Only it is now in the record that her parents are not fit for her to live with—because they wanted to put her there. It is all right for the judge to put her there.

You see, it doesn't really matter where your children go to school. All that matters is who is boss.

The parents worry about their little girl. Judges worry about power. Cari Merchant and lawyer Kuhn reportedly said after the trial, "We lost the battle but we won the war." Well, you see they are thinking about Cari, and her safety, and they won on that score. That is why Carl and Constance Merchant are smiling in that A.P. Wirephoto. But you and I, not being Cari's parents or the Merchants' lawyer, have to think, like the judges, about the strategic outcome of this thing; and what that outcome amounted to was a raw assertion of judicial power to take a child away from her father and mother—just to show that it could be done, since she ended up in the school where her parents had wanted her to go anyhow.

What the case does as a precedent is to strengthen the arm of judicial terror. Judges are not yet sending their marshals in the middle of the night to knock on your door to take away your children, and I don't say that they ever will, for the war is not over, and they may not win it . . . but we haven't won it either. I'm glad the Merchant's found a way out of the immediate problem of Cari's schooling, but they and all the rest of us lost more in that battle than anyone can yet determine.

That we have not lost with finality is best evidenced by Carl Merchant's fighting spirit. He and Constance have another daughter, Connie, age 12. She is slated to go to Jefferson Junior High in the high-crime area next September. What will you do about that?

"I'll keep her at home just like I did Cari," said Carl Merchant.[a]

* * *

Still, remember that people like Judge Barnard are on the front line of the revolution to dissolve traditional America into the world society of the hypothetical future. Front line soldiers often don't know what they are doing—except trying to stay alive and more or less obey orders. Let's drop back to the rear echelons, where the high command may be found. Sometimes it seems not to know what it is doing either, but at least strategic plans are being made. Out of a welter of staff reports and studies, campaigns will emerge which for better or worse somebody in the field will undertake.

In the forefront today—not of the physical battle line, where we left Judge Barnard, but of staff conferences in the rear or command echelons—we find such men as psychology Professor Urie Bronfenbrenner of Cornell, author of *Two Worlds of Children,* a book in which he compared Soviet and American methods of child care and development, to the considerable advantage of the former. Naturally, after such as endorsement of Communism, Professor Bronfenbrenner was signed up for a star role in the last (December 1970) White House Conference on Children, in Washington, D.C. In *Time* for December 28, 1970, following the aforesaid White House Conference on Children; there is an interview by one Ruth Galvin with Professor Bronfenbrenner.[b] *Time* quotes Bronfenbrenner as saying to Ruth Galvin:

The battle today is not between children and parents; the battle is between society on one side and families on the other, and we've got to reorder things so that human values can again get some recognition.

Now what do you suppose he means by that? What battle is he talking about? If there is a battle "between society on one side and families on the other," which side is Bronfenbrenner on? When he says, "We've got to reorder things," who are "We"?

Something Bronfenbrenner says, however, is true: "if you want to turn a society around, it's around children that you have the hope of doing it." Well, it is also true that if you want to keep a society on course, you have to do that through children, too. A lot of us don't want to turn American society around; we'd like to keep it going. But a lot of psychologists and educators and judges evidently do want to turn America around, and conferences get held at the White House where task-force leaders include men who have written books extolling the Soviet system of child development. It does look as though somebody in the educational stratosphere might like to turn American society around and give it a head start in the Soviet direction.

Urie Bronfenbrenner was one of the founders of the U.S. Project Head Start. He was also cited last fall in support of the Child Development Bill, which President Nixon vetoed for well-stated reasons, but which we may expect back. This measure was called by James Jackson Kilpatrick "the boldest and the most far-reaching scheme ever advanced for the Sovietization of American youth." Passed in the Senate December 2, 1971, by a vote of 63-17, and in the House on a vote of 210-186, it would have provided as part of a two-year, $6 billion extension of the Office of Economic Opportunity (O.E.O.), a $2 billion federal child-development and day care program.

Pressured by a flood of more than 100,000 letters, many from California, President Nixon vetoed the bill with the observation that it "would commit the vast moral authority of the national government to the side of communal approaches to child rearing against the family-centered approach," and would "create a new army of bureaucrats." The *Washington Post* said the veto was "a bone he had decided to throw to the right wing of his party," and for once there may by something to what the *Post* said. Of course, if Nixon were to be reelected this coming November, he would have no further reason to cast bones to the "right wing," since he would not be Constitutionally eligible for another term.

Columnist Paul Scott said April 19 (Patriot's Day) that the strategy of Leftist Senators Jacob Javits and Walter Mondale is "to try to get a framework child development program through Congress this year that President Nixon will not veto. Then after the 1972 election, the Senators would work to expand and radicalize the legislation to include many of the social engineering schemes that were in the vetoed measure."

The "vetoed measure" would have provided free day-care to all children in families with income up to $4320 a year, cut-rate day-care for families making up to $6960, and (perhaps in the long run most important of all) care at full cost for *all* children regardless of their families' income. The significance of the last group is very great, for it means that government propaganda would be fed to the children of the well-to-do as directly as to welfare children. As for the "free," reduced-cost, and full cost features, that is all flim-flam, for obviously the taxpayers would pay for the whole thing, one way and/or another.

The underlying purpose of all this academic-governmental interest in children was revealed in another connection some years ago by James S. Coleman, author of the famous Coleman Report on "Equality of Educational Opportunity." Writing in *The Public Interest,* Summer 1966, Coleman said:

> *For those children whose family and neighborhood are educationally disadvantaged, it is important to replace this family environment as much as possible with an educational environment—by starting school at an earlier age, and by having a school which begins very early and ends very late.*

There you have the rational basis for both busing and pre-school programs. Get those kids away from their families! "The battle today," said Dr. Bronfenbrenner, "is not between children and parents; the battle is between society on one side and families on the other." In the Soviet kindergartens which U.S. Head Start founder Bronfenbrenner so admires, the children sing:

> *We are Lenin's Grandchildren*
> *We are not yet Pioneers*
> *We are not yet Octobrists,*
> *But we know who we are for sure:*
> *We are Lenin's Grandchildren!*
> *We are Lenin's Grandchildren!*[c]

"In collective upbringing," says *Time* in its article of April 27, 1970, on Bronfenbrenner, "the family plays a decidedly secondary role. The relative significance of parents is the root difference between American and Russian child raising." That difference will disappear if federal kidnappers have their way. "We have recognized," says Senator Jacob Javits, "that the child is a care of the state."

Federal and state courts in Michigan had to go to a lot of trouble to get Cari Merchant away from her parents. Think how easy it would have been if the judges had made their move when the child was still in the nursery.

But surely any American mother, or father, would be as deeply attached to her, or his, child as was the poor harlot who came before King Solomon! No doubt. But remember that in the face of the sovereign power of the sword the woman felt that, for the child's sake, she had to give the baby up. Few parents can be as resolute in resistance to state power as were Carl and Constance Merchant.

Besides there is another side of the coin. Not only are children uniquely precious possessions—they are likewise unique responsibilities. Every young mother alternates between blissful joy and the feeling that she is in jail. The better mother she is, the more trapped she will feel in bad moments, for the more she will recognize the power of the chains that bind her. Wealth is a help—and a danger. She may buy nursemaids and governesses—and may thereby lose control of her own child. The risk, which is legitimate, is hers to take or refuse. It is her child, and her money. She may use the latter to help the former (and herself) the best way she can. Mothers without the money will sometimes envy, sometimes pity her.

But in the trials of motherhood, rich or poor, the kidnapper, the Outsider sees his opportunity. If the Outsider (of the family) be also the *Insider* (of the Conspiracy) you have the maximum threat to humanity.

Until we destroy the Conspiracy that's what we've got.

Author's Notes

a. After writing the above I had an opportunity to talk with attorney Richard Kuhn. He informed me that the Merchants definitely would appeal to the appropriate Michigan circuit court, and if necessary to the U.S. Supreme Court. Mr. Kuhn also filled me in on the details of the case as follows: Uncontradicted expert testimony showed that the Jefferson school is indeed a high-crime area. Captain Nye, head of the Pontiac Police Patrol, an officer with thirty years' experience, testified that he would not send a one-man patrol car into that area, though the officer would be armed and though one-man cars are sent to other areas of Pontiac. On cross-examination, Captain Nye was asked whether he had ever sent a one-man car into the area in question. His reply was that if that had ever occurred, or should occur, there was or would be a follow-up car directly behind the first one.

The Pontiac City Commission, possibly disturbed to have these matters aired, requested a report on incidence of crime in the Jefferson school area from eight a.m. to five p.m., Monday through Friday. At the session where this report was to be presented a member of the press was present. Reading the report began with the statement that in one week there were in the Jefferson area some twenty-seven armed robberies, as compared with one armed robbery in a more typical area of Pontiac. At this point the Commission ordered the report not be be read aloud but presented sealed for the Commission's eyes only.

The Merchants have three other children, who are being bused to other schools. Two of these children have at one time and another to get home the best way they could, because of some failure in the busing operation. This obviously could happen in the Jefferson area also. The point was brought out to refute the contention of Superintendent Whitmer that only conduct inside the school was relevant, not crime statistics in the area. Plainly, however, it would be an invitation to disaster if a thirteen-year-old girl had to walk through a ghetto area in which some twenty-seven armed robberies are committed in daylight hours in a typical five-day week.

In view of a parent's duty to protect his child as well as to see to his schooling, Mr. Merchant plainly had conflicting pressures. It was the duty of the jury, not of the judge, to decide whether he was in fact guilty of neglect. That the judge refused to let the matter go to the jury is the basis on which the Merchants are appealing this case.

b. By the way, *Time* never says *Dr.* Bronfenbrenner or *Professor* Bronfenbrenner— always just "Bronfenbrenner," which is a sort of final accolade. We say Beethoven, Shakespeare, MacArthur, Napoleon. You know.

c. Quoted from *Lenin's Grandchildren: Preschool Education in the Soviet Union*, by Kitty D. Weaver; Simon and Schuster, 1971.

YOUR FAMILY
THE FIGHT FOR AMERICA BEGINS AT HOME
Reed Benson and Robert Lee

Events of recent years have made it clear that the institution of the family is under fire as never before in our nation's history. It is now imperative that Conservatives who would preserve their families become better informed about the significance of this attack, its nature, and means which can be used to defend and strengthen this vital institution.

The family is civilization's most basic social unit. It is in the home that a child first learns the rules of conduct which shape his attitude toward the other institutions with which he comes in contact. The family provides his

From Reed Benson and Robert Lee, "Your Family: The Fight for America Begins at Home," *American Opinion* 15, no. 6 (June 1972).

food, clothing, shelter, recreation, and applies penalties for the infraction of rules which govern the home.

The family is also the child's first and most important school. It provides him with a wealth of knowledge and information before he ever enters a classroom, and it is in the home that the mother performs what must surely be the most difficult of all educational tasks—teaching the mother tongue to a child who, at the start, neither speaks nor understands a word in any language. This remarkable accomplishment is usually achieved smoothly and naturally as the response of the child to expressions of love by the mother, the most elemental of educators.

As an economic institution, there is nothing which surpasses the family. The family system in America today supports well over a hundred million individuals, ably and well, and does so in a way which tends to strengthen, rather than weaken, the social fabric. It is when the family declines and degenerates as an institution that such destructive activities as crime and juvenile delinquency begin to flourish. As the Reverend Rousas J. Rushdoony has observed:

> *In terms of sheer economic efficiency, nothing in all of history has ever equalled the family. By comparison, statist welfare and Communist take-overs of the family's economic functions are pathetic and tragic failures. Socially, this magnificent economic institution, the family, has no equal in its contribution to social stability and order.*[a]

And this is one of the key reasons why collectivists, from the fascist regime of ancient Sparta to the Communists of today, have sought to undermine the family. Dictators thrive on the conditions created by weakening the family. If millions of stable families are permitted to impart their own unique traditions and outlook to succeeding generations, the resulting variety in attitudes about everything from religion to styles of clothing to politics make it very difficult indeed for a dictatorial oligarchy to impose its collectivist program without meeting resistance at every turn. The dictators must therefore work to undermine the family's influence, making possible the eventual transfer of family responsibilities to the state, after which they rule with the common views and attitudes necessary to run the state collective with efficiency. The goal is to make everyone dependent on, and loyal to, the state rather than to such highly individual and competitive institutions as our families. And the methods used to achieve this goal are often ingenious as well as sinister. Consider, for instance, some examples found in *The Communist Manifesto.*

One of the demands made by Karl Marx in the Manifesto was for "Abolition of property in land. . . ." This would prohibit ownership by a family of its physical home, and therefore eliminate the stability that results from such ownership. It is not without meaning that in our country it is becoming increasingly difficult for our families to acquire debt-free homes, largely due to government policies of taxation and inflation.

Marx also called for "A heavy progressive or graduated income tax," such as the one with which we are afflicted today, as a means of transferring economic power and wealth from the family to the state. And he demanded "Abolition of all right of inheritance," in order to give the state additional control over family property. Taken together, these two Communist objectives greatly diminish the strength and stability of the family, and erode parental influence and authority.

Note also that the Manifesto made a plea for "Free education for all children in public schools," a recognition that the state must control what children learn if it is to eventually control what they do. The results of such "free" education in our own government schools is reflected today in the increasing number of young people who emerge from such schools with their political outlook tilted to favor programs and policies which expand the power and reach of government. For instance, what government schools in your area give students a fair and honest chance to study a Conservative view of such issues as the U.N., welfare, crime in the streets, the Federal Reserve System?

Parents have surrendered control of the education of their children to the state. This is seen in the proliferation of courses like sex education, and in policies such as forced busing, which are imposed on children by government educators despite vigorous parental opposition to such schemes.[b]

A list of other tactics and strategies now being used to undermine the family includes the following:

a) Indoctrinate children with the idea that their parents are old-fashioned, ignorant and out of touch with the collective needs of modern times.

b) Encourage sexual promiscuity (and the use of contraceptives by unmarried persons) as both healthy and fashionable, and portray chastity as a joke.

c) Promote divorce as reasonable and commonplace, adultery as psychologically helpful, and fidelity as backward and confining.

d) Use government to develop ever increasing taxation, and rocketing inflation, thus forcing more wives to work outside the home.

e) Promote schemes such as the phony Women's Liberation Movement to create sexual hostility and antagonism within families, and encourage women to abandon their maternal responsibilities.

f) Propagandize for the widespread use of contraceptives to keep children from being conceived; for abortion to prevent those conceived from being born; and for government child-care centers to replace mothers in caring for those children who are born.

g) Promote the acceptance of homosexuality and other perversions as the mark of eccentric genius, or as an exercise in "personal freedom."

h) Destroy the religious base, moral significance, and sanctity of marriage, so that the family becomes merely a temporary arrangement devoid of permanent spiritual meaning.

i) Relieve children of any feeling of responsibility for their parents, thus clearing the way for government (rather than the family unit) to assume responsibility for parents during sickness or old age.

j) And, promote the use of narcotics, alcohol, pornography, and similar destructive devices as a means of weakening family ties.

The list is by no means complete, but we think it makes our point. Certainly you needn't look far to find educators, politicians, movie stars, journalists, commentators, and other persons of influence who are busily engaged in promoting some or all of these destructive policies.

It is time for parents and young people alike to fight back. We urgently need to regain for the family the ground it has lost, and restore it to its proper place within our national life. There are many specific actions that can be taken to help achieve this important goal, one of which is so potentially beneficial that it merits special attention.

In 1915, the Church of Jesus Christ of Latter-day Saints (Mormon) introduced as an official program the policy of encouraging families within the Church to hold Family Home Evenings on a weekly basis. This project has proved worthwhile and beneficial to those families which have adopted and used it, and the underlying concept is readily applicable to the needs and circumstances of Conservative families of all faiths. Here is how it works:

One night is set aside each week, every week, during which members of the family gather together in the home. No appointments, dates or other outside engagements are scheduled by family members for that evening, and all reasonable steps are taken to avoid outside interruptions and interference.

Any list of possible Home Evening activities might be long and varied, and the following are only a few suggestions. Each family will want to add to, delete from, or modify the list to suit its own needs:

a) **Games** which develop the mental, physical and/or spiritual qualities of family members are highly desirable. Preference should be given to those which permit all family members to participate, and to those which keep the element of chance at a minimum while placing stress on the skill and ability of the participants. For couples without children, many wholesome games for two are available, including (for example) such skill-oriented table games as chess.

Just as one example of a game that would qualify as an appropriate Home Evening activity for large Conservative families, consider the following: One member of the family describes another member solely by listing his/her virtues and positive character traits, one at a time. The first to name the person being described is the winner. Activities of this nature can help to counter some of the harmful influences being promoted today (such as sensitivity training, with its stress on destructive self-criticism) by stressing the good and the positive attributes of family members.

Obviously, a little thought and ingenuity can lead to the development of many constructive games of this type, in which every member can participate.

b) **Singing songs** and hymns can be a means of bringing inspiring music into the home, and helping each child to build his own music vocabulary. Many parents have simply turned the music education of their children over to the local rock radio station, with increasingly unpleasant results. Most children are delighted to discover music of genuine merit when their parents help make it available to them. Local libraries often have record collections that include many excellent instrumental and vocal albums, as well as books containing interesting biographical sketches of great composers, singers, instrumentalists, etc. Bringing great music into the home can be an enriching and exciting experience not only for children but for parents as well.

c) **Talent Time,** to which each family member contributes a musical selection, original poem or speech recitation, story, dramatization, or craft display, can provide an enthusiastic forum for family talents. A main value of this activity is the manner in which it can help children overcome shyness and reticence when performing before an audience.

d) **Compassionate Service,** with the Home Evening devoted to helping others, can be a richly rewarding experience. One family, upon learning that a neighbor child had been hospitalized with an extremely serious illness, devoted its Home Evening to visiting the child's home in order to scrub floors, vacuum rugs, wash dishes and otherwise pitch in to help lighten the burden of the distraught parents. Such activities can help instill in young people a desire to be personally helpful to others in times of need—a character trait being destroyed in an age which tends to turn all problems over to some government agency.

e) **Spiritual and Character Guidance** may be achieved in many ways under the Home Evening program. Prayer and Spiritual readings may be given to instruct family members in matters pertaining to truth, righteousness, family love and loyalty, *etc.*

Love of our country, its Constitution, and the noble traditions of our inspired Founding Fathers should also be made an integral part of the program. A few years ago, *This Week* magazine surveyed a number of history books issued prior to 1920 and compared them with those in use which were issued since 1920. Nathan Hale's stirring, "I regret that I have but one life to live for my country," appeared in eleven of the old textbooks, but in only one of the later ones. Patrick Henry said, "Give me liberty or give me death" in twelve out of fourteen earlier texts, but in only two of forty-five recent ones. John Paul Jones proclaimed, "I have not yet begun to fight" in nine of the old texts, but in none of the recent ones. This is just one indication of the way in which the tradition, heritage, and heroes of our nation are being neglected or undermined. Fortunately, however, the reliable sources to which parents may go to fill these gaps are now increasing. Accurate history books, such as *Quest of A Hemisphere* by Donzella Cross Boyle, may now be added to home libraries and read during Home Evenings, as can inspirational and Americanist anthologies such as Professor E. Merrill Root's *America's Steadfast Dream.*[c]

In addition, examples of great poetry, classic literature, and inspiring art can be read, looked at, and discussed to add flavor to Home Evenings. Again, the local library can serve as a source for materials too expensive to purchase. In addition to their availability in book form, many worthwhile literary works are also available on record for the listening enjoyment of the family, and many libraries now lend these as well as fine reproductions of great art.

f) **Field Trips** to local historic sites, museums, zoos, art galleries, *etc.*, provide an additional means by which families may spend constructive evenings together. And they can form the basis for family reports during Home Evenings to develop writing and verbal skills.

g) **Refreshments,** served at the conclusion of the Home Evening, are especially appropriate if they are of the homemade variety (such as popcorn, cookies, ice cream, fudge, or taffy) as they can be popped, baked, churned, cooked or pulled as a family project.[d]

Specific assignments for the following week can be given to family members at the conclusion of the Home Evening, a procedure which provides everyone something private and personal to work on and prepare during the week. And a Home Evening minute book may also be compiled as a permanent record of the various activities and assignments. In addition to their regular Home Evenings each week, some families even arrange to hold a separate "business" meeting for the purpose of planning future family activities and projects. Outings, chores, home and yard improvements, schedules, and vacations are some of the topics which can be considered during this supplemental meeting.

Above all, Conservatives should remember, as a prominent church leader has said:

The home is the basis of a righteous life, and no other instrumentality can take its place nor fulfill its essential functions. The problems of these difficult times cannot better be solved in any other place, by any other agency, by any other means, than by love and righteousness, and precept and example, and devotion to duty in the home.

There is an unfortunate tendency on the part of many of us to improperly portion our time between our responsibilities to church, family, country, and profession. While each of these areas cannot receive equal time, each deserves consistent attention. The above brief outline provides an introduction to a program which can assist parents in giving needed time and attention to family duties. It is an effective potential bridge for the so-called "generation gap." Its purpose is to help family members stick together, and we encourage you to give it a try. As the popular poetic journalist Edgar Guest wrote:

The stick-together families are
*   happier by far*
Than the brothers and sisters who
*   take separate highways are.*
The gladdest people living are the
*   wholesome folks who make*

A circle at the fireside that no
*   power but death can break.*
And the finest of conventions ever
*   held beneath the sun*
Are the little family gatherings
*   when the busy day is done.*

There are rich folk, there are poor
*   folk, who imagine they are wise.*
And they're very quick to shatter
*   all the family ties.*
Each goes searching after pleasure
*   in his own selected way.*
Each with strangers like to wander,
*   and with strangers like to play.*
But it's bitterness they harvest, and
*   it's empty joy they find.*
For the children that are wisest are
*   the stick-together kind.*

There are some who seem to fancy
*   that for gladness they must roam.*
That for smiles that are the
*   brightest they must wander far from home.*
That the strange friend is the true
*   friend, and they travel far astray*
And they waste their lives in striving
*   for a joy that's far away.*
But the gladdest sort of people,
*   when the busy day is done,*
Are the brothers and sisters, who
*   together share their fun.*

It's the stick-together family that
*   wins the joys of earth*
That hears the sweetest music and that
*   finds the finest mirth;*
It's the old home roof that shelters
*   all the charm that life can give;*
There you find the gladdest
*   play-ground, there the happiest spot to live.*
And, O weary, wandering brother,
*   if contentment you could win,*

Come you back unto the fireside
and be comrade with your kin.

That is not *great* poetry, but it is great sentiment. And we Conservatives especially, dedicated and working as hard as we can to preserve and protect our republic, must remember that no other success can compensate for failure in the home. Let's strengthen the Conservative family!

Author's Notes

a. *Law and Liberty* (The Craig Press, Nutley, New Jersey: 1971). This collection of thirty-two essays, which were originally delivered as a series of radio broadcasts by the Reverend Rushdoony, contains much penetrating and worthwhile insight into the family's role in society.

b. It is important to compare the anti-family thrust of *The Communist Manifesto* with the pro-family attitude reflected in the Ten Commandments. The family is the only institution which directly appears in the Ten Commandments, and four of the Commandments specifically protect the family and property. ("Honour thy father and they mother . . .; Thou shalt not commit adultery . . .; Thou shalt not steal . . .; Thou shalt not covert *[sic]*. . . ."[)] No Commandment was given to protect the state.

c. Professor Root's series of essays on American heroes, which has been appearing monthly in *American Opinion,* provides an excellent means of keeping the record straight for young people regarding men like George Washington, Douglas Mac-Arthur, George Patton, and Robert E. Lee.

d. We believe that a useful standard for evaluating proposed Home Evening activities is contained in this wise counsel given to young John Wesley by his mother: "Would you judge of the lawfulness or unlawfulness of pleasure? Take this rule: Now note whatever weakens your reason, impairs the tenderness of your conscience, obscures your sense of God, takes off your relish for spiritual things, whatever increases the authority of the body over the mind, that thing is sin to you, however innocent it way seem in itself."

EDUCATION

One of the central issues for the right is their perception that the left controls education. The following essays note "secular humanism" and behavior modification as the main concerns. The latter has also bothered many on the left.

Liberty Lobby

A POSITIVE
PROGRAM TO
SAVE OUR SCHOOLS

Is There Any Reason Why Americans Must Tolerate the Guided Destruction of Their Youth?

. . . Or Can Something Be Done?

LIBERTY LOBBY will make the SAVE OUR SCHOOLS PROJECT its top priority. Maximum effort to accomplish the following:

1. The enforcement of existing laws on dope pushing and use, and the development and introduction of new legislation where necessary. It must be recognized at the outset that the liberal approach to the question of drugs and narcotics abuse is thoroughly fraudulent. The remedy lies not in "rehabilitation," with plush, taxpayer-financed jobs for swarms of liberal sociologists, psychiatrists, welfare workers and bureaucrats. The only way to stop or even to curtail the drugs and narcotics pestilence is to harshly punish the human fiends who sell it, with full recognition that a drug pusher is a murderer and should be dealt with as such. *Harsh penalties for pushers is the ONLY way to dry up the illegal trade!* LIBERTY LOBBY will conduct a study to review existing laws and to propose new ones, with the above as the guideline.

2. Re-institute "Operation Intercept" at the Mexican border and cut off all smuggling of dope and narcotics by rigid inspection at all borders and ports.

3. S. 1077, to prevent the Supreme Court from overruling a jury in criminal actions against pornographers, will be given strong support. In addition, legislation will be supported to raise the income tax to 100% for publishers and vendors of pornography.

4. Private schools are to be encouraged, not penalized. Legislation is needed to guarantee tax exemption and deductibility of contributions to all

From "A Positive Program to Save Our Schools" (Washington, D.C.: Liberty Lobby, [1982?], flyer).

private schools. The courts have wrongfully held that some schools do have the right.

5. Legislation will be supported to remove the National Educational Association and the AFL-CIO American Federation of Teachers from the list of tax exempt groups, and to force them to register as lobbies.

6. HEW Secretary Finch and Education Commissioner Allen, as well as other public servants who flout the law which forbids busing of students, must be fired or impeached.

7. The concept of neighborhood schools should be recognized as a desirable aim, and a permanent end must be put to forced integration and busing to achieve integration. Local authorities will be encouraged to re-draw school boundaries according to cultural consistency and neighborhood integrity.

8. Legislation will be supported to establish a NATIONAL SCHOOL SAFETY OFFICE which would hear complaints from parents where local officials failed to maintain law and order, and which would have funds available to hire local policemen to step in when necessary, with a rigid policy of arrest and punishment of agitators.

9. A mandatory loyalty oath to the Constitution should be a requirement for all teachers and employees working for any institution receiving aid from the federal government. Recognition is needed of the principle that all people who work for the taxpayers must be loyal to the government, which is the exclusive agent of the taxpayers.

10. Legislation is needed to expel from schools receiving federal assistance of all members of the Communist or Nazi Party, or teachers who refuse to take a loyalty oath.

11. Encouragement of the recital of the Pledge of Allegiance by schoolchildren, and school prayer when desired by the community.

12. An immediate halt to sex education in all schools receiving federal assistance until a local committee, composed equally of proponents and opponents, reviews the present program and establishes guidelines of an acceptable program.

13. Inasmuch as Sensitivity Training is still in the laboratory stage, with participants acting as guinea pigs, and with many participants mentally and psychologically damaged for life, it should be prohibited in all schools receiving federal assistance.

14. The establishment of a NATIONAL COUNCIL ON CURRICULA, composed of reputable Americans appointed by the S.O.S. [Save Our

Schools] Committee, to expose the poison of Leftist and revolutionary propaganda when discovered.

15. The establishment of a NATIONAL MEDIA GUIDELINES COUNCIL of reputable citizens to establish guidelines for the movie, TV, radio and publishing industry in regard to their handling of drugs, narcotics, sex and subversion themes. Constant or wilful violation of the guidelines would require the panel's recommendation as to appropriate federal action.

16. LIBERTY LOBBY will devote a special section of *Liberty Letter* every month to reporting on legislation and other matters affecting the S.O.S. Project.

17. Active cooperation with all other Conservative efforts, including the United Congressional Appeal, and the establishment of a policy to defeat at the polls congressmen and senators who do not pledge support of the S.O.S. Project.

18. LIBERTY LOBBY will step up its existing program of working with youth organizations and will mount a greater effort to attract youth to patriotism and anti-communism.

19. The S.O.S. Project will be implemented at all times to increase overall Conservative effectiveness by involving parents and taxpayers and recruiting them for political action. *It must always be borne in mind that present conditions are but the inevitable result of years of liberal indoctrination and liberal political misrule.*

John Birch Society

NEW EDUCATION
THE RADICALS ARE AFTER YOUR CHILDREN
Gary Allen

The great masses of Americans have traditionally looked upon formal education as an automatic escalator grinding upward to better jobs, higher income, and instant culture. The idea that formal education is the answer to all economic and social problems has been one of the popular heresies of the American creed since colonial days. But it was not until late in the last

From Gary Allen, "New Education: The Radicals Are After Your Children," *American Opinion* 14, no. 5 (May 1971).

century that this uncritical faith was exploited to persuade Americans to accept laws requiring compulsory education. It was a confidence game so brazenly burlesque as to drive a W.C. Fields to sobriety.

As the late Professor Richard LaPierre of Stanford University observed, the proponents of tax-supported schools argued that the "free" public schools:

> . . . *would, in a generation or two, be the cure for every recognized social ill; and that the schools would, moreover, in the course of time cost the taxpayer nothing, since the educated boys would grow up to be reasonable and honest men, and the need for public support of jails, prisons, poor farms, and homes for the aged indigent would thus be eliminated.*

Although there was a considerable number of congenital doubters at the time, there is no record of anyone having laughed himself to death at such wild promises. In retrospect such claims by Horace Mann and others seem totally absurd, but they were no more extravagant than those now being made by their modern counterparts. And, of course, they ignore how wrong history has regularly proved the predictions of educationists that their ever-revised programs would produce instant Nirvana. Again and again their lunatic schemes have been adopted with catastrophic results.

Yet our educationists are unwilling to accept any responsibility for the products of their great socialist school system. Instead they blame the parents—who, they say, are too stingy to pay for "quality education." Just what "quality education" means is usually unspecified, but it is always within a cat's breath of what you are supposed to get if you approve another tax bite for increased spending on government schools. . . .

Instead of throwing more money at a failing school system, Americans have come more and more to look at its degenerate offspring as symptoms of a disease within the system.

It is a twice-told tale, but the current malaise in public education is beyond understanding unless one reviews the thoughts and accomplishments of John Dewey, the Marxist father of modern public education. For it is the students of Dewey who are today combining the theories of their master with the concepts of behavioral scientists to create an educational system which makes the electronic totalitarianism of Big Brother seem mild by comparison.

To understand John Dewey's role one must recognize that the international Marxist conspiracy which he served has for many years been divided into Eastern and Western divisions. The East seeks to establish Marxism by the sword, while the Western branch pursues the same objectives with the pen. Readers will do well to remember that the pen is mightier than the sword.

The Western branch is known as Fabian Socialism. It was named for a Roman general who never directly engaged his enemies in all-out battle, and was founded by an odd group of radical intellectuals in London in 1884. These conspirators believed that socialism could be more effectively established through gradualism than bloody revolution. The Fabian strategy called for infiltration of education, the public media, political leadership, the clergy, and other influential bodies. The object was to establish a Marxist government by persuading the people to vote for it by degrees.

In 1905, the British Fabian Society opened an American branch known as the Intercollegiate Socialist Society. John Dewey was one of the founders. In 1921 the Society changed its name to the League for Industrial Democracy and announced the purpose of "education for a new social order based on production for use and not for profit." Dewey later became the organization's president.[a]

John Dewey developed his theories of "progressive education" while a professor at Columbia University, and he was quickly built up by collectivists on and off the American campus as a Great Authority. He taught that there is no such thing as truth, and certainly there are no eternal truths, no fixed moral laws; that man has no mind or soul as we have always understood those words, that he is nothing more than a biological organism subject to constant change, and that he is therefore wasting his time trying to find in religion or tradition the moral and ethical concepts to best guide his way on earth. "There is no God," Dewey proclaimed, "and there is no soul. Hence, there are no needs for the props of traditional religion. With dogma and creed excluded then immutable truth is also dead and buried. There is no room for fixed, natural law or permanent moral absolutes."

Comrade Dewey's job was to work out ways to use the schools as a vehicle for selling the "new society" about which he and his Fabian Socialist disciples dreamed. "They [the schools]," he proclaimed, "take an active part in determining the social order of the future . . . according as the teachers align themselves with the newer forces making for social control of economic forces." From such a starting point it was naturally easy for Dewey to arrive at the conclusion that tradition had no meaning, that history and the lessons of the past were nonsense, that stern discipline of the mind and body was foolish, and that education had only one purpose—to enable the child to be happy in his environment.

In the early 1920's, along with fellow Fabian Socialists Bertrand Russell and Harold Laski, Dewey journeyed to Russia where the Eastern arm of the

Marxist conspiracy had recently triumphed by the sword. There, for two years, John Dewey worked with the two English Fabians to help organize a Marxist educational system for the Worker's Paradise. The Dewey system produced in Russia the same sort of educational havoc that it was later to wreak on America, and in 1931 Stalin dispatched hundreds of thousands of students and their Deweyite teachers to Siberia. The Soviets went back to the Three R's—or whatever they call them in Russian. Progressive education, they decided, was fine for corrupting bourgeois capitalists, but was idiotic caprice once the dictatorship was fully in control.

Meanwhile, Dewey had returned to America to establish the system that had proved so destructive to educational quality in Russia.[b] He saw that the traditional system of American education fostered individualism and defended our system of free enterprise, both of which he had vowed to destroy. "The mere absorbing of facts and truths," he wrote, "is so exclusively individual an affair that it tends very naturally to pass into selfishness. There is no obvious social motive for the acquirement of mere learning, and there is no clear social gain in success thereat." (John Dewey, *The School And Society,* University of Chicago Press, 1915, Page 15).

Throughout the Twenties, Dewey spread his poison among his fellow college professors, but as yet the public school systems were relatively untouched. Soon, however, those who received doctorates in education at Columbia Teachers College began to occupy the chairs of education at other colleges and universities and to author textbooks extolling the virtues of "the new society." Columbia Teachers College became the most influential educational institution in the United States, and John Dewey its high guru.

One of Dewey's chief lieutenants at Columbia was Dr. George S. Counts. Like John Dewey he was frank about what "the new society" meant. In 1931, Counts authored a book called *The Soviet Challenge,* in which he proclaimed:

> *The revolutionary movement embraces much that is rich and challenging in the best sense of the word. The idea of building a new society along the lines developed by the Communists should provide a genuine stimulus to the mind and liberate the energies of millions.*

In order to bring about this revolutionary millennium, said Dr. Counts:

> *[It] would seem to require fundamental changes in the economic system. Historic capitalism, with its deification of the principle of selfishness, its reliance upon the forces of competition . . . and its exaltation of the profit motive, will either have to be displaced altogether or so radically changed in form and spirit that its identity will be completely lost. . . .*

Dr. George Counts soon wrote a book titled *Dare The Schools Build a New Social Order?*, in which he spelled out openly how the Dewey "progressive education" would be used to build a Marxist Utopia in America. Here are his words:

In the collectivist society now emerging the school should be regarded, not as an agency for lifting gifted individuals out of the class into which they were born and elevating them into favored positions where they may exploit their less-favored fellows, but rather as an agency for the abolition of all artificial social distinctions and of organizing the energies of the nation for the promotion of the general welfare. . . .

Throughout the school program the development of the social rather than egotistic impulses should be stressed; and the motive of personal aggrandizement should be subordinated to social ends. In promotion practices, in school activities, in the relations of pupils and teachers and administrators, the ideal of a cooperative commonwealth should prevail. . . . All of this applies quite as strictly to the nursery, kindergarten, and the elementary school as to the secondary school, the college, and the university. . . .

John Dewey and his colleagues, known as the "Frontier Thinkers," made little headway until they attracted the attention, and the financial support, of the powerful Carnegie and Rockefeller foundations. . . .

Following World War II, the emphasis on creating a new economic and social order in America was expanded to include the entire globe. This philosophy was officially adopted with the acceptance of U.N.E.S.C.O. source material by the N.E.A. As one textbook for teachers phrases it:

Allegiance to a nation is the biggest stumbling block to creation of international government. National boundaries and the concept of sovereignty must be abolished . . . sovereignty is to condition the young to another and broader allegiance. Opinion favorable to international government will be developed in the social studies in the elementary school.

All of this was just fine with the boys at the Rockefeller, Carnegie, and Ford foundations. The idea of world government is music to the ears of the clique of super-wealthy radicals using the socialist cant for their own purposes. If you want to establish and preserve a monopoly on a national level you need to control the national government. If you want to establish and preserve a worldwide monopoly, you must establish and control a World Government. These boys think big.

But the penthouse conspirators were not only the only ones pushing "progressive education." Dr. Bella Dodd, who for many years headed the New York City Teachers' Union while a high-ranking officer of the Communist Party, broke with the Communists after a religious conversion and testified before a Senate Committee:

> *The Communist Party as a whole adopted a line of being for progressive education. . . . [It] was eagerly seized upon and championed by the Comintern as the ideal system for limiting the ability of children in capitalistic societies to read, write, or to think for themselves or to act for themselves, and so to cause them to depend upon the state for a guaranteed livelihood and for the hazards caused by their inadequate training for the battle of life.*

. . . the term "progressive education" had by now fallen into disrepute as parents observed that their offspring, assigned by the schools to "life adjustment" classes, had neither adjusted to life nor learned to read, write, or add. It was time to change labels. While the educationists no longer praise the name of John Dewey in public, nor refer to their programs as "progressive education," both the song and the melody linger on—humming along under more "modern" aliases. . . .

The coverup was necessary because anti-Deweyism had risen to a crescendo following the Sputnik fiasco in 1957. For a time there was great rhetorical stress on academic excellence, particularly in the sciences. Then, using Sputnik as an excuse, America's first program of direct federal aid to education became law as the National Defense Education Act. Federal involvement had long been a goal of the National Education Association. Its proponents swore up and down that there would never be any federal strings attached to the federal monies. All they were interested in, they contended, was that the kiddies got a better education so that America could "catch-up" with the Russians. Such talk proved as absurd as the earlier prediction that a compulsory public school system would permit the abolition of jails. . . .

The next big step in the federalizing of education came with the 1965 appointment by President Lyndon Johnson of "Republican" John Gardner as Secretary of Health, Education and Welfare. Gardner, you will not be surprised to learn, came to H.E.W. after serving for many years as president of the Carnegie Foundation for the Advancement of Teaching. Soon the Elementary and Secondary Education Act was passed as part of L.B.J.'s "Great Society."[c] It provided Secretary Gardner with billions of dollars each year with which to implement the wild educational schemes of his friends and colleagues at the Carnegie, Rockefeller, and Ford foundations. Indeed, wherever one finds radical experiments in education designed to destroy concepts of individualism and self reliance and to promote socialism, almost inevitably one finds the names Carnegie, Rockefeller, and Ford.[d]

Today, the quest for academic excellence born in the aftermath of Sputnik has been all but abandoned. The emphasis in the journals of educational theory is now on "change." The word "change" seems to appear at least once in every sentence. The line being promoted is that technological "change" is so altering our lives that the old values of absolutes, eternal truth, traditions, and cultural standards have become obsolete. They are to be replaced by the "new morality" and "doing your own thing."

We are also told that the rapidity of technological change has "dehumanized" the individual, who can no longer function adequately in our society. In order to cope with such "change," it is necessary to develop a "relevant" curriculum. The word "relevant" now runs second only to "change" in the abracadabra of educationist incantation. . . .

Such promulgators of the "new education" are mostly behavioral scientists—sociologists, psychiatrists, psychologists. Almost without exception they are secular humanists, holding that man is his own god, and that truth, as the essence of social good, must be manipulated to support the latest social theories. Through programs pushed by such people our schools are abandoning the teaching of "facts" and substituting instruction in human relations. No longer do the educationists rationalize, stammer, and apologize for poor performance in reading; now they claim that reading is no longer important. . . .

Today's Frontier Innovators tell us that the printed word has served its purpose.[e] Oh, it has served well enough until technology gave us so many alternative forms of communication. Now, however, the printed word is increasingly *passé*. More and more schools are using records, tapes, film strips, and movies to replace the antiquated printed word. Who knows, some day books may be as rare as stereoscopes. Or so the line goes. As part of this movement many school districts are abandoning textbooks altogether and substituting class discussion.

Under such "relevant" education the class is conducted without lectures or texts according to a new system called "inquiry," which is based on endless open-ended discussions. Subject matter includes such "relevant" matters as the Vietnam War, ecology, community control, the New Left, drugs, the draft, the "peace" movement, the new morality, the pill, and abortion. These, you understand, are topics for grammar school students as well as those in junior and senior high.

In many of the "relevant" education programs the teachers prepare packets of "information" taken from a variety of periodicals on a "relevant" topic and pass them out to pupils for review and discussion. For example, students might compare treatment of a subject such as air pollution by an Establishment magazine like *Time* with the same subject as presented in a "progressive" periodical of the nature of the *New Republic* or *Village Voice* . . . so that students see "all sides" of an issue.

Just how students can be capable of reaching rational conclusions on emotionally charged political matters without a basic foundation of history, political science, economics, and morality is difficult to understand. Obviously they can't. They are being asked to accept canned "Liberal" opinions on fad subjects. The teacher guides their conclusions to what is "socially correct." Truth is redefined as a "social good." It is no wonder so many of our teenagers are intellectually confused and emotionally distraught.

In the past, parents expected teachers to reinforce parental values and discipline. Now the child is praised for his brilliance and his courage on "social" problems while the parent is ridiculed for stubborn rigidity and old-fashioned morality. Much of what we call the Generation Gap is really a teacher-parent gap. What is happening is Marxist class warfare, based on youth versus age rather than capital versus labor.

Yet those promoting the "inquiry" system under a plethora of names and guises (the most famous of which is the Glasser System)[f] claim that it teaches young people to be "problem solvers" rather than filling their heads with "useless" accumulated knowledge. . . .

But the behavioral scientists are not content merely to load the curriculum. They have introduced what can only be termed psychological brainwashing techniques in order to "change" the character and personality of students. In an article titled "Forecast For the '70's" the *N.E.A. Journal* observed in its issue for January 1969:

> *The roles and responsibilities of teachers will alter throughout the next decade. Future-think suggests that between 1970 and 1980 a number of new assignments and specialties will materialize if present trends continue.*
>
> *For one thing, the basic role of the teacher will change noticeably. Ten years hence it should be more accurate to term him a "learning clinician." This title is intended to convey the idea that schools are becoming "clinics" whose purpose is to provide individualized psychosocial "treatment" for the student, thus increasing his value both to himself and to society. . . .*

While it has many variations and aliases, sensitivity training nearly always includes group confessions and group criticism conducted by a "trained" leader. The technique is the same as that used by the Red Chinese on

American prisoners of war in Korea. It is designed to produce "change" in a person's values and even his personality. Many become psychologically hooked on sensitivity training, caught up in the fascination it holds for those with sado-masochistic tendencies. Others sustain severe emotional damage.

The National Training Laboratory, financed by the N.E.A., admits that sensitivity training "includes coercive persuasion in the form of thought reforms or brainwashing as well as a multitude of less coercive, informal patterns." Which is why socialist N.E.A. promotes it for the schools. Sensitivity training is designed to strip a person of his psychological defenses so that he has no private thoughts which are kept from the group. The group collectively decides what is right or wrong for the individual. Sensitivity programs have been financed by the Ford Foundation, the Office of Economic Opportunity, and the Department of Health, Education and Welfare. . . .

Other radical educators are not so much concerned about pumping amphetamines into their charges as they are about the fact that they do not get their hands on your child until age five. In its "Forecast For the 70's" the N.E.A. declares: "As nonschool, pre-school programs begin to operate, educators will assume a formal responsibility for children when they reach the age of two." What worries those certified government child molesters is that too many parental values are transmitted to the child during the early years.

But, of course, the child doesn't belong to the state! Really? Then why did President Nixon tell the recent convention of governors at Colorado Springs that "We have declared the first five years of a child's life to be a period of special and specific Federal concern?"

When the White House Conference on Children and Youth met in Washington last December, one of the most important matters to come before the session was that of establishing a vast grid of federally funded child care centers, a system which will probably be established this year. It would cost some $10 billion per year to operate these federally controlled centers, plus construction costs. The White House Conference even recommended that the federal government provides an "advocate" for our children who would serve as a "protector" between parent and child.

The Master Planners are also discussing other charming ideas in this field. One of them is compulsory national service at age eighteen for both males and females. Those who do not choose the military would be required to do social work as federal bureaucrats. Someone wants to make awfully sure your child has no chance for independent thinking between the ages of two and twenty one.

Among other schemes being contemplated by the illumined educationists are mandatory foster homes for children removed en masse from the influence of socially or politically unacceptable parents. Serious discussion of billeting children from poverty areas to affluent neighborhoods is already underway. There is also discussion of establishing kibbutzim where children would live in a commune, learning to be "socially acceptable." Elizabeth Koontz, president of the National Educational Association in 1968, and named head of the new network of child care centers by President Nixon, is already pushing for the establishment of this sort of arrangements for children.

These "innovative" ideas are emanating from hundreds of so-called P.A.C.E. (Programs to Advance Creativity in Education) Centers, established by Congress as part of the Elementary and Secondary Education Act. The Centers, scattered over the nation, have been funded by the Department of Health, Education and Welfare and the Ford Foundation, and are staffed by the usual radical psychiatrists, sociologists, and educators. Their job is to design experimental programs for the various school districts in their area.

In order to make sure that the "new education" juggernaut is not derailed, the National Education Association operates as one of the most potent lobbies in the country. It is a very cute operation indeed. On January 29, 1970, N.E.A. President George Fischer proclaimed: "We plan to make it political suicide to vote against [what we think is good for] the kids and education." In July of 1970, Fischer told an N.E.A. convention in San Francisco: "The world has never seen an organization of this magnitude." Mr. Fischer said that by the end of the Seventies "the President of the U.S. will consult with the officers of the united teaching profession on all issues of national importance." He did not say or else, but he added that teachers would reach their goals by strikes, contract negotiations and political action.

And the N.E.A. is well prepared with counter measures should parents try to protect their schools from attacking waves of behavioral scientists. Along with other "educational" groups the National Education Association is now conducting seminars in how to sell the new programs and head off opposition. The first tactic is always to accuse those who oppose letting teacher play psychiatrist of being some sort of extremist or religious fanatics.

Okay, what *can* parents do to protect their offspring from the Orwellian people planners? It is customary here to urge parents to become involved, to join the P.T.A., to discuss the situation with teacher, to protest at the local school board. More often than not, these are merely exercises in frustration.

In some cases it still may be possible to head off the "new education" programs if local citizens can mobilize enough pressure on the local school board. But more and more these programs are being taken out of the jurisdiction of local boards and mandated by state law or federal guidelines. Within a few years, local school boards will have no power at all and we will have a Federal School System. Even in cases where local pressure can be brought to bear, unless the pressure can be brought to bear, unless the pressure is constant, "Liberal" school boards will tend to sneak faddish programs in the back door as soon as the furor out front calms down.

It is vital for a totalitarian state to control the education and indoctrination of youth. Knowing this, the collectivist social engineers are working constantly to destroy independent private schools. They scream that it is "un-Democratic" for you to try to keep your child out of their clutches. . . .

Those who would socialize America will do anything to keep their education monopoly from being broken. They see private schools as a serious threat to their power. But so bad are the public schools that more and more parents are now willing to make the financial sacrifices necessary to keep their children out of the hands of the certified government child molesters.[g] After all, how much is it worth to keep your son or daughter from being turned into a hippie, a revolutionary, or an obedient little Marxist?

Private schools, unfortunately, cannot be a panacea. Many of us simply cannot afford them, and others live in areas so sparsely populated that maintenance of both public and private schools is not practical. Parents in these situations must run their own schools at home after regular school hours. If they are not to see their children destroyed they have no other choice.

What were once community schools, organized for the convenience of parents and supported by them, have now become government indoctrination centers, increasingly financed and controlled by Washington. Their products are the Spock-marked generation of delinquents, drop-outs and drug freaks we see all around us. Their tools are no longer those of Socrates or Christ, but of Dewey, Moreno, and the behavioral scientists. As Dr. Joseph Bean observed: "When you consider that the ultimate goal of warfare is the control of the behavior of the vanquished by the victor, you realize that we are now in the greatest conflict in the history of mankind. Welcome to World War III."

Author's Notes

a. In 1962, the League formed an action arm which is now better known than the
   parent organization. When the subsidiary, Students for a Democratic Society
   (S.D.S.), later became a hot potato, the L.I.D. freed it to go its violent way.
b. John Dewey did, however, continue to serve on the National Advisory Council for
   the University of Moscow, a group which sent American students to summer
   school sessions in the Red capital. The reader should keep in mind that educationists vehemently deny that Dewey's Marxism and virulent atheism had anything to
   do with his theories of education, or that they have had any lasting influence on
   American education.
c. A phrase coined by British Fabian Socialist Graham Wallas, and the title of a
   radical book he published in 1914.
d. One of Richard Nixon's first acts after being elected President was to appoint the
   Carnegie Corporation's president, Alan Pifer, to head his committee on national
   goals.
e. A recent Lou Harris poll showed that 18.5 percent of Americans aged sixteen or
   older are illiterate. These products of the public school system are obviously ahead
   of their time!
f. This is thoroughly described in Dr. William Glasser's book *Schools Without
   Failure*, which might also be subtitled "Schools Without Learning."
g. This is not to contend that all private schools are good schools. Many are more
   futuristic than the public schools. But when you are paying the bill *privately* you
   can pick and choose.

Committee for Positive Education

In The Name Of Education
Jo-Ann Abrigg

When school bells ring each fall, bright eyed healthy American youngsters
are sent off by loving parents to be educated in the American public school
system.

What will these children learn? What will they read? What will they
comprehend? Or, more important, what will they *not learn?* Based on the
experience of past years, what *will not be happening* in many classrooms? If

From Jo-Ann Abrigg, "In the Name of Education" (Warren, Ohio: Committee for Positive
Education, 1976, pamphlet).

statistics remain the same—and according to the series of educational reports recently published by the *Los Angeles Times*—there is no reason to expect much differentiation:

Some 35 per cent of those who have completed five years of school will be functionally illiterate. Children will not be able to add, subtract, multiply or divide. Scholastic Aptitude Tests will continue their drastic decline in scores. All the disastrous educational innovations of the 60s, found to be failures in the early 70s will still be very much in existence. Textbook publishers, responding to a changing market in college texts, will continue to use simplified language in their books because large numbers of college students simply cannot read the English language well enough to understand textbooks previously used and understood by college students. One-third of our young men will flunk the Armed Forces Qualifying Examination, which means they can neither read, write, spell, or compute on a 5th grade level. National publications and weekly magazines will continue to print articles about the shocking state of education. Brig. Gen. William Woodyard, Dean of the faculty of the Air Force Academy, has stated that more than 300 freshmen cadets will have to take remedial courses in English and mathematics.

Many students who graduated from high school with top grades will find that they can't make it in college—even with their college textbooks now written at a 9th grade level. Many college graduates who received their diplomas this year will find out that they were not actually given the academic prerequisites necessary for a productive life in the working world, but simply received their diplomas based on inflated grades of A or B, due to the fact that their college didn't give anyone a grade lower than a C, making it impossible for anyone to fail. James L. Kilpatrick, noted columnist put it quite bluntly: "We are raising a whole nation of 'culturally disadvantaged children' and 'education is a sordid, sorry racket.' "

What is actually going on across our land IN THE NAME OF EDUCATION? In a country where concerned citizens have been willing to be taxed to the tune of over $85 billion a year to provide education for the future generation, where young Americans would have had and could have had the greatest education in the history of Western civilization, how is it possible that such statistics could be making headlines?

No longer can we, who are footing the exorbitant bill for education, accept the "amazement" of the educationists as they are confronted with scholastic test results. Nor, should we, as parents, stand by silently and watch these so-called "educational experts" grasp for new and more outlandish reasons as they attempt to explain away their educational failures.

When Bishop Fulton Sheen wrote that Watergate might have been more indicative of our educational system rather than our political system, he touched on the real basis for the mess in public education. There is one very basic reason: that education has been redefined—and is rapidly being redesigned. Where once it was the responsibility of the schools to foster the intellectual development of the child by providing essential basic skills, by cultivating the mind of each child to seek the systemic knowledge produced through centuries of academic endeavor, and by instilling our heritage and our culture, the purpose of education today is to use the child as a means by which society can be changed. Education is now defined as a "change of behavior" and "to educate" means "to modify behavior." The question that logically must follow is, "change to what?" "To what extent shall we modify the child in order to change our society?"

Who is responsible for this redesigning of education in order to implement this change? The answers to these questions can be found by researching educational programs, textbooks, teachers' manuals, materials used in teacher in-service training workshops, and the NEA Journals and Task Force reports. These sources provide a clear-cut answer to the questions "Who is redesigning education and why?", "To what are we changing the behavior of the school child and why?", and "What methods will be used to bring about this change?"

BEHAVIORISM AND HUMANISM

There are two trends or movements producing the major portion of public education today; one comes from the School of Behavioral Psychology and is referred to as Behaviorism. The other finds its base in the American Humanist Association and the School of Humanistic Psychology and is referred to as Secular Humanism, or the religion of Humanism.

Behaviorism and Humanism have indeed become the major factors in public education today. As they rise to the surface, more and more parents and many dedicated teachers are becoming alarmed at just what education is producing through the adoption of these two trends. Many parents are withdrawing their children from public schools. Many concerned teachers are doing their very best to protect their own students from the influence of these trends in the program and textbooks they have been mandated by school administrations to teach.

At the same time, there are many parents, teachers, board members and administrators who are either unaware of these trends, or are initiating and promoting programs utilizing Behaviorism and Humanism without understanding their implications or ramifications.

The School of Behavioral Psychology was founded in 1913 by John B. Watson. Behaviorism stands for the extension of the methods and point of view of Animal Psychology and states that man must be regarded as simply an animal, nothing more. The Behaviorist states unequivocally that the human being has no mind, no consciousness, no soul, no instincts, no native intelligence, no special talents or inherited gifts, and no emotions. The Behaviorist believes that man is simply a whole living organism reacting to his whole natural environment, and that all of his activities can be explained by one who regards him as a stimulus response machine. According to the Behaviorist, man's whole system of behavior is built up from a few simple reactions by the important process of conditioning. The conditioning process is one of the most important factors in Behaviorism.

Conditioning is a method of learning by which a specific response is continuously given to a specific stimulus until it is learned and, therefore, becomes a conditioned reflex or response. The specific stimulus can be a material or physical stimulus (as in the often-quoted canine conditioning experiments of Pavlov, where the conditioned dog salivated simply at the sound of a bell). Or, the specific stimulus can be words, groups of words, phrases, or even a specific facial expression, which through the conditioning process will eventually elicit a specific response or reaction. Conditioning can be done on an individual basis, or it can be applied to groups. With groups, it is then referred to as "group reflexology." With "group reflexology," the individual loses his own identity and becomes one of the group, accepts the interaction of the social group or "peer group" as his own and becomes conditioned to thinking like the group and reacting with his "peer group" to a given stimulus. One very important thing to remember with conditioning is that the original response or original behavior to a specific stimulus is changed or altered or modified through the conditioning process. In other words, a Behavior Modification takes place.

BEHAVIOR MODIFICATION

Thus, from the School of Behavioral Psychology, we find the formula or method which forms the basis for Behavior Modification, which is promoted in thousands of classrooms across this country. When we talk about modifying or altering or changing behavior, we must ask, changing behavior to what and why? . . . we find in the School of Behavioral Psychology an elitist attitude that they must not be content with merely understanding the human animal and predicting and controlling him through conditioning, but the Behaviorist must also alter and "improve" man. This knowledge of conditioning must be used to manage the human race. The Behaviorist is sold on the theory that, IF he has the power to condition all human animals, then he will have the ultimate power to control mankind and design a future Utopian society.

What will this future Utopian society be like? Who is utilizing the techniques of Behavioral Psychology, such as conditioning, to design and produce a future Utopia? Most important, is it a society which we as freedom-loving, God-fearing Americans desire as a replacement for our present society, imperfect though it may be?

The second movement making a tremendous impact on education today, the American Humanist Association, is a relatively small organization. Those referred to as Third Force Psychologists and Secular Humanists actually make up a very small portion of our country's vast population. But when you delve into the backgrounds and philosophies of the nationally known spokesmen for education today, those who are writing educational books and journals, speaking at teachers conferences, designing behavior modification programs and holding the leading in-service training workshops across this country, we find that the secular Humanists, are doing an impressive job of directing public education.

THE RELIGION OF HUMANISM

Humanism is a religion, and has been so declared even by the U.S. Supreme Court. It is a way of life, a philosophy, an all encompassing ideology. The Humanist Manifesto states that there is no God, every man is his own creator, there is no right or wrong, ethics are situational, there are no absolutes, there must be no feeling of individuality, the individual must be trained to think of himself as part of a group willing to be manipulated for the good of society rather than for individual gain or achievement. Under humanism there must be no patriotism, no feeling of nationalism developed, because all society must eventually be conditioned to accept living in a global collectivist economy under a one-world government.

The first American to use public education to promote Humanism was John Dewey, who also served as president of the American Humanist Association. Horace Mann, one of the founders of public education stated: "What the church has been for medieval man, the public school must become for democratic and rational man. God would be replaced by the concept of the public good." Beginning in the early 1930s, John Dewey and his many disciples of progressive education have continually promoted and increased the impact of Humanism on public education. . . .

Because of their own alien ideology, the Humanists are designing education today from the basic premise that children, by the time they enter school, have been indoctrinated by their parents and their church with certain beliefs, attitudes, standards and values (so-called middle class values) such as belief in God, belief in moral standards of right and wrong, patriotism, individualism, competition, achievement—and that these beliefs and values have no place in a future one-world Utopian society. The Humanistic educationists have designed what they refer to as "psychological education" to develop the whole child "emotionally, socially, and psychologically." In order to accomplish this, they have "borrowed" from the Behaviorists the psychological techniques which produce conditioning.

Thus we find this psycho-social philosophy as the basis for the Hawaii Master Plan for Education which states that all classrooms must now be considered "mental health clinics," all teachers must be looked upon as ["]Mental Health Clinicians," and all students must be regarded as "patients." Then, through the use of psychological techniques which produce behavior modification, the students will be conditioned to an acceptance of the religion of Humanism, which is basic to a one-world government. . . .

SCHOOLS TURNED INTO CLINICS

Then too, the NEA followed with its report, "Education for the 70s," which said, "Schools will become clinics whose purpose is to provide individualized, psycho-social treatment for the student, and teachers must become psycho-social therapists." "This will include biochemical and psychological mediation of learning, as drugs are introduced experimentally to improve in the learner such qualities as personality, concentration, and memory. Children are to become the objects of experimentation." This has already come about with the thousands of children who have been given Ritalin and other tranquilizers to improve their classroom behavior, the endless listings and categorizing of "learning disabilities," and teachers across the country who have already adopted the role of psycho-social therapists.

The Humanists and Behaviorists with their elitist attitude believe that, if they can just take children from their parents by the age of two, it will be much easier to condition and develop children with the "right" set of attitudes and values. This philosophy is the basis for the tremendous amount of child advocacy legislation being written to promote federal day care centers, state-run nursery schools, Senator Mondale's Child and Family Services Act of 1975, and the proposal by the NEA and the American Federation of Teachers that all children begin school by the age of three.

In the meantime, the Humanists and Behaviorists continue to design programs that begin in Kindergarten. The combination of these two schools of thought have made it clear that the chief concern of the schools should not be to teach the child knowledge and skills, but to work on his psyche so that he will fit into the specific mold they have designed. These educationists endeavor to influence the child's feelings and emotions, attitudes and values, rather than teach him factual knowledge.

Is it any wonder that more and more parents and dedicated teachers are expressing alarm at what is going on IN THE NAME OF EDUCATION? Against this background of present day educational philosophy, let's take a quick look at specific programs, methods, and techniques found in the classrooms.

One of the most popular methods being utilized is called "open-ended discussions" and "problem solving group discussions." Discussions must be about "relevant" issues such as racial equality, poverty, free speech, sexual freedom, academic freedom, war, ecology, women's lib, homosexual liberation, death, abortion, the occult, witchcraft, suicide, the pill, drugs, family planning, friendship, love and taxes. These moral, emotional, or social issues either replace or are added into discussions on basic academic subjects.

TOTAL ATTITUDINAL CHANGE

The Behavior Modification that takes place is called Total Attitudinal Change, a specified goal of the Behaviorists and Humanists. During these discussions, the teacher must adopt the role of psychosocial therapist, in which he or she must remain non-directive, and non-judgmental. Without any absolutes, without any basic truths, without any guidance or direction from the non-judgmental teacher, the group of students "solves" all of these relevant issues. They bring uninformed opinions into discussion, keep exchanging them, finally come up with an uninformed answer based on nothing absolute, and feel that they have solved the relevant issues. The immensity of this modification in attitudes can be realized when you recognize the fact that these open ended discussions are utilized in sex education, drug education, family life series, and many English courses and reading series. Beginning in kindergarten and continuing through high school, these programs continuously modify the children in their attitudes, standards, values, and beliefs. They alienate them from basing any opinions or decisions on Christian-Judeo morals and values taught by the home and church.

Through these specific programs which produce Total Attitudinal Change, the Humanist philosophy of Situational Ethics is promoted to the extent that young children become conditioned to thinking only in terms of the situation rather than the Ten Commandments. The only true authority presented in the conclusion of open-ended discussions in the classroom is "What do you, the child, think?" Or, "What does the peer group decide"? There are no right and wrong answers, there are no basic truths, and there are no absolutes.

The ideas are introduced, through stories, group discussions, social studies, visual aids and reading materials, that Mothers and Fathers are old-fashioned, Mothers and Fathers have strange ideas or hang-ups about different things, the morals that Mom and Dad and the church preach are not really relevant to today's society, everything is moving so quickly today that older people just can't keep up with the changing times, and, besides, look at the mess the world is in today, and after all, who got us into all these problems! The older folks obviously don't know very much, but you young children are brighter than any other! In order to accomplish things in today's society, you must be relevant and base your thoughts and actions on the "situation"—not on old and out-moded Christian values and morals that certainly haven't solved the problems of the past and hold no hope for the future.

MODIFYING YOUR CHILD

How long do you think it will take for this type of education to modify the young child's previously held values and beliefs, particularly if the parents are unaware of what is happening in the classroom?

There are many other techniques being used to change and modify the child such as: Psychodrama, Role Playing Reversal, Soliloquy, Group Dynamics, Encounter Group sessions, Sensitivity Training Sessions, "All about me" Diaries, Daily Journals, reality therapy, magic circles, self-actualizing sessions, and values clarification programs. These techniques are incorporated into many different courses and at all different grade levels. All these techniques were designed and utilized originally by licensed psychiatrists treating emotionally disturbed patients in the controlled situation of mental clinics and hospitals. Now we find them being used in classrooms by teachers, playing the role of amateur psychologists, on normal, healthy, well-adjusted American children who have never been diagnosed as in need of psychological help.

Concerned parents in different sections of this country, while raising their voices against some of the more notorious pornographic materials found in the schools, have not, unfortunately, voiced protests against the utilization of psychological techniques being used on their children. Yet these techniques can cause irreparable emotional damage when used by amateurs and can condition our children to an anti-Christian-Judeo philosophy and religion.

ABOVE ALL, BE "RELEVANT"

Our teenagers can't discuss philosophy or the classics, or the history of our country but they know everything there is to know about sex, drugs, the problems of America, pollution, abortion, ecology, population control, and the paperback books that have made four letter words common in the classroom.

Literature which promotes the beauty of the English language, teaches our heritage, uplifts the mind and has its basis in morality, is no longer considered "Relevant" by the educationists. If children are never given good classical literature to read—only pornographic garbage; if they are never given a chance to hear and learn about good music—only hard rock; if they never have an opportunity to view good art—only mod splashes on canvas; if they are never shown the beauty of this country—only its problems; if the beauty of love and sex in marriage is never stressed—only descriptions of lust, rape, and deviate sexual activity; they will be conditioned only for the society of the Humanists and the Behaviorists.

As Bishop Fulton Sheen said, "A person who has no contact with real precious stones, has no criteria by which to judge synthetic stones." If everyone sets his own watch to suit his relevant situation, will there ever be a correct time?

After reviewing many of today's textbooks, one can't help but ponder this thought: Would we as parents knowingly hire a babysitter to come into our home and systematically teach our children the exact opposite of what we believe? Would we permit that babysitter to spoon-feed garbage to our child?

Yet—in the name of education—we, as parents, are indeed paying taxes to school systems that hire teachers and purchase educational programs that fill our children's minds with garbage and utilize psychological techniques to condition our children to an anti-Christian-Judeo philosophy and religion.

Loud cries are constantly heard about our country's monopolies—the monopolies of utilities, oil companies, and big business. These monopolies are nothing compared to the ever growing monopoly on the most precious commodity that this country has—the minds of our children. This monopoly is produced, promoted and perpetuated by the elitist Behaviorist and Humanist educationists.

When the Supreme Court took God out of the classroom, the elitist educationists replaced Him with the religion of Humanism. We the people of America, are the only ones who can protect our children from futuristic manipulation by these elitists.

But we must begin now—we can't wait for the next generation to take action. By then they will have been "educated" to conform to the new definition of education and educated to hold allegiance only to man and to a one-world government. They will never even know that they were misled. They may never know America the Beautiful. Above all, they might never know God.

Phyllis Schlafly

WHAT'S WRONG WITH SEX EDUCATION?

The major goal of nearly all sex education curricula being taught in the schools is to teach teenagers (and sometimes children) how to enjoy fornication without having a baby and without feeling guilty.

This goal explains why the courses promote an acceptance of sexual behavior that does not produce a baby, such as homosexuality and masturbation. This goal explains why they encourage abortions and all varieties of contraception. This is why they promote the acceptance of the propositions that a "sexually active" lifestyle is normal for all teenagers, and that no sex act is abnormal.

This is why the courses shred the girls of their natural modesty (a psychological defense against fornication) by forcing them to discuss sexual acts, techniques, devices, and parts of the body, with explicit vocabulary in a coed classroom. This is why they censor out from sex education courses both moral training and the truth about the physical and psychological penalties for sin.

The reason we are able to state so bluntly what are the real goals of sex education is because the U.S. Department of Health, Education, and Welfare Center for Disease Control, headquartered in Atlanta, GA, gave a large federally-funded contract to a think tank called Mathtech, Inc. of Bethesda, Maryland, to make the most comprehensive survey of sex education in the United States. The survey was designed, and is being widely used, to promote sex education courses in all the public schools from kindergarten through grade 12.

Called "An Analysis of U.S. Sex Education Programs and Evaluation Methods," the Mathtech report was written by Douglas Kirby, Judith Alter and Peter Scales. It is identified by Contract No. 200-78-0804, and was published in July 1979. This survey describes in five volumes of detail the real goals of sex education. Those goals are quite shocking, and almost completely unknown to parents or taxpayers.

"Sex education is very different from many other classes," the Mathtech

From Phyllis Schlafly, "What's Wrong with Sex Education?" *Phyllis Schlafly Report* 14, no. 7 (February 1981).

report explains. "The purposes of sex education is not simply to fill gaps in the knowledge of adolescents. . . . The goals of sex education are much more ambitious; they involve . . . the changing of attitudes and behaviors."

The Mathtech report describes with unconcealed enthusiasm how current sex education courses are "changing" students' attitudes. The goals of these changes are identified by Mathtech as "broadly humanistic."

Whether the courses are at the junior or senior high school or at the college level, the students who take sex education courses become more "liberal or tolerant of the sexual behavior" of others. They develop "a greater acceptance of homosexuality and masturbation."

They become "more comfortable" with the idea of their future marriage partners having had sexual relations with someone else. It is no accident that this is the effect on students because, as Mathtech reports, "with near unanimity, the experts believe that the discouragement of all nonmarital activity was unimportant," and some experts think it is "counterproductive."

This antagonism to premarital chastity is echoed again and again throughout the Mathtech report. The Mathtech authors warn bluntly that the goals of sex education professionals "will, of course, conflict with the belief held by some people that sex should be enjoyed only within the context of marriage. . . . Thus, policymakers and sex educators should realize that some values conveyed in sex education classes are not supported by all members of society."

That's right, they are not. But the question is do the "members of society" whose children are being subjected to this "changing" of their values know what are the real goals of the sex professionals? Do they know that the "sexperts" are teaching tolerance for homosexuality but antagonism to premarital chastity?

The more controversial and private the topic, the more the "experts" believe that it should be covered in depth and "not superficially." For example, when contraception is discussed, it is suggested that the lecture should include the advantages and disadvantages of each method, the fears and fallacies of each method and the addresses of the places where contraceptives can be obtained. Outside of the self-serving use of the words "experts" and "professionals" to describe those involved in teaching or promoting the Mathtech brand of sex education, the next most used word is "values clarification." That's the jargon which identifies the use of educational facilities to change the students' values and attitudes rather than for the traditional purpose to impart knowledge.

Another favorite word in the Mathtech report is "nonjudgmental." That means that sex education courses should promote "a reduction of sexual guilt" (for committing immoral sex acts) and "an acceptance of alternative lifestyles" (such as homosexuality).

It is clear from the Mathtech report that sex education, as conceived by the experts, extends from kindergarten through twelfth grade (K-12), and that it is integrated throughout many different courses so that parents will find it more difficult to identify. Obviously, it is easier to bring about "attitudinal change" in youngsters if the professionals can start at the earliest age and prevent the parents from knowing the goals.

One of the quickest ways to see how values and attitudes are changed is to read the questionnaires given to the pupils. The multiple-choice questions about what is assumed to be their "sexually active" lifestyle are pornographic in their explicitness. They could not help but encourage a chaste youngster to get busy and find out what he or she has been missing.

One of the major defects of sex education courses is that they assume that all teenagers are "sexually active," thereby exerting tremendous peer pressure to turn the assumption into a fact. But the assumption is false.

The eleventh annual opinion survey of the top five percent of the 6 ½ million students who were high school seniors and juniors during the 1979-80 academic year shows clearly that high achievement goes hand in hand with good moral character. The poll was taken among the students who excel in academics, extracurricular activities, community service or athletics in the nation's 20,000 public, private and parochial schools.

More than three-fourths (76 percent) of these high school leaders have not had sexual intercourse, and 59 percent say they would not live with someone prior to marriage. Teenagers should be encouraged to imitate the good character of their own peer leaders, rather than be dragged down to the assumption of the sex education courses.

CAUSE OF TEENAGE PREGNANCY

The prevailing liberal dogma is that "sex education" is the solution for teenage pregnancy, one of the nation's growing public health problems. On the contrary, it is more probable that sex education is a principal cause of teenage pregnancy.

That's the conclusion of research by Dr. Rhoda L. Lorand after reading a mammoth collection of sex education materials put out by Planned Parenthood, the Alan Guttmacher Institute, public health departments and drug companies. Dr. Lorand, Ph.D., is a practicing psychotherapist in New York City, a Diplomate in Clinical Psychology of the American Board of Professional Psychology, an expert witness before many Congressional committees, and the author of *Love, Sex and the Teenager.*

Most parents have the naive idea that sex education means telling children the anatomical and biological facts of life. Not so, Dr. Lorand says, "The message beamed to school children, often from the fifth grade up, is that everyone has the right to engage in sexual intercourse, the number of sexual partners purely a matter of personal preference."

The child is taught in explicit detail all the varieties of normal and abnormal sexual activity and sensual arousal. The child is taught that moral standards and judgments should have little or nothing to do with sexuality.

In addition to eliminating morality, the sex education advocates have deliberately concealed from the children the medical evidence of the dangerous consequences of early and permissive sexual behavior—facts which would cause any reasonably normal teenager to abstain from sexual activity, even if he had no moral scruples.

For example, there is a mountain of corroborative evidence of the direct connection between early coitus and cervical cancer in females. Yet the sex education advocates have censored all this evidence out of the materials they thrust at teenagers.

Some sex education materials mention venereal disease, but within the context of an unquestioning acceptance of promiscuity and the assertion that VD is curable.

None of the sex education materials examined by Dr. Lorand mentions the painful and dangerous VD, genital herpes, which is not curable, or that some strains of gonorrhea are penicillin-resistant and sterility may occur during the time a cure is sought. Nor do the materials tell about Cytomegalovirus, another incurable sexually-transmitted disease which cripples and retards more infants than German measles.

"The emotion of fear," Dr. Lorand points out, "is a fundamental life-protecting response to the perception of danger." It is very healthy for a young girl to be deterred from promiscuity by fear of contracting a painful, incurable disease, or cervical cancer, or sterility, or the likelihood of giving birth to a dead, blind or brain-damaged baby (even 10 years later when she may be happily married).

It is shocking that the sex education advocates promote the "everybody's doing it" syndrome without warning of the tragic consequences. It is a cheat on your teenagers who are thus led into mistakes for which they may have to pay a bitter price all the rest of their lives.

Graphs on VD in Sweden and the U.S. indicate that sex education is a cause of the epidemic rise in VD. Sweden started a steady upward climb in 1954, the year sex education became compulsory. In the United States, VD declined until the mid 60's, when it began a sharp rise upward. That was when U.S. schools introduced Swedish-style sex education.

Sweden is certainly not a model our country would want to follow. In 1976, the illegitimacy rate in Sweden was 33 per cent of all live births, even though half of all teenage pregnancies ended in abortion.

Planned Parenthood is the principal agency pushing for the most extreme Swedish-style sex education in the schools. In its Annual Report for 1978, Planned Parenthood speaks openly for its "role as agent of social and attitudinal change."

What masquerades as sex education is not education at all. It is selective propaganda which artificially encourages children to participate in adult sex, while it censors out the facts of life about the unhappy consequences. It is robbing children of their childhood. . . .

SEX EDUCATION CHECK LIST

1. Does it omit all references to moral standards of right and wrong, teaching only animal-level sex?

2. Does it urge boys and girls to seek help from or consult only or primarily public agencies rather than their parents or religious advisors?

3. Does it require instruction and discussion to take place in sex-integrated (coed) classes rather than separate classes for boys and girls?

4. Does it require boys and girls to discuss private parts and sexual behavior openly in the classroom, with explicit vocabulary, thereby destroying their natural modesty, privacy, and psychological defenses (especially of the girls) against immoral sex?

5. Does it omit mentioning chastity as a method (the only absolute method) of preventing teenage pregnancies and VD?

6. Does it try to eliminate all guilt for sin?

7. Does it assume that all boys and girls are engaging in immoral sex, thereby encouraging them to accept promiscuous sexual acts as normal?

8. Does it omit mention of the spiritual, psychological, emotional and physical benefits of premarital chastity, marital fidelity, and traditional family life?

9. Does it omit mention of the spiritual, psychological, emotional and physical penalties and risks of fornication, adultery and promiscuity?

10. Does it require boys and girls to engage in role playing (pretending one is pregnant, pretending one has to admit having VD, pretending to use various types of contraceptives), thereby encouraging peer pressure to be exerted on the side of fornication rather than chastity?

11. Does it fail to stress marriage as the most moral, most fulfilling, and/or most socially acceptable method of enjoying sexual activity?

12. Does it encourage boys and girls not to tell their parents about the sex-ed curriculum, or about their sexual behavior or problems?

13. Does it present abortion as an acceptable method of birth control?

14. Does it use materials and references from the pro-abortion Planned Parenthood?

15. Does it present homosexual behavior as normal and acceptable?

16. Does it omit mention of the incurable types of VD which today affect millions of Americans? Does it falsely imply that all VD can be cured by treatment?

17. Does it give respectability to VD by listing famous people who had it?

18. Does it omit mention of the danger of cervical cancer in females from early promiscuity?

19. Does it use a vocabulary which disguises immorality? For example, "sexually active" to mean fornication, "sexual partners" to mean sex in or out of marriage, "fetus" to mean baby, "termination of pregnancy" to mean killing a preborn baby.

20. Does it require boys and girls to draw or trace on paper intimate parts of the male and female bodies?

21. Does it ask unnecessary questions which cause boys and girls to doubt their parents' religious and social values ("is there a need for a wedding ceremony, religious or civil?")?

22. Does it force advanced concepts and vocabulary upon 5-8 year old children too young to understand or be interested? (For example, selection of mate, Caesarian, pregnancy prevention, population control, ovulation, VD, sperm, ovum.)

23. Does it constantly propagandize for limiting the size of families by teaching that having more children means that each gets fewer economic benefits?

24. Can the sex-ed curriculum reasonably be described as a "how to do it" course in sexual acts (instruction which obviously encourages individual experimentation)?

GENDER RELATIONS

The issue of gender relations deeply divides the right and the left, but the questions involved frequently divide groups within the right and the left. In addition, gender questions show clearly why libertarianism is frequently closer to the left than the right.

LIBERTARIANISM

Libertarians stress personal choice without governmental control, and this position clearly includes free choice for women in areas like abortion, contraception, lesbianism, and prostitution that the right wants governmentally controlled.

Association of Libertarian Feminists

GOVERNMENT IS WOMEN'S ENEMY
Sharon Presley and Lynn Kinsky

I ask for no favors for my sex. I surrender not our claim to equality. All I ask of our brethren is that they will take their feet off our necks, and permit us to stand upright on the ground which God has designed us to occupy.
—Sarah Grimké, *Letters on the Equality of the Sexes and the Condition of Women*, Boston, 1838.

The above words of early feminist Sarah Grimké are as good an answer now as they were then to the question. What do feminists want? We want, as women, as persons, to be free.

From Sharon Presley and Lynn Kinsky, "Government Is Women's Enemy" (New York: Association of Libertarian Feminists, 1976, pamphlet).

Feminism is a proposition that insists that no one exists for anyone else: that government, commerce, technology, education, etc. all exist as tools for people to use as they decide, not the other way around. Feminism rejects any system that keeps people tied to roles, that depends on a hierarchical oppressor-oppressed relationship in order to function.

Feminists want women to be free—free of the domination of men, free to control their bodies and psyches as they see fit, free to make their own decisions about their own lives independent of the coercive domination of others.

Unfortunately, inconsistency has crept into the modern women's movement. While rejecting patriarchal attitudes and dominating ways of interacting on a *personal* level, women's liberationists will too often ask for government favors and handouts such as free child care-centers or free abortions. Yet turning to the government just changes the *sort* of oppression women face, not the *fact*. Instead of being overburdened as mothers or wives we become overburdened as taxpayers, since child-care workers, doctors, etc. have to be paid by someone unless they are to be enslaved also! Turning to the government to solve our problems just replaces oppression by patriarchs we *know*—father, husband, boss—with oppression by patriarchs we don't know—the hordes of legislators and bureaucrats who are increasingly prying into every nook and cranny of our lives!

But there is a nonauthoritarian alternative—a philosophy that not only has goals compatible with the psychological goals of feminism, but methods more compatible with these goals than the alternatives usually touted. So it is particularly appropriate that the first woman in history to receive an electoral vote—Tonie Nathan[a]—is an advocate of this philosophy: libertarianism.

The essence of libertarianism is the belief that all social interactions should be voluntary, that no one has the right to rule another, that individuals have the right to live their lives in any manner they see fit as long as they don't initiate force or fraud against others.

Libertarians want to repeal laws, not pass them. They are not interested in stopping people from smoking pot, having abortions, *or* from spending their own money as they see fit. Libertarians just want to leave people alone. They believe that there *are* voluntary nonauthoritarian alternatives to coercive government services and institutions that will work, even in our modern complex society.

Libertarian feminists believe that we can't achieve a nonauthoritarian society by authoritarian methods. If our goals are personal autonomy and individual freedom, we can't achieve these goals by taking away individuals' rights to choose for themselves. If we pass laws that force *our* values on others, we are no better than men who have forced *their* values on us through legislation. We merely substitute our tyranny for the tyranny of men. Women's liberationist Susan Brownmiller advocating anti-obscenity laws is no better than conservative James Buckley advocating abortion laws.

GOVERNMENT IS WOMEN'S ENEMY

> **Oh! That we could learn the advantage of just practice and consistent principles! That we could understand that every departure from principle, how speciously soever it may appear to administer to our selfish interests, invariably saps their very foundation! That we could learn that what is ruinous to some is injurious to all, and that whenever we establish our own pretentions upon the sacrificed rights of others, we do in fact impeach our own liberties and lower ourselves in the scale of being!**
> —Frances Wright, *Course of Popular Lectures,* New York, 1830.

Not only on a moral and psychological level, but on a practical level as well, it would be bitterly ironic for women to turn to government for solutions to their problems. Government has harmed women far more than it has helped them. Government has in many cases, *created* the problems in the first place and still continues to perpetuate them through unnecessary and harmful legislation.

Child Care Centers

The issue of child-care is a prime example of why government is an enemy, not a friend of women. Government regulations have *created* the child-care crisis! Zoning laws, unnecessary and pointless health and safety restrictions, required licensing that is difficult to obtain—all combine to assure that people will not be able to get together to provide low-cost child care on their own.

Then when the government sees the lack of child-care facilities (caused by government restrictions), it steps in to fill the void with stolen money at costs far in excess of what perfectly adequate private child care could be provided for. Typically a large portion of the cost of child-care centers goes to line the pockets of the bureaucratic administration or to pay rent on unnecessarily expensive buildings—as a recent scandal in New York City shows so well. (Outrageously inflated rents far beyond the normal market value were paid for broken down slum buildings owned by landlords with friends at City Hall.) But parents don't need these bureaucrats and expensive buildings to provide loving care for children.

Worse yet, after forcing parents and children into the role of charity cases, the government is also in a position to control the development of children just as it does in the public schools. Government officials intend that these "child development centers" (as they like to call child-care centers) will be places where young children can be psychologically conditioned to what the administrators think are healthier attitudes.

> **There is serious thinking among some of the future oriented child development research people that maybe we can't trust the family alone to prepare young children for this new kind of world which is emerging. . . In the first 18 months of life, the brain is growing faster than it ever will again. It is then also more plastic and available to appropriate experience and corrective interventions**
> —Reginald Lowrie, President of the Joint Commission on the Mental Health of Children

Do you trust *government officials* to intervene in the lives and minds of your children?

Public Schools

If you wonder what kind of attitudes these government officials have in mind and what kinds of corrective interventions they plan, just look at the public school system. Public schools not only foster the worst of traditionalist sexist values but inculcate docility and obedience to authority with sterile, stifling methods and compulsory programs and regulations. Government has obtained frightening power over the lives of children in public schools through the use of psychological testing and "counseling," secret (and often viciously subjective) files that follow children throughout their school years, and— worst of all—compulsory drug programs for allegedly hyperactive children. All in the name of helping children, the government draws its net tighter and tighter. (That these programs are truly harmful rather than helpful is well documented in *The Myth of the Hyperactive Child, and Other Means of Child Control,* by Peter Schrag and Diane Divoky.)

These programs in the public schools are popular and widespread. It is unrealistic to assume that they won't be incorporated into government child-care centers, too. And never forget that no matter how much control you think you have over child-care centers or schools, the strings are always attached. What the government finances, it always ultimately controls.

Abortion and Contraception

The government's record on abortion and contraception is no better. Such controls could not have been instituted without the power of government in the first place. And alleged "reforms" notwithstanding, controls and restrictions still exist. The much touted 1973 Supreme Court decisions that supposedly brought "legalized abortion" still allow the government great latitude in dictating when and the conditions under which abortions may be performed; and the places where contraceptives may be sold are still limited. Whether you can even see contraceptives or ads for them is also still heavily restricted by local, state, and federal laws. But unlike the politicians of the Republican and Democratic parties, who weasel their way past the issues, the Libertarian Party calls for total repeal of abortion and contraception laws, not just wishy-washy "reforms." Libertarians believe that abortion is a matter of individual conscience and choice and that the state has no right to tell women how they may use their own bodies.

Other Government Discrimination Against Women

Much of the discrimination that women face in today's society has been enshrined and institutionalized through law and other government processes. So-called "protective" labor legislation has kept women out of certain jobs and encouraged private job discrimination. Marriage, divorce, and property laws all discriminate against women.

In the area of sexuality, government discriminates against women is particularly blatant: laws against prostitution try to dictate how women will use their own bodies and usually only the woman prostitute, not her male customer is prosecuted. "Sexual delinquency" charges are brought against young girls far more often than against boys. Lesbians and single mothers are discriminated against in child custody and adoption cases.

And most blatant of all, rape cases are treated differently from other assault cases: conviction is much harder to obtain because evidence is required that is not required for non-sexual assaults. Often not only must the victim produce a "corroborating witness," but she must also demonstrate *her* innocence as well as the rapist's guilt!

WHAT IS TO BE DONE

> **The modern conviction, the fruit of a thousand years of experience, is, that things in which the individual is the person directly interested, never go right but as they are left to his own discretion; and that any regulation of them by authority, except to protect the rights of others, is sure to be mischievous.**
> —John Stuart Mill, *On the Subjection of Women;* London, 1869.

Many feminists will say "but what we need are better laws and better politicians." Libertarians agree that the laws must change. Discrimination built into the laws, such as in the instances cited above, must go. Government is obligated to treat all citizens equally. Those laws that restrict the freedom of women to make choices about their bodies, about their lives and the lives of their dependent children, about their sexual relationship with others, must go. But while libertarian feminists uncompromisingly believe in the repeal of such restrictive laws against women, they do not believe that passing laws to obtain or extend special government privileges and handouts will solve the other problems of women. The history of government shows all too well that corruption, boondoggling, inefficiency, wastefulness, and authoritarian control are inherent in the political system. On both a moral and a practical level, women are far better off without government solutions.

We need to develop nonauthoritarian alternatives, both as substitutes for government institutions and services already in existence, and as an example to others that voluntary action does work. For instance, an excellent example of feminist voluntary action right now is the rape crisis centers. Angered by the lack of interest or inability of the police and courts to deal sensitively with the problem of rape, women in many communities have formed rape crisis centers to provide help and support for rape victims and to try and dispel the many myths about the crime of rape. The various self help medical clinics are another good example of a non-governmental solution to a problem, and schools, child-care centers, and other important services also exist on private, voluntary community bases already. Libertarians believe that many additional services can also be provided if the government will just get off our backs. We are learning to break free of big brother politically as well as psychologically. We don't need him either way.

Author's Note

a. *Ms. Nathan ran for Vice President on the Libertarian Party ticket in 1972. She and her running mate John Hospers, received a maverick electoral vote from a Virginia Republican elector, Roger MacBride. Mr. MacBride was the 1976 Libertarian Party candidate for President.*

THE RIGHT

The most outspoken person on the right regarding gender relations is Phyllis Schlafly, whose movement against the Equal Rights Amendment was very effective. In general, the right favors what it sees as the natural and only moral relationship between men and women, with the man working outside the home and the woman staying home and taking care of her husband and children. The Equal Rights Amendment was seen as a threat to this relationship.

Phyllis Schlafly

What the Equal Rights Amendment Means

ERA will make every wife in the U.S. legally responsible to provide 50% of the financial support of her family.

ERA will wipe out a woman's present freedom of choice to take a paying job *or* to be a fulltime wife and mother supported by her husband.

ERA will make women subject to the draft.

ERA will put women on warships and make them subject to combat duty on an equal basis with men regardless of whether we have a draft of not.

ERA will eliminate the preferential Social Security benefits women now enjoy.

From "What the Equal Rights Amendment Means" (Alton, Ill.: STOP ERA, [mid-1970s], broadside).

ERA will wipe out many protective labor laws which benefit women.

ERA will knock out present laws protecting women from sex crimes such as statutory rape and forced prostitution.

ERA will integrate boys' and girls' physical education classes in high schools and colleges.

ERA will jeopardize present lower life insurance rates for women.

ERA could create havoc in prisons and reform schools by preventing segregation of the sexes.

ERA will nullify thousands of present laws which protect women, and will transform every provision of law concerning women into a constitutional issue that will ultimately have to be resolved by the Supreme Court.

ERA does not guarantee better paying jobs, promotions or better working conditions. The equal employment opportunity act and other laws already guarantee women "equal pay for equal work" and need only to be enforced to ensure women equal opportunity.

What's Wrong With "Equal Rights" for Women?

Of all the classes of people who ever lived, the American woman is the most privileged. We have the most rights and rewards, and the fewest duties. Our unique status is the result of a fortunate combination of circumstances.

1. We have the immense good fortune to live in a civilization which respects the family as the basic unit of society. This respect is part and parcel of our laws and our customs. It is based on the fact of life—which no legislation or agitation can erase—that women have babies and men don't.

If you don't like this fundamental difference, you will have to take up your complaint with God because He created us this way. The fact that women, not men, have babies is not the fault of selfish and domineering men, or of the establishment, or of any clique of conspirators who want to oppress women. It's simply the way God made us.

Our Judeo-Christian civilization has developed the law and custom that, since women must bear the physical consequences of the sex act, men must be required to bear the other consequences and pay in other ways. These laws and customs decree that a man must carry his share by physical protec-

From Phyllis Schlafly, "What's Wrong with 'Equal Rights' for Women?" *Phyllis Schlafly Report* 5, no. 7 (February 1972).

tion and financial support of his children and of the woman who bears his children, and also by a code of behavior which benefits and protects both the woman and the children.

The Greatest Achievement of Women's Rights

This is accomplished by the institution of the family. Our respect for the family as the basic unit of society, which is ingrained in the laws and customs of our Judeo-Christian civilization, is the greatest single achievement in the entire history of women's rights. It assures a woman the most precious and important right of all—the right to keep her own baby and to be supported and protected in the enjoyment of watching her baby grow and develop.

The institution of the family is advantageous for women for many reasons. After all, what do we want out of life? To love and be loved? Mankind has not discovered a better nest for a lifetime of reciprocal love. A sense of achievement? A man may search 30 to 40 years for accomplishment in his profession. A woman can enjoy real achievement when she is young—by having a baby. She can have the satisfaction of doing a job well—and being recognized for it.

Do we want financial security? We are fortunate to have the great legacy of Moses, the Ten Commandments, especially this one: "Honor thy father and thy mother that thy days may be long upon the land." Children are a woman's best social security—her best guarantee of social benefits such as old age, pension, unemployment compensation, workman's compensation, and sick leave. The family gives a woman the physical, financial and emotional security of the home—for all her life.

The Financial Benefits of Chivalry

2. The second reason why American women are a privileged group is that we are the beneficiaries of a tradition of special respect for women which dates from the Christian Age of Chivalry. The honor and respect paid to Mary the Mother of Christ, resulted in all women, in effect, being put on a pedestal.

This respect for women is not just the lip service that politicians pay to "God, Motherhood, and the Flag." It is not—as some youthful agitators seem to think—just a matter of opening doors for women, seeing that they are seated first, carrying their bundles, and helping them in and out of automobiles. Such good manners are merely the superficial evidences of a total attitude toward women which expresses itself in many more tangible ways, such as money.

In other civilizations such as the African and the American Indian, the men strut around wearing feathers and beads and hunting and fishing (great sport for men), while the women do all the hard, tiresome drudgery including the tilling of the soil (if any is done), the hewing of wood, the making of fires, the carrying of water, as well as the cooking, sewing and caring for babies.

This is not the American way because we were lucky enough to inherit the traditions of the Age of Chivalry. In America, a man's first significant purchase is a diamond for his bride, and the largest financial investment of his life is a home for her to live in. American husbands work hours of overtime to buy a fur piece or other finery to keep their wives in fashion, and to pay premiums on their insurance policies to provide for her comfort when she is a widow (benefits in which he can never share).

In the states which follow the English common law, a wife has a dower right in her husband's real estate which he cannot take away from her during life or by his will. A man cannot dispose of his real estate without his wife's signature. Any sale is subject to her 1/3 interest.

Women fare even better in the states which follow the Spanish and French community-property laws, such as California, Arizona, Texas, and Louisiana. The basic philosophy of the Spanish/French law is that a wife's work in the home is just as valuable as a husband's work at his job. Therefore, in community property states, a wife owns one-half of all the property and income her husband earns during their marriage, and he cannot take it away from her.

In Illinois, as a result of agitation by equal rights fanatics, the real estate dower laws were repealed as of Jan. 1, 1972. This means that in Illinois a husband can now sell the family home, spend the money on his girl friend or gamble it away, and his faithful wife of 30 years can no longer stop him. "Equal rights" fanatics have also deprived women in Illinois and in some other states of most of their basic common-law rights to recover damages for breach of promise to marry, seduction, criminal conversation, and alienation of affections.

The Real Liberation of Women

3. The third reason why American women are so well off is that the great American free enterprise system has produced remarkable inventors who have lifted the backbreaking women's work from our shoulders.

In other countries and in other eras, it was truly said that "Man may work from sun to sun, but woman's work is never done." Other women have labored every waking hour—preparing food on wood burning stoves, making flour, baking bread in stone ovens, spinning yarn, making clothes, making soap, doing the laundry by hand, heating irons, making candles for light and fires for warmth, and trying to nurse their babies through illnesses without medical care.

The real liberation of women from the backbreaking drudgery of centuries is the American free enterprise system which stimulated inventive geniuses to pursue their talents—and we all reap the profits. The great heroes of women's liberation are not the straggly-haired women on television talk shows and picket lines, but Thomas Edison who brought the miracle of electricity to our homes to give light and to run all those labor-saving devices—the equivalent, perhaps, of a half dozen household servants for every middle-class American woman. Or Elias Howe who gave us the sewing machine which resulted in such an abundance of ready made clothing. Or Clarence Birdseye who invented the process for freezing foods. Or Henry Ford, who mass-produced the automobile so that it is within the price-range of every American, man or woman.

A major occupation of women in other countries is doing their daily shopping for food, which requires carrying their own containers and standing in line at dozens of small shops. They buy only small portions because they can't carry very much and have no refrigerator or freezer to keep a surplus anyway. Our American free enterprise system has given us the gigantic food and packaging industry and beautiful supermarkets, which provide an endless variety of foods, prepackaged for easy carrying and a minimum of waiting. In America, women have the freedom from the slavery of standing in line for daily food.

Thus, household duties have been reduced to only a few hours a day, leaving the American woman with plenty of time to moonlight. She can take a full or part-time paying job, or she can indulge to her heart's content in a tremendous selection of interesting educational or cultural or homemaking activities.

The Fraud of the Equal Rights Amendment

In the last couple of years, a noisy movement has sprung up agitating for "women's rights." Suddenly everywhere we are afflicted with aggressive females on television talk shows yapping about how mistreated American women are, suggesting that marriage has put us in some kind of "slavery," that housework is menial and degrading, and—perish the thought—that women are discriminated against. New "women's liberation" organizations are popping up, agitating and demonstrating, serving demands on public officials, getting wide press coverage always, and purporting to speak for some 100,000,000 American women.

It's time to set the record straight. The claim that American women are downtrodden and unfairly treated is the fraud of the century. The truth is that American women never had it so good. Why should we lower ourselves to "equal rights" when we already have the status of special privilege?

The proposed Equal Rights Amendment states: "Equality of rights under the law shall not be denied or abridged by the United States or by any state on account of sex." So what's wrong with that? Well, here are a few examples of what's wrong with it.

This amendment will absolutely and positively make women subject to the draft. Why any woman would support such a ridiculous and un-American proposal as this is beyond comprehension. Why any Congressman who had any regard for his wife, sister or daughter would support such a proposition is just as hard to understand. Foxholes are bad enough for men, but they certainly are not the place for women—and we should reject any proposal which would put them there in the name of equal rights.

It is amusing to watch the semantic chicanery of the advocates of the Equal Rights Amendment when confronted with this issue of the draft. They evade, they sidestep, they try to muddy up the issue, but they cannot deny that the equal rights amendment will positively make women subject to the draft. Congresswoman Margaret Heckler's answer to this question was, don't worry, it will take two years for the ERA to go into effect, and we can rely on President Nixon to end the Vietnam War before then!

Literature distributed by Equal Rights Amendment supporters confirms that "under the amendment a draft law which applied to men would apply also to women." The Equal Rights literature argues that this would be good for women so they can achieve their "equal rights" in securing veterans' benefits.

Another bad effect of the Equal Rights Amendment is that it will abolish women's right to child support and alimony, and substitute what the women's libbers think is a more "equal" policy, that "such decisions should be within the discretion of the court and should be made on the economic situation and need of the parties in the case."

Under present American laws, the man is *always* required to support his wife and each child he caused to be brought into the world. Why should women abandon these good laws—by trading them for something so nebulous and uncertain as the "discretion of the Court"?

The law now requires a husband to support his wife as best as his financial situation permits, but a wife is not required to support her husband (unless he is about to become a public charge). A husband cannot demand that his wife go to work to help pay for family expenses. He has the duty of financial support under our laws and customs. Why should we abandon these mandatory wife-support and child support laws so that a wife would have an "equal" obligation to take a job?

By law and custom in America, in case of divorce, the mother always is given custody of her children unless there is overwhelming evidence of mistreatment, neglect or bad character. This is our special privilege because of the high rank that is placed on motherhood in our society. Do women really want to give up this special privilege and lower themselves to "equal rights" so that the mother gets one child and the father gets the other? I think not.

The Right NOT to Take a Job

Passage of the Equal Rights Amendment would open up a Pandora's box of trouble for women. It would deprive the American woman of many of the fundamental special privileges we now enjoy, and especially the greatest rights of all: (1) NOT to take a job, (2) to keep her baby, and (3) to be supported by her husband. . . .

Women's Libbers Do NOT Speak for Us

The "women's lib" movement is not an honest effort to secure better jobs for women who want or need to work outside the home. This is just the superficial sweet-talk to win broad support for a radical "movement." "Women's lib" is a total assault on the role of the American woman as wife and mother, and on the family as the basic unit of society.

Women's libbers are trying to make wives and mothers unhappy with their career, make them feel that they are "second class citizens" and "abject slaves." Women's libbers are promoting free sex instead of the "slavery" of marriage. They are promoting "Federal" day care-centers for babies instead of homes. They are promoting abortions instead of families.

Why should we trade in our special privileges and honored status for the alleged advantage of working in an office or assembly line? Most women would rather cuddle a baby than a typewriter or factory machine. Most women find that it is easier to get along with a husband than a foreman or office manager. Offices and factories require many more menial and repetitious chores than washing dishes and ironing shirts.

Women's libbers do *not* speak for the majority of American women. American women do *not* want to be liberated from husbands and children. We do *not* want to trade our birthright of the special privilege of American women—for the mess of pottage called the Equal Rights Amendment.

Modern technology and opportunity have not discovered any nobler or more satisfying or more creative career for a woman than marriage and motherhood. The wonderful advantage that American women have is that we can have all the rewards of that number one career and still moonlight with a second one to suit our intellectual, cultural or financial tastes or needs.

And why should the men acquiesce in a system which gives preferential rights and lighter duties to women? In return, the men get the pearl of great price: a happy home, a faithful wife, and children they adore.

If the women's libbers want to reject marriage and motherhood, it's a free country and that is their choice. But let's not permit these women's libbers to get away with pretending to speak for the rest of us. Let's not permit this tiny minority to degrade the role that most women prefer. Let's not let these women's libbers deprive wives and mothers of the rights we now possess.

Tell your Senators NOW that you want them to vote no on the Equal

Rights Amendment. Tell your television and radio stations that you want equal time to present the case for marriage and motherhood.

Men's Rights Association

A very interesting variant on the right's approach to gender relations is found in the men's liberation movement. While there have been variants of this on the left supporting women's liberation, it originated on the right as an argument in favor of traditional roles and against the perceived destruction of men's rights.

A MANIFESTO OF MEN'S LIBERATION
R. F. Doyle

AN OVERVIEW

Objective examination demonstrates that over the past 30 years anti-male discrimination has become far greater, in scope, in degree and in damage, than any which may exist against women. It takes the form of violations of law, decency and common sense that can be described as unconscionable at best. It is most evident in the areas of domestic relations, employment and crime and punishment.

The social repercussions are predictable and catastrophic. They include:

a. The male image is becoming that of Jack the Ripper or Dagwood Bumstead.
b. The female image is emerging supreme, almost to the point of canonization.
c. Women and bureaucracies are usurping male roles and functions in family and industry.
d. The sexes are becoming indistinguishable. More and more persons are becoming sexual nonentities and homosexuals.
e. Fifty percent of marriages end in divorce.
f. A large percentage of children therefore are being deprived of normal family lives, due to divorce.

From R. F. Doyle, "A Manifesto of Men's Liberation," 3rd ed. (Forest Lake, Minn.: Men's Rights Association, 1983, pamphlet).

g. Defeated, emasculated men, in ever-increasing numbers, are matriculating into the flotsam and jetsam of skid row.
h. Immorality, neurotic instability, drug addiction, delinquency, crime and other abberations [sic] are being spawned at a disastrous rate.
i. The resultant welfare, correction and mental institution burdens are becoming staggering, actually, intolerable. . . .

FAMILIES

The institution of marriage has become a mere covenant of servitude for men. Hard working men are reduced to the position of donkeys, providing the needs and luxuries of their families without the concomitant dignity and authority. . . .

WOMEN'S LIB

The basic premise of neo-feminists is that women are more discriminated against than men. This is preposterous, if not obscene. Normal women are the most pampered creatures in western society. In fact, bluntly put, many are parasites, living off the production of men and doing little more to justify their existence than cooking and cleaning a few hours a week, and perhaps computing the value of these services as if the husband were the only beneficiary. This is called biting the hand that feeds you. The alleged discrimination against women in employment, abortion, and miscellaneous areas is insignificant compared to that against men in crime and punishment, employment and domestic relations. Braying, irrational, but widely heard neo-feminists are cluttering the women's cause with emotional trash, non-issues, impractical solutions and some dangerous policies. They need only perch glasses atop their head and babble "newspeak." People, especially the liberal press, take them seriously. . . .

Neo-feminists demand to become employed at work men can do best in numbers equal to their population. Government and industry, taking the line of least resistance, are giving women preference in hiring and promotion, regardless of qualification. This is causing hardship to male family breadwinners, especially the emerging blacks. The military and police forces are becoming weakened by an influx of women, seriously threatening this country's security. Yet not one neo-feminist in a hundred is prepared to sacrifice the privileges routinely accorded women by virtue of their sex, or to demand equal treatment with men in the areas where men are discriminated against. One never sees them clamoring for the dirty jobs men must perform or for equal representation in jails or skid row. Its a "have their cake and eat it too" situation.

Neo-feminists have conned or frightened governments and philanthropists into contributing vast amounts of money to finance their programs. A recent scheme to fund offices and staff is the proliferation of "battered women's shelters." "Mod-politicians" promote this craze, oblivious to studies showing there is as much or more violence directed at husbands by wives.

The Men's Liberation movement is a positive force, not a reaction to women's lib. However, it would be well-neigh *[sic]* impossible for these two philosophies not to conflict. We feel that women's lib should confine itself to representing those women with unrecognized and uncompensated for male characteristics, instead of trying to drag all women down to that level. Although admittedly women have problems, (but not nearly as many as claimed), being born female isn't the degradation neo-feminists claim it to be. We advocate men's rights without denying the relatively few troubles of women, like the NAACP advocates Black's rights, without denying the relatively few troubles of Whites. We are not anti-women; we are pro-justice and pro-family. We stand for the principles that made this country great (once upon a time), principles such as self-sufficiency and rugged individualism.

SELF CULPABILITY

The link between our confused society and the women's lib and other "mod" philosophies is obvious. But this is not to imply that all blame lies on the shoulders of women, judges, lawyers and institutions. Males themselves are largely responsible for allowing this sorry condition to develop, by gradually surrendering their rights, shirking their responsibilities and abdicating their trousers. Fuzzy headed housemales, purporting to represent "men's liberation," but sponsored by NOW, are denouncing their masculinity while groping at each other in "consciousness raising" sessions. The bleats of these eunuchs have been hailed as representative of men's liberation. Nothing could be further from the truth. The MRA has been championing male equality long before these camp followers ever publically admitted the urge to slip into a pair of panties. Men's liberation means establishing the right of males to be *men;* not to liberate them *from being men.*

THE SOLUTIONS

In the face of their treatment most men lie down and roll over in the manner of submissive dogs. This only encourages further tyranny. Protest must be made. Male dignity and men's rights must be restored, preserved and protected against the excesses of society, legalists, and bureaucrats. Just and competent administration of law must be implemented. The divorce racket must be "busted." "Man power" must be brought to bear to accomplish these goals, carefully avoiding reverse prejudice. This effort must be coordinated by a full time, professional organization. Anything less cannot hope to overcome the juggernaut of institutionalized opposition to reform. Failure to do so means hundred of thousands of future victims.

REFORM—APPEALS TO REASON

To fulfill the needs mentioned above, divorce and lawyer victims formed the Men's Rights Association in St. Paul, Minnesota in 1972. An outgrowth of the old divorce reform movement, but greatly expanded in purpose, it is the avant-grade *[sic]* of a national men's liberation movement. We may be running second to women's lib now, but we try harder. We ask all fellow actual and potential victims to unite with us. We have nothing to lose but our chains.

The MRA philosophy, to date, has been a non-militant appeal to reason, briefly described as follows:

1. Regarding the sexes—We maintain that males and females of every species are different physically, and anatomically, emotionally and psychologically. There are distinct, natural characteristics generally predominant in each sex. These are not the result of recent adverse sociological discrimination or conditioning, but of eons of evolution. To deny this is to deny all science, behavioral and biological, as well as the evidence of one's own eyes and ears. Because of these differences, males are usually superior in certain functions and females in other. For example, only one female horse ever won

the Kentucky Derby. Surely, that isn't the result of conditioning female horses to inferiority. Therefore, in the human realm, it is appropriate that there be male and female roles in life. Men are naturally the beef-luggers, and women the seamstresses. Nowhere in responsible biological literature can we find a single instance of the identical behavior of the males and females of any species.

This is not to imply that men are better than women, but different, and just as good. We are proud of our masculine characteristics and resultant abilities, as women should be of theirs.

2. Regarding equality—At one time the MRA was of the naive opinion that the Equal Rights Amendment implied equal rights for both sexes—thereby working to improve the position of men. However in light of recent interpretations, the only visible results of ratification has been to eliminate all distinction, however reasonable, between the sexes (unless that distinction served to further the interests of "liberated" women). Banning father-son banquets as sexist borders on the insane. Demanding access to men-only clubs, and getting it, infringes on a larger right—that to freedom of association. Requiring universities to provide athletic budgets for women equivalent to those for men is almost as preposterous as requiring hospitals to provide maternity wards for men.

Therefore we have withdrawn our support of the ERA as presently written and propose to substitute the following language

Section 1. Neither sex shall receive preferential treatment nor shall equality of rights be denied or abridged, by the United States or by any state on account of sex.

Section 2. This shall not prohibit the recognition of physical and psychological distinction between the sexes, nor prohibit the recognition of social or occupational roles derived therefrom.

Section 3. Congress shall have the power to enforce, by appropriate legislation, the provision of these articles.

Section 4. This amendment shall take effect 2 years after the date of ratification.

Of course, there are exceptions to normal sexual role adaptation, some women are superior to some men in certain masculine roles. Some men are superior to some women in certain feminine roles. These exceptional people are subjected to gross discrimination, which is regrettable and should be remedied. The MRA suggests that the way out of this social morass is to reshape our entire social-political-economic-judicial-legal-legislative-administrative philosophies along logical and practical lines. This can be done only by recognizing that men and women are normally different, by designing our social behavior and normal sexual role assignments around that undeniable fact, and by establishing true men's and women's rights. Equal rights imply equal responsibilities. If held solely responsible for financing the needs and pleasures of his family, the male must have concomitant dignity and authority. The more responsibility women reject, the more unequal they make themselves.

3. Regarding marriage and children—Theoretically marriage is the most beautiful, symbolic relationship possible. It should be a "dedicated partnership," in which spouses cheerfully accept roles adopted to their respective sexes. Just as children have a right to a complete home, including both father and mother, sustenance and guidance, parents have an inalienable right to live with and guide their children, unless proven unfit. So long as their rights are honored, it is the parents responsibility to provide that home, sustenance and guidance. Unfortunately, until equal justice for all is established, we believe the institution of marriage should be avoided.

There is no such thing as "illegitimate" children, only illegitimate parents. In view of the obvious reality that women, not men, get pregnant, the difficulty of definitely establishing paternity, and the easy availability of modern birth control methods, financial costs of such children should normally devolve upon mothers. To force alleged fathers to pay or marry amounts to entrapment.

4. Regarding divorce—Because marriage is a lifetime contract, spouses aspiring to terminate it unilaterally without very good cause should be prevented from absconding with the fruits of marriage.

Merit, not sex, must be the criteria for distribution of custody, property and money. The MRA sincerely believes that the existing pro-female prejudice serves as a bribe to divorce; that wild horses couldn't drag the average woman into divorce court without historic assurance of winning all. Therefore the incentives to divorce must be eliminated. If they were, the divorce rate would become insignificant within a few years.

We believe that the exclusively "no-fault" divorce concept is even more dangerous than exclusively "fault" divorce. We favor a "fault option" system to be adopted uniformly throughout the United States. Retaining both options would:

a. Under "fault" option—give injured parties recourse to redress in court. Injuries and culpabilities would be factors in determining awards of property and financial support.
b. Under "no-fault" option—allow couples (if both agreed) to avoid the butcherous arena of adversary courts, obtaining their divorce from a clerk of court on terms mutually consented to; much as they got married.
c. Permit the *principals* themselves to choose the option most suited to them. Obviously, to select the no-fault option, they would both have to agree.

5. Regarding custody—The automatic award of custody to mothers must terminate. Joint custody should be the preferential alternative. Where laws do not yet make provision for joint custody, the criteria of fitness and financial ability to support should be given priority over sex gender.

In sole custody states, children must be greatly deprived of either maternal qualities or of paternal qualities. It is necessary to choose the lesser of two evils. Therefore the MRA proposes that, where all other factors are equal in disputed situations, the following rule should apply: boys under seven and girls under puberty to mothers, those above said ages and when they reach said ages to fathers.

6. Regarding abortion and adoption—Without taking an official position, pro or con, on the morality or legality of abortion per se, the MRA maintains that prospective fathers, married or unmarried, have an equal right to determine the fate of their offspring, born or unborn; Supreme Court opinions to the contrary notwithstanding. Bread belongs no more to the oven than to the baker.

7. Regarding alimony—Because it is usually unfair to men and frequently equates with prostitution, it must be greatly curtailed. It should not be disguised as "child support," as is so common.

8. Regarding the courts—The courts must be cleaned up and their every move watched. Violations of human rights must be taken to appellate courts, damage courts, and to the forum of the news media. Names of offenders must be made public. They must be screamed from the rooftops if necessary.

9. Regarding lawyers—At the risk of being branded "Communists," we believe the legal profession should be socialized. Our monopolistic system of justice to the highest bidder does not operate fairly. Justice is a birthright more precious than education. Therefore the provision of legal aid to our citizens should receive a higher priority than provisions of an education.

Private tutors were replaced by public schools generations ago. We should make justice as easily obtainable as education. Socialized law is also more logical than socialized medicine. This is because government is not responsible for disease, but is quite responsible for the need of lawyers. It has imposed a complicated set of laws and procedures upon citizens and ought to provide for the free exercise and interpretation of them.

These reforms will benefit decent women as well as men. How many women want sons, brothers, and loved ones to suffer discrimination? Or the institution of marriage to disappear?

THE LEFT

The positions on the left regarding gender relations are varied. The Equal Rights Amendment is not really an issue for the left; it is seen as basically a conservative or at most liberal reform, needed but insufficient to bring about real change.

COYOTE

The sex work industry produced a trade union for prostitutes and other sex workers. COYOTE (Call Off Your Old Tired Ethics) argued for the decriminalization of prostitution.

C.O.Y.O.T.E.
CALL OFF YOUR OLD TIRED ETHICS

OUR GOALS

COYOTE'S ultimate goal is to decriminalize prostitution. Legalization, as opposed to decriminalization, requires government regulation. Decriminalization means the repeal of all criminal codes regarding voluntary prostitution, removing the existing prohibition against consenting adult activity and allowing sexworkers complete autonomy.

From "C.O.Y.O.T.E.: Call Off Your Old Tired Ethics: Our Goals" (San Francisco: C.O.Y.O.T.E., pamphlet), adopted and first printed in the 1970s and still in use in the late 1980s.

COYOTE believes that no voluntary aspects of sexwork should be a crime, including relationships between prostitutes and third party managers (pimping and pandering), renting a premise for the purpose of sexwork, residing in a place where sexwork occurs, etc.

COYOTE'S primary goal at this time is to provide an educational and support network to raise the overall self-esteem of women and men in the sex industry.

COYOTE seeks to end the stigma surrounding sexwork. Prostitution is a time honoured and historically valued profession. Sexwork in all it's variations is a valid occupational choice for women and men.

COYOTE intends to create an open dialogue about the myths and realities of sexwork. Accurate and accessible information is needed to address the misconceptions and stereotypes of sexwork.

The gay movement was and is strong on the left. Lesbians argue that it is impossible for women to fully develop all their potentials in a patriarchal society and that only in relationships with other women can women ever be truly free. Gay men have tended to be less overtly political than lesbians, at least until the AIDS crisis, but some gay male groups became involved in issues beyond those of sexual rights. Some groups, as will be seen below, have tried to combine lesbians and gay men into one organization.

Lavender Left

DRAFT STATEMENT OF UNITY

I. Who We Are

The Lavender Left is a movement of lesbian and gay male socialists which began in the United States and is attempting to organize a network of lesbian and gay socialists in the Western Hemisphere. Lesbian and gay males have always been active in the socialist and progressive movements, just as socialists and progressives have always been active in the lesbian and gay movement. However, in these movements we have too often been allowed to participate only if we remained in the closet, sexually or politically. The

From "Draft Statement of Unity" (New York: Lavender Left, [1981], flyer).

Lavender Left was formed to advance simultaneously and openly the goals of socialism and lesbian and gay liberation.

We are a multi-racial organization, made up of political independents and members of left parties, tendencies and groups. We represent a wide range of political positions, including feminists, socialists, socialist feminists, communists and anarchists. Despite our varying political perspectives, we are committed to working together towards our common goals.

II. Points of Unity

1. The overthrow of capitalism is a necessary precondition for lesbian and gay liberation. Heterosexism is inherent in the class nature of society, functioning, as do racism and sexism, as an institutionalized form of oppression. We recognize that the economic transformation of society will not in itself guarantee that liberation. Historically, we have seen that the liberation of lesbians and gay males has been most advanced where lesbian and gay male socialists have worked actively and openly in the socialist movement.

2. We therefore work to ensure that the socialist revolution will include lesbian and gay liberation by fighting against heterosexism both within and without the socialist movement. This means that we work as open lesbian and gay socialists wherever possible.

3. We are unalterably opposed to sexism and all of its forms. We are committed to fighting against sexism in all of the institutions of capitalist society. We also work on a continuing basis against male domination in the left, in the lesbian and gay movement, and in the Lavender Left.

We recognize the close relationship between the oppression of women and the oppression of lesbian and gay men and take a firm stand in solidarity with the specific struggles of lesbians. It is the responsibility of gay men to take up the struggle against sexism.

4. The struggle against racism is a priority of the Lavender Left. Racism serves to divide and disunify both the working class as a whole and the lesbian and gay movement and the capitalist class consciously maintains it as a vehicle for exploitation and domination.

We recognize the autonomous movements of Third World people and view their success as crucial to our own liberation. We actively support the struggle of the Third World people, and particularly Third World lesbians and gay males.

A necessary part of that support is that white people fight against political or personal expressions of racism. We are committed to taking up that fight in the Lavender Left.

5. Monopoly capitalism is an international economic system which takes the form of the imperialist domination, by a handful of advanced capitalist countries, of the rest of the capitalist world. Capitalism must therefore be fought on an international level. We see ourselves as part of this international struggle, and seek in particular to strengthen our ties to lesbian and gay socialists around the world.

6. Class oppression under capitalism is based on the wage system. While we as socialists work for the total abolition of wage slavery, we work now against economic oppression by supporting workers in their labor struggles and drives for unionization. We take up lesbian and gay issues in the workers' movement.

The lesbian and gay movement is itself divided by class. Knowing this, we fight for working-class positions in the lesbian and gay movement.

7. The right wing movement has set itself up as the savior of capitalism in this period of economic crisis. The left creates "moral" issues, such as abortion, busing, affirmative action, the family and homosexuality, to mobilize mass support to give the ruling class the free hand it needs to salvage the capitalist system. Besides working against progressive and for reactionary legislation, they seek out scapegoats for the alleged moral failure of liberal reformism. The right wing is responsible for the climate in which individual acts of violence against Third World people, women, workers, Jewish people, and lesbian and gay men are encouraged and sanctioned. The next step is the systematic organization of violence against these groups, as has already begun with the resurgence of the Klan and the Nazis.

The nature and the magnitude of the right is such that lesbians and gay men cannot defeat it alone. The right stands unified against Third World people, women, Jewish people, and lesbians and gay men. We must transform our negative unity as targets of the right into the positive unity of struggle which alone can defeat this threat.

8. Part of the struggle against the right involves defending hard-won reforms. We are not willing to wait for the revolution, but fight now to alleviate oppression. However, to us, as revolutionary socialists, reforms are not ends in themselves. Agitation in favor of reforms serves to educate and organize people toward the necessity of socialism and to build the power of the working people independent of the capitalist system.

Freedom Socialist Party

As was seen in the previous document, gender relations were not the only concerns of organizations on the left that focused on such issues. The following selection is a particularly good example of the issues that concerned a group that defined itself as a "socialist feminist organization."

WHAT IS FSP?

The Freedom Socialist Party is a socialist feminist organization dedicated to the replacement of capitalist rule by a genuine workers democracy that will guarantee full economic, social, and political equality to women, minorities, gays, and all people exploited and oppressed by the profit system and imperialism.

REVOLUTIONARY INTERNATIONALISM

The working class, like the capitalist class it seeks to overthrow, is an international class, bound by a common global exploitation and the task of winning liberation through socialism. A truly socialist transformation of society cannot occur in any single country; only worldwide socialism, the product of revolutions in many single countries, can insure a humane civilization freed of racism, sexism, and class oppression. We support the revolution on all its fronts, and seek to transform it into one international socialist society.

WOMEN'S LIBERATION

We organize for the total emancipation of women on every level of life. The terrible oppression and unique exploitation of women are burning injustices that intersect every other political issue and social movement. The multiple oppression of women as workers, minorities, and gays propels them into militancy and leadership; their daily struggle for survival as the most

From "What Is FSP?" *The Freedom Socialist* 2, no. 1 (Summer 1976).

oppressed of every downtrodden group steels them in their revolutionary fervor. Women, particularly minority women workers because of their double and triple jeopardy, are destined to exercise dynamic leadership in the coming American revolution.

MINORITY FREEDOM

Institutionalized racism and forced racial segregation are fundamental to the capitalist political economy of the U.S. Minority struggles against second-class social status accordingly threaten the entire system and tie in the racial freedom issue with the proletarian struggle for socialism.

Minority workers, because of dual oppression, stand in the forefront of the class struggle. All the ethnic liberation movements spur white workers, women, and other sectors of the class to an advanced political consciousness. Minorities in the U.S. are a cutting edge of the long struggle for revolutionary social change.

We stand for immediate and unconditional economic, political, and social equality for Blacks, Chicanos, Asians, Native Americans, and Puerto Ricans. We endorse the demand for self-determination by the Native American and Puerto Rican nations.

REVOLUTIONARY INTEGRATION

We advocate a revolutionary collaboration of Black militants with the general movement for socialism as the only realistic and historically validated alternative to the dead ends of separatism or reformist integration into the capitalist system. At the same time, we support independent mass organizations for Blacks and call on them to join the struggle of the working class for a socialist America and to extend their rich experience and political expertise to the general movement. Without massive involvement and leadership by Blacks, there will be no American revolution.

GAY EQUALITY

The gay revolt is essentially a deep protest against all forms of sexual repression and sex-role stereotyping. It is a key ingredient of the fight for women's equality, and the emancipation of women, in turn, is a prerequisite for the achievement of the gay movement's basic goals. Lesbians, like other minority women, provide a consistent militancy to the gay and feminist movements. Similarly, lesbians represent a significant leadership force in the overall revolutionary struggle as a result of their special oppression.

Too many socialist organizations today, steeped in traditional sexism, are unable to utilize Marxist theory for a radical analysis of the origins of gay oppression and the significance of the long history of bloody resistance to such oppression. The FSP, however, proudly affirms full support of gay liberation and calls upon gay people to join us and help develop a rich and revolutionary socialist ideology and program for sexual minorities as a basic component of the general struggle for human dignity.

THE CHILDREN QUESTION

The most hapless and vulnerable victims of capitalist degeneration are the children. Regarded as barely human appendages to adults, they are torn apart by the social, economic, and emotional chaos created by a culture that glamorizes acquisitiveness, cynicism, and brutality, and ignores the right of kids to security, love, and unhampered growth. Children are the responsibility of the total society, and need to become our first, not our last, priority. We demand a world fit for healthy children to live in.

UNION DEMOCRACY

Only the working class has the strategic power, numbers, need, and opportunity to effect a socialist transformation of society.

But the traditional organs of working class unity, the trade unions, have been reduced by the class collaborationist policies of the union bureaucrats into obstacles of working class solidarity and instruments of the bosses and the government. Only a militant struggle for internal democracy and a return to class struggle principles and tactics can rid the unions of their corrupt and dictatorial leadership, free them from the stranglehold of the capitalist Democratic Party, and transform them into fighting organs of the working class.

We hail the mounting aggressiveness of labor activists, particularly low-paid workers. We demand the end of discrimination against minorities and women by union officials and ranks. And we call for independent political action by the unions as the only way of attaining class solidarity in the voting booth.

A PARTY OF THE WORKING CLASS

History has proved that only a thoroughly democratic and centralized vanguard party can lead the working class and its allies to political victory. The Freedom Socialist Party is such a party, operating in the living tradition of Marx and Engels, Lenin and Trotsky, with the aspiration of becoming a mass workers party capable of accomplishing the American revolution. **Join Us Today!**

NOTES

1. See Jane J. Mansbridge, *Why We Lost the ERA* (Chicago: University of Chicago Press, 1986).
2. See, for example, James Combs, "Sensitivity Training," *Aryan Nations,* no. 18 (1980): 9.

7

ECONOMIC QUESTIONS

On economic issues the right has three main targets: the Federal Reserve system, the Internal Revenue Service (and the tax system in general), and "welfare," which includes a number of other issues as well. To the right, the Federal Reserve and the IRS symbolize an illegal usurpation of state powers by the national government. The right to coin (many take that word literally to exclude all printed currency) money is believed to be a constitutionally protected state authority. The income tax, as established by the Sixteenth Amendment (1913), they believe to be a violation of the Constitution. They also argue that the IRS has been allowed to act as if it is above the law, and that the IRS regularly violates the law in its efforts to collect taxes.

There are a number of proposals for replacing the income tax. Many on the right favor the sales tax, which is a regressive tax taking a higher percentage of income from the poor than from the rich. Two other proposals are seen below.

The left has no problem with the redistribution of the income tax; they generally want the rich to pay more and the poor to pay less. They also have little problem with the Federal Reserve system as such, although they would generally prefer it to be under direct legislative control rather than being independent.

"Welfare" is, of course, one of the major targets of the right, related to

the question of redistribution of money through the income tax. The argument is simply that the national government uses its power to take money from one set of people (those who earned it) to give to another set of people (those who failed to earn it). They also believe, as is seen elsewhere, that those receiving welfare are mostly African American (not in fact true); thus the racism affecting much of the right also comes into play. Welfare, it is believed, can be replaced by individual charitable giving.

For the left, welfare is a flawed but necessary means of redistributing money from the wealthy to the needy. Their major concern is with the intrusion of bureaucracy into the lives of the poor and the need to empower welfare recipients, as can be seen in the selections below.

ECONOMIC PRINCIPLES

The fundamental economic principles of the right focus on the free market and the need to rid the country of governmental regulation, but, as has been seen in earlier selections, the right is not completely unified, even on these principles. The first two selections below are good examples of the basic principles. The third is a more detailed set of suggestions for changing the overall economic system.

Individualists for a Rational Society

THE INDIVIDUALIST'S MANIFESTO
(Adopted by IFRS as its official statement of principles, April 21, 1973)
Framer: Robert James Bidinotto

We as Individuals for a Rational Society, affirm these truths:

That each man has an inalienable right to his own life;

That this right is derived from man's nature as a rational entity, and its recognition represents a necessary condition for his proper survival among

From "The Individualist's Manifesto" (n.p.: Individualists for a Rational Society, 1973, flyer).

his fellow men; that it entails man's freedom to take all actions required by his nature to maintain, further, and enjoy his existence; and that it thereby morally sanctions his freedom to act on his own judgment, in his own self-interest, for his own chosen values;

That this right to life is the source of all other rights, including the right of property; that property rights are human rights—moral guarantees of the freedom to gain, keep, use, and dispose of the material values produced by a human being to support his own life;

That one's rights can be forfeited only by and to the extent that one violates the equal rights of other men; that since, in logic, there can be no such thing as a right to violate rights, no man or men may morally initiate the use of force, coercion, or fraud against any other man or men—the only moral use of force being in retaliation against those who initiate its use;

That governments are formed when men delegate to an institution their right of retaliation, so as to obtain an impartial protection of their rights under a codified system of objective laws; that a government, as such, has no rights except those delegated to it by the citizens for a specific purpose; and that the only purpose of a moral government is the protection of individual rights;

That the sole functions of government compatible with the principle of individual rights are three: a law-making and enforcement apparatus, to protect the innocent against criminals; a national defense system, to protect the innocent against foreign aggressors; and a judiciary, to distinguish the innocent from the guilty, to bring the guilty to justice and justice to the innocent, and to arbitrate disputes among men;

That just as it is immoral for a man or group of men to infringe upon individual rights, no government—which is merely an agency of men—may morally do so; that to the extent to which governments therefore venture beyond their rightful role, they embody the very evil which they were established to eradicate; that, for these reasons, no government may morally interfere with the convictions, associations, occupations, transactions, properties, and pleasures of any peaceful and non-coercive individual;

That any government interference in the economy is inconsistent with these principles, and, unless completely eliminated, inexorably degenerates into dictatorship or chaos; that such interference is inevitably on behalf of some individuals at the expense of others, destroying the independence, initiative and integrity of all; that when the seeds of coercion are planted in the field of politics, all that grows is the strangling weed of totalitarian control;

That free trade—the uncoerced production and voluntary exchange of values—is the only method of social behavior consonant with individual rights and with the nature and needs of rational beings; that laissez-faire capitalism, entailing a total separation of economics and state, is the only social system embracing that method—and is therefore the only moral, as well as practical, social system possible to man;

That a government's foreign policy, to be both moral and practical, must likewise remain consistent with the principles of individual rights, and serve the just self-interest of the people whom that government represents; that just as a proper government does not attempt to cooperate with domestic criminals, neither should it attempt to cooperate with foreign tyrants; that to aid a despot is to tighten his grip on the chains of his slaves; that a bow to tyranny is a blow to liberty;

Finally, we dedicate ourselves to the task of advancing the principles of reason, individualism, and capitalism. With these ends, then, we pledge—as did our intellectual forefathers—to raise a standard to which the wise and honest can repair.

New Right Coalition

Regulations: How the Government Strangles Free Enterprise
Frank Peseckis

Big government has become the single greatest obstacle to economic prosperity. This obstacle consists largely of the mass of tariffs, anti-trust laws, and innumerable regulatory agencies which attempt to "run the economy" but succeed only in causing economic distress.

From Frank Peseckis, "Regulations: How the Government Strangles Free Enterprise" (Boston: New Right Coalition, [1970s], flyer).

Regulatory Agencies

There are presently more than 100 regulatory agencies in the Federal Government alone. These substantially control the communications networks, transportation systems, the production and distribution of energy and the practices of banks and investment corporations. Indeed, better than 25% of all economic activity in America is controlled outright by the State, while State control is felt to some degree in every other business.

Federal regulatory agencies continually sacrifice the well being of one businessman for the benefit of another. Unbelievable? Well, for the past two decades the Federal Communications Commission (FCC) has blocked expansion of Cable TV to "protect" local television stations from competition. Or take the case of the Interstate Commerce Commission (ICC). Since its inception the ICC has been regulating the railroads. And the more rules the ICC imposed, the less efficient and profitable the railroads became. Every failure provided the ICC with an excuse for more regulations. The result is the disastrous situation the railroads presently face. Now that it has ruined the railroads the ICC has started to regulate trucking concerns, to protect the railroads from destructive competition.

To highlight the injustice of regulatory agencies, one need only examine their method of conducting hearings on companies which have allegedly broken their rules. The agency is complainant, prosecutor, judge and jury, all wrapped in one. They're not only autocratic, but inefficient as well. Cases are backed up for years. Most businesses charged with a violation of an agency's edicts exist in a precarious position. As one prominent businessman has noted, "We no longer hope for a fair decision, we hope for any decision at all."

Regulatory agencies are responsible for flooding the market with less reliable merchandise at higher prices than would exist in a free market. They encourage inefficient businesses while destroying the competent.

Antitrust

Allegedly, antitrust laws protect individuals from any "vicious industrialist" who first, would offer such excellent goods and/or low prices that he would drive his competition out of business; and who would then use his monopolistic position to raise prices exorbitantly, thus exploiting those of us who must buy his goods. Actually, this would never happen in a free market. Suppose some "greedy" industrialist did drive his competitors out of business. Suppose he then tried to raise his prices far above the free market level. What would happen?

In a free market, every businessman invests his money in the most profitable venture he can find. If one businessman was making a 10% profit on his investments and he saw our greedy businessman making a 50% profit, he would invest his money in the same type business. Soon our "greedy" businessman would be so swamped by competition that he would be forced to lower his prices. Hence, in a free market monopolies would never raise prices unjustifiably, to do so would be a form of economic suicide. . . .

Tariffs and Import Quotas

Tariffs and import quotas are supposed to protect American jobs and industries from cheap foreign labor. Yet there is no need for this protection. The following is a typical result of import quotas. Import quotas restrict Oil Imports to 12 ½% of U.S. oil consumption per year. The President's Task Force on oil imports has ascertained that this quota has driven the price of oil from a free market level of $2.24/barrel to approximately $3.90/barrel. In other words, last year American consumers spent about $5 billion more for oil products than they would have under free enterprise. . . .

Conclusions—For a Free and Prosperous Society

State intervention is not progressive, rather it is reactionary. It's a revision to an economic barbarism which has caused hunger, disease, poverty, and has crippled countless lives. Observe that countries with the fewest restrictions on trade are also the most prosperous, while those nations which have instituted the greatest degree of economic conformity are in a state of chaos. Observe also that as America has piled up regulations on trade, and governmental bureaucracies to enforce them, we have also suffered depressions, recessions, inflation, and unemployment.

It should also be mentioned that governments cannot control the use of property without controlling the lives of men. All of us must work for a living. When the State regulates the economy, it controls business, trade, and commerce; which means it controls our means of survival; which means it controls our lives.

We must abolish these laws and agencies which are strangling man's productivity and creativity. If our goal is a free and prosperous nation, we must progress toward a society of free men, a society of laissez-faire capitalism.

Committee of the States in Congress

COMMITTEE OF THE STATES IN CONGRESS, JULY 4, 1984
THE UNANIMOUS DECLARATION OF THE FIFTY STATES OF AMERICA, ASSEMBLED.
DECLARATIONS OF ALTERATION AND REFORM

The following alterations and reform for the government of these United States of America are hereby declared ratified by the Committee of the States in Congress assembled and are held to be the "law of the land." Enforcement shall be as directed by the Committee of the States in Congress assembled.

ARTICLE I

All prior Acts of the Congress (Constitutional Congress) of the UNITED States, wherein appropriations of funds, moneys of [sic] credits have been made for other than the domestic support of the government of these United States, are hereby repealed. All unexpended funds, moneys or credits for all such appropriations shall be immediately returned to the Treasury of the United States. Organizations and functions governed by this Act of Repeal include all Multilateral International Organizations in which the United States participates. These include but are not limited to (1) The United Nations and Specialized Agencies; (2) Inter-American Organizations; (3) Foreign Aid of any kind; (4) The World Bank and all financial elements provided by the

From Committee of the States in Congress, "Declarations of Alteration and Reform," *Duck Club News Digest* 3, no. 12 (1984).

Bretton Woods Agreement Act; and (5) All purposes except for the retention of Embassies outside the territorial limits of these United States.

ARTICLE II

Effective this date, July 4th, 1984, the Federal Reserve Act (28 Stat. 251; 12 U.S.C. 221) enacted 23 December 1913, is hereby repealed. All statutes in [*sic*] enacted in pursuance thereof are hereby repealed.

All stock of the Federal Reserve System and Federal Reserve Banks shall be delivered to the Treasurer of the United States within 10 days from this date, July 4th 1984.

ARTICLE III

The Treasurer of the United States shall immediately establish a United States Bank within the Treasury Department.

ARTICLE IV

The Comptroller of the Currency shall provide for the recovery of all Federal Reserve Notes in circulation. United States Notes shall be loaned by the United States Bank to all lawfully constituted private banks which are domestically owned by citizens of these United States. A service charge on said loans shall be at an annual rate of Two Percent (2%), payable to the Treasury of the United States.

All private, domestically owned banks in the United States (National and State Banks), shall hereafter function on a "commercial" basis only and shall maintain a reserve of One Hundred Percent (100%) in cash of all Time Deposits (Savings Accounts). Demand Deposits (Checking Accounts) shall be maintained upon a commercial basis and reasonable service charges may be adopted for the performance of such banking services provided to the public by said banks.

Ex:sting private, domestically owned banks may borrow from the United States Bank, an amount not to exceed Fifty Percent (50%) of the total amount deposited in said banks by depositors with Time Deposits (Savings

Accounts), provided said loans are supported by adequate collateral from secondary borrowers (persons borrowing from the bank), and the service charge upon such secondary loans shall not exceed the annual rate of Four Percent (4%) to the secondary borrower. Borrowing from the United States Bank by said private banks shall be computed upon month-end balances of Time Deposits. Collateral requirement from secondary borrowers shall be in accord with good business practices.

ARTICLE V

The General Accounting Office shall immediately commence an audit of the Federal Reserve System and Federal Reserve Banks in its and their entirety. All funds, credits and financial transactions of the Federal Reserve System are hereby frozen pending completion of audit. In the interim, all monetary and banking functions in the United States shall be performed by the Department of the Treasury in accordance with directions of the Committee of the States in Congress assembled and with the instructions contained herein.

ARTICLE VI

The Committee of the States in Congress assembled, confirms that the Gold Reserve Act of 1934 is repealed. All statutes in pursuance thereof are by [sic] also hereby repealed.

ARTICLE VII

The bureau of the Mint, in cooperation with the Department of the Interior, shall arrange for the United States Bank to make necessary financing available to citizens of these United States for rehabilitation of the domestic Mining Industry in these United States. Domestic production of gold and silver shall be based upon a free market and a free market shall govern the production and disposition [of pre]cious metals necessary for the minting of gold and silver coins for the account of the United States Treasury. United States Notes, issued by the United States Bank, shall be redeemable in gold or silver coin to citizens of the United States at all times, but to foreign sources, at the option of the United States, in surplus commodities of these United States which are made available through foreign trade.

ARTICLE VIII

Effective immediately, all costs or obligations of the United States shall be paid by the Treasurer of the United States with United States Notes which shall be printed by the Treasury Department and be issued and or expended in payment of services, interest free. No expenditures may be made except in accordance with appropriations made by the Committee of the States in Congress assembled and in pursuance of the Constitution of these United States.

The government of the United States shall not participate in any business or commercial activity not specifically authorized by the Constitution. Where disposition of assets are necessary to comply with this injunction, disposition of all holdings and assets shall be made by the government in such a manner that proceeds will derive to the benefit of the United States.

ARTICLE IX

The Social Security Act, approved August 14th, 1935 (49 Stat. 620; U.S.C. Chap. 7) and all subsequent Acts related thereto, are hereby repealed.

All accounts of funds pertaining to the Social Security Act shall be credited to the Treasurer of the United States. The Treasury Department shall employ the records of the Bureau of Old-Age and Survivors insurance, and shall provide a monthly Old-Age Pension in the amount of Five Hundred Dollars ($500.oo) per month to each citizen of the United States who resides in the United States, who has been previously eligible for said benefits. No benefits shall be paid to citizens residing outside the continental limits of the United States or in foreign countries. Payment shall be made in United States Notes as a cost or obligation of the United States.

All Estate and Inheritance taxes are hereby repealed and no further taxes shall be paid by any citizen of the United States for the purpose of Social Security.

All personal (individual) income taxes are hereby declared unlawful and no direct tax shall be imposed upon any citizen or upon a citizen's income, any provision of Title 26, U.S.C. notwith [*sic*] standing.

In order to compensate citizens nearing the age of sixty five years (65) and who have made substantial contributions to the Social Security System during their lifetime, the Old-Age Pension in the amount of Five Hundred dollars ($500.oo) per month, shall be paid to each citizen of the United States who resides in the United States and who shall provide evidence of having reached the age of 65 years. Said Old-Age Pension shall be paid for a period of twenty (20) years from this date, (7 July 1984), after which no benefits shall accrue to anyone reaching said age. As the beneficiaries decrease, the Old-Age Pension will be phased to a completion by the government.

ARTICLE X

Effective this date (July 4, 1984), the Federal Deposit Insurance Act is hereby repealed. (The Federal Deposit Insurance Corporation was organized under authority of Sec. 12B of the Federal Reserve Act, approved June 16, 1933 (48 Stat. 162; 12 U.S.C. 264). By the Act approved Sept. 21, 1950 (64 Stat. 873; 12 U.S.C. 1811–1831), Section 12B of the Federal Reserve Act as amended was withdrawn as part of the Federal Reserve Act and was made a separate, independent law known as the "Federal Deposit Insurance Act." The act also made numerous amendments to the former Federal Deposit insurance law). All assets of the Federal Deposit Insurance Corporation will be immediately delivered to the Treasurer of the United States.

The General Accounting Office shall immediately commence an audit of the Federal Deposit Insurance Corporation. The former functions of the corporation shall be assumed by the Secretary of the Treasury of the United States.

ARTICLE XI

Effective immediately, the Export-Import Bank Act, as amended (59 Stat. 526; 12 U.S.C. 635) is hereby repealed.

All capital stock of the Export-Import Bank shall be immediately delivered to the Treasurer of the United States. The General Accounting Office shall commence an immediate audit of the Export-Import Bank and all former functions of the Bank shall be assumed by the Secretary of the Treasury of the United States.

ARTICLE XII

Effective immediately, the Federal Home Loan Bank Act, approved July 22, 1932 (47 Stat. 725; 12 U.S.C. 1461 et seq.) and Title IV of the National Housing Act, approved June 27, 1934 (48 Stat. 1255; 12 U.S.C. 1724 et seq.), to include all amendments to said Acts, [is] hereby repealed.

All assets of the Federal Savings and Loan Insurance Corporation shall be immediately delivered to the Treasurer of the United States.

The General Accounting Office shall immediately commence an audit of the Federal Savings and Loan Insurance Corporation. Former functions of the corporation shall be assumed by the Secretary of the Treasury of the United States.

ARTICLE XIII

Effective immediately, the Act of Congress of September 24, 1789 as amended (1 Stat. 92, 16 Stat. 162; 5 U.S.C. 291) and the Act of Congress of June 22, 1870 (16 Stat. 162; U.S.C. 291) are hereby amended to provide that all functions of the Department of Justice shall be administered by a sub-committee of this Committee of the States sitting as the Congress of the United States.

ARTICLE XIV

Effective immediately, the National Security Act of 1947 (61 Stat. 499 as amended; 5 U.S.C. Sup. 171) and the Reorganization Plan 6 of 1953 are hereby amended to provide that all function of the Department of Defense shall be administered by a sub-committee of this Committee of the States, sitting as the Congress of the United States.

ARTICLE XV

In accordance with Article IX of the Articles of Confederation and Perpetual Union, and the Act of Congress of September 22, 1789 (1 Stat. 70) and subsequent Acts of Congress providing Rules and Regulations for the development of the Postal System of the United States, to include the Reorganization Plan 3 of 1949, said statutes and Acts are amended herewith to provide that all functions of the U.S. Post Office Department shall be administered by a sub-committee of this Committee of the States, sitting as the Congress of the United States.

ARTICLE XVI

It is hereby declared that the Constitution of these United States is a compact (contract) by and between the People of the sovereign states of the Union. By this compact the People of the sovereign states created an "agent" commonly referred to as the "federal government" and placed this corporate entity in the District of Columbia in another corporate entity known as the City of Washington. The People as sovereign states did enumerate the powers granted to the "agent" and by the terms of the contract the states and the People retained all powers not granted. (See Amendments IX and X to the U.S. Constitution).

It is further declared that all three branches of the "agent" commonly referred to as the "federal government" have violate [*sic*] the principles of a Republic [*sic*] Form of government, usurping jurisdiction over sovereign citizens of sovereign states of the Union and usurping powers NOT GRANTED by the states and the People and therefore violating the terms of the contract (the Constitution).

These violations of the Ordinance of God for this Constitutional Republic, if continued, will bring violence and chaos upon the people and therefore upon the government. Public Servants have committed acts of SEDITION against the government (the body politic) of these United States of America and are as insolent as those of the Roman government in the days of the Apostle Paul.

It is therefore declared that all agencies, departments and/or activities of government not functioning in pursuance of the Constitution of these United

States of America, are hereby dissolved. These include, but are not limited to: (1) The Department of Health, Education and Welfare; (2) The International Cooperation Agency; and (3) All Executive Orders entered into the Federal Register wherein Congress has unlawfully delegated its mandated powers to the Executive.

Wherein, the delegates of the sovereign states of the Union do hereby declare as the COMMITTEE OF THE STATES assembled IN CONGRESS, that the above adopted Articles of the Declarations of Alteration and Reform are the "law of the land." Any interference with the implementation and execution of said Articles shall be considered an act of SEDITION against the government of these United States of America and shall be punishable under the law. Any interference or attempt to obstruct the functions of this Committee of the States or any of its delegates, shall result in imposition of the death penalty upon conviction by the Committee sitting as the Congress of the United States.

IN CAVEAT, the UNANIMOUS DECLARATION OF THE FIFTY STATES ASSEMBLED IN CONGRESS shall be delivered as constructive notice to (1) The Clerk of the House of Representatives and the President of the Senate in Washington, D.C. and the Clerk of the Legislature of each state of the Union.

AFFIRMATION

We, the People, the "body politic", citizens of the sovereign states of the Union and of the Republic known as the "United States of America", a Union under the compact known as "Articles of Confederation and Perpetual Union", hereby AFFIRM THIS INDICTMENT and further affirm that said CHARGES and the SPECIFICATIONS of the Indictment are not all inclusive, but in their limitations are considered sufficient for "aye" on the indictment and its affirmation by the Committee of the States sitting as a Grand Jury of the People (the body politic).

It is hereby declared that We, the People, the "body politic" bringing this Indictment, are the Lords and Masters of this self-governing Republic known as the United States of America, and that the Congress (Constitutional Congress) of these United States, collectively and in persona (as individuals), are employees on the public payroll, therefore subject to dismissal and removal from office and replacement by a committee of the States as provided for in Article V., Articles of Confederation and Perpetual Union of 1777 (1778), as ratified by the States of the Union formally announced to the public on March 1st, 1781. Said removal from office and replacement by the Committee of the States is hereby recommended and authorized. The effective date of such removal from office and replacement by the Committee of the States shall be declared by the Committee of the States in Comgress [*sic*] assembled.

Dated in the Year of Our Lord Jesus Christ, 4 July 1984.

TAXES

Patriot Network

As was noted earlier, the income tax is one of the primary targets of the right. The following two selections present the argument that the income tax is unconstitutional.

MUST YOU PAY INCOME TAX? FOR INDIVIDUALS, INCOME TAX IS A VOLUNTARY TAX

The above statement makes many people skeptical when they read it. However, the basic reason for the truth of the statement is really very simple.

THE U.S. CONSTITUTION **FORBIDS** THE FEDERAL GOVERNMENT TO IMPOSE ANY TAX DIRECTLY UPON INDIVIDUALS.

INDIVIDUALS VOLUNTARILY IMPOSE AN INCOME TAX UPON THEMSELVES WHEN THEY FILE AN INCOME TAX RETURN.

Read on and learn why. You will be glad you spent a few minutes to learn about these important facts.

AMERICANS ARE CONFUSED AND DECEIVED

Before World War II, individuals' wages were not considered to be subject to income taxes. During the war a "victory tax" was imposed on

From "Must You Pay Income Tax?" (Evans, Ga.: Patriot Network, [1980s], pamphlet).

wages as an emergency measure to help pay for the war. The people did not realize that government could not constitutionally impose any tax directly on them, so they assumed that individuals and their earnings could be taxed directly.

The Internal Revenue Service intentionally promoted this misunderstanding of taxing power through clever wording of its statements, publications and propaganda news releases. Consequently, Americans have been deceived into believing that they are required to pay an income tax which is laid on them directly by government. However, when the IRS's publications, U.S. Supreme Court decisions and the Internal Revenue Code (income tax law) are studied carefully, they show that for individuals, paying income tax is voluntary and that the filing of tax forms is also a voluntary action that is not required by law.

CONSTITUTIONAL LIMITATIONS ON TAXING POWER

In order to understand why paying income tax and filing tax forms are voluntary actions for individuals, it is essential to understand the limitations on federal taxation embodied in the United States Constitution. The statesmen who wrote the constitution were fully aware of the dangers to liberty in allowing a central government to impose taxes directly upon individuals or upon property.

Tyranny resulting from direct taxation of individuals had led to the American Revolution only 12 years earlier when all the taxes collected amounted to less than 5% of the colonists' earnings. This tyranny was referred to in the Declaration of Independence where in describing the reasons for the revolution the founding fathers stated: *"He* (King George III) *has erected a multitude of new offices, and sent hither swarms of officers to harass our people, and eat out their substance."*

Because of the knowledge of these facts, the framers of the constitution included not one, but two limitations in the Constitution that **absolutely forbid the federal government to impose any direct taxes upon individuals or upon property.** All direct taxes are required to be "apportioned," which means that they must be laid upon the state governments in proportion to each state's population.

The limitations forbidding direct taxation of individuals are found first in Article 1, Section 2, Clause 3, which states : *"Representatives and direct taxes shall be apportioned among the several states which may be included within this Union, according to their respective Numbers. . .*", and again in Article 1, Section 9, Clause 4, which states: "*No capitation, or other direct, tax shall be laid, unless in proportion to the census or enumeration herein before directed to be taken.*" These basic sections of the Constitution have never been repealed or amended. The Constitution still forbids direct taxation of individuals and property.

16TH AMENDMENT MISINTERPRETED (DELIBERATELY)

Deceptive statements by IRS spokesmen and other propaganda have intentionally created great confusion as to whether these limitations on direct taxes are still in effect. They incorrectly claim that the 16th amendment (the income tax amendment) changed the constitutional limitations on direct taxes and authorized an income tax as a direct tax without apportionment. The U. S. Supreme Court rejected these claims in the case of **Brushaber v. Union Pacific R.R. Co.,** 240 US 1, (1916), when they ruled that the 16th Amendment created no new power of taxation and that it did not change the constitutional limitations which forbid any direct taxation of individuals.

The Court stated that the nature of income tax is identified by the wording of the amendment itself, which says: "*The Congress shall have power to lay and collect taxes on incomes, from whatever source derived, without apportionment among the several States, and without regard to any census or enumeration.*" The Court explained that since it is a tax "without apportionment", the income tax cannot be a direct tax, because the Constitution still requires that all direct taxes must be "apportioned".

INCOME TAX IS AN EXCISE TAX

If the income tax is not a direct tax, what kind of tax is it? The Brushaber decision, which has never been overruled, cleared up the misunderstanding by stating ". . . *taxation on income was in its nature an excise. . .*" And it further stated ". . . *that taxes on such income had been sustained as excises in the past.*" The ruling established that income tax is constitutional as an excise tax, but not as a direct tax. According to the Court, the income tax is still an excise tax. The IRS relies on the Brushaber decision to prove the constitutionality of the income tax, but ignores the Court's ruling that income tax is an excise tax.

Now the question arises: can an excise tax be laid on individuals by government? The answer is definitely **NO!** Remember . . . **the Constitution absolutely forbids any federal taxes to be laid directly on individuals.** Then who or what is subject to an excise tax? The U. S. Supreme Court in **Flint v. Stone Tracy Con.,** 220 US 107, defined excises as ". . . *taxes laid upon the manufacture, sale, or consumption of commodities within the country, upon license to pursue certain occupations, and upon corporate privileges.*"

Individuals are not commodities or corporations, so the only way an individual could be even indirectly subject to an excise tax is if he were granted a license to engage in an occupation of special privilege, such as a lawyer. The Court has ruled that a lawyer is granted a license of special privilege by government to act as an officer of the Court and that money earned in the exercise of that privilege is subject to an income (excise) tax. All occupations that one could lawfully pursue without the existence of government are occupations of common right and are not subject to an income (excise) tax. For example: laborer, factory worker, salesman, plumber, electrician, doctor, merchant, nurse, secretary, truck driver, waitress, etc.

INDIVIDUALS ARE NOT "REQUIRED"

Section 6012 of the Internal Revenue Code tells who "shall" file income tax returns. Without careful analysis, the wording of the section appears to require all individuals earning $1000 or more to file returns. The section states: "*Returns with respect to income taxes under subtitle A shall be made by the following: (1) (A) Every individual having for the taxable year a gross income of $1000 or more, except . . .*" Everything that comes in to an individual is not legally defined as "income". To be "income", money must be a gain or profit made in the exercise of government granted privilege, such as lawyers' fees. The IRS Code, if carefully analyzed, clearly shows that wages, salaries and tips are not "income".

The section states that returns "shall" be made by every individual having a certain amount of "income". It does not say that returns are required to be made by them. Courts have repeatedly ruled that "shall" means "may" when used in statutes.

In the decision on **Cairo and Fulton R.R. Co. v. Hecht,** 95 US 170, the U.S. Supreme Court stated: *"As against the government, the word 'shall' when used in statutes is to be construed as may unless contrary intention is manifest."*

In the decision of **Gow v. Consolidated Coppermines Corp.**, 165 Atlantic 136, the Court stated: *"If necessary to avoid unconstitutionality of a statute, 'shall' will be deemed equivalent to 'may'."*

If you, as an individual, were required to file a return and supply information under oath, all of which could be used as evidence against you in any criminal case, the requirement would be unconstitutional because it would violate your 5th Amendment right not to be compelled to be a witness against yourself. It is clear that individuals are not required to file returns, even if they have income of $1000 or more.

DAMAGING EFFECTS OF INCOME TAX

In the past, America prospered and became the greatest and richest country in the world when individuals paid no income tax and government's revenues were raised by constitutionally authorized taxes on certain goods and services and on corporations. But, now, money is taken from [the] productive sector of society by the income tax scam to support the non-productive sector, foreign aid, give-aways and a bloated, needless bureaucracy. The income tax paid by citizens sharply reduces their earnings: they then buy less, causing business to decline, leading to unemployment and depression, thus lowering the standard of living for all Americans. The income tax has created havoc in America's economy, in addition to the loss of liberty and the harassment of our people by the IRS's oppressive collection tactics.

The collection of the income tax by extortion like methods based on deception and enforced by fear and intimidation is as un-American as the origin of the income tax itself, which is the second plank of Karl Marx's Communist Manifesto.

Abuses of the rights of American citizens by judges and bureaucrats administering the income tax law is a disgrace to our country. History has proven that governmental abuses of citizens' rights, if unchecked, always lead to tyranny. Deceiving citizens into voluntarily subjecting themselves to a tax they do not owe is a **fraud.** When individuals who do not voluntarily subject themselves to the income tax by filing returns, have assessments of tax laid on them directly, it is a **blatant violation of the constitutional limitations forbidding the direct taxation of individuals.** If the IRS then confiscates the individuals' wages or property by levy and seizure to settle the unconstitutionally laid tax claims, the action is **pure theft under color of law.**

WHAT YOU CAN DO

The U.S. Constitution is the supreme law of the land. It was written to create a government of limited powers for the primary purpose of securing citizens' rights to life, liberty, and property. The Declaration of Independence states that it is the duty of citizens to oppose and resist abuses of their rights. These violations of citizens' rights can be stopped if enough people become informed of these facts. The American people must be informed of these facts so they can take action to preserve their rights.

The Constitution is a precious document of our heritage of freedom. Its guarantees of liberty are only as effective as the will of the people to enforce them.

PORTRAIT OF AN AMERICAN TRAITOR
M. J. "Red" Beckman

American history has recorded very few cases of treason. A traitor is an enemy within and we are reminded of Abraham Lincoln who said that the only way this great nation could be destroyed was from within.

As you read this small pamphlet, this once great nation seems to be deteriorating at a very rapid pace. Government is plundering and looting over half of the wealth being produced by its creative and productive citizens. High interest rates and inflation are the concern of everyone. We are not

From M. J. "Red" Beckman, "Portrait of an American Traitor" (Evans, Ga.: Patriot Network, [1984?], flyer).

involved in any declared wars so must we not ask ourselves are we being destroyed form [*sic*] within by traitors?

the answer must surely be an emphatic YES!! Who are these traitors? Can we catch them? Can we stop them before it's too late? This great nation was to be a nation of law not men so we must assume that the law must not be effective and we must have men who have put themselves above the law. The law [of] which we are talking is the Constitution of the United States and the intent of the law was to protect 'we the people' from government.

Are 'we the people' of these United States being protected from government? No—a thousand times NO!! The people are afraid of their government in America today. The people are terrorized by the Internal Revenue Service because they are threatened with jail and total ruin if they don't comply with I.R.S. rules and codes.

Are I.R.S. agents traitors, you ask? The answer is yes, but they are not alone. We don't want to single out these people. All government employees are required to take an oath to uphold the Constitution of the United States of America. Now remember the Constitution is the law which the people wrote to govern the government and thereby protect 'we the people' from government. We have had Presidents, Congressmen, Senators, and Judges who have been violating their oath because the people are not being protected from government anymore. The oath that these men in government take says that they will uphold and defend the Constitution. That means they must do everything in their power to help protect 'we the people' from government.

Now let's explore a very simple solution to our problem. 'We the people' still have some clout and we can turn this nation around very quickly. The key is to inform a lot of people in a very short time with a very simple message. The Constitution allows the government to write criminal statutes but does not give the government any enforcement power of those statutes. Article 3, Section 2, clause 3 of the Constitution and Amendment 6 of the Bill of Rights says "that in all criminal cases there shall be the right to a Jury trial." The Constitution gives the Government power to write civil statutes but the 7th amendment of the Bill of Rights says that the citizen has the right to a jury trial if the matter in controversy exceeds $20.00. So there you have the key.

It is 'we the people' who serve on those juries. Did the I.R.S. get its power from Congress, or the Courts? NO!! It was 'we the people' on the juries who said "guilty" and it was 'we the people' who didn't protect our fellow citizen from the government. It is 'we the people' who are the traitors and 'we the people' who suffer the same fate as those throughout history who have given their power over to the government and become the pawns of dictators, despots and tyrants. The worst enemy of mankind on planet Earth has usually been his own government. Our Constitutional Republic is a system where the people by law can protect each other from bad government.

Don't curse the I.R.S. agents, the Judges, bureaucrats or the Democrats and Republicans. Just look in the mirror. Has the fellow you see been upholding and defending the Constitution of the United States of America? Have you been making the government obey the law? Do you know what the law says that governs the government?

You went to a government run school, so you were taught that only the Supreme Court could say what the Constitution means. Did it ever occur to you that there are nine lawyers on the Supreme Court who all work for the government? They are paid with government checks. How do we force these nine lawyers to obey the law?

If you are concerned about America, you will always be registered to vote. As a voter you have three votes. At the polling place you elect those you hope will serve your best interest. Your vote at the polling place can be very frustrating and many do not vote. The politician has a tendency to promise one thing and do the opposite once in office. But we must remember that this first vote is not the most important.

Your second vote is when you get called for Grand Jury duty. On the Grand Jury you get to vote on whether you approve or disapprove of the laws your elected public servants are writing. You have a check against the government and you must protect 'we the people' from government. The government will be asking for indictments against your fellow Americans and you will be in a position to protect your fellow American if you are on the Grand Jury. We have many Americans who are angry at the traitors in government and we need these angry Americans on the Grand Jury to protect 'we the people' from Government.

Your third vote is when you are called for regular Jury duty. You are the final check in our system of Checks and Balances. You must decide, is the citizen who is on trial a threat to 'we the people' or is the defendant a threat to the government? As an individual on that jury you have more power than the President of the United States, more power than all 435 Congressmen and 100 Senators and more power than the Supreme Court and all of the Federal Court System. As an American Citizen you have a lot of clout if you know how to use it. You must not let the Judge or prosecutor know that you are an informed American who now has clout. You will need a blank face and go along with the whole process because these Judges and prosecutors are government employees and they don't want anyone on the Jury who can't be manipulated. Play the game until you get into the Jury room and then vote to save this the greatest nation in history. Vote yourself free of I.R.S. tyranny by voting to free your fellow American.

Remember this simple rule—is the defendant a threat to you, your family or your community? Is the defendant a threat to the government's plan to loot, plunder and destroy 'we the people'? Vote yourself free—the polling place, the Grand Jury and the Jury, three votes in the system so that we might be able to enforce the law which we wrote to bind and control government.

'We the people' gave the I.R.S. all of its power when we said guilty on the jury and now we are going to take the power away from the I.R.S. by saying "not guilty". You may be the only one on that jury that will say "not guilty", but you have lots of clout now and you can hang that jury all by yourself. You may even be able to educate the other eleven people on the jury. Try it you'll like it.

The traitors are at work within America as you read this but we aren't going to hang a lot of people because 'we the people' did it to ourselves. This little pamphlet is the answer and you must now do everything in your power to transmit this message to every American.

Remember this fact. The people of Hitler's Germany destroyed themselves because they did exactly what government told them to do. People through blind obedience to Hitler's commands, destroyed themselves and their nation. The judges in our Courts are telling us in their instruction that we must do as the government says. 'We the people' can serve our nation and ourselves only by a critical judgement of the government and the laws which that government wishes to put on the people's backs. Is your tax-burden about to destroy you? Then vote yourself free by voting to protect 'we the people' from government, from bad government.

ALTERNATIVE MONEY SYSTEMS

In the true populist tradition, the right has developed alternatives to the current money system; below are three such proposals. The Federal Reserve system is the primary target.

Lord's Covenant Church

THE CONSTITUTIONAL WAY—EVERY CITIZEN A STOCKHOLDER
Sheldon Emry

If we would have used the Constitutional way of "creating" the money needed in the nation, the Federal Congress would spend most of its time and study on the issuance and control of an adequate supply of stable money for the people. If an increase of population and production required an increase in the medium of exchange, Congress would authorize the "coining" (i.e. printing) of the determined amount. Some could be used to pay current legitimate expenses of the Federal Government, with the balance paid directly to the citizens. Records for payment would be similar to Social Security records, except a citizen would be recorded at birth instead of when he first goes to work. Each person on the records as of the date of the Congressional authorization would receive an equal amount just as if he were a stockholder holding one share. Citizenship would be the only requirement, with no discrimination as to race, color, age, or sex.

In the above manner the nation's total money supply could be increased, with no disadvantage to anyone, and in advantage to all. All would benefit from the increased ease of exchanging goods and services with more money available. The important thing would be that the money would be debt-free, and would not have to be taxed back out of existence to pay back to the Federal Reserve Bankers. . . . it would remain in circulation for generations at no cost to the taxpayers except printing replacements for paper currency as it wears out.

Another decided benefit of the people's control of Congress, and through them, the money, would be that an adequate national military defense would be protected by the same interests. There would be no Bankers behind the scenes bribing politicians to give $100 billions of American military equipment to other nations, disarming us while alien nations prepare to attack and invade the United States of America.

From Sheldon Emry, *Billions for the Bankers Debts for the People: The Real Story of the Money-Control over America* (Phoenix: Lord's Covenant Church, [1973?]).

STABLE MONEY

Money, issued in such a way, would derive its value in exchange from the fact that it had come from the highest legal source in the nation and would be declared to be legal to pay all public and private debts. Issued by a sovereign nation, not in danger of collapse, it would need no gold or silver or other so-called "precious" metals to back it. As history shows, the stability and responsibility of the government issuing it is the deciding factor in the acceptance of that government's currency; not gold, silver or iron buried in some hole in the ground. Proof is America's currency today. Our gold and silver are practically gone, but our currency is accepted. But, if the government were about to collapse, our currency would be worthless. Also, money issued through the people's legitimate government would not be under the control of a privately owned corporation whose individual owners benefit by causing the money amount and value to fluctuate and the people to go into debt.

CITIZEN CONTROL

If the Federal Congress failed to act, or acted wrongly, in the supply of money, the citizens would use the ballot to replace those who prevented correct action with others whom the people believe and its issuance in sufficient quantity would be one of the few functions of Congress, the voter could decide on a candidate by his stand on money instead of the hundreds of lesser, and deliberately confusing, subjects he is presented with today. And since money is, and would remain, a national function, local differences or local factions would not be able to sway the people from the nation's i.e., the people's interest. All other problems, except the nation's defense would be taken care of in the State, County, or City governments and would not affect decisions on money.

A DEBT-FREE AMERICA

There would be no such thing as the Federal Income Tax, our houses would be mortgage-free with no $3000 a year payments to the Bankers, nor would they get $500 to $1000 per year from every automobile on our roads. We would need no "easy payments" plans, "revolving charge accounts," "go now-pay later" travel or loans to buy engagement and wedding rings, loans to buy furniture, loans to pay medical or hospital bills, loans to pay taxes, loans to pay for burials, and the thousand and one usury-bearing loans that suck the life-blood of American families. There would be no unemployment, inadequate pensions, destitute old people, or mounting crime, and even so-called "deprived" classes would be deprived of neither job nor money with which to buy the necessities and even the luxuries of life.

Criminals could not become politicians and politicians would not become criminals in the pay of the Money-lenders. Our elected officials, at all government levels, would be working for the people instead of being agents for Bankers, devising means to spend more money to place us further in debt to the Bankers. We would get out of the entangling foreign alliances that have engulfed us in four major wars and scores of minor wars since the Federal Reserve Act was passed, alliances which even now prevent America from preparing its own defense in the face of mounting world communist power.

A debt-free America would mean mothers would not have to work and could rear their children to be good citizens instead of juvenile delinquents. The elimination of the interest and debt would be the equivalent of a 50% raise in the purchasing power of every worker. Eliminating the over $100 billion "stolen" from the people every year by the bankers and their political apparatus, America would be prosperous and powerful beyond the wildest dreams of its citizens today. And we would be at peace!

TELL THE PEOPLE!

America will not shake off her Banker-controlled dictatorship as long as the people are ignorant of the hidden controllers. International Financiers, who control our government, as they control almost all governments in the world, and news media, have us almost completely within their grasp. They can begin and end wars at will, bring prosperity or depression to our nation, give us peace or unleash "urban guerilla warfare" on our cities. They are afraid of only one thing: an awakened Patriotic Citizenry, armed with the truth, and with a trust in Almighty God for deliverance.

Committee to Repeal, Rescind and Revoke
the Federal Reserve Act

A CONSTITUTIONAL MONEY SYSTEM
June Crem

An act to establish in the United States of America a Constitutional debt and interest free monetary system; To liberate our government out of the corporate and money-monopolists' strangle hold; To equitably dispose of the national debt[;] To eliminate the income tax, and drastically reduce most other taxes; to wipe out inflation, & halt the ever-tight business of money supply..

Be it enacted by the Senate and House of Representatives of the United States of America in Congress assembled, that: This act may be cited as the "CONSTITUTIONAL INFLATIONLESS MONEY ACT"..

Section 1..The Federal Reserve Act of 1913 and all subsequent, related codes and regulations are recinded [*sic*], revoked, repealed, and declared null and void, including the open market committee and all its operations..

Section 2..All private individuals, banking and financial institutions and other entities are henceforth prohibited from creating money or money credits in any form. All fractional reserve banking is prohibited. . . .

Section 4..As delegated in article 1 section 8 clause 5 of the United States Constitution, Congress shall commence to issue, create and provide Constitutional, national debt-free money and all money credits, for all national requirements: Backed by the same elements as our present United States Bonds..

From June Crem, "A Constitutional Convention to Real Money." Compiled from the Liberty Amendment Money Trap Published by Liberty Bell, Reedy, West Virginia. Distributed by Committee to REPEAL, RESCIND and REVOKE the Federal Reserve Act of 1913 and the Monetary Control Act of 1980 ([1980s], pamphlet).

Section 5..The Congress-issued and created National debt-free funds shall be used to finance all the National government's expenditures, obligations and appropriations in peace & war time.

Section 6..Congress (instead of the banks) shall create and make available National debt-free funds, with no conditions attached, to the state and local governments, in the form of long-term or NO INTEREST loans or grants: For social and public works, such as schools, hospitals, municiple [*sic*] transit systems, roads and freeways, land, water, forest conservation, etc..

Section 7..For the encouragement, operation and expansion of all segments of the Nation's free enterprise economy, Congress shall create and provide adequate National debt-free funds in the form of self-liquidating loans, including the banks, but no preferred rates..

Section 8..The free enterprise banks and money lending and investment institutions shall be completely free to bid and obtain their lending and investing funds in the open market, from the general public and also from the United States Treasury system, as prescribed in section 7..

The people through Congress shall establish and regulate the interest rates of all Congress-created-funds, loaned into the free enterprise economy as self-liquidating loans. The interest charges on all Congress-created and loaned funds shall be created into the general tax revenue fund, for the benefit of all the people: To reduce or eliminate the Nations Federal Taxes.. . . .

Section 10..Congress shall instruct the Secretary of the Treasury to remove out of circulation all Federal Reserve Notes currency, by exchanging it for United States Notes currency, & convert and coordinate all demand and savings deposits into Constitutional Monetary Aggregates System, ON A DOLLAR FOR DOLLAR BASIS..

Section 11..Constitutional money coordinated, bank credit loan repayment amount of funds, may again be used by the banks for re-lending and investing as prescribed in section 9. The previously bank-created funds coordinated into the Constitutional money aggregates are then considered as Congress-created and loaned funds..

Section 12..All Congress-authorized funds shall be issued or disbursed through the United States Treasury (sub and mini treasuries, deputized post offices and banks) system, in modern and convenient forms..

Section 13..Congress shall instruct the Secretary of the Treasury to keep an adequate stock of United States Notes currency on hand, and have it freely available through the Treasury system, to convert 100% of the Constitutional money credits transferrable by checks into United States Notes currency, if the public shall so demand..

Section 14..Congress through its power to tax, shall remove out of circulation and extinguish the excess government expenditures and appropriations funds, after they have accomplished their purpose..

Section 15..Congress through its power to lay & collect taxes, shall regulate and maintain an adequate and inflation-less monetary equilibrium, to maintain a healthy and robust economy..

Section 16..Congress shall create and appropriate adequate funds to carry out this act, and to equitable [*sic*] dispose of the United States debt by redeeming before or at maturity, all United States Securities purchased with EARNED funds and with Constitutional debt-free money credits, convertible into United States Notes currency, and expunge out of existence all U. S. Securities held by the Reserve and Commercial banks and associated entities which they had procured with their own created funds..

Section 17..This legislation shall become effective upon passage (not three years later)..

Frontiers of Freedom

REPORT ON THEFT

The founders of the United States wanted the people to have an honest money system. As a result they placed into the United States Constitution the following:

From *Frontiers of Freedom* (Bellevue, Wash.: n.p., [1989]).

"NO STATE SHALL MAKE ANY THING BUT GOLD OR SILVER COIN A TENDER IN PAYMENTS OF DEBTS."

To implement the Constitution and to set the standard for money and to answer the question: "What is a dollar" The Coinage Act of 1792 established a money system based on gold and silver. The Coinage Act of 1792 defined the dollar as a **UNIT OF MEASURE** like a "peck", "bushel", or "barrel". They defined A DOLLAR as 371.25 Grains of pure silver. A silver coin containing this measure of silver was called a DOLLAR.

All the conflicting legislation since 1792 contravenes the intent of the Constitution and therefore the Coinage Act of 1792 is still in effect and the money system in use today is UNCONSTITUTIONAL. . . .

In 1862, President Abraham Lincoln introduced the "Greenback" paper currency, the first United States Notes. You will note that these U. S. Notes were redeemable in silver on demand of the holder of these notes.

We also had Silver Certificates which were redeemable in silver on demand.

In 1914, the first Federal Reserve Notes were issued. You will note that these Federal Reserve Notes were redeemable in Dollars which has been defined by the Coinage Act of 1792 as 371.25 grains of silver.

We also had gold coins and gold certificates (paper notes redeemable in gold coin). However, in 1934, gold coins and gold certificates were removed from circulation. We also had United States Notes which differed from the Federal Reserve Notes by being debt free. The U. S. Note was also redeemable in silver.

In 1963, the redemption promise was no longer printed on any of our paper currency. In 1968, redemption in silver coin or bullion of the remaining Silver Certificates, Federal Reserve Notes, and United States Notes—was stopped. Today, the only paper currency in general circulation in the United States is the so-called "Federal Reserve Note." You will note that this Federal Reserve Note is not redeemable in lawful money, which is silver, therefore IT IS NOT A NOTE. A note is an I.O.U. to be redeemed at a certain date for the lawful money (Silver).

You will note at the top of this piece of paper it has the label FEDERAL RESERVE NOTE and at the bottom it says FIVE DOLLARS. **THIS IS AN ABSOLUTE FRAUD.** A note has to fulfill four requirements. 1. It has to name who it is payable to. 2. It has to state when it is due. 3. It has to state the amount payable. 4. It has to show the name of the Payer who owes the amount of the note. THIS SO-CALLED "Federal Reserve Note" does not fulfill any of these requirements and therefore is a fraud on whoever receives a "Federal Reserve Note" in payment for labor or produce.

This particular piece of paper is labeled at the bottom as FIVE DOL-LARS. It cannot be labeled FIVE DOLLARS WHEN WE HAVE SEEN THAT A DOLLAR IS DEFINED AS 371.25 GRAINS OF SILVER AND FIVE DOLLARS WOULD BE FIVE TIMES THAT AMOUNT. **YOU CAN EASILY SEE THAT THIS PIECE OF PAPER LABELED—FEDERAL RESERVE NOTE—AT THE TOP AND FIVE DOLLARS AT THE BOTTOM IS NEITHER. IT IS SIMPLY A PIECE OF PAPER THAT IS BEING USED AS MONEY AND A HORRENDOUS FRAUD ON THE AMERICAN PEOPLE.**

The Rothschilds—"HE WHO CONTROLS THE MONEY, RULES THE WORLD." . . .

HOW DOES THIS AFFECT THE AMERICAN PEOPLE?

1. THE GOVERNMENT NOW CONTROLS THE MONEY INSTEAD OF THE PEOPLE.

Previous to 1968 those people who produced silver could take it to the United States mint and have it minted into coins. Other people obtained these coins when they sold their production and received coins for their effort which was the result of production also. Inasmuch as the government did not produce anything they did not receive any money except what the people gave them for running the government. This made it hard for government to get overdeveloped because the people controlled the money and stood in the way.

However, now the United States Government simply creates these worth-less paper (notes) and spends them in to circulation. As a result they can purchase everything they want without actually producing anything. They no longer need the people to furnish them money as they simply counterfeit lawful money and spend it in to circulation for what they want. **TAXES ARE SIMPLY A METHOD THE GOVERNMENT USES TO TAKE THE COUNTERFEIT MONEY OUT OF CIRCULATION BEFORE**

THE PEOPLE CAN SPEND IT AND THUS BID UP THE PRICES ON PRODUCTION. The Government can increase in size anytime they want to by simple creating more counterfeit money.

2. THE AMERICAN PEOPLE HAVE MOVED FROM STABILITY TO INSTABILITY WITH THE ADVENT OF <u>INFLATION</u>.

Inflation is simply the fraudulent worthless money forced on us by the Government. The government forces us to use this money by making these fraudulent pieces of worthless paper legal tender against the dictates of the United States Constitution.

Each so-called Federal Reserve Note in circulation causes prices on production to increase for two reasons.

1. As the people come to the realization that these worthless Federal Reserve Notes are not redeemable in anything they proceed to buy something of value with them and thus bid up the prices.

2. As the government moves more and more of these worthless Federal Reserve Notes into circulation they increase their number against any such increase in production and prices rise because of the increased bidding for production.

It becomes easy to see how this increase in prices creates havoc with those people on a fixed income such as retirees.

INFLATION COMBINED WITH TAXATION GIVES THE BUREAUCRATS A "LEGAL" METHOD TO STEAL PROPERTY.

How is this theft accomplished? Very simply by re-assessment of the property continually upwards and thus increasing the taxation on the property. The sad part of this theft is that the bureaucrats are stealing the property of the elderly who are in no position to defend themselves. . . .

3. WE HAVE DEVELOPED A HORRENDOUS NATIONAL DEBT THAT IS PURE FRAUD ON THE AMERICAN PEOPLE.

How is this debt created? Some feel that it is created by the cost of operating the government. This is part of the debt but a minor part. To get at the base of this we have to know how the counterfeit money is created in the first place.

EXAMPLE OF HOW WE GET CHEATED

1. The United States Government needs one Billion Dollars to pay its bills.

2. It notifies the U. S. Bureau of Engraving to print one Billion Dollars in United States Bonds.

3. The United States Government delivers these one Billion Dollars in bonds to the Federal Reserve Bank as promissory notes. The U. S. Government promises to pay for these, its own bonds, when they mature.

4. The Federal Reserve Bank deposits these one Billion Dollars in U. S. Bonds, for which it paid nothing, with the Comptroller of Currency.

5. The Federal Reserve bank then receives one Billion Dollars in Federal Reserve Notes, the Dollar bills we all use, in various denominations.

Now pay attention to see how we are being cheated

6. The Federal Reserve Bank retains ownership of the one Billion Dollars in bonds, which it received without paying anything for them.

7. The Federal Reserve Bank Notes (Dollar Bills) it received are now distributed to member banks, so they have money available to pay bills of the government, cash government checks citizens receive, make loans to citizens etc. Please Note: Under present laws, a bank can loan out money up to ten times the amount it has on deposit.

8. The Federal Reserve Bank receives interest on its Bonds, for which they paid nothing. Please Note that the Federal Reserve Bank got the Billion Dollars for nothing. In the meantime they get interest on the Bonds they got for nothing. They also get one Billion Dollars when the U. S. Government redeems the bonds they gave the Federal Reserve for nothing.

PLEASE NOTE THAT THE NATIONAL DEBT CANNOT BE PAID BACK WITHOUT SOMEONE FAILING AND LOSING PROPERTY. THE REASON FOR THIS IS THAT ONLY, IN THIS CASE, ONE BILLION DOLLARS WERE PRINTED UP AND ACTUALLY THE UNITED STATES GOVERNMENT HAS TO PAY TO THE FEDERAL

RESERVE SYSTEM ONE BILLION DOLLARS <u>PLUS INTEREST</u>. AS YOU CAN SEE THIS IS AN IMPOSSIBILITY BECAUSE THAT MUCH MONEY IS NOT AVAILABLE AND AS A RESULT SOMEONE WILL HAVE TO PAY FOR THIS WITH THEIR PROPERTY.

THE MONEY SYSTEM IS DESIGNED IN SUCH A MANNER THAT A CERTAIN PERCENTAGE OF PEOPLE <u>MUST FAIL</u>. THIS IS WHERE INTEREST COMES FROM THEN. IT COMES FROM THE FAILURES OF OTHERS. WHEN A DEBT IS CONTRACTED, IT IS USUALLY USED TO PURCHASE A SPECIFIC ITEM. THE "MONEY" GOES INTO CIRCULATION TO BUY THE ITEM. WHEN THE DEBT IS DISSOLVED IN BANKRUPTCY IT DOESN'T TAKE THAT SPECIFIC "MONEY" BACK OUT OF CIRCULATION SO IT IS AVAILABLE TO PAY OFF SOMEONE ELSE'S INTEREST. IF EVERYONE WERE CURRENT ON THEIR DEBT REPAYMENTS THERE WOULDN'T BE ENOUGH "MONEY" FOR ALL OF THE PRINCIPAL AND INTEREST PAYMENTS BECAUSE ONLY THE PRINCIPAL WAS LOANED INTO EXISTENCE.

REMEMBER, INTEREST CAN ONLY BE PAID WHEN MORE MONEY IS CREATED THROUGH ANOTHER LOAN OR THE FAILURE OF OTHERS. THE U. S. GOVERNMENT IS THE BIGGEST BORROWER AND THEY PAY OFF THE NATIONAL DEBT. THE UNDERDEVELOPED NATIONS OF THE WORLD ARE BEING FORCED INTO SEVERE CONDITIONS BY THEIR LENDERS AND YOU CAN EXPECT THE SAME SEVERE CONDITIONS ON AMERICANS. THERE WILL BE A PRICE TO PAY.

You may not have had to go through the shame and humiliation of declaring bankruptcy. If not, you may be the next victim. Inflation is a tool they are using but it is not the only tool available to the Fed, they can also <u>constrict</u> the "money" supply. Several segments of our society have experienced recessions or depressions that have resulted in the loss of farms, jobs, and related businesses. The government uses inflation and its resultant increased assessments to take your property and they also use constrictions of the money supply, which they can control, to take your property away from you.

SOME PEOPLE SAY NOT TO WORRY AS IT
IS ALL RELATIVE

It is not all relative when you consider the fact that we have gone from a government controlled by the people to a government that no longer depends on the people. It could be called a Monetary Dictatorship rather than a Republic.

It is not relative when we go from a situation of security for the people to a situation of insecurity for the people.

It is not relative when the money we are to use becomes worth less and less the longer you have it and previously the situation was just the opposite.

It is not relative when we have gone from a position of one person supporting the family to the new requirement of two people needed to support the family.

It is not relative when interest rates increase from 5% to over 10%.

It is not relative when taxes increases 400% every ten years and previously before the advent of the non-redeemable notes we had tax stability.

SO SHOULD YOU CARE?

Yes, because your future or the future of someone you love is definitely hanging in the balance unless this fiat money system is replaced with the Constitutional money system based on gold and silver.

THE FREEDOM, SECURITY, PROPERTY RIGHTS, AND OPPORTUNITIES OF THE AMERICAN PEOPLE ARE BEING SYSTEMATICALLY ELIMINATED BY THOSE IN CHARGE OF THIS COUNTERFEIT MONEY SYSTEM AND AT THIS TIME OUR REPRESENTATIVES ARE DOING NOTHING ABOUT IT.

REMEMBER—THE THEORY OF COMMUNISM MAY BE SUMMED UP IN THE SINGLE SENTENCE: <u>THE ABOLITION OF PRIVATE PROPERTY</u>. . . .

Do you realize that America's property owners are now leasing the property they thought they owned.

Think about it—as long as property can be lost or taken because of non-payment of taxes, you do not actually own that property. A tax on property is no different than a rental fee. The right to private property has already been taken away.

Is America going in the direction of abolishing private property? While in office, President Carter signed two treaties at the U. N. that cancelled the right of American citizens to own private property.

If our leaders are working to abolish private property and the Soviets are planning to lease property to their citizens, is Congress helping to merge America with the Soviet Union by their continued support of failing communist governments with our tax money?

There is certainly a movement afoot at this time to develop a One World Central Bank which would then "create" its own currency.

One World Currency with the help of "Free Trade" means **ONE WORLD GOVERNMENT.** The result is the loss of National sovereignty. If that happens the liberties and rights we enjoy because of our Constitution will vanish.

IT IS OBVIOUS THAT OUR PRESENT COUNTERFEIT MONEY SYSTEM IS:

LOWERING OUR INCOME
 STEALING OUR PROPERTY
  DESTROYING OUR SECURITY
   MAKING WORLD CURRENCY POSSIBLE
    MAKING ONE WORLD GOVERNMENT POSSIBLE

THUS ELIMINATING OUR CONSTITUTION AND OUR RIGHTS AND FREEDOM

* * * * * * * * * *

THE ONE WORLD CONSPIRATORS HAVE FOUND THAT A COUNTERFEIT MONEY SYSTEM CAN CONTROL THE PEOPLE MUCH EASIER THAN THEIR PREVIOUS METHOD OF TERROR AND MURDER. THEY HAVE FOUND THAT THEY CAN CONTROL THE PEOPLE WITHOUT THE PEOPLE EVEN UNDERSTANDING HOW IT IS DONE—IT IS TIME FOR AMERICANS TO WAKE UP AND GET RID OF THE COUNTERFEIT MONEY SYSTEM WE HAVE TODAY.

WELFARE

THE RIGHT

New Right Coalition

Welfare Is Theft!
Don Feder

Is there a right to welfare? Apparently, many believe there is. Groups such as the National Welfare Rights Organization vociferously demand increased welfare payments. Not only do they have an inherent right to welfare, they proclaim, but they also have a right to enough money to maintain a "decent standard of living". Even the few conservatives who oppose welfare payments, do so on the basis that money is being wasted or that many people on relief could be working for a living. This avoids the basic question. By never challenging the socialist premise that one person has a right to that which another has earned, they implicitly endorse this concept.

In this book *The Incredible Bread Machine,* Richard Grant describes the true nature of welfare: "If a person robs you, we recognize that he has performed an immoral act. But perhaps some third party seizes your property in his behalf. Has the moral content of the act been altered? Suppose the third party is called a tax collector? Has the act of plunder suddenly become noble and humanitarian? Hardly. Yet this is the meaning of welfare legislation. To tax one man for the benefit of another is not welfare. It is legalized theft."

The funds that provide welfare payments are forcibly taken from taxpayers, by the government. The person who claims he has a right to welfare is in effect saying that he has a right to enslave the taxpayer. There is no right to welfare. Welfare is a denial of the property rights of those from whom the money for these payments is obtained. The primary right of all individuals is the right of life. Since sustaining one's life requires physical or mental labor to secure the requisites for survival the greater part of life is consumed in endeavor. A man spends his life producing that which he needs to live. The

From Don Feder, "Welfare Is Theft!" (Boston: New Right Coalition, [1970s], flyer).

property which one accumulates is the product of one's life. It is a certain number of hours, days, or years of a man's life, translated into physical form. When the government takes part of a person's wealth, through taxation, it has in effect stolen part of that individual's life. When the government gives this stolen property to the welfare recipient, it enables him to enslave the person who originally produced it.

Prior to the Civil War, certain individuals, called slaves, were forced to toil for their supposed masters. The slave owners took 100% of the material goods produced by their slaves. The fact that today the government takes only part of what the worker produces for the benefit of those who will not work means that the former is only partially enslaved. He is enslaved nonetheless! Thus, we can see that far from being a right, welfare is actually a denial of the right to life and property of those from whom welfare taxes are extorted. . . .

What would the abolition of welfare mean to those on relief? Would millions starve in the streets? Actually the abolition of welfare would mean billions of dollars which would surely create new jobs. This country has the economic potential for providing jobs for anyone who is physically able to work. It's only onerous taxation and other barriers to free trade, imposed by the government, that keep us from that goal.

But what of those on relief who absolutely can't support themselves? The answer is private charity. Now, before you cry that charity is incapable of caring for these people, please consider the following facts. If the average man was able to keep the money the government presently takes for forced charity (i.e. welfare) undoubtedly part of this would be donated to private charities. The important distinction is that the producer would be able to determine the objects of his beneficence; they wouldn't be chosen for him by the state. . . .

Private Enterprise could handle the problem. It is government that is both inadequate and incapable. The abolition of welfare would benefit those who really need assistance, as well as America's tax slaves. The only losers would be the parasites who are presently getting a free ride on welfare, the welfare bureaucrats whose jobs would be eliminated, and the politicians who would lose one of their best vote-buying devices.

THE LEFT

National Welfare Rights Organization

NWRO DEMANDS
for the
POOR PEOPLES CAMPAIGN

I. REPEAL OF THE WELFARE SECTIONS OF THE 1967 SOCIAL SECURITY AMENDMENTS (PUBLIC LAW 90–248 "ANTI-WELFARE LAW")

This law is the most regressive and racist piece of social legislation in the history of the country. Directly or indirectly, it affects the majority of residents of the ghettos and barrios of our country.

A. It freezes federal funds for millions of needy children who are desperately poor but presently receiving no public assistance.
B. It forces mothers to leave their children and accept work or training or be cut off welfare and have their children taken away from them.
C. It seriously restricts the program of aid to children of unemployed fathers.
D. It encourages welfare departments to further coerce and intimidate poor people.

II. A NATIONAL GUARANTEED MINIMUM INCOME OF $4,000 FOR EVERY AMERICAN FAMILY

Four thousand dollars per year for a family of four (with $500 per person adjustments for more or fewer family members) would be a minimum to raise families out of poverty.

From "NWRO Demands for the Poor People's Campaign" (Washington, D.C.: National Welfare Rights Organization, 1968, flyer).

The Guaranteed Minimum Income should also:

A. Provide annual cost of living adjustments.
B. Be administered by a simple affidavit, similar to the income tax.
C. Include a work incentive allowing families to keep all earnings up to 25% of their guaranteed minimum income and some portion of additional earnings.

III. FEDERAL FUNDS FOR IMMEDIATE CREATION OF AT LEAST THREE MILLION JOBS FOR MEN

There is a desperate need for jobs in the ghettos for men to permit them to assume normal roles as breadwinners and heads of families.

These job programs should:

A. Focus on building critically needed low income housing and community facilities in the ghettos.
B. Contribute manpower to extend vital human services such as health care, education and community organization.
C. Give first preference to contracts with organizations controlled by poor people.

WELFARE BILL OF RIGHTS

Welfare recipients have all the rights other citizens have plus special rights guaranteed by Federal and State welfare laws. But, like all rights, welfare rights are meaningless unless welfare recipients know their rights, demand their rights, use their rights, and protect their rights.

This is why many recipients across the country have formed Welfare Rights Organizations. Welfare Rights Organizations help their members find out what their rights are. Their members teach each other how to effectively demand and use their rights. And above all, by supporting each other and

From "Welfare Bill of Rights" (Washington, D.C.: National Welfare Rights Organization, [1980s], pamphlet).

fighting together, the members of Welfare Rights Organizations protect the rights of all welfare recipients.

The following are some of the most important rights recipients have:

1. THE RIGHT TO BE A MEMBER OF A WELFARE RIGHTS ORGA-NIZATION.

2. THE RIGHT TO FAIR AND EQUAL TREATMENT, FREE FROM DISCRIMINATION BASED ON RACE OR COLOR.

3. THE RIGHT TO APPLY FOR ANY WELFARE PROGRAM AND TO HAVE THAT APPLICATION PUT IN WRITING.

4. THE RIGHT TO HAVE THE DEPARTMENT MAKE A DECISION PROMPTLY AFTER APPLICATION FOR AID.

5. THE RIGHT TO BE TOLD IN WRITING THE SPECIFIC REASON FOR DENIAL OF AID.

6. THE RIGHT TO APPEAL A DECISION THOUGHT TO BE WRONG. INCLUDING DENIALS AND REDUCTIONS OF ASSIS-TANCE, AND TO BE GIVEN A FAIR HEARING BEFORE AN IMPAR-TIAL REFEREE.

7. THE RIGHT TO GET WELFARE PAYMENTS WITHOUT BEING FORCED TO SPEND THE MONEY AS THE WELFARE DEPARTMENT WANTS.

8. THE RIGHT TO BE TREATED WITH RESPECT.

9. THE RIGHT TO BE TREATED IN A WAY WHICH DOES NOT INVADE YOUR RIGHT TO PRIVACY.

10. THE RIGHT TO RECEIVE WELFARE AID WITHOUT HAVING THE WELFARE DEPARTMENT ASK YOU QUESTIONS ABOUT WHO YOUR SOCIAL FRIENDS ARE, SUCH AS WHO YOU ARE GOING OUT WITH.

11. THE RIGHT TO HAVE THE SAME CONSTITUTIONAL PRO-TECTIONS ALL OTHER CITIZENS HAVE.

12. THE RIGHT TO BE TOLD AND INFORMED BY THE WELFARE DEPARTMENT OF ALL OF YOUR RIGHTS, INCLUDING THE WAYS YOU CAN BEST MAKE SURE THAT YOU CAN GET YOUR WEL-FARE MONEY.

13. THE RIGHT TO HAVE, TO GET, AND TO GIVE ADVICE DUR-ING ALL CONTACTS WITH THE WELFARE DEPARTMENT, INCLUD-ING WHEN APPLYING, WHEN BEING INVESTIGATED, AND DUR-ING FAIR HEARINGS.

AN EXPLANATION OF YOUR RIGHTS

It is important for every welfare recipient to know what his rights are. It is just as important to know where those rights come from. This is important so that you can tell the welfare department why they are wrong and so that you can tell other people—such as people in your organization, people from the press, and other people who you think can help you—why your position is right and the welfare department's decision is wrong.

1. THE RIGHT TO BE A MEMBER OF A WELFARE RIGHTS ORGANIZATION.

The First Amendment to the United States Constitution guarantees all citizens the right of freedom of association, this means that welfare recipients, like all other citizens, have the right to participate in private organizations of their own choosing. Welfare recipients have the right to be members and leaders of a Welfare Rights Organization, civil rights group, or any other organization they want to participate in. It is against the law for the welfare department to take any action against a welfare recipient because of his or her participation in these organizations.

2. THE RIGHT TO FAIR AND EQUAL TREATMENT, FREE FROM DISCRIMINATION BASED ON RACE OR COLOR.

The Fourteenth Amendment to the United States Constitution guarantees that all citizens are supposed to be treated equally, not to be discriminated against on the basis of race or color. Different amounts of grant cannot be given to welfare recipients because of race; nor can welfare rooms or other facilities be segregated; nor can black welfare recipients be treated discourteously. Welfare recipients also have the right to insist that welfare case workers be hired in a way which does not discriminate and which assures that the welfare staff is completely integrated.

3. THE RIGHT TO APPLY FOR ANY WELFARE PROGRAM AND TO HAVE THAT APPLICATION PUT IN WRITING.

The Federal Handbook of Public Assistance Administration, Part IV, Section 2200 and the Social Security Act, 42 U.S.C. 602, guarantee the right of any person to make an application for aid, put it in writing, or have the assistance of a welfare worker in putting the application in writing. Once a request for aid has been made, it is the responsibility of the welfare department to put the application in writing. No discouragement by welfare workers can change the fact that the person has applied.

4. THE RIGHT TO HAVE THE WELFARE DEPARTMENT MAKE A DECISION PROMPTLY AFTER THE APPLICATION FOR AID.

The Federal Handbook of Public Assistance Administration, Part IV section 2200, requires that prompt action is to be taken on every application for welfare. This means that the welfare department can take no longer than 30 days to make its decision whether to give aid or reject giving aid. If the decision is to give aid, assistance has to be provided promptly after the decision. If the welfare department takes too long, a welfare applicant has the right to immediately request a fair hearing.

5. THE RIGHT TO BE TOLD IN WRITING THE SPECIFIC REASON FOR DENIAL OF AID.

The Federal Handbook of Public Assistance Administration, Part IV section 2200, requires that an application for aid cannot be rejected by the welfare department worker's simply telling the applicant that he or she is not eligible. The applicant must be given not only written notice of the rejection but also written notice of the specific reason for the rejection. The purpose of this right is to make it possible for the applicant to show that the reason is wrong, whether because the department's rule or policy is mistakenly applied in the case or because no such rule or policy is permissible. The applicant cannot show that the reason is wrong if she is not even told why her application was rejected.

6. THE RIGHT TO APPEAL A DENIAL OF AID AND TO BE GIVEN A FAIR HEARING BEFORE AN IMPARTIAL REFEREE.

The Social Security Act, 42 U.S.C. 602, states that a basic right of persons receiving and applying for aid is the right to object to the decision of the welfare department and to be given a fair hearing in review of that decision. The kinds of decisions which can be appealed for a fair hearing include:

— denial of aid or cutting off of aid;
— too little money in the welfare grant;
— failure to act on a request for aid within 30 days;
— giving of aid in other than money form (such as giving it directly to the owner of your land or to someone you owe money to);
— giving aid on the condition that you do work;
— any action of the welfare department which you believe fair treatment has not been given.

Hearings are not to be rubber stamps of the county welfare department's action. They are conducted by a representative of the State Department and decided by the State Board of Public Welfare. The law requires that the hearing officer, the person conducting the hearing, be impartial and someone who has not been involved in the county welfare department's decision against which the appeal has been taken. The rights of persons who ask for a hearing include:

— the right to be represented or accompanied and advised by any person, whether a lawyer or not;
— the right to bring witnesses and to cross-examine the welfare department's witnesses;
— the right to present your case in a convenient and informal way;
— the right to have the hearing held at a place reasonably near the applicant's home or, if not, to receive transportation (for the witnesses as well) to the place of the hearing;
— the right to have the hearing decision made promptly—this means that final administrative action must be taken within 60 days from the date of the request for a fair hearing;
— the right to get retroactive payments, if you win the hearing, from the date of the wrongful decision.

7. THE RIGHT TO GET WELFARE PAYMENTS WITHOUT BEING FORCED TO SPEND THE MONEY AS THE WELFARE DEPARTMENT WANTS.

The Federal Handbook of Public Assistance Administration, Part IV, Section 5100, requires that the welfare recipient is to be given his or her aid in the form of money (either cash or check). The purpose of this requirement is to enable the recipient to spend the money as he or she wants. The welfare department cannot tell the recipient how to spend his or her money: welfare recipients have the right to spend their money how and when they see fit.

8. THE RIGHT TO BE TREATED WITH RESPECT.

Like all other citizens, welfare recipients have the right to be treated with respect by the employees of their government. Welfare recipients have the right to courteous and respectful treatment by all employees of the welfare department. Courtesy title should be used by the welfare employees when they talk to you.

9. THE RIGHT TO BE TREATED IN A WAY WHICH DOES NOT INVADE YOUR RIGHT TO PRIVACY.

The Fourth Amendment to the United States Constitution protects all citizens from unlawful searches, thereby assuring the right to privacy. This means that welfare recipients can refuse to let investigators into their house at any time without jeopardizing their welfare assistance. Welfare workers should not visit your home at inconvenient times such as at night, during holidays, or on Sundays. They can be forced to make sure that they do not come by your house except at a time agreeable to you. No welfare investigator or social worker can search a recipient's home without his or her permission or without a search warrant, or remove anything from the recipient's home without permission.

10. THE RIGHT TO RECEIVE WELFARE AID WITHOUT HAVING THE WELFARE DEPARTMENT ASK YOU QUESTIONS ABOUT WHO YOUR SOCIAL FRIENDS ARE, SUCH AS WHO YOU ARE GOING OUT WITH.

Under the United States Supreme Court case <u>Smith v. King</u> and under new regulations passed by H.E.W., the welfare department cannot deny, cut off, or reduce welfare aid because you are going out with someone. A welfare recipient has an absolute right to date anyone he or she wants to without having the welfare aid affected. This means that welfare workers cannot snoop around or ask you questions about your social life that you don't want to answer. Those matters are none of their business and they cannot cut off or reduce your welfare because you do not want to answer those questions.

11. THE RIGHT TO HAVE THE SAME CONSTITUTIONAL PROTECTIONS ALL OTHER CITIZENS HAVE.

A welfare recipient cannot be made to give up or limit any constitutional right because he or she is on welfare. This means that you have the same rights to speak, practice your religion, organize people into groups or help in campaigns, refuse to make statements that will hurt you during criminal investigations, refuse to let policemen search your home or unlawfully arrest you, or to have any other rights people not on welfare receive.

12. THE RIGHT TO BE TOLD AND INFORMED BY THE WELFARE DEPARTMENT OF ALL OF YOUR RIGHTS, INCLUDING THE WAYS YOU CAN BEST MAKE SURE THAT YOU CAN GET YOUR WELFARE MONEY.

The Federal Handbook of Public Assistance Administration, Part IV, Section 220 requires that the welfare department tell welfare recipients and applicants how they may show that they are eligible, of their right to a fair hearing, of their rights in the hearing (when they request a hearing), of their right to make an application in writing and get their aid promptly or get a notice of the reasons for rejection, of their right to get aid in the form of money payments, and of their right to equal treatment without regard to race or color. All other rights should be explained as well.

13. THE RIGHT TO HAVE, TO GET, AND TO GIVE ADVICE DURING ALL CONTACTS WITH THE WELFARE DEPARTMENT, INCLUDING WHEN APPLYING, WHEN BEING INVESTIGATED, AND DURING FAIR HEARINGS.

Welfare recipients have the right to be accompanied by a lawyer, advocate, or member of a Welfare Rights Organization during all contacts with the welfare department, including application, administrative reviews, investigation and fair hearings. Welfare recipients have the right to be represented by their Welfare Rights Organization, their lawyer, or other advocate (such as a friend).

8

INTENTIONAL COMMUNITIES

Intentional communities (communes, utopian communities)[1] are generally identified with the left in the United States, but that is certainly not true today, if it ever was. William Pierce, in his essay excerpted in chapter 5, refers to the need for such a community and to some of the best-known historical examples as experiments to be emulated. Many intentional communities of all persuasions are uninterested in attention from the outside; they feel there have been too many exaggerated press reports, and too many visitors who show up expecting to be supported by the community without contributing to it.

This chapter contains selections from one now-defunct community, the Covenant, The Sword and the Arm of the Lord, and one currently existing community, the Church of Israel. The Aryan Nations compound in Hayden Lake, Idaho (presented in chapter 5) is another example.

The Covenant, the Sword and the Arm of the Lord

The Covenant, the Sword and the Arm of the Lord was an intentional community on the Missouri-Arkansas border that practiced what might be called Christian survivalism. They believed that the end was approaching in both a religious and a secular sense. The United States was threatened by racial integration and was deeply corrupt. Therefore, it was necessary to withdraw, live the best life possible, and prepare for the coming troubles.

Generally the right is not thought to produce intentional communities, which are usually identified with the historical left and with the sixties. But in fact there are a large number of such communities in the United States today, mostly quietly living in rural areas and following the teachings of their leaders. They are noticed only when an incident occurs such as that in Waco, Texas, or the demise of the Covenant, the Sword and the Arm of the Lord, whose members surrendered to a large contingent of the FBI in 1985 after a man who was on his way to the community killed a Missouri State Trooper.

The following three selections reflect their ideas and illustrate how close their beliefs were to the rest of the extreme right.

STATEMENT OF PURPOSE

"And I saw another mighty angel come down from heaven, clothed with a cloud: And a rainbow was upon His head, and His face was as it were the sun, and His feet as pillars of fire: and He had in His hand a little book open: and He set His right foot upon the sea, and His left foot on the earth, And He cried with a loud voice, as when a LION roareth: and when He cried, seven thunders uttered their voices." Revelation 10:1–3

The Lamb of God who died for the sins of the world is returning to judge sin as the Lion of the Tribe of Judah. His name is Faithful and True, The Word of God, King of Kings and Lord of Lords. The armies of heaven which are with Him are clothed in white, judging and making war in righteousness, ready to rule the nations with a rod of iron.

Across the Aryan Nations, a remnant is rising in power and anointing, which the gates of hell shall not prevail against—a power and anointing which no man shall stand up to, which no enemy shall smother, which no kingdom can resist.

By faith we sojourn in a land of promise, as in a strange country. For we look for a city which has foundations, whose builder and maker is God. We have seen the promises afar off and now are persuaded of them and embrace them, confessing that we are strangers and pilgrims upon the earth. For we

From "Statement of Purpose," *Zarephath-Horeb: C.S.A. Journal,* no. 10 [1982].

that say such things declare plainly that we seek a country. For now we desire a better country, that is, a heavenly: wherefore God is not ashamed to be called our God: for he has prepared for us a city. For here we have no continuing city, but we seek one to come (Hebrews 12:9, 10, 13–16; 13:14)

We do therefore declare ourselves a Nation within a Nation, whose citizenship is of the Kingdom of God and of our Saviour Jesus Christ, and not that of this perverse and crooked generation. A stone is being cut out without hands, which shall smite the Beast image and shall become a great mountain, and fill the whole earth. The God of Heaven shall set up a Kingdom which shall never be destroyed, but it shall break in pieces and consume all kingdoms, and it shall stand forever. (Daniel 2)

The Lion of the Tribe of Judah roars, for this is His Kingdom and Domain. The seven thunders, which are the perfected voices of God's Anointed, utter their voices against the enemies of God, against sin, proclaiming to all creation the plan and purpose of God.

As is recorded for us in the Holy Word of God, in Isaiah 62:1, "For Zion's sake will I not hold my peace, and for Jerusalem's sake I will not rest, until the righteousness thereof go forth as brightness, and the salvation thereof as a lamp that burneth," so these words are engraved in our hearts, burning a direction and a vision in us that we shall not rest nor shall we hold our peace, until holiness and righteousness be established upon this war-torn, sin-infested, enemy-controlled world.

This we, those of us of Zarephath-Horeb and C.S.A., pledge.

Who We Are

Our group began in 1971. We have been at our present location since the summer of 1976. We have 224 acres on the Arkansas/Missouri border. The terrain is wooded hills with a creek on our property and Bull Shoals lake about a half mile away. Wild game include deer, rabbit, squirrel, coon, possum, and turkey. The fishing and trapping are also good here, with plenty of edible wild plants.

We are a hard-working, dedicated group of Christians, whose purpose is to build an Ark for god's people during the coming tribulations on the earth.

From "Who We Are," *Zarephath-Horeb: C.S.A. Journal,* no. 7 [1982].

We come from various walks of life. We range in ages from newborn to 75 years of age. The average adult is about 30.

Our church . . . is Zarephath-Horeb. God's purpose here is to purge the sins, worldly and fleshly desires, and various spirits out of us, in order that we may know His voice and be conformed into His image. To us, the highest relationship with God possible, which is to be as he is, is the mark we press towards.

Our church is governed by a group of God-anointed individuals called Elders. The elders make the major decisions of the group and are the Spiritual leaders and overseers, as well. Decisions are on a unanimous basis, not a majority vote. Deacons and Deaconesses also aid in the edifying of the Body, by overseeing the natural ministries.

We have a common financial pot here, with everyone's needs met and seen to. No one is required to give all his possessions to us when he joins us. As his dedication increases, so does his giving. Ours is a 100% devotion. If someone comes here and later decides to leave, he takes with him what is his, and we bless him whatever way we can.

We believe in the Holy Bible as the inspired Word of God, with the experience of Salvation and the Baptism of the Holy Spirit as essential to spiritual growth.

Our military aspect stems from obedience to the Lord concerning watching and being prepared. The Arm of God in strength and anointing shall administer judgment in the days to come. We are Christians first, survivalists second. We have a good relationship with the local people and law-enforcement personnel in our county. We absolutely love this country.

We build our own houses for each other, with the Carpenter crew working full-time. We also have a Mechanic crew, farm crew, timber crew, office crew, and construction crew.

Our bond is LOVE. Love for Christ Jesus and for each other. We are a family, enduring and growing together. This group is a Prophetic outreach of God's ministry on the earth. This outreach causes us to move the love, holiness, and commitment that is here, out to all ends of the earth. We are here to help people to prepare spiritually and physically, as a beacon of light to this country of ours. We are here to manifest Jesus, His love, and His purpose.

We have an extremely high standard of righteousness here, allowing no smoking, drinking, cussing, chewing, etc. in those who desire to abide with us. The inward motives are dealt with by the Lord after we seriously forsake the outward manifestations of sin.

This place is only one of many like it. This place is not meant for everyone. God's purpose here for right now is for the totally serious, dedicated ones whose only desire is to please Him. Later on when the Ark opens its doors before the coming flood, many will come in whose dedication may not be as severe.

What We Believe

The following is a purely basic digest of our understanding in the scriptures:

1) We believe the Holy Bible to be the inspired Word of God, written down for us for our admonition, correction, instruction, doctrinal standard, and example. It is to be believed and followed as a Holy document.
2) We believe there to be one God, our Father, who is omnipotent, omnipresent, unchangeable, all-knowing, all-loving, full of grace and mercy.
3) We believe that Jesus Christ is the Son of God, who died for our sins as the Passover Lamb of God, was buried, and rose from the dead on the third day, and is now sitting at the right hand of the throne of God.
4) We believe that the white race is the Israel race of God and is the superior race on this earth. We are not against any of the other pure races, we do not hate them, nor do we hold them back from knowing God as their Creator.
5) We believe that the experience of being "born again" by grace through faith upon repentance of sins and the Baptism of the Holy Spirit are mandatory experiences for the growth of the individual. We believe in the gifts of the Spirit (healing, tongues, etc) as power-gifts available to God's sons.

6) We believe that God is raising up a remnant out of the nations, giving them the spirit of Sonship, to grow them into perfection, to be manifested as mature Sons of God, who walk in His image upon this earth, and who will rule and reign upon earth as His Elect.

7) We believe judgment to be coming upon the earth by God and His chosen because of the sins of the world and the hardness of the people. This judgment is due to God's love for us and will in turn guide His people back to Him.

8) We believe that the commonly-called Jews of today are not God's chosen people, but are in fact, an antichrist race, whose purpose is to destroy God's people and Christianity, through its Talmudic teachings, forced inter-racial mixings and perversions.

9) We believe in the sexual separation of the races and that each race is to do as God created that race for, which is for the white race to have dominion over all things, and for the other races to serve in love.

10) We believe in the Declaration of Independence and the Constitution of these United States of America as inspired documents of God, along with the Bill of Rights. We hold that these documents have become a farce today because of evil forces in our government.

11) We believe in the Restitution of all Things in the ages to come and that all shall be gathered into Christ. This time period is known in the Bible as the Dispensation of the Fullness of Times.

12) We believe in a literal spiritual being known as the devil, along with his demons; however, we do not believe him to be all-powerful, all-knowing, and all-present as is taught by traditional churches. He is simply a tool in the hands of God, created by God, for the perfecting of the saints, and has never nor will ever thwart the will of God at any time.

13) We believe the Scandinavian-Germanic-Teutonic-British-American people to be the Lost Sheep of the House of Israel which Jesus was sent for.

14) We believe that we have the God-given right to defend ourselves against the enemies of God, and that the time is coming when God's saints shall take and then possess the kingdom of this earth, at which time the kingdoms of this world will become the kingdoms of our Lord and his Christ.

15) We believe it to be mandatory to come out of the confusion of Babylon and its political, religious, worldly, city, sinful systems, and not to touch these unclean things, that God may receive us as Sons and Daughters and may be a Father to us.

Women <u>do</u> Have a Part in the Days Ahead

A lot of women feel they don't have a place, in the days of war that lie ahead. But be assured, women, that if you let yourself, you can play a very important part even if you never pull a trigger, by being a support and encouragement to your husband and family.

Start <u>now</u>. Since it's commonly the women's job to buy the food, be wise. Start storing food. For what a few T.V. dinners cost, you could have a whole bunch of pinto beans. Also make yourself a "ready pack" with first-aid, food matches, etc. in case you have to leave in a hurry. There are many books to help you prepare in this area.

Next and very important are your children. Are they obedient to you? It may be a matter of life and death in hard times if your children are not trained to obey. Prepare them, properly. Teach them to love and trust the Lord God to prepare their minds and then prepare them physically by going on hikes and such. Don't have time? How much time do you spend watching soap operas? How much time do you spend getting your hair done or buying new clothes? *Make* time.

It's a good idea that every woman know how to shoot, clean and care for her husband's weapons. It's even better if you have your own. Practice, get good so you can make your shot count. You may never have to use it but what if your husband goes down and you must take over? A lot of women are afraid of guns—guns don't have brains! If you learn how to use one right it can be a lot of confidence for you.

Probably the most important thing you could do if you don't do anything else is to trust, support and encourage you husband. Give him a good reason to fight. Nothing will give a man more spunk than to know he's got a woman back there cheering him on. Pray for him every day. Be submissive and understanding. (Ephesians 5:22–23) It's not your job to tell him what to do; it's the Lord's. If he's tuned-in to that special channel, he'll hear that still small voice. If you're in the right spirit, God will bless you abundantly for simply submitting. What bigger blessing could we ask? We, the Israelite women bring forth the seed of our fathers—Abraham, Isaac, and Jacob. That's quite an honor, don't you think? You see, we're bringing forth out of

From "Women *do* Have a Part in the Days Ahead," *Zarephath-Horeb: C.S.A. Journal,* no. 9 [1982].

our husbands' loins and our wombs an army for His Name sake. We do have a part, let's make an effort to do the best we can! (Prov. 31:10–31)

Thank You Jesus

Church of Israel

The Church of Israel, of Schell City, Missouri, can be treated as an intentional community even though there is no community property (except church property) and its ideology strongly favors private property. In fact, its leader speaks of "Christian Covenant Settlements," and argues that communities of believers should be established in isolated rural areas.[2]

A Church With a Standard of Truth
Dan Gayman

The Church of Israel at Schell City stands unique among the churches of North America and the Western World. Unlike the denominational churches of the modern Christian world the Church of Israel at Schell City has preserved the faith of our Christian fathers and the truth of the Holy Bible. The message that is preached from this Pulpit, the Sacraments that are administered from this Altar, and the standard of truth upon which this Church is grounded reaches back to the time of Jesus Christ and the Apostles, and before that to the Prophets and Patriarchs of the earliest beginnings of our race. In 1971 the Vernon County Courthouse sought to silence this Church by taking the Sanctuary and most of the property from the Congregation. The Church survived and continued to teach the truth. In 1976 an army of Federal, State and County police units entered into the Sanctuary, locked up the Ministers and sought to silence the Church. The Church survived and continued to teach the truth. In 1980 NBC Television Crews, under the direction of Brian Ross, NBC Newsman, spent thousands of dollars coming onto the property of the Church, with sophisticated Television Cameras, Camera crews on the ground and in the air, and in a well orchestrated effort that reached from NBC offices in New York City all the way to Los Angeles, California, NBC did a National Television Smear against the Church on prime time television, on the 6:00 P.M. John Chancellor News Cast, and

From Dan Gayman, "A Church With a Standard of Truth," *The Watchman* 8, no. 14 (Fall 1984).

then again on August 5, 1980 on the TODAY program with Tom Brokaw and Jane Pauley, NBC run a smear campaign against the Church. Millions of Americans were programmed to look upon the Church of Israel with hatred and hostility. The Church survived and continues to teach the truth. Jesus Christ declared that upon this rock He would build His Church and the gates of hell would not prevail against it. We believe that by the Grace of Jesus Christ and the protection of Yahweh . . . this Church continues to stand in the earth today and teach the Faith of our Christian Fathers. You may wish to examine a few of the many great doctrines that the CHURCH OF ISRAEL at Schell City stands for.

1) WE BELIEVE IN ONE TRUE AND EVERLOVING, SELF-EXISTING UNCREATED GOD, WHOSE NAME IS YAHWEH, AND IN THE UNITY OF HIS BEING, THERE EXIST THREE SUBSISTENCES OF ONE ESSENCE, SUBSTANCE, POWER AND ETERNITY, THE FATHER, SON, AND HOLY GHOST, ALL ONE GOD, WORLD WITHOUT END.

2) WE BELIEVE IN ONE JESUS CHRIST, ETERNALLY BEGOTTEN OF THE FATHER, VERY GOD AND VERY MAN AND IN THIS ONE JESUS CHRIST THERE EXISTS TWO PERFECT NATURES, INSEPARABLY UNITED, WITHOUT DIVISION, CHANGE, CONFUSION OR COMMINGLING.

3) WE BELIEVE IN THE LITERAL AND HISTORICAL VIRGIN BIRTH, CRUCIFIXION, RESURRECTION, AND BODILY ASCENSION OF JESUS CHRIST AND THAT HE WILL LITERALLY COME AGAIN TO RULE UPON THIS EARTH IN A KINGDOM THAT WILL FILL THIS EARTH.

4) WE BELIEVE IN THE SOVEREIGN WORK OF ELECTION BY THE FATHER, THE REDEMPTION GRACE OF THE SON, AND THE SANCTIFICATION THAT IS MADE EFFECTUAL BY THE HOLY GHOST.

5) WE BELIEVE THAT THE ELECT ARE JUSTIFIED BY THE BLOOD OF JESUS CHRIST AND THAT SALVATION IS A GIFT AND NOT A REWARD EARNED THROUGH GOOD WORKS.

6) WE BELIEVE THAT THE ELECT ARE SANCTIFIED BY THE EFFECTUAL POWER OF THE HOLY SPIRIT IN OBEDIENCE TO THE LAW AND THAT GOOD WORKS IN THE LIFE OF THE BELIEVER BECOME THE FRUITS OF THEIR ELECTION IN CHRIST.

7) WE BELIEVE THAT THE LAW OF YAHWEH IS IMMUTABLE AND IRREVOCABLE AND THAT THE COMMANDMENTS, STATUTES, ORDINANCES AND JUDGMENTS MUST BE EMBRACED BY THE CHRISTIAN CLERGY, TAUGHT TO THE CONGREGATION AND THAT CHRISTIANS BEAR THE RESPONSIBILITY TO SEE THAT GOD'S LAW IS THE LAW OF EVERY CHRISTIAN STATE.

8) WE BELIEVE THAT CHRISTIANS MUST ENDURE TRIBULATION IN THIS LIFE, THAT THE TRUE CHURCH HAS ALWAYS BEEN PERSECUTED AND THAT THE RAPTURE IS A MYTH INVENTED BY THE ENEMIES OF CHRIST AND OF HIS CHURCH TO NEUTRALIZE CHRISTIAN PEOPLE AND RENDER THEM USELESS IN THE FIGHT FOR CHRISTIAN DOMINION OF THE EARTH.

9) WE BELIEVE THAT ADAM IS THE FATHER AND BEGINNING OF THE CAUCASIAN RACE AND OF NO OTHER RACE. WE BELIEVE THAT ALL OF THE NON-WHITE RACES WERE ON THE EARTH BEFORE ADAM.

10) THE CHOSEN PEOPLE OF GOD ARE ISRAELITES AND ALL ISRAELITES ARE DESCENDED FROM ADAM. ISRAELITES ARE ADAMITES, SHEMITES, AND HEBREWS, ARE ALL CAUCASIAN AND ARE IDENTIFIED TODAY AMONG THE ANGLO-SAXON-GERMANIC-SCANDINAVIAN-SLAVONIC KINDRED PEOPLES OF THE EARTH.

11) THE PEOPLE CALLED JEWS TODAY BY MOST CHRISTIANS ARE NOT ISRAELITES, ARE NOT OF ADAM'S RACE AND ARE NOT OF THE TRIBE OF JUDAH. THE JEWS OF TODAY ARE THE CANAANITE, EDEMITE, AMALEKITES AND OTHER RELATED PEOPLES IDENTIFIED IN THE WORLD TODAY AS ZIONISTS, KHAZARS AND OTHER RELATED TERMS.

12) THE NON WHITE RACES ALL CREATED GOOD IN THE ORIGINAL CREATIONS, WERE NOT GIVEN THE LAW AND WILL NOT STAND IN JUDGMENT UNDER LAW. REPRESENTATIVES OF ALL THESE RACES IN THEIR ORIGINAL RACIAL PURITY, WILL BE IN THE KINGDOM IN THE HABITAT ORIGINALLY ASSIGNED TO THEM.

13) WE BELIEVE IN THE LITERAL REGATHERING OF ALL THE TRIBES OF ISRAEL TO THE LANDS APPOINTED OF GOD FOR THEIR KINGDOM HABITAT AND THAT THIS REGATHERING

WILL TAKE PLACE AT THE SECOND COMING OF JESUS CHRIST TO HIS EARTH.

14) WE BELIEVE THAT THE KINGDOM WILL BE RESTORED TO ISRAEL, THAT JESUS CHRIST WILL RULE FROM THE THRONE OF DAVID IN THE CAPITOL CITY OF THE NEW JERUSALEM, THAT ISRAELITES WILL OCCUPY MANY AREAS OF THE EARTH INCLUDING ALL THE LAND ORIGINALLY DEEDED TO FATHER ABRAHAM.

15) WE BELIEVE THAT THE KINGDOM OF GOD IS A LITERAL THEOCRATIC KINGDOM THAT WILL BE COMPLETE WHEN JESUS CHRIST RETURNS TO RULE UPON THE THRONE OF DAVID AND THAT THE ELECT IN CHRIST, ALL ISRAELITES, WILL BE THE SUBJECTS AND ADMINISTRATORS OF THAT KINGDOM.

16) WE BELIEVE THAT THE UNITED STATES OF AMERICA IS THE BIRTHRIGHT LAND OF BIBLE PROPHECY THAT AMERICA IS MANASSEH, AND THAT THE BRITISH COMMONWEALTH OF NATIONS, ALL PART OF THE BIRTHRIGHT FAMILY OF NATIONS, IS EPHRAIM ON THE WORLD STAGE.

17) WE BELIEVE THAT THE SCEPTRE STILL BELONGS TO JUDAH, THAT THE ROYAL HOUSE OF DAVID IS STILL IN POSSESSION OF THE THRONE OF DAVID AND THAT THE ROYAL FAMILY OF GREAT BRITAIN IS THE CONFIRMATION OF THIS DAVIDIC SEEDLINE IN THE EARTH.

18) WE BELIEVE THAT NATURAL BORN ISRAELITES MUST BE BORN ANEW OF THE SANCTIFYING GRACE OF JESUS CHRIST AND THAT THIS SPIRITUAL BIRTH IS MADE POSSIBLE THROUGH THE EFFECTUAL POWER OF THE HOLY SPIRIT WORKING UPON THE HEART OF THE BELIEVER.

19) WE BELIEVE IN THE SEVEN HISTORIC SACRAMENTS OF THE APOSTOLIC, CHURCH, BAPTISM, CONFIRMATION, AND HOLY EUCHARIST, HOLY ORDERS, MATRIMONY, UNCTION FOR THE SICK AND DYING AND PENANCE FOR THOSE WHO SIN AGAINST GOD IN VIOLATION OF HIS LAW.

20) WE BELIEVE THAT THE COVENANTS, CHARTERS AND GUARANTEES GIVEN TO ISRAEL ARE STILL HONORED BY YAHWEH AND THAT THE UNCONDITIONAL COVENANTS ARE THE ASSURANCE THAT ISRAEL SHALL NEVER PERISH FROM EARTH.

21) WE BELIEVE IN THE CHRISTIAN EDUCATION OF ALL CHIL-

DREN AND THAT CHRISTIAN CHILDREN AND THEIR EDUCA-
TION IS THE RESPONSIBILITY OF THE PARENTS AND NOT THE
GOVERNMENT.

22) WE BELIEVE THAT THE CHURCH IS CHARTERED BY JESUS
CHRIST AND THAT THE CHURCH CANNOT BE LICENSED BY
THE STATE WITHOUT FORFEITING ITS CALLING IN JESUS
CHRIST.

23) WE BELIEVE THAT CHILDREN CANNOT BE GIVEN VACCINA-
TIONS WITHOUT VIOLATING THE RELIGIOUS AND SCRIP-
TURAL CONVICTIONS SET FORTH IN GOD'S IMMUTABLE
LAW.

24) WE BELIEVE THAT YOUNG MEN ARE ELIGIBLE TO FIGHT IN
WARS ONLY AS SET FORTH IN BIBLE LAW, AND THAT WHEN
GOVERNMENTS WAGE WAR IN VIOLATION OF GOD'S LAW,
CHRISTIAN BOYS MUST STAND TRUE TO THEIR RELIGIOUS
CONVICTIONS AND REGISTER AS CONSCIENTIOUS OBJEC-
TORS. WOMEN AND GIRLS ARE PROHIBITED FROM THE MILI-
TARY AND CANNOT PARTICIPATE IN ANY TYPE OF MILITARY
SERVICE ANY TIME OR PLACE.

The Duties of Christian Citizenship
Dan Gayman

The Church of Israel believes in and encourages all of its members to
walk in Christian dominion of this earth. We do not teach "**passive occupation,**" and we do not believe that Christians should refrain from becoming
active in the Christian dominion of government at every level of operation.
We believe that Christians owe their God and their country the duties of good
citizenship. Accordingly the following duties of a Christian Citizen are
presented as a guide to good citizenship.

1) Israelite Christians should walk in Christian Dominion of the earth
(Genisis [sic] 1:28) and bring all areas of life under Jesus Christ and His
Law (Psalms 8:4–6, Matt. 5:13–16).

From Dan Gayman, "The Duties of Christian Citizenship," *The Watchman* 12, no. 1 (Spring 1989).

2) Christian Israelites are to practice self-government in their own lives in the fear of God, and keep His commandments. Christians must live in accountability to God for every thought, word, deed, attitude, and motive of the heart (II Cor. 5:10, Exod. 18:21).

3) Christians should vote and encourage Christians to run for office at every level of government (St. Luke 19:13).

4) Christians should pray for the President, the Governor of their state, and local authorities of government and all who are in authority (I Timothy 2:1–3).

5) Christians should seek to keep good government in their personal lives, in the family structure, and bring forth a good witness in their marriage and in the behaviour of their children (Eph. 5&6).

6) Christians should protest sin and wickedness through every lawful means available to them (I Sam. 8:9, Psm. 97:10).

7) Christians should remember that wickedness in a nation can be corrected only when the hearts of sinful men are turned in repentance to Jesus Christ, confession of sin is made, and restoration to God and His law is complete (St. Mark 7:21–23, St. John 3:3–5).

8) Christians should use the initiative to introduce good legislation either to the legislature or directly to the voters (Proverbs 28:4).

9) Christians should exercise referendum whereby bad laws are submitted to a direct vote of the people (Psalms 119:45, 46, 126, & 142).

10) Christians should petition and appeal in Godly and fearful remonstrance in seeking to address wickedness in government (Psalms 94:16).

11) Christians should exercise recall in removing bad authorities from office (Psalm 139:21, 22).

12) Christians should obey the magistrate, walk in submission to authority and teach their children to have reverence for those in authority (Titus 3:1).

13) Christians should refrain from taking the law into their own hands and entering into acts of unlawful resistance (Romans 13:2 & Proverbs 29:1).

14) Christians should pray, read their Bibles, receive counsel from their Minister, and know when it is time to obey God rather than man (Acts 5:29).

15) Christians should always seek to bring honor to the name and reputation of Jesus Christ (Matt. 5:16).

For the Wise and the Prudent Only
Dan Gayman

We are not living in normal times. The present scenario developing in the United States of America should cause every Christian Family to immediately take their place at the Family Altar, Open their Bibles, Petition Almighty God and move forward to act upon the Scriptures read and the Prayer of Petition made to Jesus Christ. We must move forth to set our Houses in order. We are moving into a time of unprecedented trouble in this country. No organization now in existence can save us! There is no program on the scene of history that can deliver us from the time of trouble that is coming upon this nation. Our hope is in Jesus Christ and our Faith must rest in HIM alone! The Word of God is the only anchor that will hold in this storm of the ages. The winds of this storm are picking up with gale forces and a real hurricane can be expected to lash out across this nation. The United States of America is a nation under siege. We are being overrun by aliens from every corner of the world. The aliens are pouring into this country faster than any one can calculate. They are streaming into this country from every major airport in the land! Moreover, the industrial power of the United States is being dismantled and our factories and jobs are being exported out of this country and into foreign lands. The Standard of Living is plunging in this country and middle class families will find it increasingly more and more difficult to make ends meet as we watch America being transformed into a THIRD WORLD NATION.

The $200 billion deficit, coupled with the astronomical INTEREST ON THE NATIONAL DEBT, together with a plunging industrial output, will bring about the economic collapse of this nation. Any recovery is only temporary. We are living on borrowed time and those with wisdom and the providential blessing of the ETERNAL GOD to guide them, will take and act upon the knowledge of what is about to happen in this country to the end that their loved ones can be spared at least a portion of the pain that will be inflicted upon this country. As the third world swarms within the folds of this American Nation, the Children of God, the ELECT IN CHRIST must take careful and prudent steps to insulate themselves against the horrors that will

From Dan Gayman, "For the Wise and the Prudent Only," *The Watchman* 8, no. 12 (Spring 1984).

be developing in this country. The unemployed will grow into the multiplied millions. Jobs already scarce will become more and more difficult to find. Caucasian males will be at the bottom of the employment list. Inflation and taxation will confiscate much of the wealth that is left in the hands of the Middle Class. The Government is going to take steps to curtail and control the underground economy in this country. More and more government controls will be reaching out from Washington, D.C. with an ever greater army of government agents to enforce these administrative decrees. Our cities will become third world beehives of people. Moral standards already plunging will continue to get worse! You can expect FOOD, WATER AND ENERGY COSTS to take a greater and greater bite out of the family income. We are being planned for systematic bankruptcy in this country.

Because this period of time is known as the TIME OF JACOB'S TROUBLE the people of Jacob-Israel, the Elect in Christ, must Petition the God of our Fathers for DIVINE GUIDANCE in this time of National and World Trouble. This time of unprecedented trouble will continue to accelerate until the return of JESUS CHRIST to establish His Kingdom in this earth. There will be no PEACE until the return of the Prince of Peace to establish his theocratic government in this earth. When the politicians cry peace and safety . . . you can prepare for sudden destruction to come upon this land. America is a nation under judgment! The curses of God's Law are now upon this land. Weather will become a greater and greater factor in our daily lives. Food shortages and water shortages will become acute. We must take steps to act and pray that we will have the GUIDANCE OF THE HOLY SPIRIT to make Right and proper decisions. We must foresee that which is coming upon this land and take appropriate steps to insure the safety of our family and loved ones: **"By faith Noah, being warned of God of things not seen as yet, moved with fear, prepared an ark to the saving of his house; by the which he condemned the world, and became heir of the righteousness which is by faith."** Heb. 11:7. It is recommended that you give your attention to the following course of action:

1) Repent before Jesus Christ and make proper restitution for all known sins.

2) Set your spiritual house in order by acknowledgement of Sin and making a proper approach to Jesus Christ.

3) We should begin a prayer life and a Bible reading program in our private lives that will bring us into harmony with God and in communion with the Holy Spirit.

4) We should begin a plan of corporate worship with others of like precious mind and faith and blood.

5) We should give careful consideration to living near those of like mind, faith and blood, and/or preparing a "place" to move to in fast order at some future time.

6) You should own a small acreage in the rural areas of America, with a modest home, and in an area that is as Caucasian and non-industrialized as possible.

7) You should take immediate steps to clear away personal debts.

8) You should purge yourselves of credit cards and credit paper trails.

9) You should be careful to invest your money in land, tools and the means of procuring food or in a food storage program.

10) You should consider getting your children into a Christian School at once. Be careful of enrolling them in a private Christian School that will not scramble their minds as to the Bible.

11) You should make every effort to modify your life style to a point where you are less and less dependant upon the world system to find comfort, happiness and the necessities of life.

12) You should be able to defend your family and property against those who would seek to render harm in times of trouble.

13) You should begin to think of organization into Christian Communities throughout the United States where Christian men and women and children of like MIND, FAITH, AND BLOOD, can live their lives according to the Laws of the Bible and in harmony with Jesus Christ.

14) We should begin to teach our young men trade skills with their hands so that they can function independent of the "world system" at least to a limited extent.

15) Christian parents should use their energy, initiative and creative talent in forming independent small business operations that will employ our young people, develop skills and talents and give them "independence" from the World System of Large Corporations where they are mortgaged body, soul and spirit.

16) Our Christian schools should encourage and promote the development of trade skills for our young men that will enable them to become independent of the large Corporate Firms. Fathers have a responsibility of teaching their son a skillful trade that will encourage self-employment.

17) Parents should take the initiative in encouraging their young sons and

daughters to seek mates among those of like mind, faith and blood. This is imperative!

18) Our young married families should not delay bringing forth children into this world. Children represent the future of Christ's Church in this earth. Our willingness to bring forth children is the evidence of our faith and truth in a Sovereign God. It is a requirement of the Dominion Mandate given our Adamic Race in Genesis 1:8 and 9:1.

19) It is imperative that we determine what type of "life style" we want to live in this present passing world system. Our "life style" should be one which eliminates most if not all the frills of the Babylonian System. This is not to say that we are to live without the comforts of this life. We are to live in the world, and we are to be "witnesses of the truth" while living in this world, but we are not to become a part of this world. So long as we live in bodies of clay we must remain in the world and find our place in this world to the glory of Jesus Christ.

20) We are to "occupy" until He comes. This means that every generation of Christians must Occupy for Jesus Christ and the truth of His Kingdom.

21) We are to live in harmony with God, be obedient unto his commandments and seek to exercise Christian Dominion of the earth to His glory and Kingdom. This dominion begins with our personal lives, extends to the entire family and then to the community about us.

We must prepare for the most unprecedented time of trouble in the history of our race. The time of Jacob's Trouble is upon us. Let us keep our eye on the North Star for light and direction. That North Star being Jesus Christ. With His unfailing grace to keep us, and His Word to light our path we will not fail. The Church of Israel at Schell City sends the love and prayers of all this congregation to the Elect in Christ, joined together by Faith, and Truth and Blood throughout the United States of America and throughout all the nations of the world where Israel is in dispersion.

The publications of the Church of Israel range widely over contemporary issues. For example, in an article entitled "The Bible Solution To the Farm Problem," Pastor Dan Gayman argues that the destruction of the family farm in America is part of the "COMMUNIST PLAN for the conquest of America" and says that belief in God and observance of Biblical farming practices would solve our agricultural problems. He cites passages from

Leviticus, Deuteronomy, Exodus, Proverbs, and Malachi for specific Biblical injunctions regarding farming.[3]

In "Blueprint For American Survival," he lays out a detailed plan for the reconstruction of America based on Biblical law and various positions of the extreme right—such as closing all public schools, ending the Federal Reserve System, and returning manufacturing by American companies to America—but also including the abolition of alcohol, tobacco, and all other drugs, the immediate deportation of all non-white aliens, and the replacement of taxation with mandatory tithing.[4]

NOTES

1. For definitions of this concept, see Lyman Tower Sargent, "The Three Faces of Utopianism Revisited," *Utopian Studies* 5, no. 1 (1994): 1–37.
2. *The Watchman* 8, no. 15 (Winter 1985): 1–8.
3. *The Watchman* 8, no. 21 (Summer 1986): 13–16.
4. *The Watchman* 11, no. 1 (Summer 1987): 1–9.

9

RADICAL DECENTRALIZATION

An area where some of the left and some of the right seem to come together is in the idea that the real solution to our problems is moving power back as closely to the people as possible.

Posse Comitatus

The Posse Comitatus, also known as the Citizens Law Enforcement and Research Committee (founded in 1969 in Portland, Oregon, by Henry L. Beach, who had been a member of the Silver Shirts) is the best example of extreme right decentralism. The members of the Posse Comitatus believe that the locus of government should be the county and that the county sheriff should be the highest government official. They have had regular conflicts with the state and federal governments over taxes and weapons.[1]

Posse Comitatus----The Power of the People.

The Posse Comitatus is all the men of the county that a sheriff may call to his assistance in the discharge of his official duty, as to quell a riot or to

From "Posse Comitatus—The Power of the People" (Portland, Ore.: C.L.E.R.C., [1980s], pamphlet).

make an arrest. County Sheriffs must be advised of the instances where unlawful acts of officials or agencies of government are committed or unlawful acts of any kind. It is the duty of the Sheriff to protect the local citizens from such unlawful acts. Once he has been advised and refuses to perform his lawful duty in respect to the matter, the Posse Comitatus has the lawful right under natural law to act in the name of the Sheriff to protect local jurisdiction. They may make arrests, the accused being given into the custody of the County Sheriff for trial by a Citizen Jury empanelled by the Sheriff from citizens of the local jurisdiction.

The Posse acts only within the County; they are not considered a part of the military; and they are not subject to military law, since they have never been enlisted by the state and are not under their authority. It includes all the men of the County between the ages of 18 and 45 and others may volunteer!! The Posse and the Militia have essentially the same purpose; they are men who act in the execution of the law. . . .

But there are many . . . benefits to be derived from a Posse Comitatus. How peaceful and lawabiding our communities would suddenly become if there were several hundred posse members in a county whose business it was to enforce the law!! Would it not be an advantage in holding down the costs of government? Are there not many emergencies when the Sheriff or officers of the law can be in only one place at a time???

There have been recent instances of group action by neighbors with firearms who were successful in preventing violations of the law, and those who were protected were very thankful for the action taken. Why should we endure lawless communities and lawless government? Every county should have, and is entitled to a POSSE COMITATUS!!!

It would be ridiculous to suppose that those who fought so valiantly for freedom would intend to leave the counties defenseless except for a county sheriff, who must often have many square miles of territory under his jurisdiction. This inalienable right of defense was intended to be left to the descretion [*sic*] of the men of the county to organize their own self-defense without interference from either the state or federal governments. . . .

It should be obvious that a Posse Comitatus would be a deterent [*sic*] to despots, and a valuable aid in the preservation of freedom and liberty. Ever worsening affairs in the field of American Government at all levels should be a warning to the People that they must not delay in asserting their sovereignty.

IT IS THE DUTY OF GOVERNMENT TO PREVENT INJUSTICE—NOT TO PROMOTE IT.
The Posse Comitatus
by the authority of
The Constitution Of The United States

In the formation of this constitutional republic, the county has always been and remains to this day, the TRUE seat of the government for the citizens who are the inhabitants thereof. The County Sheriff is the only legal law enforcement officer in these United States of America.

The Sheriff can mobilize all men between the ages of 18 and 45 who are in good health and not in the federal military service. OTHERS CAN VOLUNTEER! This body of citizens is the Sheriff's Posse. Each must serve when called by the Sheriff. The title of this body is the Posse Comitatus.

The Posse is the entire body of those inhabitants who may be summoned by the Sheriff, or who may volunteer, to preserve the public peace or execute any lawful precept that is opposed. Since the Sheriff is the servant of the citizens who are inhabitants of the County, it is not his choice as to whether or not the Posse is organized and brought into being. It is only his Choice as to whether or not he wishes to use it.

Since the formulation of our Republic, the local County has always been the seat of government for the people. A county government is the highest authority of government in our Republic as it is closest to the people, who are in fact, the government. The County Sheriff is the only legal law enforcement officer in the United States of America. He is elected by the people and is directly responsible for law enforcement in his County. It is his responsibility to protect the people of his County from unlawful acts on the part of anyone, including officials of government. His oath of office is to uphold, preserve and defend the constitution of these United States and the State in which his County Exists. He may be required to do no less and no

From "It Is the Duty of Government to Prevent Injustice—Not to Promote It" (Portland, Ore.: C.L.E.R.C., [ca. 1975], pamphlet).

more in the performance of his official duties. It should be emphasized that this protection extends to Citizens who are being subjected to unlawful acts even by officials of government, whether these be judges of courts or Federal or State Agents of any kind whatsoever.

The County Sheriff must be advised of the instances where unlawful acts are committed. It is the duty of the Sheriff to protect the local citizens from such unlawful acts. Once he has been advised and refuses to perform his lawful duty in respect to the matter, the Posse Comitatus has the lawful right under natural law to act in the name of the Sheriff to protect local jurisdiction. Since the Second Amendment to the Constitution says, "the right of the people to keep and bear arms shall not be infringed." In the execution of the law, arrests may be made. The criminal may be remanded to the custody of the County Sheriff for trial by a citizen jury empaneled by the Sheriff from citizens of the local jurisdiction, instead of by the Courts as is the current procedure in most Counties and which has no basis under law, any act of any legislature or directives issued by the judiciary or Executive notwithstanding.

The unlawful use of County Sheriffs as LACKEYS of the Courts should be discontinued at once. There is no lawfull authority, for Judges and the Courts to direct the law enforcement activities of a County Sheriff. The Sheriff is accountable and responsible only to the citizens who are the inhabitants of his County. He is under oath of office and need not receive unlawful orders from Judges or the Courts. They are the Judiciary but the Sheriff is the Executive branch of our government. He is responsible to protect citizens, even from unlawful acts of officials of government. If he refuses to do so, he should be removed from office promptly.

The prerequisite to proper guidance is the basic understanding of Common Law and a background knowledge of the United States Constitution, as well as the Republican form of government created thereby. Such knowledge is considered essential to good citizenship and fulfillment of the responsibilities by true Christians to their God and Country.

The Supreme Court of the United States formally declared this Republic to be a Christian nation. In a case involving the Holy Trinity Church vs United States, 143 US 471, on the 28th of Feb. 1892. The Court, after mentioning various circumstances, added the following words; "and these and many other matters which might be noticed, add a volume of unofficial declarations to the mass of organic utterances, that this is a Christian Nation."

The Constitution was lifted from the articles of Confederation, therefore the Constitution's source is the Holy Bible. By this contract the States, representing the people, created an agent of the States known as the Federal Government. The people, as States, gave certain powers to this "agent" and by the 9th and 19th Amendments, made it clear that this agent had only those powers which have been enumerated for it in the contract between the States. All others remain with the States and the people. The Federal Government is not above States which created it.

The constitution is a simple document. It says what it means and means what it says. It means today what it meant when it was written. It is the SUPREME LAW for the States of the Union as well as for the Federal Government, which has been created by the States and the people, existing as States, which are separate sovereign Republics within the United States, it should be made clear that the Federal Government is a servant of the States and the people, not their master. The 9th Amendment States clearly, "The enumeration in the Constitution of certain rights shall not be construed to deny or disparage others retained by the people." This simply means that because the contract enumerated rights for the States, that the listing of these rights does not mean that the same must be done for the people but that the people retain all rights without having them enumerated in the contract. The 10th Amendment says: "The powers not delegated to the United States by the Constitution, nor prohibited by it to the States, are reserved to the States respectively, or to the people." This simply means that the Federal Government has only those powers which have been listed in the Constitution. If the power is not listed, then the Federal Government DOES NOT HAVE IT. All powers not listed for the Federal Government in the contract, remain with the States or to the people. Prior to the existence of the United States, each State was, and remains to this day, a separate sovereign Republic. The Governor of each State was and remains to this day, the Chief Executive Officer of his State. He is the only officer of the Government within the United States, who had and has to this day, "military power and military authority." He is commander and chief of his State Militia. He is the only officer of Government in the United States who has the lawful authority to declare martial law." No officer of the Federal Government has such power. Any act of Congress or Judicial ruling not-withstanding. (10th Amendment). The governor of a State had such military power prior to the existence of the union and he retains such power today. It was never delivered to the Federal Government by either the State or the People.

Article 4, Section 4 of the U.S. Constitution makes it clear that the agent created by the States, the Federal Government referred to as the United

States, as well as all State Governments, shall guarantee to every State in the Union, a Republican form of Government. (A Government of Law, not of men nor the opinions of men, nor a democracy, which is mob rule).

Dear Patriot:

From time to time we receive inquires relative to the authority for the Posse Comitatus, as a citizen's organization. The law sets forth clearly that the Sheriff has this authority. . . . It also sets forth the responsibilities of citizens to act upon the request of the Sheriff. Further, it sets forth the responsibilities of the citizen in upholding the law, even to the authority for citizens to make citizen's arrests, also that ignorance of the law is no excuse. A law which not only applies to the citizen, but also applies to our officials, regardless of their position.

. . . our officials and their lackeys are violating the law, and our tolerance of such action makes us equally guilty, by permitting such unlawful action. If you do not wish to be guilty by association, it becomes your duty to protest. Since the protest of an individual gets no recognition from the type of officials we are now plagued with, it makes good sense to bring the matter to their attention.

In areas where the Posse numbers in the hundreds, they are being heard, with both respect and fear. Our officials know when they are wrong and have a great deal of respect for those who challenge them.

We are facing a lawless group in power who are in the process of destroying our freedoms and making us serfs of a ONE-WORLD GOVERNMENT, ruled by the ANTI-CHRIST. It is time we stand up and be counted. This is no game for weak-knees or panty-waists. This calls for men with guts; men who will fight to protect their rights and God-given heritage, not those who would feed their neighbors to the crocodiles in hopes that the crocodiles would eat them last.

The formation of the posses are not in opposition of the law. Rather, it shows an intent to uphold and maintain the law, which is the duty of all CITIZENS. We do not want mobs to form in the name of the Posse Comitatus. We want

From untitled letter (Portland, Ore.: C.L.E.R.C., [ca. 1976], broadside with illegible signature).

only intelligent individuals who will stick together and use the law to maintain Constitutional law in our land. We do not need to go outside the law to be effective. All we need to do is to let it be known that we will no longer tolerate those who subvert the law in administration of the needs <u>of the people</u>.

There is no place in our Constitution or laws of our land, giving the President, Congress or any appointees the authority to <u>change our forms of government</u>. This action is in violation of our Constitution, without a vote of the people and the ratification of same by ¾ of the states. It is not the duty of the Government to tell the states and the people what is best for them; rather, it is the duty of the Government to administer the wishes <u>of the people and the states</u> and nothing more.

To stand idly by and tolerate this usurpation of power makes us equally guilty of violating Constitutional law. Individually, our opposition has little influence, but collectively our voice <u>will be heard.</u> Forming Posses is one of the most effective methods we have found to date, especially in areas where the Posse Charter is registered at the county seat, and steps are taken to let it be known publicly that we mean business. If you don't stand up and be counted, you will richly deserve the fate in store for you.

POSSE INSTRUCTIONS

The purpose of the Posse Comitatus movement is to place pertinent information regarding existing laws into the hands of concerned patriots, and to point out that there is a method of combatting the subverters. We suggest the manner of organizational procedure to keep these laws in your favor. It is imperative that we combat those who, under the guise of public servants, are more interested in the destruction of our Republic, rather than representing the people.

The patriots of 1776 knew their enemy, while we are just beginning to know ours. They also had an advantage in the fact that their enemy in red was easy

From "Posse Instructions" (n.p.: n.p., [1980s], broadside with illegible signature).

to identify, while we may have our enemy living next door, perhaps someone we call friend. Not necessarily the kind that our President chooses to call friend! Our enemy has openly stated that they intend to take us over, either peacefully or by force. If they choose to do so by force, there will be bloodshed and suffering on a large scale, perhaps more than any nation has yet witnessed. MAY GOD HAVE MERCY ON US!

It is our hopes and prayers that enough patriots can be rallied in time to recover the liberties and freedoms that our forefathers left to us at the expense of their fortunes and lives, so courageously.

Week by week it looks as tho' we have less chance of making the recovery as gentlemen and in honor. It is beginning to look as tho' the Judiciary has been taken over completely and our chance of recovering justice is a thing of the past. There is no indication that things are going to get better, and if anything, progressively worse.

The Posse concept is now becoming a nation-wide movement, and to date we have posses in nearly every state. In some cases we are supplying the books to sheriffs' departments and in one case to a judge which is actively interested.

We recommend sending one of the Posse books to every sheriff in your state, also the governor, legislators, and every commissioner. It is effective, and is causing them to take a second look at their activities, which they know are actions of treason.

Left Green Network

The following is an example of a proposal for decentralization from the left. While the principles endorsed here are clearly different from those of the Posse Comitatus, the desire for radical decentralization is the same. In both cases, the groups feel that the people, given a chance, will be on their side.

PRINCIPLES OF THE LEFT GREEN NETWORK

1. ECOLOGICAL HUMANISM

Left Greens stand for the creation of a society for human liberty, equality, and solidarity in ecological harmony with nature. We seek to realize the highest democratic and libertarian ideals of the American Revolution and to create the social conditions for life, liberty, and the pursuit of happiness. We share the Revolution's humanistic premise: that all humans are endowed by nature with the capacity for reason, empathy, and free choice and therefore have a natural right to democratic self-government and to basic freedoms, as well as to economic rights.

The humanism that the Left Greens stand for, however, is an ecological humanism. We reject the antinaturalism of traditional humanisms that have sought to create a social "realm of freedom" by means of dominating a natural "realm of necessity." We also reject the antihumanism of ecophilosophies that, in reaction to the destruction of the environment, seek to protect nature by constricting human freedom.

Left Greens oppose all forms of domination, of both human and nonhuman nature, and believe that human liberation and ecological harmony are inextricably connected. We call for a reharmonization of humanity with nature on the basis of a new harmonization of human with human. We seek a social and ecological ethics for a society in which each individual is free to reach his or her full potential; a free, egalitarian, nonhierarchial society of self-governing communities that are humanly scaled, bioregional integrated, and cooperatively confederated; a society that is a partner with the rest of nature.

2. SOCIAL ECOLOGY

Humanity has reached a point in history where the boldest concepts of utopia are possible, yet we remained mired in the legacy of domination, and even the very survival of humanity is now in question. The ecological

From "Principles of the Left Green Network" (West Lebanon, N.H.: Left Green Network, 1989, pamphlet).

provision of material security for every human being is readily achievable, yet we remain trapped in a social megamachine that pits humans against each other and devours both people and nature for its own purposes.

Left Greens are social ecologists. We root the ecological crisis in its systemic social causes—capitalism in particular and hierarchy and domination in general. The present competitive society's war on the natural world is an extension of the war of each against all that it fosters among humans—as well as a war of each against his or her own nature. Left Greens oppose the misanthropic orientations that blame human nature, human rationality, or "overpopulation" for the ecological crisis. We believe that a radical transformation of this society is not only possible but imperative for survival as well as to continue natural and social evolution.

Human liberation and the protection of nonhuman life are not merely compatible—both are necessary. The Left Greens seek to unite social and environmental movements in order to change society. As social ecologists, we stand with every struggle for human freedom, equality, and solidarity, for the liberation of women, people of color, gays and lesbians, working people, young people, old people, peoples dominated by foreign powers, and ordinary people in all walks of life who are weighed down by the institutions and culture of domination.

Left Greens also stand with every struggle for the protection of nonhuman life. As social ecologists, we embrace the conservation of species diversity, habitats, and ecosystems and the expansion of wilderness areas. We call for ecotechnologies based on renewable, organic, and nontoxic materials, energy sources, and production processes that harmonize community-controlled economies with the ecology of their bioregions.

3. RACIAL EQUALITY

Left Greens oppose any compromise with racism in any form. We support affirmative action to create substantive equality and every effort of racially oppressed groups to achieve community empowerment and self-determination. We seek to help an independent "rainbow" movement develop from below in which independent community-based organizations in all of North America's diverse ethnic and social communities join together on the basis of substantive equality, mutual aid, and grassroots control of the movement.

4. SOCIAL ECOFEMINISM

Left Greens are committed to the liberation of women, to their basic reproductive rights as well as to their full participation in all realms of social life. We believe in a social ecofeminism that seeks to understand and uproot the social origins of patricentric structures of domination. Unlike other eco-feminisms that accept patriarchal myths and cultural definitions of women as more "natural" than men and as existing outside culture, social ecofeminism regards women as cultural beings, as well as biological beings, and seeks to understand and change the social *realities* of the relationships between women, men, the political realm, the domestic realm, and all of these to nature.

5. GAY AND LESBIAN LIBERATION

Left Greens demand the sexual and social emancipation of people of all sexual preferences. We support every effort by lesbians and gay men to achieve substantive equality and civil rights in all areas, such as jobs, housing, and child custody, as well as anti-AIDS funding. We recognize that lesbians and gay men are demanding not only their own freedom and dignity but that of all people, for as long as sexuality is not free, people are doomed to thwart their most basic desires for love, pleasure, and creativity.

6. GRASSROOTS DEMOCRACY

A society in which human beings cooperatively control their own destinies must be the product of the self-activity of a popular majority of the people. Because this kind of society cannot, by its very nature, be legislated from the top down, Left Greens do not want to get elected into the existing power structure. Rather we want to restructure political institutions along lines that will replace the centralized state with a confederal participatory democracy. Our goal is base democracy, in which public policy at all jurisdictional scales is determined by community assemblies, such as town meetings, that are open to all citizens. Confederations of these community assemblies will coordinate public policy from below. Representatives to the larger scales of confederal self-government will receive ongoing instructions from the base assemblies and will be subject to immediate recall by the base.

7. COOPERATIVE COMMONWEALTH

The Left Greens seek to bring the economy under the control of the grassroots democracy. We call for a cooperative commonwealth—a fundamental alternative to both the private-corporate-market system of the West and the state-bureaucratic-command system of the East. The world economy today, under both corporate capitalism and state-"socialism," is an interconnected system based on the exploitation of the many. Its goal is not to meet human needs in harmony with nature, but the investment of capital to create more capital in order to satisfy the profit and power motives of the elite few that control the means of production and militaristic nation-states. Endless growth-for-growth's-sake is thus structured into this economic system, making it deadly to the planetary biosphere. It is inherently anti-human and anti-ecological. It degrades social and moral bonds into depersonalized, amoral market and bureaucratic relationships. It calls upon the basest of human attributes to motivate economic activity. To attempt to humanize and ecologize this system is like asking a plant to stop photosynthesizing.

Society's common wealth—the land and natural resources; the banks and the material infrastructure of production—is the creation of natural evolution and the labor of millions, not of the ruling elites that now control most of it. As our common heritage, Left Greens believe that this social wealth should be held in common and used cooperatively for the common good of people and their ecological context.

In a cooperative commonwealth, people democratically and cooperatively own and control their economy. Global corporations and centralized state enterprises should be broken up and replaced by individual and family enterprises, cooperatives, and decentralized publicly-owned enterprises. Basic industries and services would be socialized through municipalization into community ownership and control, not nationalized into bureaucracy. Confederations of communities would own larger facilities regionally, and confederations of regions would coordinate the economy from below at still larger jurisdictional scales.

This kind of democratized economic system will uncouple the exploitative growth dynamic of today's economic megamachine and make possible an ecological economy in dynamic equilibrium with the environment. It will empower people to define their own needs and then produce what is needed to satisfy them in harmony with nature. It will enable society to replace the growth-oriented exploitative economy that blindly devours the environment with a need-oriented moral economy that consciously establishes a dynamic equilibrium with the biosphere.

8. HUMAN RIGHTS

Left Greens envision a world where each individual is free to develop his or her full potential because each individual enjoys basic political, economic, and individual human rights. Left Greens make no compromises in the defense of civil liberties. But formal civil liberties are undermined as effectively by the burdens of economic deprivation as they are by overt political repression. Left Greens therefore call for the creation of a moral economy that insures that every person's basic material needs are met as a human right. We call for a guaranteed income sufficient to support a decent standard of living and for a just distribution of available work for all willing and able. We demand shorter work weeks and call for the free provision, under community control, of education, health care, public transportation, and other basic goods and services. These social responsibilities would be funded through steeply progressive taxation, revenues from public enterprises, and voluntary contributions to public funds.

9. NON-ALIGNED INTERNATIONALISM

Left Greens support human rights according to one universal criterion—freedom—without regard for national boundaries or the military blocs of the Cold War. They actively solidarize with non-aligned peace, ecology, democracy, worker, feminist, anti-racist, anti-militarist, and anti-imperialist movements in every country—East bloc, West bloc, Third World. They envision a world without borders, a world of decentralized regions composed of confederations of self-governing communities.

Left Greens demand that every nuclear power initiate immediate unilateral nuclear disarmament and conversion to nonprovocative, home-based defense based on both voluntary conventionally-armed militia and nonviolent social defense. These forms of defense should be strictly accountable to civilian authority. Left Greens demand that every country recall all armed forces from stations abroad and use the savings from military spending for social and ecological reconstruction. Only such measures can create the just, democratic, and ecologically sustainable conditions necessary for a durable peace.

10. INDEPENDENT POLITICS

Grassroots movements for fundamental change need an independent political vehicle. The Democratic Party has been the graveyard for every popular movement of the 19th century to the labor movement of the 1930's and, increasingly, the new social movements since the 1960's. Left Greens reject the dependent politics of lobbying and compromising inside the establishment parties, the Democrats and Republicans, which are dominated by the vested interests connected to big business and the military. We oppose any support for their candidates, including "progressive" Democrats who run against more moderate elements of the party establishment. Instead, Left Greens seek independent organization and action outside ruling-class structures. We support Greens who run on an independent Green ballot line as mandated and recallable representatives who are fully accountable to the program and membership of the Green political organization. Left Greens cooperate with and seek to develop unity with other independent political organizations on the basis of compatible political principles.

11. DIRECT ACTION

Voting is not enough. Global corporations hold a private economic veto over public policy through threats of disinvestment. The bureaucratic and military structures of the state can veto radical legislative initiatives through bureaucratic inertia and, as a last resort, military repression. Broad, popular direct action is thus needed to counter private corporate power, bureaucratic inertia, and, ultimately, violent repression by the military. Movements from below are the basis for Green political organization. Left Greens help build independent direct action movements that can lay the basis for an independent electoral alternative. Left Green direct action takes many forms: from nonviolent resistance to existing abuses to reconstructive action to build alternatives. The Left Greens call for extending the extra-parliamentary movement into electoral/legislative arenas, not for the purpose of getting into the existing power structure, but to restructure that power fundamentally. We seek to create direct action in its highest form—direct democracy.

Left Greens do not limit their goals to the "left wing of the possible." We aim to change what is possible. We refuse to compromise our program in order to achieve short-term "influence" inside the establishment. Capitalism and hierarchical society generally cannot be transformed incrementally from the top down. Although Left Greens may enter legislatures to advance their program, they refuse the formal executive power of government until the majority of people not only vote for a program of basic social change but are ready to take direct action to insure that the program is implemented.

12. RADICAL MUNICIPALISM

Left Greens "think globally" to understand the large-scale social forces that must be transformed, while we "act locally" to create a local framework through which grassroots people can participate directly in democratic transformation. For Left Greens, community empowerment does not mean electing better representatives to govern us, but literally the empowerment of every community to practice self-government.

Left Greens call for a radical municipalist strategy that will run independent Green candidates in cities and towns across the continent on a program of building up a popular counterpower based on movements from below, on democratizing municipalities, and on creating municipal confederations that bring increasing political and economic power under community control. We hold that community empowerment must be created throughout the land in order to build up a dual power in society that can initially resist and ultimately replace nation-states and global corporations.

13. STRATEGIC NONVIOLENCE

Left Greens are committed to a strategy of nonviolent revolution, but we affirm the right of self-defense. We practice critical solidarity with legitimate freedom struggles, although we may not agree with every tactic or programmatic goal of such movements. Left Greens work toward a society in which political disputes are solved nonviolently. We understand that this is not currently the case, and that the central reason for this fact is the existence of social hierarchies based on racial domination, patriarchal authority, class exploitation, and an unjust world order maintained by militaristic nation-states. The inevitable instances of violence arising from the conflicts between these structures and their subjects are to be blamed on the structures of domination, not those who resist domination. Such structural violence will be eliminated only by the elimination of these structures of domination.

14. DEMOCRATIC DECENTRALISM

Left Greens believe in democratic decentralism. Our organizational forms demand strict accountability of representatives, spokespeople, candidates, and elected officials to policies set by the membership. At the same time, we believe in pluralism among the membership, including the freedom to dissent and full ongoing discussion of all positions taken by the organization. Outside of the binding agreements of the Principles and Bylaws that constitute conditions for membership, members are free to abstain from the implementation of majority decisions with which they disagree and to publicly dissent from them. Although Left Green representatives, Spokespeople, candidates, and elected officials are required to act in a manner consistent with imperative mandates from the membership, they are free to publicly express their own dissenting views when they differ from such mandates. Left Greens believe in seeking to arrive at decisions by consensus if possible. But when differences exist, majorities should be accorded the right to make decisions in the name of the organization. Minorities remain free to abstain from the implementation of majority decisions with which they disagree and to publicly dissent from them.

Students for a Democratic Society

The organization Students for a Democratic Society (SDS) based its most general position on a form of radical decentralization, spelled out here in its most famous document.

Port Huron Statement

In a participatory democracy, the political life would be based in several root principles:

"Port Huron Statement" (n.p.: Students for a Democratic Society, [1962], flyer).

that decision-making of basic social consequence be carried on by public groupings;

that politics be seen positively, as the art of collectively creating an acceptable pattern of social relations;

that politics has the function of bringing people out of isolation and into community, thus being a necessary, though not sufficient, means of finding meaning in personal life;

that the political order should serve to clarify problems in a way instrumental to their solution; it should provide outlets for the expression of personal grievance and aspiration; opposing views should be organized so as to illuminate choices and facilitate the attainment of goals; channels should be commonly available to relate men to knowledge and to power so that private problems—from bad recreation facilities to personal alienation—are formulated as general issues.

The economic sphere would have as its basis the principles:

that work should involve incentives worthier than money or survival. It should be educative, not stultifying; creative, not mechanical; self-directed, not manipulated, encouraging independence, a respect for others, a sense of dignity and a willingness to accept social responsibility, since it is this experience that has crucial influence on habits, perceptions and individual ethics;

that the economic experience is so personally decisive that the individual must share in its full determination;

that the economy itself is of such social importance that its major resources and means of production should be open to democratic participation and subject to democratic social regulation.

NOTE

1. See James Corcoran, *Bitter Harvest. Gordon Kahl and the Posse Comitatus: Murder in the Heartland* (New York: Viking, 1990).

10

TACTICS

American Militia Organization

The following selection from a leader of the American Militia Organization includes a plan for taking over the United States that combines electoral politics and force. The best-known scenario for such a takeover by the right is the race war envisaged in William Pierce's Turner Diaries.[1]

IF THIS BE REBELLION
George E. Pittam

Poets and martyrs may glamorize the "good fight", the sacrificial struggle against hopeless odds, the dramatic dying words of the last survivor. Having no taste for heroics or elusive fame, I've no interest in theatrics. Tactics that produce dead heroes have no appeal. Pity is of no use to the living or dead. The good fight is the one that offers a chance of success. If it does not, then it isn't a good fight at all, it's a gesture. The sooner we recognize who is directing this losing fight the sooner we'll recognize the reasons for persisting

From George E. Pittam, "If This Be Rebellion" (Spokane, Wash.: American Militia Organization, [1976], pamphlet).

on the losing course, the sooner we'll change that course to one that offers a chance at WINNING. Then and only then does the fight become interesting.

We've tried waiting for our congressman. We've worked hard in the "party of our choice". We've written letters to the editor. We've participated in talk shows. We've donated to every effort from anti-fluoridation to getting the U.S. out of the U.N. Someone (you know who) said, in effect, that if we enlighten enough people soon enough, the whole conspiracy will evaporate overnight. DO TELL!

Education must never cease but if education is both the means and the end, there is no victory. Dead heroes are just dead, educated or ignorant.

I know that everyone here recognizes that we're in trouble. I doubt that anyone here now fails to recognize that our dilemma is the result of planning. Does anyone think it is the result of mistakes, poor judgement? It would be nice if we all had clearly analyzed every facet of every scheme and had what it takes to stamp out every one of their programs. We don't. BUT WE DO HAVE A PLAN. We intend to win with that plan. Someone said that politics is the art of the possible. — So is war and our plan involves both politics and war. Our plan calls for both caution and haste. We have much to do in a very short period of time. We have a nucleus of very good and capable men. We have a larger list of good prospects and we need many more. We will get them.

Do you realize that right here in this room and in hundreds of similar assemblages all across this land are the most important people in the world? Don't look at the person behind you. If there will be anything of value left of this nation, which we inherited, to pass on to our children and theirs, it will be because of our efforts. You say you're JUST a farmer, JUST a merchant, JUST a policeman? Who do you suppose ARE the important people? Your governor? Your senator? Your mayor? No. These are our employees. We hired them. How did this thing get turned around? How is it that we attend luncheons and rallies and we gather round and fawn over these people as though they somehow became superior to their employers? I've seen men all but wag their tails when publicly recognized by a politician with a title. Of course, they ignore our instructions. Not only do we re-elect them after they issue unconstitutional and illegal directives to their employers, we actually obey them! No wonder we have Women's Lib. I use the term "we" loosely. I don't fawn over them. You don't either. Nor do an increasing number of your neighbors.

Have you noticed that people like us are no longer the fanatics, the extremists[.] Men listen now when we speak. All but fools know we're in a desperate crises *[sic]* and they're listening for solutions. Now, let's be very sure of our statements and, in our haste, not lose any of the support we've gained. Let's be careful that we're not intolerant and obnoxious in our superior knowledge and dedication. We who think of ourselves as informed, especially if just recently enlightened, are inclined to be overly critical of all who do not share our enlightenment. Impatience is entirely understandable. Certainly, we are at a time of extreme emergency. There is every reason to be in frantic haste but in our rush to do something, let's not drive everything and everybody into resistance against us. Just because we haven't heard of decisive action by an individual, let's not assume that he has been inactive. Before we condemn the inactivity of *[sic]* ineffectiveness of another, let's take stock of our own successes. There is a time for belligerence. In the face of deliberate, willful treason and conscious connivance with our enemies, sweet rationalization and friendly persuasion have no place. Tear 'em apart! So often, though, we've seen overzealous patriots create antagonism when a smile and a word of explanation would have won a friend. That's a double loss. We lost a friend and gained an enemy. I've even seen fellow patriots neutralized by bellicose "hang the sheriff" zealots. To opine that every elected official is a traitor or fool is to utterly condemn the whole elective process. Granted that we've lost our voice in the selection of our top federal officials without immediate prospect of regaining that voice. But if we have not influenced, even controlled, the election of ALL our county and city officials, that's our fault!

Now unless we are prepared to claim that we have enough power to do just that with the people in this room acting independently, then we had better become allied and form some more alliances. We *can* form those alliances, not by shouting abuses at those who are hesitant to cooperate with us, but by calm presentation of fact and reason. I don't stick out my neck in programs I don't understand or even in those I do understand if I think that the methods do not offer a reasonable chance for success. We can almost carelessly join the American Legion, the VFW or the John Birch Society or all of them with almost complete safety. But if, by the education we receive in those associations or otherwise, we engage in activities threatening our plotter's plan for our future, it's a brand new ball game. True, we don't need cowards but if you're not scared, you're not informed. So don't be too severe with those who don't rush into every endeavor just because YOU say it's the only way. That's why I've advocated the formation of tight, small organizations composed of personal acquaintances before any mass appeal for membership. We don't want crackpots, fools or infiltrators. All are dangerous and destructive. We can control or eject the fools and crackpots if we organize properly. We will never have a FOOLPROOF system for elimination of subversives but vacancies we create in their ranks will become increasingly hard to fill, as our strength grows.

I wonder if we realize the potential for this organization. We are not joined together for social activity. We will have no tea parties—unless of the Boston variety. We will NOT have cookie sales, gossip parties or jockeying for pretentious positions. We WILL promote our associates and friends for political office but we will not be used by political opportunists. We have definite purpose and we will not depart from it. Idle men are of little use. It's the busy men and women who get things done and busy people have little time for trivialities. We are living in a time of extreme peril, probably the most dangerous period of our history. How to survive, to protect our families, to regain control of our nation, to restore our national morality, within the very limited time remaining to us, should occupy our constant thoughts, our most serious and urgent study and activity. We will have a busy program. We fervently hope, we earnestly pray, that we avoid violence. There's no pleasure in taking human life. Therefore, we endeavor with all cautious haste to do that which we are capable of doing in the political sphere. As I've stated, we CAN elect our favorite to the offices of local government. Elections are almost upon us. First, let's select and ELECT our sheriffs. If we have a good sheriff, let's be SURE he's re-elected. If he is of good moral character but not well informed, inform him and ELECT him. Our sheriffs are the most important men in government. Let's get with him and him with us! If he is a fool, a tool of our enemies—get rid of him. A handful of literate, informed men and women can contact every voter. Pick your man. Support him. Finance him. Promote him. ELECT him. Coroners replace incapacitated sheriffs. See to those offices. County commissioners—very important people. They have the power to defeat the land use scheme. They have many other important powers. Re-elect them or defeat them. This year, because of the time element, state offices will be more difficult but with enough arms, created fast enough, we can handle some of them. Let's get at it.

Before anyone starts thinking this is another political party or that politics is our sole consideration—here's the rest of it. I quote again: "History tells us that oppressive governments do not simply wither away. Never in all recorded history have the frontiers of freedom been pushed forward a single inch without the use of violence. Political and educational efforts may be of some assistance but these things alone can never achieve victory. These things by themselves can never replace an oppressive government with one more favorable to its citizens. These things alone cannot reduce the size of a governing bureaucracy that is arrogant and unresponsive to the needs of those who must submit to its directives."

Nothing would be more pleasant than to create the first instance in all recorded history of a reversal of course without bloodshed. History does not have to repeat itself but we had best be prepared for the probable. Political victory on a national scale can be considered a practical impossibility. There will be violence. There will be gun confiscation laws. When the traitors who control our federal government determine that the tide is running against them, that we, the people, the true seat of government, will no longer submit to unconstitutional directives, that we will not submit weakly to regimentation of weaklings or execution of patriots, there will be violence. Nothing would be more ridiculous than to believe that after slaughtering millions of Russians, Germans, Hungarians, Czechs, Poles, Chinese, Koreans, Poles, Yugoslavs, Romanians, Vietnamese, etc., and the meticulous step by step planning for America's subjugation, the plotters will give up and resign their posts because of popular protest.

To say that the odds are in favor would be a lie. In complete honesty, we DO plan to win. Only cowards will submit to disarming. Therefore, after government demands for our private firearms, all except cowards will still be armed. We still have time to instruct members and friends how to obtain, effectively use, preserve and conceal their weapons. With little effort, we can accumulate, preserve and secretly store all necessary provisions. In cooperation with our sheriffs, we have time to selectively recruit, equip and train a formidable militia, fully capable of resisting and arresting illegal representatives of illegal bureaucrats attempting to enforce illegal federal directives. We will take no premature action. We will not be baited into ill-advised or ruinous activities. We will not alienate responsible citizens. We can indoctrinate our sons who are in the armed services as to their real responsibilities. Except for the minuscule criminal element, few American boys will murder their friends and relatives, regardless of orders from superiors. Time, for the first time, may be in our favor. Each day, understanding increases. Admittedly, modern Americans are short on bravery—but so are their masters. When their puppets refuse to obey and they, themselves, are faced with death we'll wonder how we could have feared such disgusting, crawling carrion. . . .

Ours is the American Militia Organization—"A.M.O."

Our motto:
"When, in the pursuit of evil purpose, evil men conspire for dominion, all who would thereby be dominated must unite and conquer or destroy such conspirators or accept the classification of coward and forever forfeit their birthright and all claim to dignity and respect."

Our resolution:
"Since each state of the union is sovereign and supreme and since the powers of the federal government are those and only those authorized and clearly delineated in the Constitution of the United States, it therefore follows that any and all activities of the federal government not consistent with those limitations are of a criminal nature. Further, although the powers of sovereign states are more broad than those granted federal government, they are yet clearly limited by the Constitutions of those states and of the United States. It further follows that since any law, edict or ruling not in harmony with the provisions and limitations of the foregoing documents are null and void, therefore, any act in furtherance of the provisions of such illegal directives or obedience thereto are, themselves, criminal in nature, subjecting the perpetrators thereof to arrest and prosecution. Further, since enforcement of law is the responsibility of law enforcement officials duly elected by the people, it is incumbent upon such officials, assisted as necessary by every able bodied adult elector, to impartially enforce the law. In order to prevent the triumph of lawlessness, chaos and oppression, it is the duty of all citizens to effect the replacement of officials and employees who are derelict in their duties or, in the event of extreme emergency, to perform for such officials and employees those functions which the citizens, themselves, authorized."

Our objectives:
1) To recruit a force of men and women with courage, with devotion to family, country, co-patriots and God and with the stature to subjugate selfish interests to that devotion.
2) To demonstrate to local, elected officials, notably law enforcement officers, that we are an association of intelligent, trustworthy citizens for the

maintenance and enforcement of constitutional law and for protection from those who would impose their illegitimate will, be they agents of rampant government or any other criminals.

3) To cooperate in every lawful and just endeavor with law enforcement and court officials.

4) To train, equip and maintain our militia in the elements of self defense, mutual assistance and resistance to invasion, oppression and tyranny.

5) To effect the replacement of corrupt local officials with those of sound principle.

6) By all the foregoing, to avoid both governmental tyranny and anarchy and, in cooperation with like associations, domestic and foreign, to eventually remove all places of power and influence, those international conspirators who clearly plot our subjugation.

7) So far as is humanly possible, to restore peace and freedom throughout the world—'til He comes.

Advantages of membership in A.M.O. vs those offered elsewhere:

1) Objectives and appeal less limited in scope, yet confined to areas wherein our efforts and influence will be effective.

2) Starting from scratch but with a considerable roster of good men and women as prospects.

3) All members suspected of disloyalty or of activities detrimental to our cause will be called before a hearing committee for adjudication, as will be their accusers if charges are found to be fraudulent or trivial. . . .

5) Traitors and infiltrators will be dealt with according to circumstances.

NOTE

1. William Pierce [Andrew Macdonald, pseud.], *The Turner Diaries,* 2d ed. ([Washington, D.C.]: National Alliance, 1978).

BIBLIOGRAPHY

Abcarian, Gilbert. "Political Deviance and Social Stress: The Ideology of the American Radical Right." In *Social Control and Social Change*, edited by John Paul Scott and Sarah F. Scott, 137–61. (Chicago: University of Chicago Press, 1971).

Adamic, Louis. *Dynamite: The History of Class Violence in America*. Rev. ed. New York: Viking, 1935.

Adelson, Alan. *SDS: A Profile*. New York: Charles Scribner's Sons, 1972.

Aho, James A. *The Politics of Righteousness: Idaho Christian Patriotism*. Seattle: University of Washington Press, 1990.

Albares, Richard P. *Nativist Paramilitarism in the United States: The Minutemen Organization*. Working Paper No. 109. Chicago: Center for Social Organization Studies, University of Chicago, 1968.

Alinsky, Saul D. *Reveille for Radicals*. Chicago: University of Chicago Press, 1946.

Allen, Gary. *None Dare Call It Conspiracy*. Rossmoor, Ca.: Concord Press, [1971]. On the Council on Foreign Relations.

Allen, Marilyn R. *America Forever: Judaic-Communism versus Christian-Americanism*. Salt Lake City: n.p., 1946.

Allen, Mary L. *Education or Indoctrination*. Caldwell, Idaho: Caxton Printers, 1955. The latter.

Anbinder, Tyler. *Nativism and Slavery: The Northern Know Nothings and the Politics of the 1850s*. New York: Oxford University Press, 1992.

An Answer to Father Coughlin's Critics. By Father Coughlin's Friends. Royal Oak, Mich.: Radio League of the Little Flower, 1940.

App, Austin J. *Autobiography: German-American Voice for Truth and Justice*. Takoma Park, Md.: Boniface Press, 1977. John Birch Society publication concerned with the Captive Nations.

Armstrong, Geo[rge] W. *The Zionists.* Fort Worth, Tex.: Judger Armstrong Foundation, [1950].

Armstrong, Herbert W. *The United States and British Commonwealth in Prophecy.* Pasadena, Ca.: Ambassador College Press, 1967.

Aronica, Michele Teresa. *Beyond Charismatic Leadership: The New York Catholic Worker Movement.* New Brunswick, N.J.: Transaction, 1987.

Avrich, Paul. *The Haymarket Affair.* Princeton: Princeton University Press, 1984.

———. *Sacco and Vanzetti: The Anarchist Background.* Princeton: Princeton University Press, 1991.

Bacciocco, Edward J., Jr. *The New Left in America: Reform to Revolution 1956 to 1970.* Stanford: Hoover Institution Press, 1974.

Baritz, Loren, ed. *The American Left: Radical Political Thought in the Twentieth Century.* New York: Basic Books, 1971.

Barkun, Michael. "'Coxey's Army' as a Millennial Movement." *Religion* 18 (1988): 363–89. Reprinted in *Popular Culture and Political Change,* edited by Ronald Edsforth and Larry Bennett, 17–40. Albany: State University of New York Press, 1991.

———. "Divided Apocalypse: Thinking about the End in Contemporary America." *Soundings* 66, no. 3 (Fall 1983): 257–80. Discusses secular apocalypticism.

———. "Millenarian Aspects of 'White Supremacist' Movements." *Terrorism and Political Violence* 1 (1989): 409–34.

———. "Racist Apocalypse: Millennialism on the Far Right." *American Studies* 31, no. 2 (Fall 1990): 121–40.

———. *Religion and the Racist Right: The Origins of the Christian Identity Movement.* Chapel Hill: University of North Carolina Press, 1994.

Beam, Louis R., Jr. *Essays by a Klansman: Being a Compendium of Ku Klux Klan Ideology, Organizational Methods, History, Tactics, and Opinions, with Interpolations by the Author.* Hayden Lake, Idaho: A.K.I.A. Publications, 1983.

Bell, Daniel, ed. *The Radical Right: "The New American Right" Expanded and Updated.* Garden City, N.Y.: Doubleday, 1963.

Bell, Leland. *In Hitler's Shadow: The Anatomy of American Nazism.* Port Washington, N.Y.: Kennikat Press, 1973.

Bennett, David H. *The Party of Fear: From Nativist Movements to the New Right in American History.* Chapel Hill: University of North Carolina Press, 1988.

Benson, Ezra Taft. *A Nation Asleep: Addresses Given at General Conference, April 8, 1962, October 5, 1962, and April 17, 1963.* Salt Lake City: Bookcraft, 1963.

———. *The Red Carpet: A Forthright Evaluation of the Rising Tide of Socialism—The Royal Road To Communism.* Derby, Conn.: Monarch Books, 1963.

———. *This Nation Shall Endure.* Salt Lake City: Deseret Book, 1979.

Billington, Ray Allen. *The Protestant Crusade, 1800–1860.* New York: Macmillan, 1938.

Blacklisted News, Secret History . . . From Chicago, '68 to 1984. The New Yippie! Book. N.p.: Bleecker Publishing, 1983.

Blanshard, Paul. *American Freedom and Catholic Power.* 2nd ed. rev. and enl. Boston: Beacon, 1958.

————. *Communism, Democracy, and Catholic Power*. Boston: Beacon, 1951.

Blee, Kathleen M. *Women of the Klan: Racism and Gender in the 1920s*. Berkeley: University of California Press, 1991.

Brinkley, Alan. *Voices of Protest: Huey Long, Father Coughlin, and the Great Depression*. New York: Alfred A. Knopf, 1982.

Brissenden, Paul F. *The I.W.W.: A Study of American Syndicalism*. New York: Russell and Russell, 1957.

Broehl, Wayne G., Jr. *The Molly Maguires*. Cambridge: Harvard University Press, 1965.

Bromley, David G., and Anson Shupe, eds. *New Christian Politics*. Mercer, Ga.: Mercer University Press, 1984.

Brown, Elaine. *A Taste of Power: A Black Woman's Story*. New York: Pantheon, 1992. Black Panthers.

Broyles, J. Allen. *The John Birch Society: Anatomy of a Protest*. Boston: Beacon, 1964.

Bruce, Andrew A. *Non-Partisan League*. New York: Macmillan, 1921.

Bruce, Steve. *The Rise and Fall of the New Christian Right: Conservative Protestant Politics in America 1978–1988*. Oxford, England: Clarendon, 1990.

Buck, Solon J[ustus]. *The Agrarian Crusade: A Chronicle of the Farmer in Politics*. New Haven: Yale University Press, 1920.

————. *The Granger Movement: A Study of Agricultural Organization and Its Political, Economic and Social Manifestations 1870–1880*. Cambridge: Harvard University Press, 1913. Reprint, Lincoln: University of Nebraska Press, 1963.

Buckley, William F., Jr. *Up from Freedom*. New York: Hillman Books, 1961.

————. *Up from Liberalism*. 25th anniversary ed. New York: Stein and Day, 1984.

Buhle, Mari Jo. *Women and the American Left: A Guide to Sources*. Boston: G. K. Hall, 1983.

Buhle, Paul. *Marxism in the United States: Remapping the History of the American Left*. Rev. ed. London: Verso, 1991.

Bunzel, John H. *New Force on the Left: Tom Hayden and the Campaign Against Corporate America*. Stanford: Hoover Institution Press, 1983. Anti-Hayden.

Burbank, Garin. *When Farmers Voted Red: The Gospel of Socialism in the Oklahoma Countryside, 1910–1924*. Westport, Conn.: Greenwood, 1976.

Burlingame, Roger. *The Sixth Column*. Philadelphia: J. B. Lippincott, 1962. Against the radical right.

Cain, Edward. *They'd Rather Be Right: Youth and the Conservative Movement*. New York: Macmillan, 1963.

Canovan, Margaret. *Populism*. New York: Harcourt Brace Jovanovich, 1981.

Cantor, Milton. *The Divided Left: American Radicalism 1900–1975*. New York: Hill and Wang, 1978.

Capell, Frank A. *The Threat from Within: The Truth about the Conspiracy to Destroy America*. New York: Herald of Freedom, 1963.

Capps, Walter H. *The New Religious Right: Piety, Patriotism, and Politics*. Columbia: University of South Carolina Press, 1990.

Carr, William Guy. *The Red Fog over America*. Willowdale, Ontario, Canada: National Federation of Christian Laymen, 1955.

Carto, Willis A., ed. *Profiles in Populism*. Old Greenwich: Flag Press, 1982.

Casillo, Robert. *The Genealogy of Demons: Anti-Semitism, Fascism, and the Myths of Ezra Pound*. Evanston, Ill.: Northwestern University Press, 1988.

Caute, David. *The Fellow-Travellers: Intellectual Friends of Communism*. Rev. ed. New Haven: Yale University Press, 1988.

———. *The Great Fear: The Anti-Communist Purge under Truman and Eisenhower*. New York: Simon and Schuster, 1978.

Clabaugh, Gary K. *Thunder on the Right: The Protestant Fundamentalists*. Chicago: Nelson-Hall, 1974.

Clark, Elmer T. *The Small Sects in America*. Nashville: Cokesbury Press, 1937.

Clymer, R. Swinburne. *The Age of Treason: The Carefully and Deliberately Planned Methods Developed by the Vicious Element of Humanity for the Mental Deterioration and Moral Debasement of the Mass as a Means to Their Enslavement Based on Their Own Writings and Means Already Confessedly Employed. Destroy the Mind and Feelings of Man and Nothing Else Matters*. Quakertown, Pa.: Humanitarian Society, 1957. Opposed to fluoridation of water, food additives, vaccinations, and integration; believes that there is a huge conspiracy, led by communists, to control the world. Master race can be created.

Coán, Blair. *The Red Web: An Underground Political History of the United States from 1918 to the Present Time Showing How Close the Government is to Collapse and Told in an Understandable Way*. 1925. Reprint. Boston: Western Islands, 1969.

Cohen, Norman J., ed. *The Fundamentalist Phenomenon: A View from Within; A Response from Without*. Grand Rapids, Mich.: William B. Eerdmans, 1990.

Coleman, Patrick K., and Charles R. Lamb, comps. *The Nonpartisan League 1915–1922: An Annotated Bibliography*. St. Paul: Minnesota Historical Society Press, 1985.

Comparet, Bertrand L. *Your Heritage: An Identification of the True Israel through Biblical and Historic Sources*. Hayden Lake, Idaho: Church of Jesus Christ Christian, [1960s?].

Conover, Pamela Johnston, and Virginia Gray. *Feminism and the New Right: Conflict over the American Family*. New York: Praeger, 1983.

Conway, Flo, and Jim Siegelman. *Holy Terror: The Fundamentalists' War on America's Freedoms in Religion, Politics and Our Private Lives*. Garden City: Doubleday, 1982.

Cook, Fred J. *The Ku Klux Klan: America's Recurring Nightmare*. New York: Julian Messner, 1980.

Corcoran, James. *Bitter Harvest: Gordon Kahl and the Posse Comitatus: Murder in the Heartland*. New York: Viking, 1990.

Coughlin, Charles E. *Eight Lectures on Labor, Capital and Justice*. Royal Oak, Mich.: Radio League of the Little Flower, 1934.

———. *A Series of Lectures on Social Justice*. Royal Oak, Mich.: Radio League of the Little Flower, 1935.

Courtney, Kent, and Phoebe Courtney. *The Conservative Political Action Handbook.* New Orleans: Conservative Society of America, 1962.

―――. *The Silencers.* New Orleans: Conservative Society of America, 1965. Contends that the left is trying to muzzle the right.

Crawford, Alan. *Thunder on the Right: The "New Right" and the Politics of Resentment.* New York: Pantheon, 1980.

Critchlow, Donald T., ed. *Socialism in the Heartland: The Midwestern Experience, 1900–1925.* Notre Dame: University of Notre Dame Press, 1986.

Crosby, Donald F. *God, Church, and Flag: Senator Joseph R. McCarthy and the Catholic Church 1950–1957.* Chapel Hill: University of North Carolina Press, 1978.

Crosby, Percy. *Would Communism Work Out in America?* McLean, Va.: Freedom Press, 1938.

Curry, Richard Orr, comp. *Conspiracy: The Fear of Subversion in American History.* New York: Holt, Rinehart and Winston, 1972.

Curtiss, John S. *An Appraisal of the Protocols of Zion.* New York: Columbia University Press, 1942.

David, Henry. *The History of the Haymarket Affair: A Study in the American Social-Revolutionary and Labor Movements.* New York: Russell and Russell, 1958.

Davis, David Brion. "Some Themes of Counter-Subversion: An Analysis of Anti-Masonic, Anti-Catholic, and Anti-Mormon Literature." *Mississippi Valley Historical Review* 47, no. 2 (September 1960): 205–24.

Davis, John, ed. *The Earth First! Reader: Ten Years of Environmental Radicalism.* Salt Lake City: Gibbs Smith, 1991.

Day, Dorothy. *From Union Square to Rome.* Silver Spring, Md.: Preservation of the Faith Press, 1939.

―――. *Houses of Hospitality.* New York: Sheed and Ward, 1939.

―――. *The Long Loneliness.* New York: Harper and Brothers, 1952.

Debs, Eugene Victor. *Walls and Bars.* 1927. Reprint, Chicago: Charles H. Kerr, 1973.

DeLeon, David. *The American as Anarchist: Reflections on Indigenous Radicalism.* Baltimore: Johns Hopkins University Press, 1978.

DeLorme, Roland L., and Raymond G. McInnis, eds. *Antidemocratic Trends in Twentieth-Century America.* Reading, Mass.: Addison-Wesley, 1969.

DePugh, Robert Bolivar. *Beyond the Iron Mask.* Norborne, Mo.: Salon Publishing Co., 1974. Prison reform.

―――. *Blueprint for Victory.* Norborne, Mo.: n.p., 1966. 4th ed., Norborne, Mo.: Salon Publishing Co., 1978.

―――. *Can You Survive? Guidelines for Resistance to Tyranny For You and Your Family.* Los Angeles: Noontide Press, 1973.

Destler, Chester McArthur. *American Radicalism 1865–1901: Essays and Documents.* 1946. Reprint, New York: Octagon Books, 1965.

Diamond, Sander A. *The Nazi Movement in the United States 1924–1941.* Ithaca, N.Y.: Cornell University Press, 1974. German-American Bund.

Diamond, Sara. *Spiritual Warfare: The Politics of the Christian Right.* Boston: South End Press, 1989.

Diggins, John P. *The American Left in the Twentieth Century.* New York: Harcourt Brace Jovanovich, 1973. Expanded as *The Rise and Fall of the American Left.* New York: W. W. Norton, 1992.

Dilling, Elizabeth (Mrs. Albert W. Dilling). *The Red Network: A "Who's Who" and Handbook of Radicalism for Patriots.* Kenilworth, Ill.: n.p., 1934.

———. *The Roosevelt Red Record and its Background.* Kenilworth, Ill.: n.p., 1936.

Does the American Civil Liberties Union Serve the Communist Cause What Do You Think? Phoenix, Ariz.: FACT—a Committee For All Comprehensive Truth, 1963. Their answer is yes.

Dolgoff, Sam. *Fragments: A Memoir.* Cambridge, England: Refract Publications, 1986.

Dombrowski, James. *The Early Days of Christian Socialism in America.* New York: Columbia University Press, 1936. Reprint, New York: Octagon Books, 1966.

Dorman, Morgan J. *Age Before Booty: An Explanation of the Townsend Plan.* New York: G. P. Putnam's Sons, 1936.

Draper, Theodore. *The Roots of American Communism.* New York: Viking, 1957.

Dunbar, Anthony P. *Against the Grain: Southern Radicals and Prophets 1929–1959.* Charlottesville: University Press of Virginia, 1981.

Egbert, Donald Drew, and Stow Persons, eds. *Socialism and American Life.* 2 vols. Princeton: Princeton University Press, 1952.

Ellsworth, Ralph E., and Sarah M. Harris. *The American Right Wing: A Report to the Fund for the Republic.* Washington, D.C.: Public Affairs Press, 1962.

Elmer, Glaister A., and Evelyn E. Elmer. *Sociobiology and Immigration: The Grim Forecast for America.* Monterey, Va.: American Immigration Control Foundation, 1984.

Elmhurst, Ernest F. *The World Hoax.* Asheville, N.C.: Pelley Publishers, 1938.

Elsner, Henry, Jr. *The Technocrats: Prophets of Automation.* Syracuse: Syracuse University Press, 1967.

Emry, Sheldon. *The Bible Says: Russia Will Invade America! (And Be Defeated).* 1968. Rev. and enl. ed., Phoenix, Ariz.: America's Promise Radio, 1977.

Epstein, Barbara. *Political Protest and Cultural Revolution: Nonviolent Direct Action in the 1970s and 1980s.* Berkeley: University of California Press, 1991.

Epstein, Benjamin R., and Arnold Forster. *The Radical Right: Report on the John Birch Society and Its Allies.* New York: Random House, 1967.

———. *Report on the John Birch Society 1966.* New York: Vintage Books, 1966.

Erb, Nary Barclay. *Invasion Alert: Rising Tides of Aliens in Our Midst.* Washington, D.C.: Goetz Company Press, 1965.

Extremism on the Right: A Handbook. New York: Anti-Defamation League of B'nai B'rith, 1983.

Falwell, Jerry. *Listen America!* Garden City: Doubleday, 1980.

———, ed., with Ed Dobson and Ed Hindson. *The Fundamentalist Phenomenon: The Resurgence of Conservative Christianity.* Garden City: Doubleday, 1981.

Felsenthal, Carol. *The Sweetheart of the Silent Majority: The Biography of Phyllis Schlafly*. Garden City: Doubleday, 1981.

Finch, Phillip. *Gods, Guts, and Guns*. New York: Seaview/Putnam, 1983. Contemporary right.

Fire by Night and Cloud by Day: A History of Defenders of the Christian Faith. Wichita, Kans.: Mertmont Publishing Co., 1966.

Fisher, William H. *The Invisible Empire: A Bibliography of the Ku Klux Klan*. Metuchen, N.J.: Scarecrow Press, 1980.

Flake, Carol. *Redemptorama: Culture, Politics, and the New Evangelicalism*. Garden City: Doubleday, 1984.

Flynn, Elizabeth Gurley. *Words on Fire: The Life and Writings of Elizabeth Gurley Flynn*. New Brunswick: Rutgers University Press, 1987.

Flynn, Kevin, and Gary Gerhart. *The Silent Brotherhood: Inside America's Racist Underground*. New York: Free Press, 1989.

Forster, Arnold, and Benjamin R. Epstein. *Danger On the Right*. New York: Random House, 1964.

Foster, Catherine. *Women for All Seasons: The Story of the Women's International League for Peace and Freedom*. Athens: University of Georgia Press, 1989.

Fried, Albert. *Socialism in America from the Shakers to the Third International: A Documentary History*. Garden City: Anchor Books, 1970.

Fried, Richard M. *Men against McCarthy*. New York: Columbia University Press, 1976.

George, John, and Laird Wilcox. *Nazis, Communists, Klansmen, and Others on the Fringe: Political Extremism in America*. Buffalo: Prometheus Books, 1992.

Gerber, David A., ed. *Anti-Semitism in American History*. Urbana: University of Illinois Press, 1986.

Gillespie, J. David. *Politics at the Periphery: Third Parties in Two-Party America*. Columbia: University of South Carolina Press, 1993.

Gladstein, Mimi Reisel. *The Ayn Rand Companion*. Westport: Greenwood, 1984.

Goldberg, Robert Alan. *Hooded Empire: The Ku Klux Klan in Colorado*. Urbana: University of Illinois Press, 1981.

Goldwalter, Walter. *Radical Periodicals in America 1890–1950 with a Genealogical Chart and a Concise Lexicon of the Parties and Groups which Issued Them: A Bibliography with Brief Notes*. New Haven: Yale University Library, 1966.

Goodman, Mitchell, comp. *The Movement toward a New America: The Beginnings of a Long Revolution (A Collage) A What? 1. A Comprehension 2. A Compendium 3. A Handbook 4. A Guide 5. A History 6. A Revolution Kit 7. A Work-In-Progress*. Philadelphia and New York: Pilgrim Press and Alfred A. Knopf, 1970.

Goodman, Paul, ed. *Seeds of Liberation*. New York: George Braziller, 1964.

Goodwyn, Lawrence. *Democratic Promise: The Populist Movement in America*. New York: Oxford University Press, 1976.

Grieb, Conrad. *American Manifest Destiny and the Holocausts: Millions of People Exterminated. Where It Happened. When It Happened. How It Happened. Who*

Made It Happen. An Historical and Sociological Encyclopedia of Domestic and Foreign Affairs. New York: Examiner Books, 1979. Anti-Semitic.

Griffin, Des. *Descent into Slavery?* South Pasadena, Calif.: Emissary Publications, 1980. International bankers part of "the Illuminati plot to create a totalitarian One World government."

Griffith, Robert. *The Politics of Fear: Joseph R. McCarthy and the Senate.* Lexington: University of Kentucky Press, 1970.

Hall, Gus. *Labor Up-Front in the People's Fight against the Crisis.* New York: International Publishers, 1979. Report to the 22nd Convention of the Communist Party, U.S.A. Detroit, Mich., August 23, 1979.

Hansen, George. *To Harass Our People: The IRS and Government Abuse of Power.* Washington, D.C.: Positive Publications, 1984.

Hargis, Billy James. *"Communism, the Total Lie."* Tulsa, Okla.: Christian Crusade, 1963.

———. *Communist America . . . Must It Be?* Tulsa, Okla.: Christian Crusade, 1960.

———. *The Far Left.* Tulsa, Okla.: Christian Crusade, 1964.

Hargis, Billy James, with Julian Williams. *The Facts About Communism and Our Churches.* Tulsa, Okla.: Christian Crusade, 1962.

Haynes, John Earl. *Communism and Anti-Communism in the United States: An Annotated Guide to Historical Writings.* New York: Garland, 1987.

Heale, M. J. *American Anticommunism: Combating the Enemy Within 1830–1970.* Baltimore: Johns Hopkins University Press, 1990.

Heath, G. Louis, ed. *Off the Pigs! The History and Literature of the Black Panther Party.* Metuchen, N.J.: Scarecrow Press, 1976.

Hess, Karl. *Dear America.* New York: William Morrow, 1975.

Hesseltine, William Best. *Third-Party Movements in the United States.* Princeton: Van Nostrand, 1962.

Hicks, John D. *The Populist Revolt: A History of the Farmer's Alliance and the People's Party.* 1931. Reprint, Lincoln: University of Nebraska Press, 1959.

Higham, John. *Strangers in the Land: Patterns of American Nativism 1860–1925.* New Brunswick: Rutgers University Press, 1955.

Hilliard, David, and Lewis Cole. *This Side of Glory: The Autobiography of David Hilliard and the Story of the Black Panther Party.* Boston: Little, Brown, 1993.

Hixson, William B., Jr. *Search for the American Right Wing: An Analysis of the Social Science Record, 1955–1987.* Princeton: Princeton University Press, 1992.

Hoffman, Abbie [Free, pseud.]. *Revolution for the Hell of It.* New York: Dial, 1968.

Hoffman, Abbie. *Woodstock Nation: A Talk-Rock Album.* New York: Vintage Books, 1969.

Hofstadter, Richard. "The Paranoid Style in American Politics." In *The Paranoid Style in American Politics and Other Essays,* 3–40. New York: Alfred A. Knopf, 1966.

Holtzman, Abraham. *The Townsend Movement: A Political Study.* New York: Bookman Associates, 1963.

Hoover, J. Edgar. *Masters of Deceit: The Story of Communism in America and How to Fight It.* New York: Henry Holt, 1958.

Horn, Max. *The Intercollegiate Socialist Society, 1905–1921: Origins of the Modern American Student Movement.* Boulder, Colo.: Westview, 1979.

Hospers, John. *Libertarianism: A Political Philosophy for Tomorrow.* Santa Barbara: Reason Press, 1971.

Howard, Peter. *Design for Dedication.* Chicago: Henry Regnery, 1964. Anti-communist.

Howe, Irving. *Socialism and America.* San Diego: Harcourt Brace Jovanovich, 1977.

————, ed. *The Radical Papers.* Garden City: Doubleday, 1966.

Hunt, H. L. *Fabians Fight Freedom.* Dallas: H. L. Hunt Press, n.d.

————. *Why Not Speak?* Dallas: H. L. Hunt Press, 1964.

The International Jew: The World's Foremost Problem. Being a Reprint of a Series of Articles Appearing in the Dearborn Independent from May 22 to October 2, 1920. [Dearborn, Mich.: Dearborn Publishing Co.], 1920.

Jacker, Corrine. *The Black Flag of Anarchy: Antistatism in the United States.* New York: Scribner's, 1968.

Jackson, Rebecca. *The 1960s: An Annotated Bibliography of Social and Political Movements in the United States.* Westport: Greenwood, 1992.

Jacobs, Harold, ed. *Weatherman.* N.p.: Ramparts Press, 1970.

Jacobs, Paul, and Saul Landau. *The New Radicals: A Report with Documents.* New York: Random House, 1966.

Jaffe, Harold, and John Tytell, eds. *The American Experience: A Radical Reader.* New York: Harper and Row, 1970.

Jaher, Frederic Cople. *A Scapegoat in the New Wilderness: The Origins and Rise of Anti-Semitism in America.* Cambridge: Harvard University Press, 1994.

Jeansonne, Glen. *Gerald L. K. Smith: Minister of Hate.* New Haven: Yale University Press, 1988.

Jewett, Robert. *The Captain America Complex: The Dilemma of Zealous Nationalism.* Santa Fe: Bear and Co., 1984.

Jewish Activities in the United States. Volume II of The International Jew. Being a Reprint of a Second Selection from Articles Appearing in the Dearborn Independent from Oct. 9, 1920 to March 19, 1921. [Dearborn, Mich.: Dearborn Publishing Co., 1921].

Johanningsmeier, Edward P. *Forging American Communism: The Life of William Z. Foster.* Princeton: Princeton University Press, 1994.

Johnpoll, Bernard K., and Lillian Johnpoll. *The Impossible Dream: The Rise and Demise of the American Left.* Westport: Greenwood, 1981.

Johnson, Frank Woodruff. *The Octopus.* Omaha: n.p., 1940. B'nai B'rith.

Johnson, George. *Architects of Fear: Conspiracy Theories and Paranoia in American Politics.* Los Angeles: J. P. Tarcher, 1983.

Johnson, Guion Griffis. "The Ideology of White Supremacy, 1876–1910." In *Essays in Southern History,* edited by Fletcher Melvin Green, 124–56. Chapel Hill: University of North Carolina Press, 1949.

Jones, J. Harry, Jr. *The Minutemen.* Garden City: Doubleday, 1968.

Jones, Kitty, and Robert Olivier. *Progressive Education Is REDucation.* Boston: Meador Publishing Co., 1956.

Jorstad, Erling. *The New Christian Right 1981–1988: Prospects for the Post-Reagan Decade.* Lewsiton, Maine: Edwin Mellen Press, 1987.

Kamp, Joseph P. *Lawless Tyranny: An American Conspiracy against We, the People. PLUS Behind-the-Scenes FACTS about the RED-LED RACIST Revolution.* New Fairfield, Conn.: Headlines, 1966.

———. *We Must Abolish the United States: The Hidd. ⁿ Facts behind the Crusade for World Government.* New York: Hallmark Publishers, 1950.

Kann, Mark E. *The American Left: Failures and Fortunes.* New York: Praeger, 1982.

Kater, John L., Jr. *Christians on the Right: The Moral Majority in Perspective.* New York: Seabury Press, 1982.

Kaub, Verne P(aul). *Communist-Socialist Propaganda in American Schools: A Documented Study of the Role National Education Association is Taking in the Indoctrination of the Youth of Our Country with the Ideology of Communism-Socialism.* Boston: Meador Publishing Co., 1953.

Kehde, Ned, comp. *The American Left, 1955–1970: A National Union Catalog of Pamphlets Published in the United States and Canada.* Westport: Greenwood, 1976.

King, Dennis. *Lyndon LaRouche and the New American Fascism.* New York: Doubleday, 1989.

Kinzer, Donald Louis. *An Episode in Anti-Catholicism: The American Protective Association.* Seattle: University of Washington Press, 1964.

Kiser, Fred H. *The Hidden Power of Money.* Los Angeles: Wetzel Publishing Co., 1941. Against the national bank (seen as the privatization of money) and the New Deal.

Kittrie, Nicholas N., and Eldon D. Wedlock, Jr. *The Tree of Liberty: A Documentary History of Rebellion and Political Crime in America. A Legal, Historical, Social, and Psychological Inquiry into Rebellion and Political Crimes, Their Causes, Suppression, and Punishment in the United States.* Baltimore: Johns Hopkins University Press, 1986.

Klassen, Ben. *Nature's Eternal Religion In Two Books.* bk. 1, *The Unavenged Outrage.* bk. 2, *The Salvation.* Lighthouse Point, Fla.: Church of the Creator, 1973.

Klatch, Rebecca E. *Women of the New Right.* Philadelphia: Temple University Press, 1987.

Klehr, Harvey. *Far Left of Center: The American Radical Left Today.* New Brunswick: Transaction, 1988.

Klehr, Harvey, and John Earl Haynes. *The American Communist Movement: Storming Heaven Itself.* New York: Twayne, 1992.

Kolko, Gabriel. *The Triumph of Conservatism: A Re-interpretation of American History.* New York: Free Press of Glencoe, 1968.

Kovel, Joel. *Red Hunting in the Promised Land: Anticommunism and the Making of America.* New York: Basic Books, 1994.

Kunen, James Simon. *The Strawberry Statement: Notes of a College Revolutionary.* New York: Random House, 1968.

Lader, Lawrence. *Power on the Left: American Radical Movements Since 1946.* New York: W.W. Norton, 1979.

La Follette, Robert M. *La Follette's Autobiography: A Personal Narrative of Political Experiences.* New ed. Madison: University of Wisconsin Press, 1960.

LaRouche: Will This Man Become President? By the Editors of Executive Intelligence Review. EIR. New York: New Benjamin Franklin House, 1983.

LaRouche, Lyndon H., Jr. *Imperialism: The Final Stage of Bolshevism.* New York: New Benjamin Franklin House, 1984.

———. *The Power of Reason: 1988. An Autobiography.* Washington, D.C.: Executive Intelligence Review, 1988.

———. *What Every Conservative Should Know About Communism.* New York: New Benjamin Franklin House, 1980.

———. *Will the Soviets Rule During the 1980s?* New York: New Benjamin Franklin House, 1979.

Larson, Martin A. *The Continuing Tax Rebellion or What Millions of Americans Are Doing to Restore Constitutional Government in the United States.* Old Greenwich: Devin-Adair, 1979.

———. *Tax Revolt: U.S.A.! Why and How Thousands of Patriotic Americans Refuse to Pay Income Tax. A Study in The Public Debt The Federal Reserve System Income Taxation and Rebellion.* Washington, D.C.: Liberty Lobby, 1973.

Laslett, John H. M., and Seymour Martin Lipset, eds. *Failure of a Dream? Essays in the History of American Socialism.* Rev. ed. Berkeley: University of California Press, 1984.

Lay, Shawn, ed. *The Invisible Empire in the West: Toward a New Historical Appraisal of the Ku Klux Klan of the 1920s.* Urbana: University of Illinois Press, 1992.

Lens, Sidney. *Permanent War: The Militarization of America.* New York: Schocken, 1987.

———. *Radicalism in America.* New ed. New York: Thomas Y. Crowell, 1969.

———. *Unrepentent Radical: An American Activist's Account of Five Turbulent Decades.* Boston: Beacon, 1980.

Lepanto, Paul. *Return to Reason: An Introduction to Objectivism.* New York: Exposition Press, 1971.

Lernoux, Penny. *People of God: The Struggle for World Catholicism.* New York: Viking Penguin, 1989.

Liebman, Robert C., and Robert Wuthnow, eds. *The New Christian Right: Mobilization and Legitimation.* New York: Aldine Publishing Co., 1983.

Lipset, Seymour Martin. *Rebellion in the University.* Boston: Little, Brown, 1971.

Lipset, Seymour Martin, and Earl Raab. *The Politics of Unreason: Right-Wing Extremism in America, 1790–1970.* New York: Harper and Row, 1970.

Long, Priscilla, ed. *The New Left: A Collection of Essays.* Boston: Porter Sargent Publishers, 1969.

Loomis, Mildred J. *Go Ahead and Live!* New York: Philosophical Library, 1965.

Loomis, Mildred J., and R. Bruce Allison, eds. *Toward a Human Future: Some Imaginative Alternatives. The Complete Proceedings of the Conference on Ade-*

quate Action for a Human Future. Sponsored by the School of Living Mildred J. Loomis, General Chairman Camp Eder, Fairfield, Pa. September 3–6, 1971. Spring Grove, Pa.: School of Living Press, 1972.

Luthin, Reinhard Henry. *American Demagogues: Twentieth Century.* Boston: Beacon, 1954.

Lynd, Staughton. *Intellectual Origins of American Radicalism.* New York: Pantheon, 1968.

MacLean, Nancy. *Behind the Mask of Chivalry: The Making of the Second Ku Klux Klan.* New York: Oxford University Press, 1994.

Major Speeches and Debates of Senator Joe McCarthy Delivered in the United States Senate 1950–1951: Reprint from the Congressional Record. Washington, D.C.: U.S. Government Printing Office, n.d.

Malcolm, Andrew H. *Final Harvest: An American Tragedy.* New York: Times Books, 1986.

Manion, Clarence. *The Conservative American: His Fight for National Independence and Constitutional Government.* New York: Devin-Adair, 1964.

Marcus, Sheldon. *Father Coughlin: The Tempestuous Life of the Priest of the Little Flower.* Boston: Little, Brown, 1973.

Martin, Len. *Why "They" Wanted to Get Gordon Kahl.* Detroit Lakes, Minn.: Pro-America Press, 1983.

Martin, Rose L. *Fabian Freeway: High Road to Socialism in the U.S.A. 1884–1966.* Chicago: Heritage Foundation, 1966.

Martinez, Thomas, with John Gunther. *Brotherhood of Murder: How One Man's Journey Through Fear Brought The Order—The Most Dangerous Racist Gang in America—To Justice.* New York: McGraw-Hill, 1988.

Marvin, Fred R. *Our Government and Its Enemies.* New York: Educational Committee of the American Coalition of Patriotic Societies, 1932. Series of lectures against socialism, including a chapter on the Illuminati as the forerunner of socialism.

————. *Ye Shall Know the Truth.* 2nd ed. New York: n.p., 1926. Emphasizes how communism has infiltrated American institutions, making U.S. defense inadequate.

May, George S. "Ultra-Conservative Thought in the United States in the 1920's and 1930's." Ph.D. diss., Michigan, 1954.

McCarthy, Joe. *McCarthyism: The Fight for America. Documented Answers to Questions Asked by Friend and Foe.* New York: Devin-Adair, 1952.

————. *The Story of General George C. Marshall.* N.p.: n.p., 1952.

McEvoy, James, III. *Radicals or Conservatives? The Contemporary American Right.* Chicago: Rand McNally and Co., 1971.

McIntire, Carl. *Servants of Apostasy.* Collingswood, N.J.: Christian Beacon Press, 1955. World Council of Churches. Against plot for one-world church and one-world government.

McMillen, Neil R. *The Citizen's Council: Organized Resistance to the Second Reconstruction, 1954–64.* Urbana: University of Illinois Press, 1971.

McMurry, Donald L. *Coxey's Army: A Study of the Industrial Army Movement of 1894*. 1929. Reprint, Seattle: University of Washington Press, 1968.

McVey, Frank L. "The Populist Movement." *Economic Studies* 1, no. 3 (August 1896). Also separately published, New York: American Economic Association, 1896.

Metz, Howard. *The Social Security and Pension Conspiracy: The Illegal Operation of the Federal Reserve System*. East Rockaway, N.Y.: n.p., 1981.

Miceli, Vincent P. *The Antichrist*. West Hanover, Mass.: Christopher Publishing House, 1981.

Miles, Michael W. *The Odyssey of the American Right*. New York: Oxford University Press, 1980. New Deal to Nixon.

Miller, Albert Jay. *Confrontation, Conflict, and Dissent: A Bibliography of a Decade of Controversy, 1960–1970*. Metuchen, N.J.: Scarecrow Press, 1972.

Mintz, Frank P. *The Liberty Lobby and the American Right: Race, Conspiracy, and Culture*. Westport: Greenwood, 1985.

Moen, Matthew C. *The Transformation of the Christian Right*. Tuscaloosa: University of Alabama Press, 1992.

Montgomery, G. H. *Gerald Burton Winrod: Defender of the Faith*. Wichita, Kans.: Mertmont Publishers, 1965.

Moore, R. Laurence. *European Socialists and the American Promised Land*. New York: Oxford University Press, 1970.

Morlan, Robert L. *Political Prairie Fire: The Nonpartisan League 1915–1922*. 1955. Reprint, St. Paul: Minnesota Historical Society Press, 1983. Group centered in North Dakota that advocated publicly owned enterprises. Managed to elect state government and establish their program.

Mote, Carl H. *The New Deal Goose Step*. New York: Daniel Ryerson, 1939.

Moving into the Front Ranks of Social Change: Complete Proceedings of the Labor Day '73 Conference, Henry George Schools & The School of Living. Mildred Loomis Conference Chairman. Hinsdale, Ill.: R. Bruce Allison SOL Press, [1973].

Muggeridge, Anne Roche. *The Desolate City: Revolution in the Catholic Church*. San Francisco: Harper and Row, 1986.

Mugglebee, Ruth. *Father Coughlin, the Radio Priest, of the Shrine of the Little Flower. An Account of the Life, Work and Message of Reverand Charles E. Coughlin*. Garden City: Garden City Publishing Co., 1933.

Murch, James DeForest. *The Protestant Revolt: Road to Freedom for American Churches*. Arlington, Va.: Crestwood Books, 1967. Against the National Council of Churches.

Murray, William H. *The Negro's Place in Call of Race: The Last Word on Segregation of Races Considered in Every Capable Light as Disclosed by Experience*. Tishomingo, Okla.: William H. Murray, 1948. Author was Governor of Oklahoma, 1931–35.

Newman, Edwin S., ed. *The Hate Reader: A Collection of Materials on the Impact of Hate Movements in American Society, Including Excerpts and Commentary of*

Eminent Political and Social Scientists. Dobbs Ferry, N.Y.: Oceana Publications, 1964.

Newton, Michael, and Judith Ann Newton. *Racial and Religious Violence in America: A Chronology.* New York: Garland, 1991.

O'Brien, Michael. *McCarthy and McCarthyism in Wisconsin.* Columbia: University of Missouri Press, 1980.

Oliver, Revilo P. *All America Must Know the Terror That Is upon Us.* Bakersfield, Calif.: Conservative Viewpoint, 1966. Speech given to the DAR, March 12, 1959.

———. *Christianity and the Survival of the West.* Sterling, Va.: Sterling Enterprises, 1973.

———. *Conspiracy or Degeneracy? The Complete Text of an Address Given at the New England Rally for God, Family, and Country in Boston, Massachusetts, July 2, 1966 Together with Documentary and Supplemental notes.* Nedrow, N.Y.: Power Products, 1967.

Origin, History, and Methodology of the "Front" Movement in America. Pasadena, Calif.: Institute for Special Research, n.d.

Oshinsky, David M. *A Conspiracy So Immense: The World of Joe McCarthy.* New York: Free Press, 1983.

Overdyke, W. Darrell. *The Know-Nothing Party in the South.* Baton Rouge: Louisiana State University, 1950. Reprint, Gloucester, Mass.: Peter Smith, 1968.

Overstreet, Harry, and Bonaro Overstreet. *The Strange Tactics of Extremism.* New York: W. W. Norton, 1964.

Pace, James O. *Amendment to the Constitution: Averting the Decline and Fall of America.* Los Angeles: Johnson, Pace, Simmons and Fennell Publishers, 1985.

Penabaz, Fernando. *"Crusading Preacher From the West": The Story of Billy James Hargis.* Tulsa, Okla.: Christian Crusade, 1965. Hagiography.

Piehl, Mel. *Breaking Bread: The Catholic Worker and the Origin of Catholic Radicalism in America.* Philadelphia: Temple University Press, 1982.

Powderly, T.V. *Thirty Years of Labor 1859–1889, In Which the History of the Attempts to Form Organizations of Workingmen for the Discussion of Political, Social and Economic Questions is Traced. The National Labor Union of 1866, the Industrial Brotherhood of 1874, and the Order of the Knights of Labor of America and the World. The Chief and Most Important Principles in the Preamble of the Knights of Labor Discussed and Explained, With Views of the Author on Land, Labor and Transportation.* 1890. Rev. ed., New York: Augustus M. Kelley, 1967.

Powers, Thomas. *Diana: The Making of a Terrorist.* Boston: Houghton Mifflin, 1971.

Prairie Fire: The Politics of Revolutionary Anti-Imperialism. Political Statement of the Weather Underground. San Francisco: Prairie Fire Organizing Committee, 1974.

Pranaitis, I. B. *The Talmud Unmasked: The Secret Rabbinical Teachings Concerning Christians.* 1892. Reprint, n.p.: n.p., 1964.

Preston, William. *Aliens and Dissenters: Federal Suppression of Radicals, 1903–1933*. Cambridge: Harvard University Press, 1963.

Quint, Howard H. *The Forging of American Socialism*. Indianapolis: Bobbs-Merrill, 1953.

The Radical Right: Proceedings of the Sixth Annual Intergroup Relations Conference at the University of Houston, Houston, Texas, March 27, 1965. Houston: n.p., 1965.

Redekop, John Harold. *The American Far Right: A Case Study of Billy James Hargis and Christian Crusade*. Grand Rapids, Mich.: William B. Eerdmans, 1968.

Reeves, Thomas C. *The Life and Times of Joe McCarthy: A Biography*. New York: Stein and Day, 1982.

Ribuffo, Leo P. *The Old Christian Right: The Protestant Far Right from the Great Depression to the Cold War*. Philadelphia: Temple University Press, 1983.

Ridgeway, James. *Blood in the Face: The Ku Klux Klan, Aryan Nations, Nazi Skinheads, and the Rise of a New White Culture*. New York: Thunder's Mouth Press, 1990.

Robinson, David. *Herbert Armstrong's Tangled Web: An Insider's View of the Worldwide Church of God*. Tulsa, Okla.: John Hadden Publishers, 1980. Anti.

Robertson, Wilmot. *The Dispossessed Majority*. 1972. Rev. ed., Cape Canaveral, Fla.: Howard Allen, 1973.

———. *Ventilations*. Cape Canaveral, Fla.: Howard Allen, 1974.

Rocker, Rudolf. *Pioneers of American Freedom: Origin of Liberal and Radical Thought in America*. Los Angeles: Rocker Publications Committee, 1949.

Rockwell, George Lincoln. *Legal, Psychological and Political Warfare: Complete Course of 26 Lessons*. Arlington, Va.: American Nazi Party, 1965.

———. *This Time the World*. 2nd ed., New York: Parliament House, 1963. 3rd ed., Liverpool, W. Va.: White Power Publications, 1979.

———. *White Power*. 2nd ed., Dallas: Ragnarok Press, 1967. Reprinted in part as [George Lincoln Rockwell]. *The White Primer: A Dynamic Racial Analysis of Present Day American From the Viewpoint of the White Majority*. N.p.: C. W. Bristol, [1977 or 1978].

Rogin, Michael Paul. *The Intellectuals and McCarthy: The Radical Specter*. Cambridge: M.I.T. Press, 1967.

Roof, Wade Clark. "The New Fundamentalism: Rebirth of Political Religion in America." In *Prophetic Religions and Politics: Religion and the Political Order*, edited by Anson Shupe and Jeffrey K. Hadden, 18–34. New York: Paragon House, 1986.

Rothbard, Murray N. *Conceived in Liberty*. 3 vols. New Rochelle, N.Y.: Arlington House, 1975–76. History of the United States from the earliest colonies to 1775 from a libertarian perspective.

———. *For a New Liberty*. New York: Macmillan, 1973.

———. *Power and Market: Government and the Economy*. Menlo Park, Calif.: Institute for Humane Studies, 1970.

Rubin, Jerry. *Do It! Scenarios of the Revolution*. New York: Simon and Schuster, 1970.

382 *Bibliography*

————. *We Are Everywhere*. New York: Harper and Row, 1971.
Rushdoony, Rousas J. *Intellectual Schizophrenia: Culture, Crisis and Education*. Philadelphia: Presbyterian and Reformed Publishing Co., 1961.
————. *The Messianic Character of American Education: Studies in the History of the Philosophy of Education*. Nutley, N.J.: Craig Press, 1963.
————. *The Myth of Over-Population*. Nutley, N.J.: Craig Press, 1969.
————. *The Politics of Pornography*. New Rochelle, N.Y.: Arlington House, 1974.
Sanders, Ronald. *Lost Tribes and Promised Lands: The Origins of American Racism*. Boston: Little, Brown, 1978.
Sargent, Lyman Tower. *New Left Thought: An Introduction*. Homewood, Ill.: Dorsey Press, 1972.
Scarce, Rik. *Eco-Warriors: Understanding the Radical Environmental Movement*. Chicago: Noble Press, 1990.
Scharf, Lois, and Joan M. Jense, eds. *Decades of Discontent: The Women's Movement, 1920–1940*. Westport: Greenwood, 1982.
Schlafly, Phyllis. *A Choice Not an Echo*. Alton, Ill.: Pere Marquette Press, 1964.
Schomp, Gerald. *Birchism Was My Business*. New York: Macmillan, 1970.
Schultz, Bud, and Ruth Schultz. *It Did Happen Here: Recollections of Political Repression in America*. Berkeley: University of California Press, 1989.
Schuster, Eunice Minette. *Native American Anarchism: A Study of Left-Wing American Individualism*. 1930. Reprint, New York: Da Capo Press, 1970.
Schwarz, Fred. *You Can Trust the Communists (to be Communists)*. Englewood Cliffs: Prentice-Hall, 1960.
Search, R. E. *Lincoln Money Martyred*. 1935. Reprint, Hawthorne, Calif.: Omni Publications, 1967.
Selzer, Michael, ed. *"Kike": A Documentary History of Anti-Semitism in America*. New York: World Publishing, 1972.
Sherman, Ray W. *How to Win an Argument with a Communist*. New York: E. P. Dutton, 1950.
Sherwin, Mark. *The Extremists*. New York: St. Martin's Press, 1963.
Shover, John L. *Cornbelt Rebellion: The Farmer's Holiday Association*. Urbana: University of Illinois Press, 1965. Depression-era movement to withhold farm products from the market. Centered in Iowa.
Silverman, Henry J., ed. *American Radical Thought: The Libertarian Tradition*. Lexington: D.C. Heath, 1970.
Simpson, William Gayley. *Which Way Western Man?* Washington, D.C.: National Alliance, 1978.
Sims, Patsy. *The Klan*. New York: Stein and Day, 1978.
Singular, Stephen. *Talked to Death: The Life and Murder of Alan Berg*. New York: Beech Tree Books, 1987.
Sirgiovanni, George. *An Undercurrent of Suspicion: Anti-Communism in America during World War II*. New Brunswick: Transaction, 1990.
Skousen, W. Cleon. *The Making of America: The Substance and Meaning of the Constitution*. Washington, D.C.: National Center for Constitutional Studies, 1985. American history/government text from the viewpoint of the right.

————. *What Is behind the Frantic Drive for a New Constitution: Full Text and Analysis.* Provo, Utah: Freemen Institute, [1970]. Attack on Rexford Tugwell's proposal in *The Center Magazine* (September–October 1970). Author is descibed as "the former editorial director of the Nation's leading professional police magazine, *Law and Order.*"

Smith, Geoffrey S. *To Save a Nation: American Countersubversives, the New Deal, and the Coming of World War II.* New York: Basic Books, 1973.

Smith, Gerald L. K. *Besieged Patriot: Autobiographical Episodes Exposing Communism, Traitorism and Zionism from the Life of Gerald L. K. Smith,* edited by Elna M. Smith and Charles F. Robertson. Eureka Springs, Ark.: Christian Nationalist Crusade, 1978.

————. *Satan's New Testament. The Devil's Bible. A Sensational Analysis Of the Zionist Jew Plan For World Order.* Los Angeles: Christian Nationalist Crusade, 1975.

————. *White Man Awaken!!* Los Angeles: Christian Nationalist Crusade, [1960s?].

Smoot, Dan. *The Invisible Government.* Dallas: Dan Smoot Report, 1962. Council on Foreign Relations.

Sombart, Werner. *Why Is There No Socialism in the United States?* Translated by Patricia M. Hocking and C. T. Husbands. Edited by C. T. Husbands. White Plains: International Arts and Sciences Press, 1976.

Spivak, John L. *Shrine of the Silver Dollar.* New York: Modern Age Books, 1940. Coughlin.

Stang, Alan. *It's Very Simple: The True Story of Civil Rights.* Belmont, Mass.: Western Islands, 1965. Claims civil rights movement was communist-inspired.

Steffgen, Kent H. *The Bondage of the Free.* Berkeley: Vanguard Books, 1966. Against the civil rights movement.

Steichen, Donna. *Ungodly Rage: The Hidden Face of Catholic Feminism.* San Francisco: Ignatius Press, 1991. Anti-feminist.

Steinbacher, John. *Bitter Harvest.* Whittier, Calif.: Orange Tree Press, 1970. Against César Chavez.

Stern, Susan. *With the Weathermen: The Personal Journal of a Revolutionary Woman.* Garden City: Doubleday, 1975.

[Stormer, John A.] *Anatomy of a Smear: An Analysis of the Attacks and Smears on the Book "None Dare Call It Treason."* Florissant, Mo.: Liberty Bell Press, [1964].

————. *The Death of a Nation.* Florissant, Mo.: Liberty Bell Press, 1968.

————. *None Dare Call It Treason.* Florissant, Mo.: Liberty Bell Press, 1964.

Strong, Donald Stuart. *Organized Anti-Semitism in America: The Rise of Group Prejudice during the Decade 1930–40.* Washington, D.C.: American Council on Public Affairs, 1941.

Swing, Raymond. *Forerunners of American Fascism.* New York: J. Messner, 1935.

Teodori, Massimo, ed. *The New Left: A Documentary History.* Indianapolis: Bobbs-Merrill, 1969.

Thayer, George. *The Farther Shores of Politics: The American Political Fringe Today.* New York: Simon and Schuster, 1967.

Thompson, Franklin. *America's Ju-Deal.* New York: Community Press, 1935.

Thompson, Jerry. *My Life in the Klan*. New York: G. P. Putnam's Sons, 1982.

The Truth about the United Nations: The Speeches, Findings, and Resolutions of The Congress of Freedom, Inc. Assembled in Convention in Veteran's War Memorial Auditorium, San Francisco, April 25–30, 1955. N.p.: n.p., n.d.

Tuccille, Jerome. *Radical Libertarianism: A Right Wing Alternative*. Indianapolis: Bobbs-Merrill, 1970.

Tucker, Benjamin R. *Individual Liberty: Selections from the Writings of Benjamin R. Tucker*, edited by C.L.S. New York: Vanguard Press, 1926.

Tull, Charles J. *Father Coughlin and the New Deal*. Syracuse: Syracuse University Press, 1965.

Turner, Capstan, with A. Jay Lowery. *There Was a Man: The Saga of Gordon Kahl. A True Story*. Nashville: Sozo Publishing Co., 1985.

Vander Zanden, James W. "The Ideology of White Supremacy." *Journal of the History of Ideas* 20 (June–September 1959): 385–402.

Vennard, Wickliffe B., Sr. *The Federal Reserve Hoax (Formerly The Federal Reserve Corporation): The Age of Deception*. 11th ed. Boston: Forum Publishing Co., 1963.

Vickers, George R. *The Formation of the New Left: The Early Years*. Lexington: Lexington Books, 1975.

Viguerie, Richard A. *The New Right: We're Ready to Lead*. Falls Church, Va.: Viguerie Co., 1981.

von Hoffman, Nicholas. *We Are the People Our Parents Warned Us Against*. Greenwich: Fawcett, 1968.

Wade, Wyn Craig. *The Fiery Cross: The Ku Klux Klan in America*. New York: Simon and Schuster, 1987.

Webber, E. F. *United Nations Exposed*. Fort Dodge, Iowa: Walterick Printing Co., [1955].

Weinberg, Leonard. "The American Radical Right: Exit, Voice, and Violence." In *Encounters With the Contemporary Radical Right*, edited by Peter H. Merkl and Leonard Weinberg, 185–203, 256–58. Boulder: Westview, 1993.

Welch, Robert. *Again, May God Forgive Us*. Belmont, Mass.: Belmont Publishing Co., [1960s?]. On Chiang Kai-shek, China.

———. *The Blue Book of the John Birch Society*. Boston: Western Islands, 1961.

———. *The Neutralizers*. Belmont, Mass.: John Birch Society, 1963. Those membrs of Society who undermine the message. Anti-Semites, religious, academic, and political neutralism. British-Israelites.

———. *The New Americanism and Other Speeches and Essays*. Boston: Western Islands, 1966.

———. *The Politician*. Belmont, Mass.: n.p., 1963. Eisenhower as tool of communism.

Whitaker, Robert W., ed. *The New Right Papers*. New York: St. Martin's Press, 1982.

Wilcox, Clyde. *God's Warriors: The Christian Right in Twentieth Century America*. Baltimore: Johns Hopkins University Press, 1992.

Wilcox, Laird. *Guide to the American Left: Directory and Bibliography 1993.* Olathe, Kans.: Editorial Research Service, 1993.

————. *Guide to the American Right: Directory and Bibliography 1993.* Olathe, Kans.: Editorial Research Service, 1993.

Willoughby, William. *Does America Need the Moral Majority?* Plainfield, N.J.: Have Books, 1981. Answer is yes.

Winrod, Gerald B. *Adam Weishaupt: A Human Devil.* Metairie, La.: Sons of Liberty, n.d. [1960s?].

————. *Communism in Prophecy History and America.* Wichita, Kans.: Defender Publishers, 1946.

————. *Hitler in Prophecy.* Wichita, Kans.: Defender Publishers, 1933.

————. *The Truth about the Protocols.* Hollywood: Sons of Liberty, n.d. [1970s?].

Wolfskill, George. *The Revolt of the Conservatives: A History of the American Liberty League 1934–1940.* Boston: Houghton Mifflin, 1962.

Wolves in Sheep's Clothing: An Authentic Portrayal of the Perfidious Proposals of COMMUNISM and SOCIALISM In their Real Setting, as Masks and Devices, Employed by Amazingly Organized and Financially Powerful Occult Forces, Bent Upon World Conquest. Washington, D.C.: Sodality Union, 1937.

Young, Alfred F., ed. *Dissent: Explorations in the History of American Radicalism.* DeKalb: Northern Illinois University Press, 1968.

Zeskind, Leonard. *The "Christian Identity" Movement: A Theological Justification for Racist and Anti-Semitic Violence.* Atlanta: Center for Democratic Renewal. Published by the Division of Church and Society of the National Council of the Churches of Christ in the U.S.A., 1986.

Zwier, Robert. *Born-Again Politics: The New Christian Right in America.* Downers Grove, Ill.: InterVarsity Press, 1982.